Software Engineering: Design, Theory and Practice

Software Engineering: Design, Theory and Practice

Edited by **Tom Halt**

New York

Published by NY Research Press,
23 West, 55th Street, Suite 816,
New York, NY 10019, USA
www.nyresearchpress.com

Software Engineering: Design, Theory and Practice
Edited by Tom Halt

International Standard Book Number: 978-1-63238-480-5 (Hardback)

The publisher's policy is to use permanent paper from mills that operate a sustainable forestry policy. Furthermore, the publisher ensures that the text paper and cover boards used have met acceptable environmental accreditation standards.

Trademark Notice: Registered trademark of products or corporate names are used only for explanation and identification without intent to infringe.

Printed in the United States of America.

Contents

Preface

This book has been a concerted effort by a group of academicians, researchers and scientists, who have contributed their research works for the realization of the book. This book has materialized in the wake of emerging advancements and innovations in this field. Therefore, the need of the hour was to compile all the required researches and disseminate the knowledge to a broad spectrum of people comprising of students, researchers and specialists of the field.

Software Engineering refers to that branch of engineering which deals with developing, implementing, designing and maintaining of software. It has many sub-divisions like embedded software, software design, software configuration management, software durability, etc. This book will trace the progress made in this field and highlight some of the key concepts and applications related to it. It will provide detailed explanation of the various applications in this area. Different approaches, evaluations and methodologies have also been included. This book aims to present researches that have transformed this discipline and aided its progress. Those with an interest in software engineering will find this book helpful. It will serve as a valuable source of reference for students and researchers alike.

At the end of the preface, I would like to thank the authors for their brilliant chapters and the publisher for guiding us all-through the making of the book till its final stage. Also, I would like to thank my family for providing the support and encouragement throughout my academic career and research projects.

Editor

Single-Phase Velocity Determination Based in Video and Sub-Images Processing: An Optical Flow Method Implemented with Support of a Programmed MatLab Structured Script

Andreas Nascimento[1], Edson Da Costa Bortoni[2], José Luiz Gonçalves[2], Pedro Antunes Duarte[2], Mauro Hugo Mathias[1]

[1]Departamento de Mecânica, Faculdade de Engenharia, Câmpus de Guaratinguetá (FEG), Universidade Estadual Paulista (UNESP), Guaratinguetá, Brazil
[2]Universidade Federal de Itajubá (UNIFEI), Itajubá, Brazil
Email: andreas.nascimento@gmail.com

Abstract

Important in many different sectors of the industry, the determination of stream velocity has become more and more important due to measurements precision necessity, in order to determine the right production rates, determine the volumetric production of undesired fluid, establish automated controls based on these measurements avoiding over-flooding or over-production, guaranteeing accurate predictive maintenance, etc. Difficulties being faced have been the determination of the velocity of specific fluids embedded in some others, for example, determining the gas bubbles stream velocity flowing throughout liquid fluid phase. Although different and already applicable methods have been researched and already implemented within the industry, a non-intrusive automated way of providing those stream velocities has its importance, and may have a huge impact in projects budget. Knowing the importance of its determination, this developed script uses a methodology of breaking-down real-time videos media into frame images, analyzing by pixel correlations possible superposition matches for further gas bubbles stream velocity estimation. In raw sense, the script bases itself in functions and procedures already available in MatLab, which can be used for image processing and treatments, allowing the methodology to be implemented. Its accuracy after the running test was of around 97% (ninety-seven percent); the raw source code with comments had almost 3000 (three thousand) characters; and the hardware placed for running the code was an Intel Core Duo 2.13 [Ghz] and 2 [Gb] RAM memory capable workstation. **Even showing good results, it could be stated that just the end point correlations were actually getting to the final solution. So that, making use of self-learning functions or neural network, one could surely enhance the capability of the application to be run in real-time without getting exhaust by iterative loops.**

Keywords

Optical Flow, Single-Phase Velocity, Video and Image Processing, Sensing, MatLab Script

1. Introduction

The industry began to be interested in developing multi-phase-flow-meters, also just called as MPFMs, early in 1980s, since priory, single-phase measurements alone were sufficient to meet the industry's needs. Since 1994, MPFM installation numbers have been steadily increased as technology in the field, with substantial growth witnessed from 1999 onwards [1]. Moreover, in any extension, a solution for detecting single-phase motions embedded in a multi-phase-flow environment may still have its importance and engineering impact.

Studies have shown that non-intrusive flow meters may be more adequate in activities where intrusive ones may affect the effectiveness of the process itself, or where further effort in terms of system re-engineering may show to be necessary, since situations can lead to metering damaging, more frequent maintenance necessity, etc. [2].

Furthermore, since the treatment of the information of this specific idea can be done and run on top of algorithm and media processing, it allows a more reliable real-time data sensing, keeping itself as a very good alternative to be implemented in complex areas or environment where size and intrusiveness of the measuring method may play a bigger role, being these the main motivation of the experiments carried out and detailed in the presented work.

For the developed experiment and simulation, a two-phase flow pattern (clean water and gas bubbles) was used as main fluid combination together with a high resolution recording camera pointing to a transparent tubing. So that non-intrusively, one could record a video from the stream, and subsequently, get the recorded media treated by the developed MatLab script, yielding with the gas bubbles flowing phase velocity determination.

2. Pixels Correlation Methodology

Considering that after images treatment one can have in a black-white representative matrix some Booleans specifying what actually represents the effective image and what represents the background, it is possible to have a virtual representation of the gas bubbles in terms of mathematical matrixes.

From the **Figure 1** presented, it is possible to see in general what the ideas behind all are. Considering that **Figure 1(a)** represents one broken-down image from the video media and the **Figure 1(b)** its subsequent broken-down image, one can understand that the number 01s (ones) represent the gas bubbles, and so, by trying to accommodate both on top of each other (each matrix position represents one pixel), it is possible to see that **Figure 1(b)** advanced in 01 (one) pixel position towards, being its displacement for the final match.

From **Figure 2**, it is possible to see how the iterative process was developed in order to accommodate the images and the processing basing in pixel correlations on top of each other. Starting from the lowest edge of the matrix, moving column by column from the right to the left and from the downside to the top side, one can see

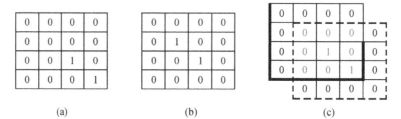

(a)   (b)   (c)

Figure 1. Main schematic of the correlation matching idea.

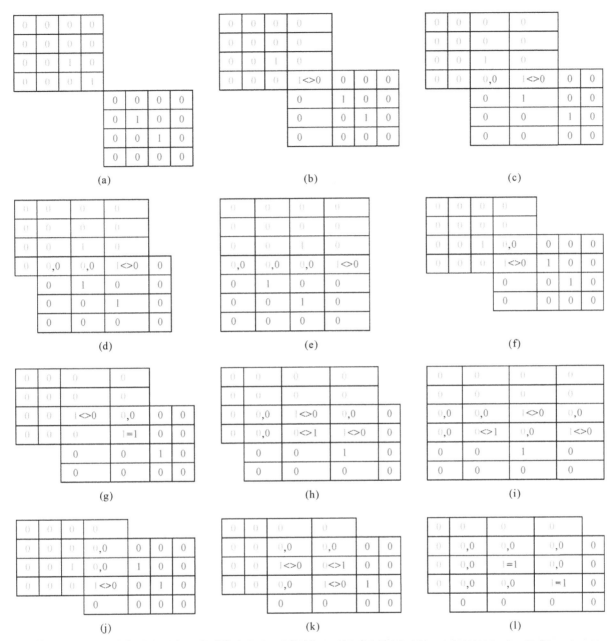

Figure 2. Example of iterative process from beginning up to the processing end match.

the first match appears by **Figure 2(g)**, and the maximum match with the total superposition at the **Figure 2(l)**, which comes to represent the final correlative position for the displacement accountability for further velocity calculation and determination.

Since velocity is not more than a displacement over a specific time-range, putting this information together with the video recording rate in use, one can come-up with the actual effective gas bubbles single-phase stream velocity. Important to notice is that since the background represents the water, for example, it is estimating the total velocity and not the relative velocity on top of the water flow.

3. MatLab Media Processing Treatments

The media processing started transforming the images from RGB 3D format (**Figure 3(a)**) to 2D images, since it has shown to be necessary to have them as singles colors "RGB2GRAY (image)" (**Figure 3(b)**).

Sequentially, it was necessary to eliminate isolated pixels in order to allow distinguishing from gas bubbles background using the function "EDGE (image, 'sobel')", and also perform a bordering quality enhancement in order to allow a better delimitation of the bubbles itself (**Figure 3(c)**).

Finally as a final step, it is always better and necessary to have some pictures boundaries cropped-out, having a better and smoother image to be feeding the script, accomplished using the function IMCROP.

4. Algorithm Script Schematics Summary Flow-Chart

From **Figure 4** shown, it can be seen how the logic behind the developed algorithm is. The source code itself has been hidden due to specific purposes.

Throughout the analysis and comparison developed with the results, could be verified that this developed methodology and source code script can help as a non-intrusive method of measuring gas bubbles stream velocity in a two-phase or even multi-phase flow environment.

There were two main factors affecting the results that could for sure be enhanced in a next research: better definition of the bubbles sharpness and processing by eliminating the isolated pixels, and guaranteeing to have just perfect ellipses or circles left to be representative so that just raw bubbles would be compared for the pixel superposition matching, allowing a much better accuracy. Furthermore, one can interpret that the matches happens

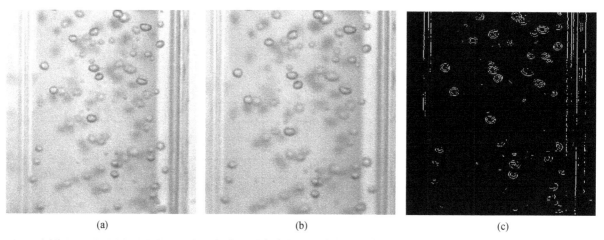

| (a) | (b) | (c) |

Figure 3. Media processing from raw 3D format (a) [3] up to final enhanced quality before cropping (c).

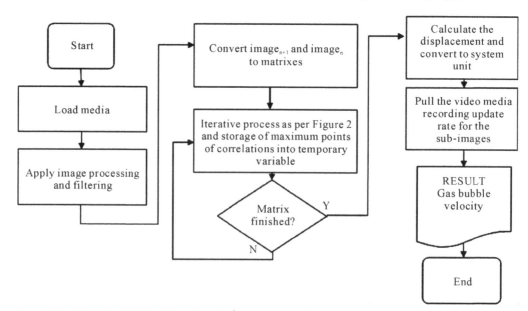

Figure 4. MatLab algorithm flow-chart representation.

normally on the lasts superposition pixels, so that may not really be necessary to run the correlation code throughout the whole image matrix, but just after a certain specific matrix position. These could lead to source code optimization and results accuracy.

Nevertheless, it allowed an estimation of the stream velocity with an accuracy of around 97% for the tests run, what is considerable in terms of the necessary work-around implied over these studies and processing.

5. Conclusions and Discussion

Throughout the analysis and comparison developed with the results, it could be verified that this developed methodology and source code script can help as a non-intrusive method of measuring gas bubbles stream velocity in a two-phase or even multi-phase flow environment.

There were two main factors affecting the results that could for sure be enhanced in a next research: better definition of the bubbles sharpness and processing by eliminating the isolated pixels, and guaranteeing to have just perfect ellipses or circles left to be representative so that just raw bubbles would be compared for the pixel superposition matching, allowing a much better accuracy. Furthermore, one can interpret that the matches happen normally on the last superposition pixels, so that it may not really be necessary to run the correlation code throughout the whole image matrix, but just after a certain specific matrix position. These could lead to source code optimization and results accuracy.

Nevertheless, it allowed an estimation of the stream velocity with an accuracy of around 97% for the tests run, what was considerable in terms of the necessary work-around implied over these studies and processing.

Acknowledgements

This publication has the financial support from the Brazilian Federal Agency for Support and Evaluation of Graduate Education (Coordenação de Aperfeiçoamento de Pessoal de Nível Superior—CAPES, scholarship process no BEX 0506/15-0) and the Brazilian National Agency of Petroleum, Natural Gas and Biofuels (Agência Nacional do Petróleo, Gás Natural e Biocombustíveis—ANP), in cooperation with the Brazilian Financier of Studies and Projects (Financiadora de Estudos e Projetos—FINEP) and the Brazilian Ministry of Science, Technology and Innovation (Ministério da Ciência, Tecnologia e Inovação—MCTI) through the ANP's Human Resources Program of the State University of São Paulo (Universidade Estadual Paulista—UNESP) for the Oil and Gas Sector PRH-ANP/MCTI no 48 (PRH48). Thanks also to the Center of Excellence in Energy Efficiency (Centro de Excelência em Eficiência Energética—EXCEN) from the Federal University of Itajuba (Universidade Federal de Itajubá—UNIFEI).

References

[1]   Mehdizadeh, P. (2006) Worldwide Multiphase and Wet Gas Metering Installations. Production Technology Report 03232007, 2007.

[2]   Zuzunaga, A., *et al*. (2013) A Survey of Non-Invasive and Semi-Invasive Flow Meters for Mining Applications: Understanding and Selecting the Right Technology for the Application. BI0497. *International Meeting on Mining Plan Maintenance* (*MAPLA*), Santiago.

[3]   Zheng, Y. and Zhang, Q. (2004) Simultaneous Measurement of Gas and Solid Holdups in Multiphase Systems Using Ultrasonic Technique. *Chemical Engineering Science*, **59**, 3505-3514. http://dx.doi.org/10.1016/j.ces.2004.05.016

Vision-Based Hand Gesture Spotting and Recognition Using CRF and SVM

Fayed F. M. Ghaleb[1], Ebrahim A. Youness[2], Mahmoud Elmezain[2], Fatma Sh. Dewdar[2]

[1]Faculty of Science, Mathematices Department, Ain Shams University, Cairo, Egypt
[2]Faculty of Science, Computer Science Division, Tanta University, Tanta, Egypt
Email: Mahmoud.Elmezain@tuscs.com

Abstract

In this paper, a novel gesture spotting and recognition technique is proposed to handle hand gesture from continuous hand motion based on Conditional Random Fields in conjunction with Support Vector Machine. Firstly, YC_bC_r color space and 3D depth map are used to detect and segment the hand. The depth map is to neutralize complex background sense. Secondly, 3D spatio-temporal features for hand volume of dynamic affine-invariants like elliptic Fourier and Zernike moments are extracted, in addition to three orientations motion features. Finally, the hand gesture is spotted and recognized by using the discriminative Conditional Random Fields Model. Accordingly, a Support Vector Machine verifies the hand shape at the start and the end point of meaningful gesture, which enforces vigorous view invariant task. Experiments demonstrate that the proposed method can successfully spot and recognize hand gesture from continuous hand motion data with 92.50% recognition rate.

Keywords

Human Computer Interaction, Conditional Random Fields, Support Vector Machine, Elliptic Fourier, Zernike Moments

1. Introduction

The task of locating the start and the end points that correspond to a gesture of interest is a challenging task in Human Computer Interaction. We define a gesture as the motion of the hand to communicate with a computer. The task of locating meaningful patterns from input signals is called pattern spotting [1] [2]. In gesture spotting, an instance of pattern spotting, it is required to locate the start point and the end point of a gesture. The gesture spotting has two major difficulties: segmentations [3] [4] and spatio-temporal variabilities [5] [6]. The segmentation problem is how to determine when a gesture starts and when it ends in a continuous hand trajectory. As the gesturer switches from one gesture to another, his hand makes an intermediate move linking the two gestures. A gesture recognizer may attempt to recognize this inevitable intermediate motion as a meaningful one. Without segmentation, the recognizer should try to match reference patterns with all possible segments of input signals. The other difficulties of gesture spotting are that the same gesture varies dynamically in shape and duration; even of the same gesturer. Therefore, the recognizer should consider both the spatial and the temporal variabilities simultaneously. An ideal recognizer will extract gesture segments from the input signal, and match them with reference patterns regardless of the spatio-temporal variabilities. Tracking methods that depend entirely on an image-plane representation of the hand have been worked on extensively. Typically such systems are computationally less expensive than those methods that use a 3D model. Moment invariants, as discriminative feature descriptors, have been used for shape representation for many years. The shape-based image invariants can be divided into two different categories: boundary based image invariants such as Fourier descriptors; region-based image invariants included various moment-based invariants such as Zernike moments. There are two types of shape-based image invariants: boundary-based and region-based. The boundary based image invariants focus on the properties contained in the image's contour while the region-based image invariants take the whole image area as the research object.

Boundary-based invariants such as Fourier descriptors explore only the contour information; they cannot capture the interior content of the shape. On the other hand, these methods cannot deal with disjoint shapes where single closed boundary may not be available; therefore, they have limited applications. For region-based invariants, all of the pixels of the image are taken into account to represent the shape. Because region-based invariants combine information of an entire image region rather than exploiting information just along the boundary pixels, they can capture more information from the image. The region-based invariants can also be employed to describe disjoint shapes.

Lee, H.-K. and Kim, J.H. [7] develope a new method by using the Hidden Markov Model based technique. To handle non-gesture patterns, they introduce the concept of a threshold model that calculates the likelihood threshold of an input pattern and provides a confirmation mechanism for the provisionally matched gesture patterns. *Yang, H.-D., Sclaroff, S. and Lee, S.-W.* [8] propose a novel method for designing threshold models in a conditional random field (CRF) model which performs an adaptive threshold for distinguishing between signs in a vocabulary and non-sign patterns. These methods have the following consequent drawback to detect the reliable end point of a gesture and find the start point by back-tracking. Therefore, the delayed response may cause one to wonder whether one's gesture has been recognized correctly or not. For that reason, the systems in [7] [8] are not capable for real-time applications.

To face the mentioned challenges, CRF forward gesture spotting by using Circular Buffer method is proposed, which simultaneously handles the hand gesture spotting and recognition in stereo color image sequences without time delay. A hand appearance-based sign verification method using SVM is considered to further improve sign language spotting accuracy. Additionally, a depth image sequence is exploited to identify the Region of Interest (ROI) without processing the whole image, which consequently reduces the cost of ROI searching and increases the processing speed. Our experiments on own dataset, showed that the proposed approach is more robust and yields promising results when comparing favorably with those previously reported throughout the literature.

2. Hand Gesture Spotting and Recognition Approach

An application of gesture-based interaction with Arabic numbers (0 - 9) is implemented to demonstrate the co-action of suggested components and the effectiveness of gesture spotting & recognition approach (**Figure 1**).

2.1. Preprocessing

Automatic segmentation and preprocessing is an important stage in our approach. The segmentation of the hand takes place using color information and 3D depth map. Firstly, the hand is segmented (*i.e.* Area of interest (AOI)) using Gaussian Mixture Model (GMM) over YC_bC_r color space, where Y channel represents brightness and (C_b, C_r) channels refer to chrominance [9]. Channel Y is eliminated to reduce the effect of brightness variation and only the chrominance channels are employed that fully represent the color information. Accordingly, Image acquisition includes 2D image sequences and depth image sequences, which devised by an algorithm of passive stereo measuring based on mean absolute difference and the known calibration data of the cameras. The

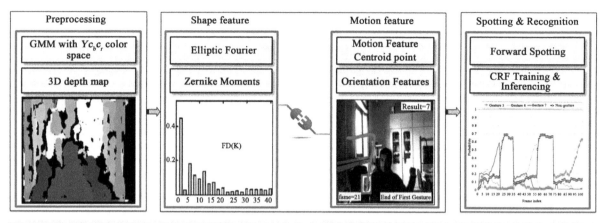

Figure 1. Hand gesture spotting and recognition concept.

depth map is to neutralize complex senses background to increase the robustness of skin segmentation for AOI completely (**Figure 2**).

2.2. Tracking and Feature Extraction

To retrieve the extracted features during occlusion, a robust method for hand tracking is considered using Mean-shift analysis in conjunction with depth map. The motivation behind mean shift analysis is to achieve accurate and robust hand tracking. Mean-shift analysis uses the gradient of Bhattacharyya coefficient [10] as a similarity function to derive the candidate of the hand which is mostly similar to a given hand target model. This structure correctly extracts a set of hand postures to track the hand motion. After that, two types of feature are employed to correctly spot and recognize hand gesture. The orientation features of hand image sequences are extracted by the trajectory of the hand motion centroid. Additionally, the shape features are considered with a variety of invariant descriptors such as elliptic Fourier's descriptors and invariant Zernike moments.

2.2.1. Orientation Features

The orientation gives the direction of the hand when traverses in space during the gesture making process. A gesture path is spatio-temporal pattern that consists of centroid points (xhand, yhand). Therefore, orientation feature is based on; the calculation of the hand displacement vector at every point which is represented by the orientation according to the centroid of gesture path (θ_{1t}), the orientation between two consecutive points (θ_{2t}) and the orientation between start and current gesture point (θ_{3t}).

$$\theta_{1t} = \tan^{-1}\left(\frac{y_{t+1} - c_y}{x_{t+1} - c_x}\right), \quad \theta_{2t} = \tan^{-1}\left(\frac{y_{t+1} - y_t}{x_{t+1} - x_t}\right), \quad \theta_{3t} = \tan^{-1}\left(\frac{y_{t+1} - y_1}{x_{t+1} - x_1}\right) \tag{2.1}$$

$$\left(c_x, c_y\right) = \frac{1}{n}\left(\sum_{t=1}^{n} x_t, \sum_{t=1}^{n} y_t\right) \tag{2.2}$$

where (c_x, c_y) refers to the centroid of gravity at n points, and T represents the length of hand gesture path such that $t = 1, 2, \cdots, T-1$.

In this manner, gesture is represented as an ordered sequence of feature vectors, which are projected and clustered in space dimension to obtain discrete code words. This is done using k-means clustering algorithm [11], which classifies the gesture pattern into K clusters in the feature space.

2.2.2. SVM-Based Dynamic Affine-Invariants Features

The shape flow as the global flow of hand is characterized and stated by the elliptic Fourier descriptors and Zernike moments $G_i = \left[C_{xk}, C_{yk}, z_{00}, z_{11}, z_{22}\right]^T$ that described as follows:

The elliptic Fourier descriptors for action silhouettes are obtained using a trigonometric form of the shape curve C_k.

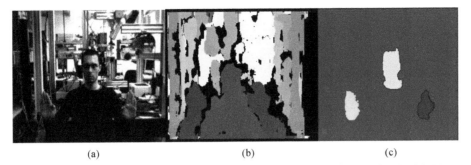

(a)   (b)   (c)

Figure 2. (a) Source image frame; (b) Depth value from the Bumblebee stereo camera system; (c) Skin color segmentation of hands.

$$C_k = C_{xk} + jC_{yk} \tag{2.3}$$

where

$$C_{xk} = \frac{1}{T}\int_0^T x(t)e^{-jk\omega t}, \; C_{yk} = \frac{1}{T}\int_0^T y(t)e^{-jk\omega t} \tag{2.4}$$

ω defines the fundament frequency and is equal to $T/2\pi$. T referents the function period and k refers to a harmonic number. It can be verified that this choice of coefficients guarantees that the resulting curve descriptors are invariant to shape translation, rotation and scaling, and they are independent from the choice of starting point on a contour [12].

Invariance of hand image can be achieved by using Zernike moments, which give an orthogonal set of rotation-invariant moments. Additionally, scale and translation invariance can be implemented using moment normalization [13]. More simply, the complex Zernike moment (Z_{pq}) with an order p and repetition q of image intensity function $f(\rho,\theta)$ is:

$$Z_{pq} = \frac{p+1}{\delta_N}\sum_{x=0}^{N-1}\sum_{y=0}^{N-1}f\left(\frac{x}{a}+\overline{x}, \frac{y}{a}+\overline{y}, t\right)R_{pq}(\rho)e^{-jq\theta} \tag{2.5}$$

Here, δ_N is a normalization factor, p is a positive integer while q either negative or positive integer subject to the constraints $p - |q| =$ even and $|q| \le p$. The function f is normalized with respect to scale and translation by using the center of silhouette image $(\overline{x},\overline{y})$ and the scale factored a. $R_{pq}(\rho)$ represents are dial polynomial [12].

Thus, the Zernike moment features invariant along with geometric features to shape translation, rotation and scaling with remarkable similarity to the Hu invariant moments is assigned by $G_z = [z_{00}, z_{11}, z_{22}]$.

2.3. Spotting and Recognition

To spot meaningful gestures of numbers (0 - 9), which are embedded in the input video stream accurately, a two-layer CRF architecture is applied (**Figure 3**). In the first layer a stochastic method for designing a non-gesture model with CRF is proposed without training data. CRF is capable of modeling spatio-temporal time series of gestures effectively and can handle non-gesture patterns. The non-gesture model provides a confidence measure that is used as an adaptive threshold to find the start and the end point of meaningful gestures. As, a forward spotting technique in conjunction with a Differential Probability (DP) value and circular buffer is employed to discriminate between meaningful gestures and non-gesture patterns. In the second layer, CRF are used to find the maximal gesture, which having the largest value among all ten labels gestures. Finally, SVM decide the final decision based on the building dataset of hand shape with elliptic Fourier and Zernike moments.

2.3.1. Spotting with CRFs

CRFs are a framework based on conditional probability approaches for segmenting and labeling sequential data. CRFs use a single exponential distribution to model all labels of given observations. Therefore, there is a trade-off in the weights of each feature function, for each state. In our application, each state corresponds to segments of the number. In addition, each label in CRFs is employed as exponential model to conditional probabilities of

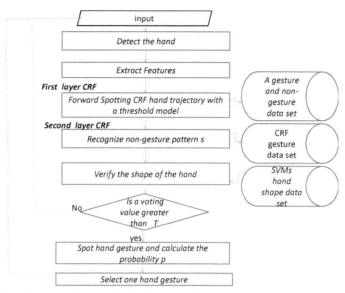

Figure 3. A two layer flow chart for spotting meaningful gestures based on CRFs and SVMs.

the next label for a given current label.

(1) Spotting with CRFs

Conditional Random Fields were developed for labeling sequential data (*i.e.* determining the probability of a given label sequence for a given input sequence) and are undirected graphical models (*i.e.* discriminative models). The structure of current label is design to form the chain with an edge between itself and previous label. Moreover, each label corresponds to a gesture number. The probability of label sequence y for a given observation sequence O is calculated as:

$$P\left(y|O,\theta\right)=\frac{1}{Z\left(O,\theta\right)}\cdot\exp\left(\sum_{i=1}^{n}F_{\theta}\left(y_{i-1},y_{i},O,i\right)\right) \tag{2.6}$$

where parameter $\theta=\left(\lambda_{1},\lambda_{2},\cdots,\lambda_{N_{f}};\mu_{1},\mu_{2},\cdots,\mu_{N_{g}}\right)$, the number of transition feature function represents by N_{f}, the number of state feature function represents by N_{g} and the length of observation sequence O is n.

F_{θ} is defined as:

$$F_{\theta}=\sum_{f}\lambda_{f}t_{f}\left(y_{i-1},y_{i},O,i\right)+\sum_{g}\mu_{g}s_{g}\left(y_{i},O,i\right) \tag{2.7}$$

where a transition feature function at position i and $i-1$ is $t_{f}\left(y_{i-1},y_{i},O,i\right)$ (*i.e.* represents the weight on the transition from label i to label $i-1$ when the current observation is O). State feature function at position i is sg (y_{i}, O, i) (i.e. represents the weight on the label i when the current observation is O). λ_{f} and μ_{g} represent the weights of the transition and state feature functions, respectively. $Z(O, \theta)$ is the normalized factor and is calculated as follows:

$$Z\left(O,\theta\right)=\sum_{y}\exp\left(\sum_{i=1}^{n}F_{\theta}\left(y_{i-1},y_{i},O,i\right)\right) \tag{2.8}$$

The CRFs are initially built without label for non-gesture pattern; Because CRFs use a single model for the joint probability of the sequences $p(y|O, \theta)$.

Using gradient ascent with the BFGS optimization technique with 300 iterations is used for trained CRFs to achieve optimal convergence. Therefore, the labels of CRFs are $y=\left\{Y_{0},Y_{1},\cdots,Y_{9}\right\}$. To create the Non-gesture model (*N-CRFs*) using the weights of transition and state features function of initial CRFs all other patterns than gesture patterns are modeled by adding a label (*N*) for non-gesture patterns. Moreover, $y_{N}=\left\{Y_{0},Y_{1},\cdots,Y_{9},Y_{N}\right\}$ are the labels of *N-CRFs*. The proposed *N-CRFs* model does not need non-gesture patterns for training and also can better spot gestures and non-gesture patterns.

(2) N-CRFs Model Parameters

The label of non-gesture pattern is created, by using the weight of state and transition feature function of the initialized CRFs model. There are two main parameters of CRFs named state feature function and transition feature function as in Equation (2.7). From the idea of Dugad et $al.$ [14] who propose an adaptive threshold model based on the mean and the variance of sample, the weight of state feature function is computed as:

$$\mu_g(N) = \overline{\mu_g} + T_N \sqrt{\sigma_g} \tag{2.9}$$

where $\overline{\mu_g}$ is the mean of state feature functions of the labels of initial CRFs from Y_0 to Y_9 and σ_g represent the variance of the gth state feature functions T_N reflects the width of state features function in some way. The optimal value of T_N is 0.7 and is determined by multiple experiments which have been conducted with a range of values on a training data set.

It is difficult to spot and recognize short gestures because short gestures have fewer samples than long gestures. A challenging problem is caused by the fact that there is a quite bit of variability in the same gesture even for the same person. A short gesture detector is added to avoid this problem, where the weights of self-transition feature functions are increased as follows:

$$\lambda_f(Y_l, Y_l) = \begin{cases} \lambda_f(Y_l, Y_l) + \Psi_f(y_l), & \text{if Cond 1} \\ \lambda_f(Y_l, Y_l), & \text{otherwise} \end{cases} \tag{2.10}$$

Such that:

$$\Psi_f(y_l) = \frac{\left(\overline{N}_{frame} - \sigma_{N_{frame}}\right) - N_{frame}(Y_l)}{\max_l N_{frame}(Y_l)} \tag{2.11}$$

and

$$\text{Cond 1}: N_{frame}(Y_l) < \left(\overline{N}_{frame} - \sigma_{N_{frame}}\right) \tag{2.12}$$

where $N_{frame}(Y_l)$ is the average frame number of a gesture Y_l, $\sigma_{N_{frame}}$ represents the average frame number of all gestures from Y_0 to Y_9 and $\sigma_{N_{frame}}$ is the variance of them. $\psi_f(y_l)$ is additional weight of the gesture Y_l notable in case of a short length gesture.

The weight of the self-transition feature function of the label of non-gesture patterns is approximately assigned with the maximum weight of transition feature functions to initialize CRFs as follows:

$$\lambda_f(Y_N, Y_N) = \max_l \lambda_f(Y_l, Y_l) + \frac{\sum_{i=1}^{l} \sum_{g=1}^{N_g} \mu_g(Y_l)}{\overline{N}_{state\_feature}} \tag{2.13}$$

where $\overline{N}_{state\_feature}$ is the average number of transition feature functions in which the weight is greater than zero. As described above about the transition parameters of non-gesture model, a method is employed to compute the weights of transition feature functions between the labels of gesture models and the label of non-gesture patterns. Therefore, the weights of transition feature functions from the non-gesture label to other labels are computed by the following equation:

$$\lambda_f(Y_N, Y_i) = \frac{\lambda_f(Y_N, Y_N)}{l}, \quad \forall i \in \{1, 2, \cdots, l\} \tag{2.14}$$

Additionally, the weights of transition feature functions from the gesture labels to non-gesture label occurs by the given equation below:

$$\lambda_f(Y_i, Y_N) = \frac{\lambda_f(Y_i, Y_i)}{l}, \quad \forall i \in \{1, 2, \cdots, l\} \tag{2.15}$$

As a result, the $N\text{-}CRFs$ model can better spot gestures and non-gesture patterns.

2.3.2. CRF Forward Spotting via Circular Buffer

Several samples of each gesture in the gesture vocabulary are stored in the database to be used in training the classifier. A gesture is stored as a sequence of (x, y, t) joint coordinates. In recognition mode, a circular buffer is used to temporarily store the real-time information. The circular buffer contains a number of sequential observations instead of a single observation. It is used to reduce the impact of observation changes for a short interval which are caused by incomplete feature extraction. The circular buffer is set to store 13 frames. The size of the circular buffer is chosen to be equal to the shortest gesture (*i.e.* gesture "1" represents a shortest gesture in our system). This ensures that at some stage during a continuous motion, the buffer will be completely filled with gesture data, and will not contain any transitional motion data. In addition, a maximum of one complete gesture can be stored in the buffer at one time.

Figure 4 illustrates the operation of the circular buffer in gesture segmentation. At $t = t_1$ the buffer contains transitional data and gesture data. At $t = t_2$, the buffer is filled entirely with data from Gesture 2, and contains no transitional motion data. The gesture recognition module is activated after detecting the start point from continuous image sequences. The main objective is to perform the recognition process accumulatively for the segmented parts until it receives the end signal of key gesture.

Assume that, the size of circular buffer is initialized with the input observation sequence with length $T = 13$ as in our system, $O = \{o_1, o_2, \cdots, o_T\}$. The *DP* value is equal to difference observation probability between the maximal gesture labels and the Non-gesture label.

When the value of $DP(t)$ at time t is negative, the start point in this case is not detected and therefore the circular buffer is shifted on unit (*i.e.* $O_{t+1} = o_{t+1}, o_{t+2}, \cdots, o_{T+1}$). This process is repeated until *DP* value is positive. In the case of DP value is positive; assume that A1 represents the first partial key gesture segmented. Then, the observed key gesture segmented is represented by union of all possible partial gesture segments $A = \{A_1 \bigcup A_2 \bigcup \cdots\}$.

At each step, the gesture type of A is determined. When the value of *DP* becomes negative again or there is no gesture image, the final gesture label type of observed gesture segment A is determined. When there is more gesture images, the previous steps are repeated with re-initializing the circular buffer at the next time t. Therefore, a forward scheme has the ability to resolve the issues of time delay between gesture spotting and recognition.

2.3.3. SVMs-Based Gesture Verification

The main motivation behind using SVMs-based gesture verification to decide whether or not to accept a gesture spotted. This helps to discriminate gestures which may have similar hand motions but different hand shapes. SVMs are trained with a set of images of a gesture hand shape according to the extracted features via elliptic Fourier and Zernike moments. Therefore, the histograms of gradient features are extracted for training SVM from training samples [15].

In our work, the hand shape at the start of the gesture is verified. Then the hand appearance is verified over a period of several frames. As a result, voting value over frames is used to consider whether to accept or reject the gesture. If voting value is greater than a specific threshold, which experimentally determined, then the candidate gesture is chosen be a meaningful gesture.

3. Experimental Results

The input images were captured by Bumblebee stereo camera system which has 6 mm focal length at 15FPS with 240×320 pixels image resolution, Matlab implementation. Classification results are based on our database that contains 600 video samples for isolated gestures (*i.e.* 60 video samples for each gesture from 0 to 9) which are captured from three persons. Each isolated number from 0 to 9 was based on 42 videos for training CRF and SVMs. Additionally, the database contains 280 video samples of continuous hand motion for testing. Each video sample either contains one or more meaningful gestures.

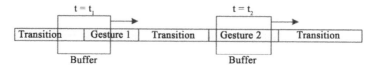

Figure 4. Gesture segmentation by circular buffer.

On a standard desktop PC, training process is more expensive for CRFs since the time which the model needs ranges from 20 minutes to several hours based on observation window. On the contrary, the inference (*i.e.* recognition) process is less costly and very fast for all models with sequences of several frames.

In automatic gesture spotting task, there are three types of errors called Insertion (I), Substitution (S) and Deletion (D). The insertion error is occurred when the spotter detects a nonexistent gesture. It is because the emission probability of the current state for a given observation sequence is equal to zero. A substitution error occurs when the key gesture is classified falsely (*i.e.* classifies the gesture as another gesture). This error is usually happened when the extracted features are falsely quantized to other code words. The deletion error happens when the spotter fails to detect a key gesture. In order to calculate the recognition ratio (Rec.) (Equation (3.2)), insertion errors are totally not considered. However, insertion errors are probably caused due to substitution and deletion errors because they are often considered as strong decision in determining the end point of gestures to eliminate all or part of the meaningful gestures from observation. Deletion errors directly affect the recognition ratio whereas insertion errors do not. However, the insertion errors affect the gesture spotting ratio directly. To take into consideration the effect of insertion errors, another performance measure called reliability (Rel.) is proposed by the following equation:

$$Rel. = \frac{\#\,correctly\ recognized\ gestures}{\#\,test\ gestures + \#\,Inseration\ errors} \times 100 \tag{3.1}$$

The recognition ratio and the reliability are computed based on the number of spotting errors (**Table 1**).

$$Rec. = \frac{\#\,recognized\ gestures}{\#\,test\ gestures} \times 100 \tag{3.2}$$

Experimental results of CRF show that the proposed method automatically recognizes meaningful gestures with 92.50% recognition (**Table 1**). It is noted that the proposed method achieved good recognition r ate due to a good election for the set of feature candidates to optimally discriminate among input patterns. In addition, A short gesture detector has the ability to efficiently alleviate spatio-temporal variability. Thus, this system is capable for real-time applications and resolves the issues of time delay between spotting and recognition tasks.

Lee, H.-K. and Kim, J.H. [7] developed a new method using the Hidden Markov Model based technique. To handle non-gesture patterns, they introduce the concept of a threshold model that calculates the likelihood threshold of an input pattern and provides a confirmation mechanism for the provisionally matched gesture patterns. For gesture segmentation, it detects the reliable end point of a gesture and finds the start point by back-tracking the Viterbi path from the end point (*i.e.* backward technique). The model performs gesture spotting with recognition

Table 1. Meaningful gesture spotting results for gesture numbers from "0" to "9".

Gesture path	Train data	Meaningful gestures spotting results						
		Test	I	D	S	Correct	Rec. (%)	Rel. (%)
"0"	42	28	1	0	1	27	96.43	93.10
"1"	42	28	1	0	0	27	96.43	93.10
"2"	42	28	1	1	1	26	92.86	89.65
"3"	42	28	1	1	1	26	92.86	89.65
"4"	42	28	1	2	1	25	89.93	86.21
"5"	42	28	1	1	1	26	92.86	89.65
"6"	42	28	1	1	1	26	92.86	89.65
"7"	42	28	1	2	1	25	89.93	86.21
"8"	42	28	1	2	1	25	89.93	86.21
"9"	42	28	1	1	1	26	92.86	89.65
Total	420	280	10	11	9	259	92.50	89.31

rate 93.14%. However, the proposed method has a problem in that the system cannot report the detection of a gesture immediately after the system reaches its end point. It is because the endpoint detection process post-pones the decision until the detection of the next gesture in order to avoid premature decision. The delayed response may cause one to wonder whether one's gesture has been recognized correctly or not. For that reason, their system is not capable for real-time applications.

Yang, H.-D., Sclaroff, S. and Lee, S.-W. [8] proposed a novel method for designing threshold models in a conditional random field (CRF) model which performs an adaptive threshold for distinguishing between signs in a vocabulary and non-sign patterns. A short-sign detector, a hand appearance-based sign verification method, and a sub-sign reasoning method are included to further improve sign language spotting accuracy. Their experiments demonstrate that their system can spot signs from continuous data with an 87.00% spotting rate. In order to spot signs from continuous data, a two-layer CRF architecture is applied with a sub-sign reasoning method, a short-sign detector, and an appearance-based shape verification method. In the first layer, in-vocabulary signs and non-sign patterns are discriminated by a threshold model with CRF. Spotted signs in the first layer are temporarily saved. Subsequent to detecting a sign sequence, the second layer CRF is applied to find sub-sign patterns. Sub-sign patterns within signs are modeled with a CRF. The input sequence of the second layer CRF includes more than one sign. The results of the second layer CRF are used to find the candidate label with the maximum probability. Finally, the appearance-based sign verification method is performed for the selected candidate sign. These steps are employed with end point detection technique that is not suitable for real-time applications.

Elmezain, M., Al-Hamadi, A. and Michaelis, B. [16] proposed a stochastic method for designing a non-gesture model with Hidden Markov Models (HMMs) versus Conditional Random Fields (CRFs). He used as an adaptive threshold to find the start and the end point of meaningful gestures, which are embedded in the input video stream. Also, he employed the forward spotting technique with sliding window with size ranging from 1 to 7 to empirically decide the optimal value. Their system was enhanced using relative entropy measure and increasing self-transition weight for HMMs and CRFs short gesture, respectively. The experiments of them could can successfully spot and recognize meaningful gestures with 93.31% and 90.49% reliability for HMMs and CRFs respectively.

In the light of this comparison (**Table 2**), it is being notice that the proposed approach performs competitively with another state-of-the-art method [7] [8] [16] in addition to carry out without sacrificing real-time performance. To assess the efficiency of the proposed method, the obtained results have been compared with those of other previously published studies in the literature, as shown in **Table 2**. From this comparison, it turns out that our approach performs competitively with other state-of-the-art approaches, and its results compared favorably with previously published results. Notably, all the methods that we compared our method with have used nearly similar experimental setups. Thus, the comparison is meaningful.

The image sequences depicted in **Figure 5** contain three key gestures "7", "6" and "5". The above graph of this figure considers only the temporal evolution of the probabilities of gestures "7", "6", "5" and non-gesture (for simplicity, the other curves are eliminated because their probabilities are low). The gesture "7" ends at frame index 21. Between frame index 22 and frame index 34, the highest priority is assigned to non-gesture label which means that the start point of second key gesture is not detected. At frame index 35, a new key gesture is started where the probability value of non-gesture label is not the highest value as compared to the other gesture labels. The gesture "6" ends at frame index 57. Between frame index 58 and frame index 73, the highest priority is assigned to non-gesture label. The gesture "5" starts at frame index 74 and ends at frame index 102.

Table 2. Comparison with the state-of-the-art.

Method	Recognition rate
Our method	92.50%
Lee, H.-K. and Kim, J. H. [7]	93.14%
Yang, H.-D., Sclaroff, S. and Lee, S.-W. [8]	87.00%
Elmezain, M. Al-Hamadi, A. and Michaelis, B. [16]	90.49%

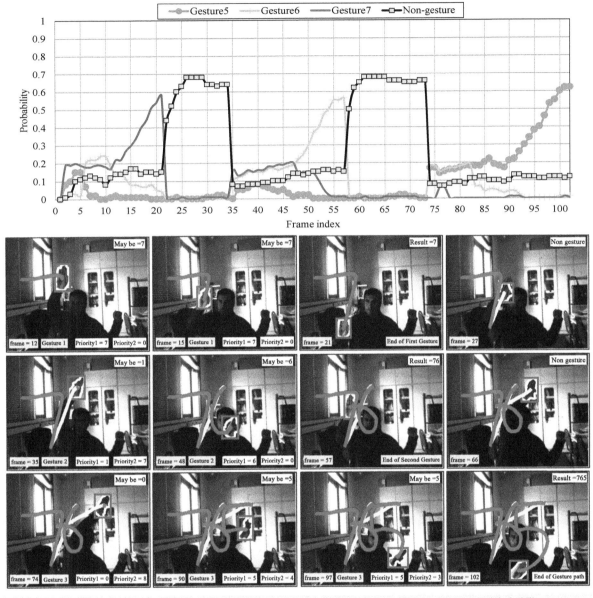

Figure 5. Temporal evolution of the probabilities of the gesture numbers "5", "6", "7" and non-gesture label "N".

4. Conclusion

This paper proposed a novel gesture spotting and recognition technique, which handled hand gesture from continuous hand motion based on Conditional Random Field in conjunction with Support Vector Machine. 3D depth map was captured by bumblebee stereo camera to neutralize complex background sense. Additionally, dynamic affine-invariants features like elliptic Fourier and Zernike moments, in addition to three orientations motion features were employed to CRF and SVMs. Finally, the discriminative model of CRF performed the spotting and recognition processes by using the combined of orientation features. Accordingly, Support Vector Machine verified the hand shape at the start and the end point of meaningful gesture by using elliptic Fourier and Zernike moments features. Experiments showed that our proposed method could successfully spot hand gesture from continuous hand motion data with 92.50% recognition rate.

References

[1]   Rose, R.C. (1992) Discriminant Word Spotting Techniques for Rejection Non-Vocabulary Utterances in Unconstrained

Speech. *IEEE International Conference on Acoustics, Speech, and Signal Processing*, **2**, 105-108.

[2]   Chen, F.R., Wilcox, L.D. and Bloomberg, D.S. (1993) Word Spotting in Scanned Images Using Hidden Markov Models. *IEEE International Conference on Acoustics, Speech, and Signal Processing*, **5**, 1-4. http://dx.doi.org/10.1109/icassp.1993.319732

[3]   Starner, T., Weaver, J. and Pentland, A. (1998) Real-Time American Sign Language Recognition Using Desk and Wearable Computer Based Video. *IEEE Transaction on Pattern Analysis and Machine Intelligence*, **20**, 1371-1375. http://dx.doi.org/10.1109/34.735811

[4]   Takahashi, K., Seki, S. and Oka, R. (1992) Spotting Recognition of Human Gestures from Motion Images. Technical Report IE92-134, 9-16.

[5]   Baudel, T. and Beaudouin, M. (1993) CHARADE: Remote Control of Objects Using Free-Hand Gestures. *Communications of ACM*, **36**, 28-35. http://dx.doi.org/10.1145/159544.159562

[6]   Wexelblat, A. (1994) Natural Gesture in Virtual Environments. *Proceedings of Virtual Reality Software and Technology Conference*, Singapore, 23-26 August 1994, 5-16. http://dx.doi.org/10.1142/9789814350938_0002

[7]   Lee, H.-K. and Kim, J.H. (1999) An Hmm-Based Threshold Model Approach for Gesture Recognition. *IEEE Transactions on Pattern Analysis and Machine Intelligence*, **21**, 961-973. http://dx.doi.org/10.1109/34.799904

[8]   Yang, H.-D., Sclaroff, S. and Lee, S.-W. (2009) Sign Language Spotting with a Threshold Model Based on Conditional Random Fields. *IEEE Transactions on Pattern Analysis and Machine Intelligence*, **31**, 1264-1277. http://dx.doi.org/10.1109/TPAMI.2008.172

[9]   Elmezain, M. (2013) Adaptive Foreground with Cast Shadow Segmentation Using Gaussian Mixture Models and Invariant Color Features. *International Journal of Engineering Science and Innovative Technology (IJESIT)*, **2**, 438-445.

[10] Elmezain, M., Al-Hamadi, A., Niese, R. and Michaelis, B. (2009) A Robust Method for Hand Tracking Using Mean-Shift Algorithm and Kalman Filter in Stereo Color Image Sequences. *International Conference on Computer Vision, Image and Signal Processing, PWASET*, **59**, 355-359.

[11] Ding, C. and He, X.F. (2004) K-Means Clustering via Principal Component Analysis. *Proceedings of the 21st International Conference on Machine Learning*, New York, 225-232.

[12] Nixon, M.S. and Aguado, A.S. (2002) Feature Extraction and Image Processing. Newnes, Central Tablelands.

[13] Ahmad, M. and Lee, S.-W. (2008) Human Action Recognition Using Shape and Clg Motion Flow from Multi-View Image Sequences. *Journal of Pattern Recognition*, **41**, 2237-2252. http://dx.doi.org/10.1016/j.patcog.2007.12.008

[14] Dugad, R., Ratakonda, K. and Ahuja, N. (1998) Robust Video Shot Change Detection. *Workshop on Multimedia Signal Processing*, Redondo Beach, 7-9 December 1998, 376-381. http://dx.doi.org/10.1109/mmsp.1998.738965

[15] Dalal, N. and Triggs, B. (2005) Histograms of Oriented Gradients for Human Detection. *IEEE Computer Society Conference on Computer Vision and Pattern Recognition*, San Diego, 25-25 June 2005, 886-893. http://dx.doi.org/10.1109/cvpr.2005.177

[16] Elmezain, M., Al-Hamadi, A. and Michaelis, B. (2010) Robust Methods for Hand Gesture Spotting and Recognition Using Hidden Markov Models and Conditional Random Fields. *IEEE Symposium on Signal Processing and Information Technology (ISSPIT)*, Luxor, 15-18 December 2010, 131-136. http://dx.doi.org/10.1109/ISSPIT.2010.5711749

3

An Integration of UML Sequence Diagram with Formal Specification Methods— A Formal Solution Based on Z

Nasir Mehmood Minhas, Asad Masood Qazi, Sidra Shahzadi, Shumaila Ghafoor

University Institute of Information Technology, PMAS-University Institute of Information Technology, Rawalpindi, Pakistan
Email: nasirminhas@uaar.edu.pk, asad.masood@dpskw.com, sidra.shahzadi363@gmail.com, shumailaghafoor90@gmail.com

Abstract

UML Diagrams are considered as a main component in requirement engineering process and these become an industry standard in many organizations. UML diagrams are useful to show an interaction, behavior and structure of the system. Similarly, in requirement engineering, formal specification methods are also being used in crucial systems where precise information is required. It is necessary to integrate System Models with such formal methods to overcome the requirements errors *i.e.* contradiction, ambiguities, vagueness, incompleteness and mixed values of abstraction. Our objective is to integrate the Formal Specification Language (Z) with UML Sequence diagram, as sequence diagram is an interaction diagram which shows the interaction and proper sequence of components (Methods, procedures etc.) of the system. In this paper, we focus on components of UML Sequence diagram and then implement these components in formal specification language Z. And the results of this research papers are complete integrated components of Sequence diagram with Z schemas, which are verified by using tools and model based testing technique of Formal Specifications. Results can be more improved by integrating remaining components of Sequence and other UML diagrams into Formal Specification Language.

Keywords

Formal Specifications, Software Requirement Specifications, Formal Notations

1. Introduction

Formal Methods are based on mathematical techniques, which can be used in any phase of Project life cycle, especially in an initial stage. When requirements are gathered from clients, project team has to know about the system. There are many techniques of formal methods, like Model based Languages, Process Oriented and Algebraic Specifications.

In Software Engineering, formal specifications and UML Diagrams are very useful to understand the requirements and specifications of the system. Formal specifications and UML are used since many years in Software Engineering, and UML diagrams are considered as a standard tool in many organizations. There is a complete method in Software Engineering named as "Clean Room Software Engineering" [1] basically based on formal specifications. The idea behind the Clean Room SE is "Do it Right, at first Time". It is composed of gathering requirements, and then transforms them into statistical methods, so there will no need of unit testing.

UML diagrams are important to understand the complexity of system. UML describes the behavior and structure of a program. Also, they describe the interaction of components with the system. These include Use Case, Class, Activity and many other diagrams. UML diagrams are easy to understand by the users, developers and domain experts whereas the formal methods are difficult to understand by the users, domain experts and developers as well.

Before go forward, we also need to know that where the specification part lies actually in the Requirement engineering process. A brief detail of requirement engineering process is given below:

Software requirement engineering involves requirements elicitation, requirements specification, requirements validation and requirements management [2] [3]. Requirements elicitation involves the ways of gathering the requirements which include many traditional, cognitive, model based techniques etc.

Whereas, the requirements Specification (where analysis and negotiation of requirements are performed), requirements of users are specify to make them understandable and meaningful for developers. Specifications can be formal as well as non-formal [4]. Formal techniques include the set of tools and techniques based on mathematical models whereas informal techniques are based on modeling the requirements in diagrams or making architecture of system. There are many techniques in both types of specification. Like in formal techniques of specifications, we have different formal specification languages like Z, VDM etc. and in in-formal or non-formal techniques, we have UML diagrams which include use-cases, sequence diagrams, collaboration and interaction diagrams etc.

In Requirements validation, the completeness of the requirements being checked which means either gathered requirements are correct, complete or not. The main objective to analyze the validation and verification of RE process to identify and resolve the problems and highly risk factors of software in early stages to make strengthen the development cycle [5]. Finally, in Requirements management phase, issues and conflicts of users are resolved. According to Andriole [6], the requirement management is a political game. It is basically applied in such cases where we have to control the expectations of stakeholders from software, and put the requirements rather than in well-meaning by customers but meaning full by developers, so they can examine that, they actually full fill the user's requirements.

Authors of [7] include the Requirement change management under the Requirement Engineering process. RCM is a term which is used as the history or previous development of the similar software product (s). On the basis of historical development, we investigate the need of RCM or not.

Unique Features of Sequence Diagrams

There are some unique features of Sequence diagrams and also reasons for choosing sequence diagrams for this research purpose, which are:
- Sequence Diagrams are used to show the priorities of steps/modules of system, Lower step denotes to the later.
- Reverse Engineering of UML sequence diagrams are used to support reverse engineering in software development process [8].
- It shows a dynamic behavior of system and considered as good system architecture design approach [9].
- Sequence diagrams include the Life line of the objects, and it can be easily integrated because of Time dimension [10].
- We can use messages to make it understandable by all stakeholders.
- We can also use loops, alternatives, break, parallelism between complex components of system and many more [10].

Our Idea is to work on integration of UML Sequence Diagram's attributes with formal specification methods like Z notations to bridge a gap between both (formal and informal) methods. So, once we make a sketch of any system in to Sequence diagram to show its sequence of steps, requirement priorities, time bar information and others, then we will transform these attributes into Z schemas. So it will be an easy for developers, to develop system if they had requirements in proper mathematical forms. Also, there was a research gap of properly integration of Sequence diagrams with formal specifications.

2. Related Work

The Integration of formal and in formal methods of specification is not a new area, it is being used by many software industries as well as there is a complete area of research in Software engineering to tackle the limitations of both techniques and transform them into an intermediately solution. Many studies are there which are helpful to integrate the Z notations with Scrum, requirement elicitation and many other areas.

In [11], authors represents a conceptual solution to formalize the Class Diagrams, in which they formalize the class diagrams through steps including representing classes in Z, representing associations in Z representing aggregation in Z and then represent generalization of classes in Z.

Similarly, in [12] researchers represent a conceptual solution to integrate XP methodology with Z. They work on user stories phase, where user stories will be verified through Formal Verification techniques. It can also be observed from [13] in which integration of the Z notations into Use case Diagram, because use case diagrams are very common in software development companies, as these are easy to understand by all stakeholders, so they apply Z on them, to bridge a gap between formal and informal techniques. It has been observed from [14], which is study on an Integration of formal methods into agile methodology that formal methods can lead towards a better software development solution. In [15], they apply formalization in the requirement specification phase of Requirement Engineering Process. They describe an analyzing phase, in which they will focus on such a specification which is being analyzed early.

Concept of making Z schemas of UML class and sequence diagrams on the basis of some semantic rules can also be found in the [16] [17]. Firstly, a Video on Demand case study is been taken in this study, then authors draw its class structure diagram to shows the hierarchy of the classes, and then Z schemas are defined. Secondly, sequence diagram is generated on same case study, furthermore its objects are defined in a complete way using Z schemas.

Tony Spiteri [18] takes a case study, transform it into UML diagrams, and then implement the specifications into formal method languages, then apply optimization methods to minimize the computing resources; total time and total cost. in [19]-[21] z notations based schemas are applied in some real life examples and case studies, furthermore, the authors also uses z/eves tool for formal model check as well as z schemas verification. In [11], very important concept can be found related to this study, in which sequence diagram is analyzed through the states of the system and their relationship according to the message using state transitions graphs.

3. Expectations from System Specifications

In any system development, we gather the requirements from users and then we try to understand "What" should be done, but formal specification methods also specify "Why" should be done. For moving from analysis to implementation we have to identify these (and many else) variables from [22]-[24].

3.1. Domain Knowledge

Understanding about the system as well as its context, and it should be known by all stakeholders. For example for Library management system, there should be complete understanding about the library environment and ordinary procedures followed by Library. Similarly for Airline reservation system, there should be a complete knowledge about its possible components like scheduling, ticketing boarding etc.

3.2. User's Requirements

These are the requirements which are not the requirements of system. Actually, these requirements are defined by the client or user to make it efficient or easy to use, like cost, ease of use etc. are the examples of user's requirements.

3.3. System Requirements

These requirements are purely related to the system, which must be included in the system. For example a flight reservation system must include the flight place with time and date.

3.4. System Specification

To specify the gathered requirements, software engineers' uses many ways to transform the story based requirements into a meaningful form for developers. These specifications are not basically dependent to any design, these can be in form of abstract prototypes, formulas procedures or else. In this part, specifications are sent to the developers to implement them, and testers to test them and to the users to verify them.

3.5. Design Structure

In design structure, we have to focus on "How" part. For example how the functionality is allocated to the system component, how the system's components will communicate each other etc.

3.6. Problem Refinement

Formal notation methods like VDM and Z helps the software engineers to refine the problem. In user's stories which problem look more complex, and involve complex mathematical structure, we refine it by using formal methods, so by specify the relationship between components problem becomes in more refined shape.

4. Proposed Solution

Formal specifications use mathematical notation and provide state requirements and mechanism for the verification of system correctness. Z specification provides a mathematical technique to model relation via predicate calculus that has states and relational functions [9]. Our Research will basically focus on implementation of UML Sequence diagram into Z. So, to implement our problem we proposed some sequence of steps which is given in **Figure 1**.

5. Formalization of Flight Reservation System

5.1. UML Sequence Diagram as an Input

A flight reservation system may contain the records of flights, which includes the place, date and time of flight, airline name, number of seating capacity or number of tickets, list of users etc. Now on the basis of this given data, following operations can be performed like Creation of Reservation, Cancel the reservation, Sign In/Sign Up etc. UML sequence diagram for Flight reservation system can be seen in **Figure 2**.

5.2. States-Transition Diagram

To set some grammar rules we have to identify the state transition graph or diagram. So, on the basis of these grammar rules we can formalize our sequence diagram's components. The State UML diagram is given in **Figure 3**.

5.3. Define Grammar Rules

In transformation procedure from state to grammar development is given in **Table 1**. In transformation

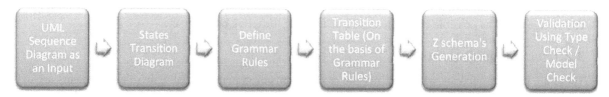

Figure 1. Proposed solution steps to integrate UML sequence architecture with formal specification methods.

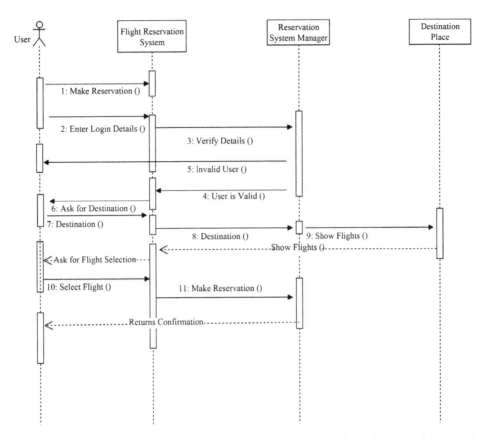

Figure 2. UML sequence architecture of flight reservation system.

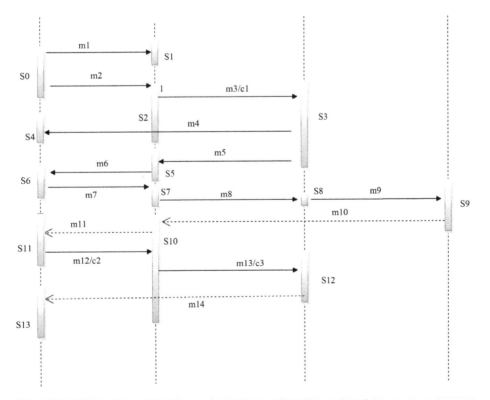

Figure 3. State Transition graph/diagram on the basis of UML sequence diagram.

Table 1. States-transition table with their termination conditions.

Sr.#	STATES/MESSAGE	OUTPUT
1	S0, m1, S1, null	S0 $\Rightarrow$ m1S1, null
2	S0, m2, S2, null	S0 $\Rightarrow$ m2S2, null
3	S2, m3, S3, c1	S2 $\Rightarrow$ m3S3, c1
4	S3, m4, S4, null	S3 $\Rightarrow$ m4S4, null
5	S3, m5, S5, null	S3 $\Rightarrow$ m5S5, null
6	S5, m6, S6, null	S5 $\Rightarrow$ m6S6, null
7	S6, m7, S7, null	S6 $\Rightarrow$ m7S7, null
8	S7, m8, S8, null	S7 $\Rightarrow$ m8S8, null
9	S8, m9, S9, null	S8 $\Rightarrow$ m9S9, null
10	S9, m10, S10, null	S9 $\Rightarrow$ m10S10, null
11	S9, m10, S10, null	S9 $\Rightarrow$ m10S10, null
12	S10, m11, S11, null	S10 $\Rightarrow$ m11S11, null
13	S10, m12, S11, c2	S10 $\Rightarrow$ m12S11, c2
14	S10, m13, S12, c3	S10 $\Rightarrow$ m13S12, c3
15	S12, m14, S13, null	S12 $\Rightarrow$ m14S13, null

there are certain states regarding each object and messages execute from one state another state, a production rule is created, for the execution of message if there is no condition null condition is supposed. We can elaborate this concept with the help of example for this consider row 1 where m1 (message 1: make reservation) execute from state S0 to S1 here no condition is imposed for execution so, there is null condition. We can determine final states from given table where S2, S10 are final states and rest of all are failure of operation.

Using **Table 1**: After constructing rules regarding each message now, here for the termination of the process the null production are added, represented by derivation tree for parsing of a scenario.

Rule (r1): S0 $\Rightarrow$ m1S1, null|m2S2, null,
Rule (r2): S1 $\Rightarrow$ $\in$,
Rule (r3): S2 $\Rightarrow$ m3S3, c1,
Rule (r4): S3 $\Rightarrow$ m4S4, null|m5S5, null,
Rule (r5): S4 $\Rightarrow$ $\in$,
Rule (r6): S5 $\Rightarrow$ m6S6, null,
Rule (r7): S6 $\Rightarrow$ m7S7, null,
Rule (r8): S7 $\Rightarrow$ m8S8, null,
Rule (r9): S8 $\Rightarrow$ m9S9, null,
Rule (r10): S9 $\Rightarrow$ m10S10, null|m10S10, null,
Rule (r11): S10 $\Rightarrow$ m11S11, null|m12S11, c2.

To check validation we can derive by above diagram which we have constructed in grammar rules, here is only the validation for S0, we can check for all states like this way:

According to r1 S0 $\Rightarrow$ m2S2, now if we apply r3 we get m3S
S0 $\Rightarrow$ m2S2
(By applying r3 on S2 we get m3S3)
$\Rightarrow$ m2m3S3
(By applying r4 on S3 we get m5S5)
$\Rightarrow$ m2m3m5S5
(By applying r6 on S5 we get m6S6)
$\Rightarrow$ m2m3m5m6S6
(By applying r7 on S6 we get m7S7)
$\Rightarrow$ m2m3m5m6m7S7

(By applying r8 on S7 we get m8S8)
⇒m2m3m5m6m7m8S8
(By applying r9 on S8 we get m9S9)
⇒m2m3m5m6m7m8m9S9
(By applying r10 on S9 we get m10S10)
⇒m2m3m5m6m7m8m9m10S10
(By applying r11 on S10 we get m11S11)
⇒m2m3m5m6m7m8m9m11S11

5.4. State-Transition Table

Rules for Constructing Z Schemas:

Rule 1:

S0 ∧ S1 € states, if current (state) = i then new (state) = i+1, condition c = null for the execution, message = m1 will move from S0 to S1. Creation and termination time of object (passenger) is between start and end time of S0, S1, and same in the case of message m2.

Rule 2:

S2 ∧ S3 € states, if current (state) = i then new (state) = i+1, condition c = c1 for the execution, message = m3 will move from S2 toS3 regarding objects flight reservation system and reservation system manager. Termination and creation time of these objects (o1, o2) must not be greater than the time require for the start and end of states S2, S3.

Rule 3:

S3 ∧ S4 € states, if current (state) = i then new (state) = i+1, condition c = null for the execution, message = m4 will move from S3 toS4 regarding objects flight reservation system and reservation system manager. Termination and creation time of these objects (o2 to o1) must not be greater than the time require for the start and end of states S3, S4.

Rule 4:

S8 ∧ S9 € states, message m9 execute by fulfilling condition c9. Termination and creation time of these objects (o3 to o4) must not be greater than the time require for the start and end of states.

5.5. Z Schemas Generation

In schema generation, we are using Z as formal specification language. The schema's mentioned below are the schemas of the sequence diagram of flight reservation system, which are based on the set of grammar rules, which we define earlier. Schemas are defined at the Appendix.

6. Testing and Verification

We have taken a small case study to work on this particular area, so we can test and validate our schemas and model efficiently. Our Z schemas are written in Z word tool, in which there is an option for type checking Z schemas using tool fuzz. Our grammar rules are semantic based solutions, which can be clearly seen in our state transition diagram. For model check we have used the same tool. Our resultant schemas are error free, but the results can also be improved through using other tools and techniques like Z/eves, CZT and many others.

The procedure of our testing was based on Z word tool which uses fuzz tool for type checking. The tool can be downloaded from Internet, and after installing we can use following procedure as described in **Figure 4** for Type Check.

By executing schemas, we achieve correctness of our schemas as described in **Figure 5**.

7. Limitations and Future Work

The case study, which we take as a reference is a simple study, and does not cover all the features of Z, also this integration make the system more complex for understandable to normal stake holders like Users. Although a sequence diagram is decomposed into parts, which means modules, sub modules, their relations etc. are extracted but overall cost of system in terms of time and money can be increased, that is why, formal specifications were not cordial welcomed by software industry. But now in this study and related previous (referenced) studies

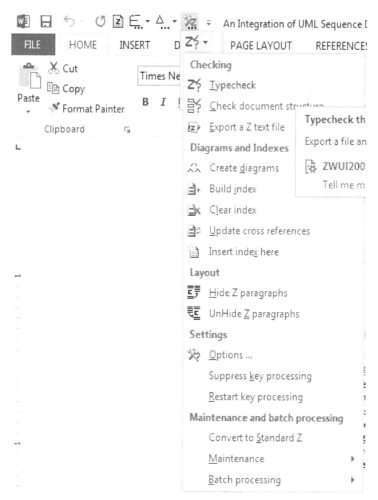

Figure 4. Type check specification.

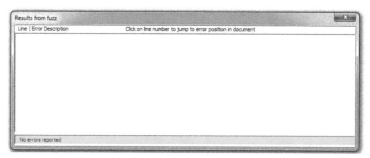

Figure 5. On Execution of Schemas the correctness is shown.

a gap between formal and informal methods of requirement engineering and specifications are bridged.

Furthermore, there are many other informal techniques which are needed to be formalized like many development models, requirement elicitation techniques which are typically based on user stories etc. Also we can improve the results by using other formal and mathematical techniques and algorithms to optimize the results and decrease the overall cost of system.

8. Conclusions

In this paper, we have focused on the integration of UML sequence diagram into using Z specification language. For this we take a system "the Flight Reservation System" by following all procedure as described in our methodology, we formalize our system into Z specification as well as we try to accommodate maximum features of UML diagrams into our proposed solution by applying some grammar rules, which are used in our semantic based solution.

Our formal specification method is based on the UML diagrams include sequence and state diagrams, and our objective is to integrate them using Z schemas notations. But it was not an easy task to include all the features and applications in one paper or one solution. But overall Z schemas are analyzed and tested using fuzz as a type checking.

References

[1] Selby, R.W., Basili, V.R. and Baker, F.T. (2006) Cleanroom Software Development: An Empirical Evaluation. *IEEE Transactions on Software Engineering*, **SE-13**, 1027-1037.

[2] Chikh, A. (2011) A Knowledge Management Framework in Software Requirements Engineering Based on SECI Model. *Journal of Software Engineering and Applications*, **4**, 718-728. http://www.SciRP.org/journal/jsea http://dx.doi.org/10.4236/jsea.2011.412084

[3] Flores, F., Mora, M., Álvarez, F., *et al.* (2010) Towards a Systematic Service Oriented Requirement Engineering Process (S-SoRE). *Proceedings of the International Conference, CENTERIS* 2010, Viana do Castelo, 20-22 October 2010, 111-120. http://dx.doi.org/10.1007/978-3-642-16402-6_12

[4] Batra, M., Malik, A. and Dave, M. (2013) Formal Methods: Benefits, Challenges and Future Direction. *Journal of Global Research in Computer Science*, **4**.

[5] Boehm, B.W. (1984) Verifying and Validating Software Requirements and Design Specifications. *IEEE Software Journal*, **1**, 75-88.

[6] Andriole, S. and Safeguard Sci. Inc. (1998) The Politics of Requirements Management. *IEEE Software Journal*, 15, 82-84. http://dx.doi.org/10.1109/52.730850

[7] Flores, F., Mora, M., Álvarez, F., O'Connor, R. and Macias, J. (2008) Handbook of Research on Modern Systems Analysis and Design Technologies and Applications. In: Global, I.G.I., Ed., *Chapter VI: Requirements Engineering: A Review of Processes and Techniques*, Minnesota State University; Mankato, 96-111.

[8] Rountev, A. and Connell, B.H. (2005) Object Naming Analysis for Reverse-Engineered Sequence Diagrams. *Proceedings of the International Conference on Software Engineering*, St. Louis, 15-21 May 2005, 254-263.

[9] Zafar, N.A. and Alhumaidan, F. (2013) Scenarios Verification in Sequence Diagram. *The Journal of American Science*, 9, 287-293. http://www.jofamericanscience.org

[10] UML Basics: The Sequence Diagram. http://www.ibm.com/developerworks/rational/library/3101.html

[11] Shroff, M. and France, R.B. (1997) Towards a Formalization of UML Class Structures in Z. *The 21st Annual International Computer Software and Applications Conference, 1997 (COMPSAC' 97)*, Washington DC, 11-15 August 1997, 646-651. http://dx.doi.org/10.1109/cmpsac.1997.625087

[12] Sgafiq, S. and Minhas, N.M. (2014) Integrating Formal Methods in XP—A Conceptual Solution. *Journal of Software Engineering and Applications*, 7, 299-310. http://dx.doi.org/10.4236/jsea.2014.74029

[13] Sengupta, S. and Bhattacharya, S. (2006) Formalization of UML Use Case Diagram—A Z Notation Based Approach.

[14] Black, S., Boca, P.P., Bowen, J.P., Gorman, J. and Hinchey, M. (2009) Formal versus Agile: Survival of the Fittest? *IEEE Computer*, **42**, 37-45. http://dx.doi.org/10.1109/MC.2009.284

[15] Fernández-y-Fernández, C.A. and José, M.J. (2012) Towards an Integration of Formal Specification in the Áncora Methodology.

[16] Spivey, J.M. (1998) The Z Notation: A Reference Manual. Prentice Hall International, Oxford.

[17] El Miloudi, K., El Armani, Y. and Attouhami, A. (2013) Using Z Formal Specification for Ensuring Consistency in Multi View Modeling. *Journal of Theoretical and Applied Information Technology*, **57**, 407-411.

[18] Staines, T.S. (2007) Supporting UML Sequence Diagrams with a Processor Net Approach. *Journal of Software*, **2**, 64-73. http://dx.doi.org/10.4304/jsw.2.2.64-73

[19] Alhumaidan, F. and Zafar, N.A. (2013) Automated Semantics Treatment of Sequence Diagram Defining Grammar Rules. http://worldcomp-proceedings.com/proc/p2013/FCS7057.pdf

[20] Zafar, N.A. (2006) Modeling and Formal Specification of Automated Train Control System Using Z Notation. *IEEE Multi-Topic Conference (INMIC'06)*, Islamabad, 23-24 December 2006, 438-443. http://dx.doi.org/10.1109/inmic.2006.358207

[21] Zafar, N.A., Khan, S.A. and Araki, K. (2012) Towards the Safety Properties of Moving Block Railway Interlocking

System. *International Journal of Innovative Computing, Information & Control*, **8**, 5677-5690.

[22] Heitmeyer, C.L., Jeffords, R.D. and Labaw, B.G. (1996) Automated Consistency Checking of Requirements Specifications. *ACM Transactions on Software Engineering and Methodology*, **5**, 231-261.
http://dx.doi.org/10.1145/234426.234431

[23] Hall, A. (1996) Using Formal Methods to Develop an ATC Information System. *IEEE Software*, **13**, 66-76.
http://dx.doi.org/10.1109/52.506463

[24] Bano, M. and Zwoghi, D. (2013) User's Involvement in Requirement Engineering and System Success. *IEEE 3rd International Workshop on Empirical Requirement Engineering*, Rio de Janeiro, 15 July 2013, 24-31.

Appendix

Schemas for object in sequence diagram

```
┌─ Passenger ──────────────────────────
│ pname:PName
│ pstart,pend:Time
│ states:seq state
│ attributes:□Atributes
│ function: Atributes□Atributes
├──────────────────────────────────────
│ states ≠ <>
│ n-states≥1
│ ⇒(∃ s0,s1:state | s0∧ s1∈active stats
│ .states0= s0∧states(n-states)=s1
│ ⇒pstart ≤ s0.stime  ∧  s1.etime ≤ oend)
│ ∀ i:ℕn-states ≥ 1∧I ∈ 1.........n-states-1
│ According to  rule 1
│ .∃s0,s1:states
│ .states i= s0∧staes (i+1)=s1⇒s0.etime ≤ s1.stime
│ ∀ input , output:Atributes | (input,output) ∈functions
│ .input ∈  atributes ∧ output ∈ atributes
└──────────────────────────────────────
```

Schemas for Messages in Sequence Diagram

Condition: = NULL |TRUE| FALSE

```
┌─ Enter-Id ──────────────────────────
│ Starttime ,end time:ℕ
│ condition: Condition
│ from s0 to s1 :states
├──────────────────────────────────────
│ starttime<end time
│ s0.stime ≤ starttime ∧ end time ≤ s1 . etime
│ according to rule 1
└──────────────────────────────────────
```

Schemas for Sequence Diagram

```
┌─ Flight Reservation system ──────────
│ objects : □Object
│ messages:□ Messages
├──────────────────────────────────────
│ ∀ o1 ,o2 :object | o1 ∧o2 ∈objects
│ ∃ s1, s2 : state | s1∧s2 ∈ran  o1.state∧o2 . states
│ ∃ m: Message | m∈ messages .m from = s1 ∧m. to =s2
│ ∀ m : Message | m ∈ messages
│ According to rule 2
│ ∃ o1 , o2 : object | o1 ∧o2 ∈objects
│ ∃ s1 ,s2 : state | s1∈ran.. o1 .staes ∧ s2 ∈ran o2. Staes
│ Where s1 = m. from ∧ s2 m. to
└──────────────────────────────────────
```

Operations in Reservation System

_Show Flight_____

Ξ *Flights*

Place? : Place

Date! : Date

Time !: Time

Starttime ,end time:$\mathbb{N}$

condition: Condition

from s8 to s9 :states

Place? $\in$ *Known*

Date! = Flights (Date?) $\wedge$

Time! = Flights (Time?)

starttime<end time

s8.stime $\leq$ starttime $\wedge$ end time $\leq$ s9 . etime

_Login System_____

Ξ *Users Initialization*

Usr ?: USERS

Res ?: RESOURCES

Result! REPORT

Starttime ,end time :$\mathbb{N}$

condition :C1

from s0 to s1 :states

Usr ? $\in$ Users

Res ?$\in$Resources

Result! = Welcome

Start −time <end time

S0.stime $\leq$ start time $\wedge$ end time $\leq$ s1.time

_Sign up users_____

Δ *Users Initialization*

Us ? : User

Crdls ?? : $\mathbb{P}$*CEDENTIAL*

U ? $\in$ users

U ? $\in$ registered users

Registered_users'   = Registered_Users $\cup$

{ (U? $\leftrightarrow$ crdls

4

Test Suite Design Methodology Using Combinatorial Approach for Internet of Things Operating Systems

Abhinandan H. Patil[1], Neena Goveas[1], Krishnan Rangarajan[2]

[1]Department of Computer Science and Information Systems, Birla Institute of Technology and Science, Goa, India
[2]Department of Information Science, Dayanand Sagar College of Engineering, Bangalore, India
Email: P2013408@goa.bits-pilani.ac.in, Neena@goa.bits-pilani.ac.in, Krishnanr1234@gmail.com

Abstract

In this paper we describe how the test design can be done by using the Combinatorial Testing approach for internet of things operating systems. Contiki operating system is taken as a case study but we discuss what can be the approach for RIOT and Tiny OS operating systems. We discuss how the combinatorial coverage measurement can be gathered in addition to the traditional metrics code coverage. The test design generated by using Advanced Combinatorial Testing for Software is analyzed for Contiki operating system. We elaborate the code coverage gathering technique for Contiki simulator which happens to be in Java. We explain the usage of Combinatorial Coverage Measurement tool. Although we have explained the test design methodology for internet of things operating systems, the approach explained can be followed for other open source software.

Keywords

CT, ACTS, CCM, Code Cover, Contiki, Cooja

1. Introduction

Our previously published paper touches upon the test design using combinatorial testing approach for Contiki operating system [1]. In this paper we intend to extend the concept and explain what can be done for the Internet of Things (IoT) operating systems which do not have standard regression test suites viz. RIOT and Tiny OS. We analyze the Advanced Combinatorial Testing for Software (ACTS) generated test suite design and explain how the traditional effective metrics, code coverage can be gathered in addition to more relevant combinatorial coverage measurements using combinatorial coverage measurement tool (CCM) .

While we want to have minimal overlap of this paper with the one published already [1], we may re-visit few sections and elaborate more. At places, we get specific and explain implementation part of testing (such as what changes are done to the test setup for gathering the data).

National Institute for Standards and Technology (NIST) has been actively supported combinatorial testing. The research carried out by NIST has been well documented [2] [3]. NIST has made several tools which are available to public [4]. C Nie *et al.* conducts a survey of combinatorial testing and the same is available as part of survey report [5]. Software testing is inarguably essential part of all software development cycles and the same is discussed at high levels by several papers [6]. While few papers discuss software testing techniques at very high level [7], we get specific and discuss combinatorial testing in this paper.

Combinatorial testing is not only adopted by researchers, and evidence shows the adoption by large organizations [8]. Few papers have different perspectives about testing at large [9]. Test suite and test oracles are integral part of testing these days [10]. NIST tools for combinatorial testing take these test suites and test oracles as input entities. NIST tools are an integral part of combinatorial testing and many users have been using them successfully in testing activities of research/industry. ACTs and CCM aid the combinatorial testing immensely. ACTs has been tested with self [11]. CCM's success is documented [12]. While abstracting the formal specifications to generate software tests is an old concept [13], it is being still researched. Few researchers are focusing on different fields of combinatorial testing [14], we in this paper focus on classic approaches of combinatorial testing techniques. A general strategy for t-way software testing is documented in few papers [15] and their through put is documented in few papers [16].

As mentioned earlier, this paper focuses on classic approaches of combinatorial testing and the same is being elaborated in the following sections.

2. Typical Workflow for Base-Lining the Regression Test Suite

Figure 1 depicts the typical flow of work when we want to ascertain the effectiveness of the test suite using combinatorial approach. First step is choosing the operating system for Internet of Things. Then traverse through the source code of the open source code base folders to see if the test suite exists. If it exists gather the coverage data using the code coverage tools.

If the gathered data indicates inadequate test suite, redesign the test suite using the combinatorial approach and gather the data. If the coverage data is less, it calls for re-visiting the test design. Base line the test suite once the adequate test criterion is met.

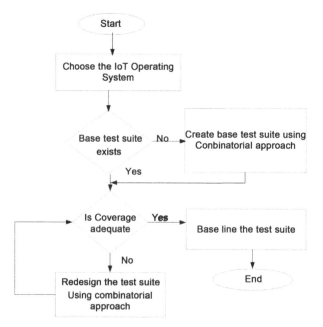

Figure 1. Typical work flow for base lining the test suite.

As can be seen from the diagram it can be iterative process. We document the process that was used for case study operating system in further sections. We describe the approach to be followed when the test suite already exists and when it does not. Section 3 is for the case when the base test suite already exists and Section 4 is for the case when the test suite does not exist.

3. Process of Redesigning the Regression Test Suite If It Already Exists

Figure 2 depicts the process in the case when test suite already exists. This section is for the case when the base lined test suite already exists as in the case of Contiki operating system version 2.7. We can use the either parameter based re-design or configuration based re-design as explained in the book and manual [1] [2] or combination of both. The coverage can be gathered using CCM and traditional coverage tools such as CodeCover. We did preliminary investigation using freely available tool CodeCover for the existing test suite. The coverage was less than 20%. **Appendix B** gives the data gathered using the CodeCover.

Then we visited the existing test suite to know the reason for low coverage. Few areas of improvements were observed in the existing test suite.
- No formal test design document existed.
- It appears that the test cases were concentrated around few mote types (hardware or configurations in the context of combinatorial testing).

We went through the whole regression test suite to extract the configurations supported and input parameters being used. We came up with **Table 1** to be populated in the ACTS test model. When the ACTS was populated using these set of values, the generated test design document is as shown in **Appendix A**.

Contiki Specific Details

Contiki is open source operating system widely used and accepted for Internet of Things. It has base-lined regression test suite for version 2.7. Contiki gives the user friendly operating system in the form of instant Contiki which has Ubuntu like the feel with the tool chains to make the iterative development easy. The developers can use the instant Contiki to test the patches and testers can use the same environment for ascertaining the reliability of the operating system without procuring the hardware for all the mote types.

Contiki gives the simulator which is called Cooja. The Cooja simulator talks to the Contiki using Java Native Interface (JNI). The test cases are called csc files which are understandable by Cooja. We found Eighty three test cases of this type in the regression folder. However, these test cases were concentrated around few mote types.

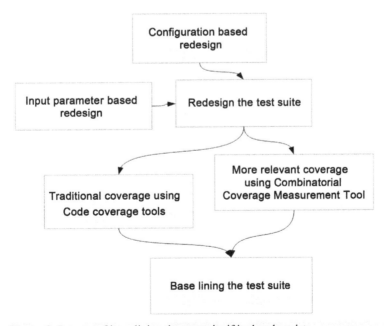

Figure 2. Process of base lining the test suite if it already exists.

Table 1. Acts input parameters.

Parameters	Parameter Values
Platform	Exp5438, z1, wismote, micaz, sky, jcreate, sentilla-usb, esb, native, cooja
base	Multithreading, coffee, check pointing
Rime	collect, rucb, deluge, runicast, trickle, mesh
Net Performance	Net Perf, Net Perf-lpp, Net Perf-cxmac
collect	shell-collect, shell-collect-lossy
ipv4	telnet-ping, webserver
ipv6	ipv6-udp, udp-fragmentation, unicast-fragmentation, ipv6-rpl-collect
RPL	up-root, root-reboot, large-network, up and down routes, temporary rootloss, random rearrngement, rpl-dao
ipv6apps	servreg-hack, coap

As already mentioned, **Appendix A** gives the test design generated using ACTS for **Table 1** input. Let us visit the column 2 of the design. We can see that the generated test cases are spread across the mote (hardware) types. Further, the generated test design takes care of the input parameters as well for the test cases.

Now the task at hand is mapping these generated test cases to functional test cases (xml files called csc) which are understandable by Cooja and gathering the coverage data again. The coverage data should improve in principle. We are working on this.

4. Process of Designing the Regression Test Suite If It Does Not Exist

Figure 3 depicts the case when test suite does not exist. This process is more suited for operating systems which do not have standard regression test suite viz. RIOT and TinyOS. Since the functional specification and test design are both missing in case of these operating systems, we will have to come up with the functional specification document first. This will be our understanding of the functionality that these operating systems support. Once the functionality of these operating systems is understood we will have to come up with the test design. Configuration to be supported and input parameters to be supplied for each test case will act as starting point for populating the ACTS test model. Once test design is generated, we will have to understand the test environment for these operating systems and the test design need to be mapped to functional test cases to be executed for gathering the coverage data. The CCM coverage will not be appropriate as the test cases generated using ACTS tool will always give 100% combinatorial coverage. Traditional coverage such as code coverage may be handy.

5. Contiki Environment Specific Changes to Be Done

In this section we document the changes that we did in the Contiki environment for the tasks at hand. Since we get implementation specific for case study operating system, this section can be conveniently skipped by the readers who are not interested in specific details for given operating system.

1. Log in as user in the instant Contiki environment.
2. Search for the .travis. yml
3. Add the build type you are interested in:
- BUILD_TYPE = "ipv6-apps"
- BUILD_TYPE = "CT"
-BUILD_TYPE = "compile-8051-ports"
4. Under the directory../contiki-2.7/regression-tests create a folder 02-CT
5. Under contiki-2.7/regression-tests/02-CT directory create *.csc files you are interested in viz. 01-custom.csc 02-custom.csc
6. The Make file should look like include../Makefile. simulation-test
7. Create a 01-custom.csc file in the Cooja tool. Use the test script editor to create a java script which will be essential while running the test case from command line using the makefile.

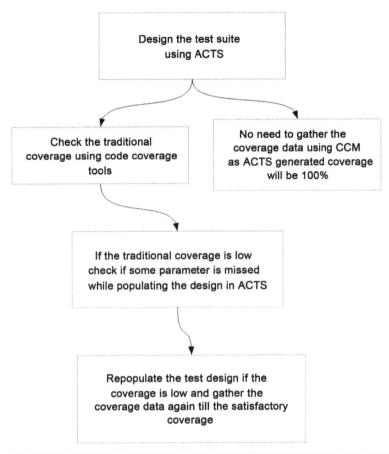

Figure 3. Process of base-lining the test suite if it does not exist.

8. Modify the build.xml suitably as explained in **Appendix C**.
9. Run the regression test suite as usual.
10. Test run will create many *.clf files.
11. Create a script for analyze, merge and generate report.

6. Conclusion

In this paper we presented the approaches that could be employed for designing the regression test suite using combinatorial approach. We explained how the bench marking of the regression test suite could be done using the traditional approaches such as code coverage in addition to coverage gathered using combinatorial coverage measurement tools.

7. Future Work

In this paper we investigated how the combinatorial approach could be applied for the cases when the regression test suite already existed viz. Contiki case. We were working on ascertaining the gain due to Combinatorial testing.

We were planning to explore the Combinatorial testing for the cases when the regression test suite did not exist viz. RIOT and TinyOS.

Further we were planning to model the System Under Test (SUT) and use New Symbolic Model Verifier (NuSMV) in conjunction with ACTs.

References

[1]   Patil, A.H., Goveas, N. and Rangarajan, K. (2015) Re-architecture of Contiki and Cooja Regression Test Suite Using

Combinatorial Testing Approach. *ACM SIGSOFT Software Engineering Notes*, **40**, 1-3.

[2]   Richard Kuhn, D., Kacker, R.N. and Lei, Y. (2013) Introduction to Combinatorial Testing. Text Book.

[3]   Richard Kuhn, D., Kacker, R.N. and Lei. Y. (2013) Practical Combinatorial Testing Manual. NIST Special Publications 800-142.

[4]   NIST. http://csrc.nist.gov/groups/SNS/acts/index.html

[5]   Nie, C., *et al.* (2011) A Survey of Combinatorial Testing. ACM Computing Surveys, Vol. 43, No. 2, Article 11.

[6]   Ammann, P. and Offutt, J. (2008) Introduction to Software Testing. Cambridge University Press, New York. http://dx.doi.org/10.1017/CBO9780511809163

[7]   Beizer, B. (1990) Software Testing Techniques. 2nd Edition, Van Nostrand Reinhold, New York.

[8]   ASTQB (2014) Introducing Combinatorial Testing in Large Organizations.

[9]   Bach, J. and Shroeder, P. (2004) Pairwise Testing—A Best Practice That Isn't. *Proceedings of 22nd Pacific Northwest Software Quality Conference*, Portland, 180-196.

[10] Baresi, L. and Young, M. (2001) Test Oracles. Department of Computer and Information Science, University of Oregon, Eugene. http://www.cs.uoregon.edu/michal/pubs/oracles.html

[11] NourozBorazjany, M., Yu, L., Lei, Y., Kacker, R.N. and Kuhn, D.R. (2012) Combinatorial Testing of ACTS: A Case Study. 2012 *IEEE 5th International Conference on Software Testing, Verification and Validation*, 17-21 April 2012, Montreal, 971.

[12] Combinatorial Coverage Measurement NASA IV&V Workshop, 11-13 September 2012.

[13] Ammann, P. and Black, P.E. (1999) Abstracting Formal Specifications to Generate Software Tests via Model Checking. *Proceedings of 18th Digital Avionics Systems Conference*, **2**, 10.A.6.1-10.A.6.10. http://dx.doi.org/10.1109/dasc.1999.822091

[14] Kuhn, D.R., Higdon, J.M., Lawrence, J.F., Kacker, R.N. and Lei, Y. (2012) Combinatorial Methods for Event Sequence Testing. 5*th International Workshop on Combinatorial Testing*, Montreal, 17-21 April 2012, 601-609.

[15] Lei, Y. (2007) IPOG—A General Strategy for t-Way Software Testing. 14*th Annual IEEE International Conference and Workshops on the Engineering of Computer-Based Systems*, Tucson, 26-29 March 2007, 549-556.

[16] Price, C., Kuhn, R., *et al.* (2013) Evaluating the t-Way Technique for Determining the Thoroughness of a Test Suite. *NASA IV&V Workshop*, Fairmont, September 2013.

Appendix A: ACTS generated test design for Contiki Operating System

Column1	Column2	Column3	Column4	Column5	Column6	Column7	Column8	Column9	Column10
Test Case#	Platform	base	Rime	NetPerformanc	collect	ipv4	ipv6	RPL	ipv6apps
0	Exp5438	coffee	rucb	NetPerf-lpp	shell-collect-lossy	webserver	udp-fragmentation	up-root	coap
1	Exp5438	checkpointing	deluge	NetPerf-cxmac	shell-collect	telnet-ping	unicast-fragmentatic	root-reboot	servreg-hack
2	Exp5438	Multithreading	runicast	NetPerf	shell-collect-lossy	telnet-ping	ipv6-rpl-collect	large-network	coap
3	Exp5438	coffee	trickle	NetPerf-cxmac	shell-collect	webserver	ipv6-udp	upanddownroutes	servreg-hack
4	Exp5438	checkpointing	mesh	NetPerf	shell-collect	webserver	udp-fragmentation	temporaryrootloss	coap
5	Exp5438	Multithreading	collect	NetPerf-lpp	shell-collect	webserver	unicast-fragmentatic	randomrearrngement	servreg-hack
6	Exp5438	checkpointing	rucb	NetPerf-cxmac	shell-collect-lossy	telnet-ping	ipv6-rpl-collect	rpl-dao	servreg-hack
7	z1	Multithreading	deluge	NetPerf	shell-collect-lossy	telnet-ping	ipv6-udp	up-root	coap
8	z1	coffee	runicast	NetPerf-lpp	shell-collect	webserver	udp-fragmentation	root-reboot	servreg-hack
9	z1	checkpointing	trickle	NetPerf-lpp	shell-collect-lossy	telnet-ping	unicast-fragmentatic	large-network	coap
10	z1	Multithreading	mesh	NetPerf-cxmac	shell-collect-lossy	telnet-ping	ipv6-rpl-collect	upanddownroutes	coap
11	z1	coffee	collect	NetPerf	shell-collect-lossy	telnet-ping	ipv6-udp	temporaryrootloss	servreg-hack
12	z1	checkpointing	rucb	NetPerf	shell-collect	telnet-ping	ipv6-udp	randomrearrngement	coap
13	z1	Multithreading	deluge	NetPerf-lpp	shell-collect	webserver	udp-fragmentation	rpl-dao	coap
14	wismote	checkpointing	runicast	NetPerf-cxmac	shell-collect	webserver	unicast-fragmentatic	up-root	servreg-hack
15	wismote	Multithreading	trickle	NetPerf	shell-collect-lossy	webserver	ipv6-rpl-collect	root-reboot	coap
16	wismote	coffee	mesh	NetPerf-lpp	shell-collect	telnet-ping	ipv6-udp	large-network	servreg-hack
17	wismote	checkpointing	collect	NetPerf-cxmac	shell-collect-lossy	telnet-ping	udp-fragmentation	upanddownroutes	coap
18	wismote	Multithreading	rucb	NetPerf	shell-collect-lossy	telnet-ping	unicast-fragmentatic	temporaryrootloss	coap
19	wismote	coffee	deluge	NetPerf-lpp	shell-collect-lossy	webserver	ipv6-rpl-collect	randomrearrngement	servreg-hack
20	wismote	coffee	runicast	NetPerf	shell-collect-lossy	telnet-ping	ipv6-udp	rpl-dao	coap
21	micaz	checkpointing	trickle	NetPerf-cxmac	shell-collect	webserver	udp-fragmentation	up-root	servreg-hack
22	micaz	coffee	mesh	NetPerf-lpp	shell-collect-lossy	telnet-ping	unicast-fragmentatic	root-reboot	coap
23	micaz	Multithreading	collect	NetPerf-cxmac	shell-collect	webserver	ipv6-rpl-collect	large-network	coap
24	micaz	checkpointing	rucb	NetPerf	shell-collect	telnet-ping	ipv6-udp	upanddownroutes	coap
25	micaz	checkpointing	deluge	NetPerf-lpp	shell-collect-lossy	webserver	ipv6-rpl-collect	temporaryrootloss	servreg-hack
26	micaz	checkpointing	runicast	NetPerf-cxmac	shell-collect	telnet-ping	udp-fragmentation	randomrearrngement	servreg-hack
27	micaz	checkpointing	trickle	NetPerf-cxmac	shell-collect	webserver	unicast-fragmentatic	rpl-dao	servreg-hack
28	sky	coffee	mesh	NetPerf	shell-collect-lossy	webserver	ipv6-rpl-collect	up-root	servreg-hack
29	sky	checkpointing	collect	NetPerf-lpp	shell-collect	telnet-ping	ipv6-udp	root-reboot	coap
30	sky	Multithreading	rucb	NetPerf-cxmac	shell-collect	webserver	udp-fragmentation	large-network	servreg-hack
31	sky	checkpointing	deluge	NetPerf-lpp	shell-collect-lossy	telnet-ping	unicast-fragmentatic	upanddownroutes	servreg-hack
32	sky	checkpointing	runicast	NetPerf-cxmac	shell-collect	telnet-ping	unicast-fragmentatic	temporaryrootloss	coap
33	sky	checkpointing	trickle	NetPerf	shell-collect	webserver	ipv6-rpl-collect	randomrearrngement	coap
34	sky	coffee	mesh	NetPerf-lpp	shell-collect-lossy	telnet-ping	ipv6-rpl-collect	rpl-dao	coap
35	jcreate	coffee	collect	NetPerf	shell-collect-lossy	webserver	ipv6-rpl-collect	up-root	servreg-hack
36	jcreate	checkpointing	rucb	NetPerf-lpp	shell-collect	telnet-ping	ipv6-udp	root-reboot	coap
37	jcreate	Multithreading	deluge	NetPerf-cxmac	shell-collect	webserver	udp-fragmentation	large-network	coap
38	jcreate	Multithreading	runicast	NetPerf-lpp	shell-collect	webserver	unicast-fragmentatic	upanddownroutes	servreg-hack
39	jcreate	checkpointing	trickle	NetPerf-lpp	shell-collect-lossy	webserver	ipv6-udp	temporaryrootloss	coap
40	jcreate	coffee	mesh	NetPerf-cxmac	shell-collect	telnet-ping	ipv6-udp	randomrearrngement	servreg-hack
41	jcreate	checkpointing	collect	NetPerf-cxmac	shell-collect	webserver	unicast-fragmentatic	rpl-dao	servreg-hack
42	sentilla-usb	coffee	rucb	NetPerf	shell-collect-lossy	webserver	ipv6-rpl-collect	up-root	servreg-hack
43	sentilla-usb	checkpointing	deluge	NetPerf-lpp	shell-collect	telnet-ping	ipv6-udp	root-reboot	coap
44	sentilla-usb	Multithreading	runicast	NetPerf-cxmac	shell-collect	webserver	udp-fragmentation	large-network	coap
45	sentilla-usb	coffee	trickle	NetPerf	shell-collect-lossy	webserver	unicast-fragmentatic	upanddownroutes	coap
46	sentilla-usb	coffee	mesh	NetPerf-lpp	shell-collect	telnet-ping	ipv6-udp	temporaryrootloss	coap
47	sentilla-usb	Multithreading	collect	NetPerf	shell-collect-lossy	telnet-ping	ipv6-udp	randomrearrngement	coap
48	sentilla-usb	Multithreading	collect	NetPerf-cxmac	shell-collect	webserver	unicast-fragmentatic	rpl-dao	servreg-hack
49	esb	coffee	rucb	NetPerf	shell-collect	webserver	ipv6-rpl-collect	up-root	servreg-hack
50	esb	checkpointing	deluge	NetPerf-lpp	shell-collect	telnet-ping	ipv6-udp	root-reboot	coap
51	esb	Multithreading	runicast	NetPerf-cxmac	shell-collect-lossy	webserver	udp-fragmentation	large-network	servreg-hack
52	esb	Multithreading	trickle	NetPerf	shell-collect-lossy	webserver	unicast-fragmentatic	upanddownroutes	servreg-hack
53	esb	coffee	mesh	NetPerf-lpp	shell-collect	webserver	ipv6-rpl-collect	temporaryrootloss	servreg-hack
54	esb	Multithreading	collect	NetPerf	shell-collect	webserver	ipv6-udp	randomrearrngement	coap
55	esb	coffee	trickle	NetPerf-cxmac	shell-collect	telnet-ping	udp-fragmentation	rpl-dao	servreg-hack
56	native	coffee	rucb	NetPerf	shell-collect-lossy	webserver	ipv6-rpl-collect	up-root	servreg-hack
57	native	checkpointing	deluge	NetPerf-lpp	shell-collect	telnet-ping	ipv6-udp	root-reboot	coap
58	native	Multithreading	runicast	NetPerf-cxmac	shell-collect	webserver	udp-fragmentation	large-network	servreg-hack
59	native	coffee	trickle	NetPerf-lpp	shell-collect-lossy	webserver	unicast-fragmentatic	upanddownroutes	coap
60	native	coffee	mesh	NetPerf-cxmac	shell-collect	webserver	unicast-fragmentatic	temporaryrootloss	servreg-hack
61	native	Multithreading	collect	NetPerf-cxmac	shell-collect	telnet-ping	ipv6-udp	randomrearrngement	coap
62	native	checkpointing	rucb	NetPerf-cxmac	shell-collect-lossy	webserver	ipv6-rpl-collect	rpl-dao	coap
63	cooja	coffee	rucb	NetPerf	shell-collect-lossy	webserver	ipv6-rpl-collect	up-root	servreg-hack
64	cooja	checkpointing	deluge	NetPerf-lpp	shell-collect	telnet-ping	ipv6-udp	root-reboot	coap
65	cooja	Multithreading	runicast	NetPerf-cxmac	shell-collect	telnet-ping	udp-fragmentation	large-network	servreg-hack
66	cooja	Multithreading	trickle	NetPerf	shell-collect-lossy	telnet-ping	unicast-fragmentatic	upanddownroutes	servreg-hack
67	cooja	coffee	mesh	NetPerf-cxmac	shell-collect-lossy	telnet-ping	ipv6-udp	temporaryrootloss	coap
68	cooja	Multithreading	collect	NetPerf-lpp	shell-collect-lossy	telnet-ping	ipv6-rpl-collect	randomrearrngement	coap
69	cooja	checkpointing	collect	NetPerf	shell-collect	webserver	udp-fragmentation	rpl-dao	coap

Appendix B: Code Coverage data gathered for existing test suite of Contiki and Cooja using CodeCover

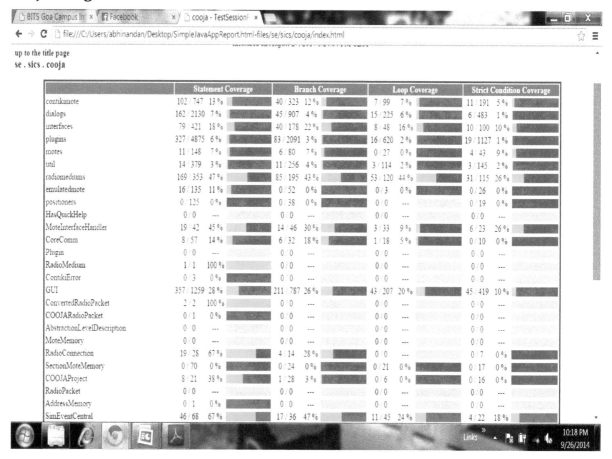

Appendix C: Tweaking of Ant Build.xml for Gathering the Coverage Data

```
<?xml version="1.0"?>
<project name="COOJA Simulator" default="run" basedir=".">
<property name="java" location="java"/>
.
.
.
<property name="args" value=""/>
<property name="codecoverDir"
value="/home/user/Desktop/CodeCover/codecover-batch-1.0/lib"/>
<property name="sourceDir" value="/home/user/contiki-2.7/tools/cooja/java"/>
<property name="instrumentedSourceDir" value="instrumented"/>
<property name="mainClassName" value="se.sics.cooja.GUI"/>
<taskdef name="codecover" classname="org.codecover.ant.CodecoverTask"
classpath="${codecoverDir}/codecover-ant.jar"/>
<target name="clean">
<delete>
<fileset dir="." includes="*.clf"/>
</delete>
<delete file="codecover.xml"/>
<delete file="report.html"/>
<delete dir="report.html-files"/>
</target>
```

```
<target name="instrument-sources" depends="clean">
<codecover>
<instrument containerId="c" language="java"
destination="${instrumentedSourceDir}" charset="utf-8"
copyUninstrumented="yes">
<source dir="${sourceDir}">
<include name="**/*.java"/>
</source>
</instrument>
<save containerId="c" filename="codecover.xml"/>
</codecover>
</target>
<target name="compile-instrumented" depends="instrument-sources">
<javac srcdir="${instrumentedSourceDir}" destdir="${instrumentedSourceDir}"
encoding="utf-8" target="1.7" debug="true"
classpath="${codecoverDir}/lib/codecover-instrumentationjava.
jar:/home/user/contiki-2.7/tools/cooja/lib/log4j.jar:/home/user/contiki-
2.7/tools/cooja/lib/jdom.jar:/home/user/contiki-2.7/tools/cooja/lib/jsyntaxpane.jar"
includeAntRuntime="false"></javac>
</target>
<target name="run-instrumented" depends="compile-instrumented, copy configs">
<java classpath="${instrumentedSourceDir}:${codecoverDir}/lib/codecoverinstrumentation-
java.jar:/home/user/contiki-
2.7/tools/cooja/lib/log4j.jar:/home/user/contiki-
2.7/tools/cooja/lib/jdom.jar:/home/user/contiki-2.7/tools/cooja/lib/jsyntaxpane.jar"
fork="true" failonerror="true" classname="${mainClassName}">
<jvmarg value="-Dorg.codecover.coverage-log-file=test.clf"/>
</java>
</target>
<target name="create-report" >
<codecover>
<load containerId="c" filename="codecover.xml"/>
<analyze containerId="c" coverageLog="*.clf" name="Test Session"/>
<save containerId="c" filename="codecover.xml"/>
<report containerId="c" destination="report.html"
template="/home/user/Desktop/CodeCover/codecover-batch-1.0/reporttemplates/
HTML_Report_hierarchic.xml">
<testCases>
<testSession pattern=".*">
<testCase pattern=".*"/>
</testSession>
</testCases>
</report>
</codecover>
</target>
<target name="help">
<echo>
.
.
<target name="copy configs" depends="init">
<mkdir dir="${build}"/>
<copy todir="/home/user/contiki-2.7/tools/cooja/instrumented">
<fileset dir="${config}"/>
```

```
</copy>
.
.
.

<target name="jar_cooja" depends="init, compile, copy configs, compile instrumented
">
<mkdir dir="${dist}"/>
<jar destfile="${dist}/cooja.jar" base dir="/home/user/contiki-
2.7/tools/cooja/instrumented">
<manifest>
<attribute name="Main-Class" value="se.sics.cooja.GUI"/>
<attribute name="Class-Path" value=". lib/log4j.jar lib/jdom.jar
lib/jsyntaxpane.jar"/>
</manifest>
</jar>
<mkdir dir="${dist}/lib"/>
<copy todir="${dist}/lib">
<fileset dir="${lib}"/>
</copy>
</target>
</project>
```

5

An E-Negotiation Agent Using Rule Based and Case Based Approaches: A Comparative Study with Bilateral E-Negotiation with Prediction

Sheetal R. Vij[1], Amruta More[1], Debajyoti Mukhopadhyay[2], Avinash J. Agrawal[3]

[1]Department of Computer Engineering, Maharashtra Institute of Technology, Pune, India
[2]Department of Information Technology, Maharashtra Institute of Technology, Pune, India
[3]Department of Computer Science and Engineering, Ramdeobaba College of Engineering and Management, Nagpur, India
Email: sheetal.sh@gmail.com, moreamruta930@gmail.com, debajyoti.mukhopadhyay@gmail.com, agrawalaj@rknec.edu

Abstract

The research in the area of automated negotiation systems is going on in many universities. This research is mainly focused on making a practically feasible, faster and reliable E-negotiation system. The ongoing work in this area is happening in the laboratories of the universities mainly for training and research purpose. There are number of negotiation systems such as Henry, Kasbaah, Bazaar, Auction Bot, Inspire, and Magnet. Our research is based on making an agent software for E-negotiation which will give faster results and also is secure and flexible. The negotiation partners and contents between the service providers change frequently. The negotiation process can be transformed into rules and cases. Using these features, a new automated negotiation model for agent integrating rule based and case based reasoning can be derived. We propose an E-negotiation system, in which all product information and multiple agent details are stored on the cloud. An E-negotiation agent acts as a negotiator. Agent has user's details and their requirements for a particular product. It will check rules based data whether any rule is matching with the user requirement. An agent will see case based data to check any similar negotiation case matching to the user requirement. If a case matches with user requirement, then agent will start the negotiation process using case based data. If any rule related requirement is found in the rule base data, then agent will start the negotiation process using rule based data. If both rules based data and cases based data are not matching with the user requirement, then agent will start the negotiation process using Bilateral Negotiation model. After completing negotiation process, agent gives feedback to the user about whether negotiation is successful or not. The product details, rule based data, and case based data will be stored on the cloud. So that system automatically becomes flexible. We also compare E-negotiation agent automated negotiation and behavior prediction system to prove that using rule based and case based approaches system should become fast.

Keywords

Automated Negotiation, Multi-Agent, Rule Based Reasoning, Case Based Reasoning, Cloud Computing

---

1. Introduction

Practically "negotiation" can be defined as an iterative process which aims to achieve a mutually beneficial deal for the seller and buyer [1]. The automation saves human negotiation time and computational negotiators are better at finding deals in combinatorial and strategically complex settings. The rapid success of online auctions clearly shows that E-negotiation will eventually become the basis of e-commerce. Whether it is a case of B to B purchase or a case of online shopping, it is required to make the traditional negotiation pricing mechanism automated and intelligent [2].

Cloud computing is innovation that uses advanced computational power and improved storage capabilities. Cloud computing is a new processing scheme in which computer processing is performed in the network. This means that users need not concern themselves with the processing details. Although Cloud computing enables more flexible, easier and faster computing [3].

Case Based Reasoning (CBR) is a problem solving paradigm where the solution of new problem is based on solution of similar past problem. We use Rule Based Reasoning (RBR) concept, where there are some rules such as discount, festival offers etc.

In this system, we are introducing an E-negotiation agent based system using Rule Based Reasoning and Case Based Reasoning. Due to the use of Rule Based Reasoning and Case Based Reasoning, system becomes faster. In this system, all data that is product detail, case base data and rule base data are stored on cloud. Therefore system becomes flexible.

2. Literature Review

In this section, we are presenting literature survey related to only rule based and case based reasoning. In our previous paper [4], we have referred ten papers related to automated negotiation in the literature survey.

Liu Xiaowen and Yu Jin [5] introduced automated negotiation model for tourism industry. To improve the negotiation efficiency and success rate, this system proposed RBR and CBR. The model employs CBR method to support an automated negotiation by past successful negotiation cases used for those negotiation partners that have no contract rule existing in each other. This system does not support multi party multi issue negotiation.

Mohammad Irfan Bala, Sheetal Vij and Debajyoti Mukhopadhyay [6] introduced, E-negotiation system with behavior prediction. This work reviews the various methods used for predicting the opponent's behavior and then proposes architecture for behavior prediction using artificial neural networks. It proposes the use of database for storing the results and suggests various issues that can be taken into consideration while predicting the opponent's behavior.

Mira Vrbaski and Dorina Petriu [7] proposed Context-aware systems which use Rule Based Reasoning engines for decision making without involving explicit interaction with the user. It is difficult to rank suitable solutions based on unclear, qualitative criteria with a rule based approach, while rule based systems excel in filtering out unsuitable solutions based on clear criteria.

Leen-Kiat Soh and Costas Tsatsoulis [8] use Case Based Reasoning (CBR) and utility to learn, select, and apply negotiation strategies. Agent uses Case Based Reasoning (CBR) approach to solve new problem of negotiation strategy which based on previous similar past problem. Agent also learns from its previous negotiation experience.

P. Maes, R. Guttman, A. Moukas [9] introduced a Kasbah negotiation model. In this system, agents can only negotiate over the single issue of price. However, B2B negotiations often involve multiple issues. Moreover, the Kasbah agents can only act according to one of their pre-defined negotiation strategies which may not lead to the optimal negotiation results.

P. Wurman, M. Wellman, W. Walsh [10] introduced the Michigan AuctionBot is a general purposed Internet-based auction server hosted by the University of Michigan. Sellers can create new auctions on AuctionBot by choosing from a set of pre-defined auction types and then enter their specific auction parameters such as clearing time, minimum bid increment and whether proxy bids are allowed. E-bay is the example of AuctionBot negotiation system.

Some of above papers support multi party multi issue negotiation Rule Based Reasoning and Case Based Reasoning. Our negotiation system is a bilateral, muti-party, multi issue negotiation model. In this system, buyer and seller negotiate o multiple issues at a time and when both buyer and seller comes to final decision, then only negotiation process will be stopped.

3. Proposed System

3.1. Problem Statement

For negotiation process, more than two parties come together to reach mutually beneficial outcome. For similar negotiation case, there is no need to do negotiation process again due to use of case based approach. We also provide some rules related to negotiation process which makes successful negotiation process. Due to use of rule based and case based approaches, negotiation system become faster. We also use Cloud computing concept, to store all organizations' product data. Hence, maintenance of organizations' data is reduced.

3.2. Mathematical Model

The given mathematical model is for bilateral negotiations where an agent can negotiate about multiple issues. It also supports learning from the previous negotiation rounds. The mathematical model for the proposed work is as follows:

$$N = \{A, U, R, D, T\}$$

A: A is an agents which will participate in the negotiation.

U: The set of users that will participate in the negotiation. This set consists of both sellers and buyers.

$U = \{u_1, u_2, \cdots, u_m\}$ represents m number of users.

R: The set of requirement which are given by users to their respective agents. This set consists of both sides' seller side and buyer side requirements.

$R = \{r_1, r_2, \cdots, r_i\}$ represents i number of requirements that is "R" represents total number of requirements which are available at current stage.

D: The set of database which is used for matching the users' requirement with rule based and case based databases.

T: The time limit for the negation.

Whole process of negotiation should complete before the time limit.

Constrains:

In previous we can use R for set of requirements but requirement of particular user is become a constrain.

Algorithms:

A_1 = A single user gives his requirements to respective agent.

$$N = \{A, U, R\}$$

$$A_1 = \{A, U_1, R_1\}$$

Here, mapping of R_1 to R, U_1 to U.

A_2 = Agent checks the user requirements with rule based and case based databases

A_3 = After checking databases, agent will start actual negotiation process.

A_4 = Total time of negotiation process should be less than or equal to T.

$$T \leq N_{\text{time}}$$

where, N_{time} is the total time of negotiation process.

Flow diagram of mathematical model is shown in **Figure 1**.

4. System Architecture

The architecture of E-negotiation agent system is shown in **Figure 2**.

Working of E-negotiation agent system:

1) Databases on cloud

- Product detail: used to store organizations' product detail like product name, price, quantity;
- Case base: used to store experience of agent about negotiation process;
- Rule base: used to store rules related to product like discount, festival offers.

2) Seller and Buyer: Users of the system

3) Agent: An agent acts as a negotiator

Negotiation Process: After receiving Seller's and Buyer's requirement, agent will start negotiation process. For negotiation process, agent will check three conditions.

- Case based: An agent will see case based data to check any similar negotiation case is matching to the user requirement. If a case matches with user requirement, then agent start the negotiation process using case based data.
- Rule based: It will check rules based data whether any rule is matching with the user requirement. If any rule related requirement is found in the rule base data, then agent will start the negotiation process using rule based data.
- Bilateral Negotiation model: If both rules based data and case based data are not matching with the user requirement, then agent will start the negotiation process using Bilateral Negotiation model.

4) Feedback: After completing negotiation process, agent gives feedback to the user about whether negotiation is successful or not.

Flow chart of E-negotiation agent system is shown in **Figure 3**.

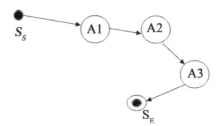

Figure 1. Flow diagram of mathematical model of E-negotiation agent system.

Buyer Gives the Requirements to agent and Agent gives feedback

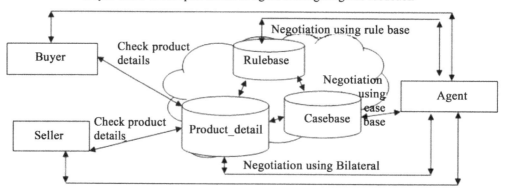

Seller gives the Requirements to agent and Agent gives feedback

Figure 2. System architecture of E-negotiation agent system.

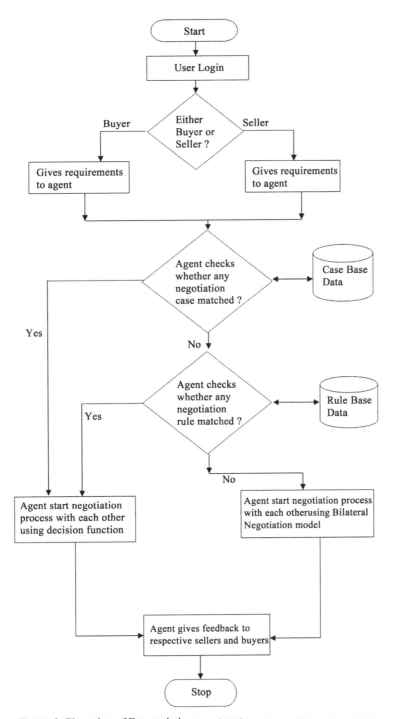

Figure 3. Flow chat of E-negotiation agent system.

Components of the System

For this system, we can use three components. Using these components, system becomes easy to use and work efficiently.

1) *Store data on cloud*: For storing data, we can use Open Stack cloud. Open Stack is a Cloud computing project to provide an IaaS. It is free open source software released under the terms of the Apache License.

In this module, all data which is required for negotiation process like product data, rule base data and case base data is stored on cloud.

2) *Negotiation process*: For negotiation process [4], seller and buyer give their requirements to agent in encrypted format that is generate the hash code of that requirement and encrypt that hash code using user's public key. User's public key is known to Agents.

$$\text{Buyer or seller requirement} = E\{H(m), U_{pk}\}$$

where, for generating hash function MD5 algorithm is used.

U_{pk} is user's public key.

We can use encryption for security purpose, in this process, we can use digital signature concept.

Same as seller, buyer can do same process for generating hash code of his requirement.

After getting requirement, agent decrypt the hash code using his private key and calculate the hash code for checking whether this message comes from appropriate seller or buyer and whether it is modified or not.

$$\text{Agent receive requirements} = D\{A_{pri}, H(m)\}$$

where, A_{pri} is agent's private key.

After getting the requirement, agent checks the user requirements whether any rule related to requirement is found in the rule base data then only agent will start the negotiation process using decision function [11].

- Decision Function: After getting the requirement, agent checks the user requirements whether any rule related to requirement is found in the rule base data then only agent will start the negotiation process using decision function. The negotiation .model introduces a decision function [11] for supplier and buyer first. Seller's agent responds at t_n to buyer's agent offer sent at time t_{n-1} and total profit is defined as Equation (1). Similarly, buyer's agent also has a decision function to respond at t_n to seller's agent offer sent at time t_{n-1} and total cost is shown in Equation (2).

$$D^S(t_n) = \begin{cases} \text{terminate} & \text{if } t_n > t_{max} \\ \text{accept} & \text{if } TP\left(x_J^{B \to S}(t_{n-1})\right) \leq TP\left(x_J^{S \to B}(t_n)\right) \\ \text{otherwise} & \left(x_J^{S \to B}(t_n)\right) \end{cases} \tag{1}$$

$$D^B(t_n) = \begin{cases} \text{terminate} & \text{if } t_n > t_{max} \\ \text{accept} & \text{if } TC\left(x_J^{S \to B}(t_{n-1})\right) \geq TP\left(x_J^{B \to S}(t_n)\right) \\ \text{otherwise} & \left(x_J^{B \to S}(t_n)\right) \end{cases} \tag{2}$$

The buyer uses Equation (2) to decide whether he should accept suppliers' proposal or not. Similarly, using a decision function Equation (1) a supplier can make decision.

- Bilateral Negotiation model: If both rules based data and case based data are not matching with the user requirement, then Buyer's agent and Seller's agent will start the negotiation process with each other using Bilateral Negotiation model.

For negotiation process, we can use the Bilateral Negotiation model [12].

Let x represents the buyer agent $\left(x \in \{x_1, x_2, \cdots, x_m\}\right)$ and y $\left(y \in \{y_1, y_2, \cdots, y_m\}\right)$ be the supplier agent. And

let then i $\left(i \in \{i_1, i_2, \cdots, i_n\}\right)$ be the issues under negotiation, such as price, volume, duration, quality and so on. Each agent assigns to each issue i a weight W_i, denoting the relative importance of that issue to the agent. Here, we consider quality as a weight. Hence, W_i^x represents the importance of issue i to agent x, therefore the overall utility function of an offer O is

$$U(O) = \frac{\sum_{i=1}^{m} W_i u_i(x_i)}{\sum_{i=1}^{m} W_i} \tag{3}$$

where the overall utility is denoted as $U(O)$ for the offer $O\left(= [O_1, \cdots, O_m]^T\right)$, and $u_i(x_i)$ is the individual utility function for issue i for $u_i \in [0, 1]$ and the preference degree of an agent to an issue I is denoted as $W_i \in [0, 9]$.

Each agent also specifies a minimum acceptable utility level [U_{max}, U_{min}] to determine if an offer is acceptable.

Hence, for benefit-oriented, the utility function $U_i(x_i)$ is computed as follows :

$$U_i(x_i) = \frac{x_i - x_{\{min\}}}{x^i_{\{max\}} - x^i_{\{min\}}} \quad (4)$$

For cost oriented however, the utility function can be as follows:

$$U_i(x_i) = 1 - \frac{x_i - x_{\{min\}}}{x^i_{\{max\}} - x^i_{\{min\}}} \quad (5)$$

3) *Feedback*: When negotiation process was finished. Agent gives feedback to appropriate seller or buyer about negotiation whether it is successful or not.

5. Experimental Analysis and Results

We implemented E-negotiation agent system using rule based and case based approaches. We took a system (automated negotiation and behavior prediction) [6] as an existing system.

Mohammad Irfan Bala implemented an automated negotiation and behavior prediction system. In this system, during negotiation the agent will store the offers received and predict the preferences of the opponent based on these offers. The negotiation protocol determines the overall order of actions during a negotiation and the agents are obliged to stick to this protocol. In the bilateral alternating offers protocol two parties—agent A and agent B—take turns. Agent A starts the negotiation. Each turn an agent presents one of the three possible actions:

Accept: This action indicates that agent accepts the opponent's last bid.

Offer: This action represents the bid made by an agent.

End negotiation: This action indicates that the agent terminates the negotiation.

We compared E-negotiation agent using rule based and case based approaches system with automated negotiation and Behavior Prediction system based on response time.

Table 1 shows the response time values of both systems. We calculated response time value of both the systems up to 300 users. Therefore we can say that, using rule based and case based approaches E-negotiation process requires less time as compared to existing system.

Figure 4 shows the comparison graph based on response time.

In E-negotiation agent using rule based and case based approaches system, all the data which is required for E-negotiation process such as product detail, rule base data, case base data is stored on cloud. Automated negotiation and Behavior Prediction system does not use Cloud computing concept to store negotiation process.

We calculated CPU utilization (in percentage) and Memory utilization (in percentage) of both systems up to 300 users.

Table 2 shows the Memory utilization values (in percentage) of both systems.

Therefore we can say that, due to use of Cloud computing E-negotiation agent using rule based and case based approaches system requires less CPU utilization and Memory utilization as compared to existing system.

Table 3 shows the CPU utilization values (in percentage) of both systems.

Figure 5 shows the comparison graph based on Memory utilization.

Figure 6 shows the comparison graph based on CPU utilization.

Table 1. Response time values of both systems.

No. of Users	Response Time (E-Negotiation Agent)	Response Time (Existing System)
50	256	360
100	591	641
150	723	803
200	1138	1157
250	1364	1513
300	1681	1741

Table 2. Memory utilization values of both systems.

No. of Users	Memory% (E-Negotiation Agent)	Memory% (Existing System)
50	9%	12%
100	10%	13%
150	12%	16%
200	15%	19%
250	18%	23%
300	21%	27%

Table 3. CPU utilization values of both systems.

No. of Users	CPU% (E-Negotiation Agent)	CPU% (Existing System)
50	17%	20%
100	34%	43%
150	52%	61%
200	66%	73%
250	71%	82%
300	89%	93%

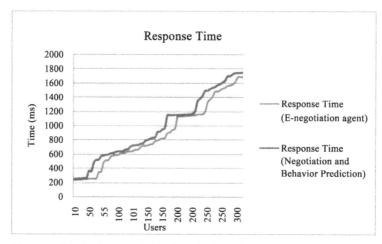

Figure 4. Comparison graph based on response time.

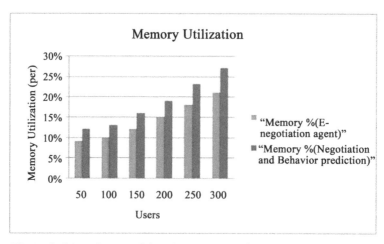

Figure 5. Comparison graph based on memory utilization.

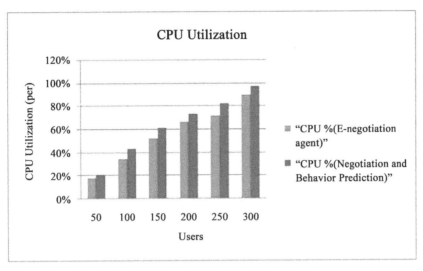

Figure 6. Comparison graph based on CPU utilization.

6. Conclusion and Future Scope

In order to make faster E-negotiation process, we use the rule base and case based approaches. Two or more parties are coming together during the negotiation process. And there are organizations to maintain data of the negotiation process and product data. But this maintenance is a very tedious job. In order to overcome this problem, all organizations' product data are stored on cloud. So that system should become flexible.

This system is a Bilateral Negotiation model. In future this system can be implemented as multilateral negotiation model, behavior prediction and also uses the concept of expert system for increasing success rate of negotiation process.

References

[1]   Jennings, N.R., Faratin, P., Lomuscio, A.R., Parsons, S., Sierra, C. and Wooldridge, M. (2002) Automated Negotiation: Prospects, Methods and Challenges. *Group Decision and Negotiation*, **10**, 199-215.
       http://dx.doi.org/10.1023/A:1008746126376

[2]   Mukun, C. (2010) Multi-Agent Automated Negotiation as a Service. *7th International Conference on Service System and Service Management* (*ICSSSM*), Tokyo, 28-30 June 2012, 308-313.

[3]   Singh, J., Kumar, B. and Khatn, A. (2012) Securing Storage Data in Cloud Using RC5 Algorithm. *International Journal of Advance Computer Research*, **2**, 94-98.

[4]   More, A., Vij, S. and Mukhopadhyay, D. (2013) Agent Based Negotiation Using Cloud—An Approach in E-Commerce. *Proceedings of* 48*th Annual Convention of the Computer Society of India*, Visakhapatnam, 13-15 December 2013, 489-496.

[5]   Liu, X.W. and Yu, J. (2012) Hybrid Approach Using RBR and CBR to Design an Automated Negotiation Model for Tourism Companies. 2012 *International Conference on Management of E-Commerce and E-Government*, **21**, 197-201.

[6]   Bala, M.I., Vij, S. and Mukhopadhyay, D. (2013) Negotiation Life Cycle: An Approach in E-Negotiation with Prediction. *Proceedings of* 48*th Annual Convention of the Computer Society of India*, Visakhapatnam, 13-15 December 2013, 505-512.

[7]   Vrbaski, M. and Petriu, D. (2012) Tool Support for Combined Rule-Based and Goal-Based Reasoning in Context-Aware Systems. *Requirement Engineering Conference* 2012, Chicago, 24-28 September 2012, 335-336.

[8]   Soh, L.-K. and Tsatsoulis, C. (2001) Agent-Based Argumentative Negotiations with Case-Based Reasoning. AAAI Technical Report FS-01-03.

[9]   Maes, P., Guttman, R. and Moukas, A. (1999) Agents That Buy and Sell. *Communications of the ACM*, **42**, 81-91.
       ttp://dx.doi.org/10.1145/295685.295716

[10]   Wurman, P., Wellman, M. and Walsh, W. (1998) The Michigan Internet AuctionBot: A Configurable Auction Server for Human and Software Agents. In: Sycara, K.P. and Wooldridge, M., Eds., *Proceedings of the 2nd International*

Conference on Autonomous Agents, ACM Press, New York, 301-308. http://dx.doi.org/10.1145/280765.280847

[11] Rau, H., Chen, C.-W. and Shiang, W.-J. (2009) Development of an Agent-Based Negotiation Model for Buyer-Supplier Relationship with Multiple Deliveries. *Proceedings of the 2009 IEEE International Conference on Networking, Sensing and Control*, Okayama, 26-29 March 2009, 308-312.

[12] Ateib, M.T. (2010) Agent Based Negotiation in E-Commerce. *International Symposium on Information Technology* 2010, **2**, 861-868.

6

Hand Gesture Recognition Approach for ASL Language Using Hand Extraction Algorithm

Alhussain Akoum, Nour Al Mawla

Department GRIT, Lebanese University, Beirut, Lebanon
Email: Hussein_akoum@hotmail.com

Abstract

In a general overview, signed language is a technique used for communicational purposes by deaf people. It is a three-dimensional language that relies on visual gestures and moving hand signs that classify letters and words. Gesture recognition has been always a relatively fearful subject that is adherent to the individual on both academic and demonstrative levels. The core objective of this system is to produce a method which can identify detailed humanoid nods and use them to either deliver ones thoughts and feelings, or for device control. This system will stand as an effective replacement for speech, enhancing the individual's ability to express and intermingle in society. In this paper, we will discuss the different steps used to input, recognize and analyze the hand gestures, transforming them to both written words and audible speech. Each step is an independent algorithm that has its unique variables and conditions.

Keywords

Hand Gesture, American Sign Language, Gesture Analysis, Edge Detection, Correlation, Background Modeling

1. Introduction

Gestures are meaningful body movements which are capable of expressing something in a communication, although gesture finds a place to catalogue itself into non-verbal communication, it prominently reaches well to the other end of communication. Gesture is motion of body that contains information [1]. The straightforward purpose of a gesture is to express gen or interrelate with the surroundings. Motionless gestures are those that undertake a precise posted stance. Activity contains a gesture movement that is distinct. Based on the locality of initiation of sign in the body, it can be considered a hand, an arm, a head or a face gesticulation. This paper is exerted on the first type *i.e.* hand gestures. The probable sub-divisions on the hand gestures are static gesture, dynamic gesture, and static and dynamic gesture [2]. Gesture research is termed as a complex research area, as there exists many-to-one mappings from concepts to gestures and gestures to concepts. The major drawback in pursuing research with gestures is that they are ambiguous and incompletely specified [3].

Natural HGR is one of the very active research areas in the Computer Vision field. It provides the easiness to interact with machines without using any extra device and if the users don't have much technical knowledge about the system, they still will be able to use the system with their normal hands. Gestures communicate the meaning of statement said by the human being. They come naturally with the words to help the receiver to understand the communication. It allows individuals to communicate feelings and thoughts with different emotions with words or without words [4].

In our due time, software for sign language recognition is very imperative and is receiving great attention. Such software not only enhances communication between talking people and silent people, but also provides deaf people the ability to interact quickly and professionally with computers and machines using nothing but their hands. American Sign Language (ASL) is a complete system that is considered both simple and complex. It uses 26 different hand signs each indicating a letter. ASL is more than 200 years old. It was the preferable language of 500,000 deaf throughout the United States which rated it as the fourth most-used language.

This language is gaining attractiveness since it supports and enhances communication with an automated system or human located at a distance. Once the user finishes the gesture, the system needs to be capable of identifying it instantly. This is known as "Gesture Recognition". The target of this effort is to construct a system which can classify particular hand gestures and extract the corresponding literatures. This dynamic system is based on the American Sign Language alphabets (**Figure 1**).

2. Overview on the Process

Computers are invariably used by everyone extensively in today's world; one of the major areas of prominence is the human computer interface. Attempts in making a computer understand facial expressions, speech, and human gestures are paving to create a better human computer interaction [5]. Most of the researchers classified gesture recognition system into mainly three steps after acquiring the input image from camera(s) (**Figure 2**), videos or even data glove instrumented device. These steps are: Extraction Method, features estimation and extraction, and classification or recognition as illustrated in figure below [6].

2.1. Similar Systems

The representation captures the hand shape, position of the hand, orientation and movement (if any). The region of interest *i.e.* hand was identified, from where feature vector was to be framed [7]. The feature vector composed for the American Sign Language standard database samples stored consists of. jpg files of existing database along with a few real-time or home-made images. The keypoints derived from the image are placed in an array. All image pixel values that are greater than zero are considered as keypoints and the keypoints array gets generated (**Figure 3**). The match performance based on similarity measures is not made for every point; instead a dimensionality reduction is done. It is taken as the final feature vector. Only retain the keypoints in which the ratio of the vector angles from the nearest to the second nearest neighbor is more [8].

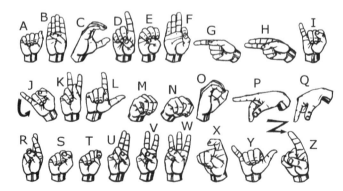

Figure 1. The 26 hand signs of the ASL Language.

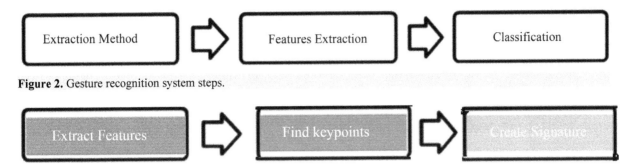

Figure 2. Gesture recognition system steps.

Figure 3. Basic flow of vector composition.

The SIFT detector extracts from an image a collection of frames or keypoints. These are oriented disks attached to blob-alike structures of the image. As the image translates, rotates and scales, the frames track these blobs and thus the deformation. By canonization, *i.e.* by mapping the frames to a reference (a canonical disk), the effect of such deformation on the feature appearance is removed. The SIFT descriptor is a coarse description of the edge found in the frame. Due to canonization, descriptors are invariant to translations, rotations and scaling and are designed to be robust to residual small distortions.

Considering the experimental results of the system above, 80% of the test sample was used for training and 20% for testing. The implementation gave 100% accuracy in identifying the test sample for this dataset only for sample images shown in **Figure 4**. The recognition percentage started to gradually decrease reaching 0% in letters that has almost identical shape such as "M" "N" and "S" (**Figure 4**).

However, the system that we worked on proved to follow a different approach to realize a more precise result. Though our method is more divergent and somehow complicated in terms of code, it is as simple as moving the hand in terms of usage. There are two methods used in building our input data (images), Samples (training) and Live Camera (testing), and our database is wide and variant it covers almost all possible hand positions and skin color (**Figure 5**).

The following flow chart demonstrated in **Figure 6** presents the whole arrangement of the algorithms.

2.2. Creating Database

Image databases pose new and challenging problems to the research community. Over the past 40 years, database technology has matured with the development of relational databases, object-relational databases, and object-oriented databases. The core functionalities of classical databases, however, are tailored toward simple data types and do not extend gracefully to nonstructural information. Digital images have a predominant position among multimedia data types. Unlike video and audio, that is mostly used by the entertainment and news industry [9].

Our database contains about 1200 images composed for the American Sign Language standard samples all in the .bmp format and of dimensions 100 × 100. It is important to mention that having a big database means more accuracy, which is likely to increase the recognition percentage. However, working on software, we must take into consideration the quality of the image as well as the overall size of the program. Since all what we care about in the input image is the hand, which won't exceed 100 × 100 dimensions, we resized the database to fit the description, and thus dramatically decreasing the size of the overall code. Note that later in the code, all images would be changed form "(R. B. G.)" to "Binary", so having the images in. bmp format reduces the image's size while preserving all the information we require from the gesture.

2.3. Camera

By camera we are referring to images captured from the digital camera. It is important to mention that the hardware we are working on, especially the camera, is neither professional nor has any profitable aims. Thus, facing certain obstacles and errors is inescapable. Such errors are not the results of the code but the technical insufficiency. After capturing the image from the camera, the followed steps are:

Feature capture and extraction: Diminish the amount of data by extracting relevant information, which is the hand. In this step it is necessary to detect only the hand and to remove all other features for the image captured

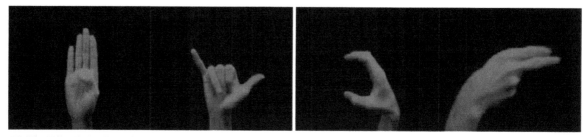

Figure 4. Successful samples.

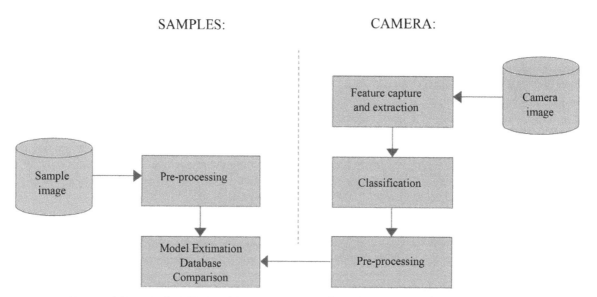

Figure 5. Image classification process.

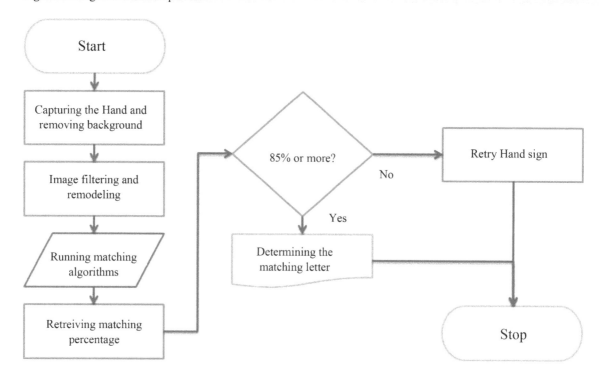

Figure 6. Flow chart of the process.

in the camera. Stabilizing the structures is necessary for distance measurements, *i.e.* the distance between the hand and the camera.

Classification: Before attempting to find a match, the input image must pass through particular functions that change certain properties (color type for example).

Pre-processing: In this step, certain modifications are done on the input image until it is in the appropriate form needed. This step includes trimming, cropping, lining and resizing the image. Given a segmented (isolated) part of the image, features for recognition that should be taken into consideration in a 2-D image are [10]: Total mass (number of pixels in a binarized image), Centroid-Center of mass, Elliptical parameters, Eccentricity (ratio of major to minor axis), Orientation (angle of major axis), Skewness, Kurtosis, Higher order moments, Hough and Chain code transform and Fourier transform and series.

Model Estimation (Database Comparison): Compare the extracted feature image to the various models included in the database and finds the closest match (**Figure 7**).

3. Input Image via Camera

The first step is to capture a plain image of the background before entering the hand gesture. This step is necessary for the upcoming algorithms. The second step is choosing the desired hand gesture. Face the hand straight in front of the camera and make sure your hand is straight and not more than few centimeters away from the camera.

The human steps are done, now it's time for the algorithms to work. Different algorithms and functions are executed after capturing the two required image. The first step is to crop and resize the images.

Removing Background

Background extraction is an important part of moving object detection algorithms that are very useful in surveillance systems. Moving object detection algorithm will be simple by background subtraction when a clean background image is available. The method of extraction the background during training sequence and updating it during the input frame sequence is called background modeling. The main challenges in moving object detection is to extract a clean background and its updating [11].

Thus, removing the background after capturing the image would preserve only the hand (**Figure 8**). The mechanism functions depending on the number of layers, (R. B. G.) Euclidian threshold and fraction of observed color accumulating in the background.

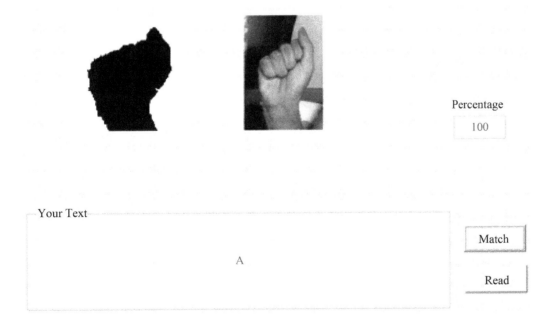

Figure 7. Input camera example.

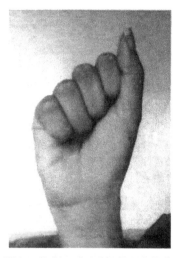

Figure 8. Input hand before and after background removing.

The above function removed the background but resulted in loss in parts of the hand. This error is mostly due to camera. It is necessary to restore the small area subsequent to the hand itself. To do so, the algorithm changes the image type from (R. B. G.) to "Binary" and applies filtering at different levels. Converting images to binary type is done by replacing all pixels according to the specified luminance with either white (logical 1) if the pixel is equal or greater that the level or black (logical 0) otherwise. Specified level should belong to the range [0, 1]. This level differs from one image to another. Though it can be manually assigned, using the function "Graythresh" to compute it gives better results. The function "Graythresh" function uses Otsu's system in order to determine the threshold of the image and to minimize the interclass modification of the black and white pixels. Multidimensional sections are altered to 2-D arrays The "Graythresh" function overlooks any nonzero invented part of the image. If not specified, the default value of the level is 0.5 (**Figure 9**).

The next step is removing small connected components and objects from binary image. Those objects have fewer pixels than the specified threshold. Since we are working on a 2 dimensional image from a law quality webcam, there is no need to specify any connectivity level. We work with the default connectivity which is 8. Removing the noise in the image is one of the most important and most difficult of the pre-handling techniques. This noise is designated as an unsystematic discrepancy of brightness or color gen through the image's background. 2-D median filtering is one of the most effective functions to overcome many filtering errors. It performs average filtering of the pixels' matrix in both directions. The output pixel comprises the average value of all pixels of the 3-by-3 neighboring region. The procedural steps for 2D median filtering are summarized in the following chart (**Figure 10**).

4. Montage

Perhaps the greatest advantage of our system is that it recognizes not only letters, but also full words. Creating a word using ASL Language means that we need to orderly join multiple images in a single frame. Typically made for this use, we used the montage function, which display all of the structures of a multi-frame image in a particular entity, positioning the frames so that they crudely form a square. What is does is demonstrating a chronological assortment of the specified input images, in other words it changes an array of images into a solo image entity. This function also assembles the borders so that they approximately construct a square. Images can be a series of binary, grayscale, or true-color images. The advantage of this technique is on one hand its ability to specify the word's length, minimizing spelling mistakes, and on other hand preserving all hand gestures and thus reviewing the hand's shape and form throughout the procedure (**Figure 11**).

5. Image Matching

Our task is to recognize a sign based on the input sequence of gestural data, so this is a multiclass classification problem (95 classes). We need to identify the basic characteristics of sign language gestures in order to choose a good classification method. Each sign varies in time and space. Also, the signing speed can differ significantly.

Figure 9. Difference between binary image with (1) Graythresh level (~0.7) and (2) Level = 0.3.

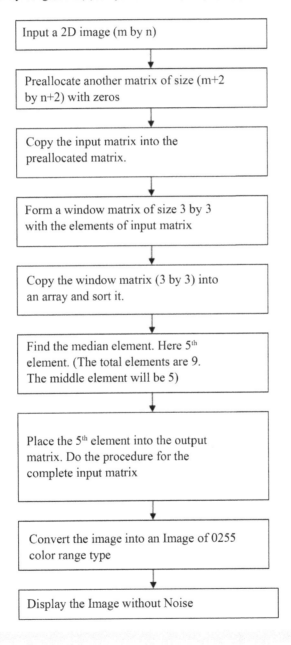

Input a 2D image (m by n)

Preallocate another matrix of size (m+2 by n+2) with zeros

Copy the input matrix into the preallocated matrix.

Form a window matrix of size 3 by 3 with the elements of input matrix

Copy the window matrix (3 by 3) into an array and sort it.

Find the median element. Here 5th element. (The total elements are 9. The middle element will be 5)

Place the 5th element into the output matrix. Do the procedure for the complete input matrix

Convert the image into an Image of 0255 color range type

Display the Image without Noise

Figure 10. Median filtering.

Figure 11. Creating the word "Love".

Even if one person performs the same sign, the speed and position can differ [12].

After creating the database and obtaining the final filtered input image, it's time compare the input image with all images in the database in order to find the closest match. To insure the best results and to receive the closest image after running the matching algorithm, matching is done via 3 different independent methods: 2-D correlation coefficient, Edge detection and Data Histogram.

The matching percentage between input image and each image in the database is stored and eventually the image with highest matching results is chosen.

5.1. Matching via Our Method 1 (2-D Correlation Coefficient)

The correlation coefficient is an integer signifying the resemblance between 2 images regarding their pixel strength. The equation to calculate this coefficient is:

$$r = \frac{\sum_m \sum_n \left(Amn - \overline{A}\right)\left(Bmn - \overline{B}\right)}{\sqrt{\left(\sum_m \sum_n \left(Amn - \overline{A}\right)^2\right)\left(\sum_m \sum_n \left(Bmn - \overline{B}\right)^2\right)}} \tag{1}$$

where $\overline{A} = \text{mean2}(A)$ and $\overline{B} = \text{mean2}$ (2)

A and *B* are the images meant for matching, while *m* and *n* refer to the pixel position in the image Equations (1) and (2). Due to this formula, the size of the two images must be identical, otherwise the result would not be anywhere near accuracy. What the algorithm does is calculate, for every pixel position in both images, the intensity value and compare it to the mean intensity of the whole image. This is type of stabilization method which considers the pixel intensity as the variable to be studied. Eventually, the closer this coefficient is to 1, the closer are the two images. Breaking down an image into blocks before calculating the correlation coefficient reduces the code's elapsing time if the images are relatively large. However, if the correlation coefficient is equal for 2 blocks of images, this doesn't necessarily indicate that images are identical. Using small size images in the database is less likely to cause any error even if resizing a picture may lead to information loss. This method is the one with the most precise results. It provides recognition up to 80% with some errors in extremely close signs. To increase the accuracy, we apply a second level of matching.

5.2. Matching via Our Method 2 Edge Detection

Edge detection is an image handling procedure for finding the borders of entities within images. The mechanism it uses is detecting breaks in the image's illumination. Edge detection is used for image dissection and data abstraction in image processing, computer visualization, and instrumental vision. Applying this method increased matching accuracy from 60% to 80%.

As the name of the method dictates, the matching is based upon finding the image's boundaries. It divides the image pixel by pixel, find the number of white points (*i.e.* 1 logical) and finally determine the match depending on the average of the number found. The key objective of the edge function is to find the edges intensity of the image. As simple as it may sound, this method is very accurate. Though two images may have same number of white pixels, they are meant to have different edges, and thus are at a certain level of dissimilarity. Using this method to compare one image with a large database of images is quite useful and precise.

Common edge recognition algorithms contain Sobel, Canny, Prewitt, Roberts, and Fuzzy logic methods. Choosing the suitable algorithm for your function is as important as specifying the image's threshold, which identifies its sensitivity (**Figure 12**).

That the system explained above used the Sobel method in the SIFT function. This is an important improvement we provided in our system. It enhanced recognition by 2% - 4%.

Canny edge detection: The explanation of canny procedure is done based on Prof. Thomas Moeslund's research on digital image processing in Indian Institute of Technology [13]. There are five overall steps:

Gaussian filter: As all edge detection consequences are certainly affected by image noise, it is vital to filter out the noise to avoid false recognition (**Figure 13**). This step will faintly level the image to diminish the effects

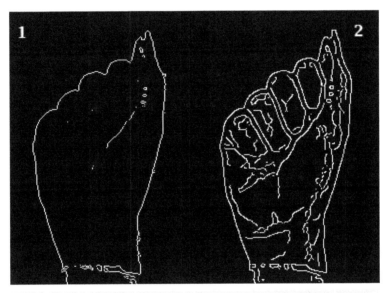

Figure 12. Edge difference between Sobel method (1) and canny method (2).

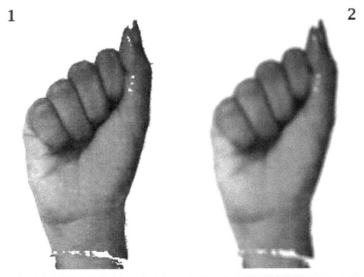

Figure 13. The image before (1) and after (2) a 5 × 5 Gaussian filtering.

of noise during the procedure. The Gaussian filter removes any noise and rough parts of the image.

Intensity Gradient: This step is similar to edging using Sobel method. An edge might point in a range of guidelines, so the Canny algorithm uses four filters to spot horizontal, vertical and diagonal edges in the hazy image resulting from the Gaussian filtering. For each pixel, 2 dimensional convolution matrices are created and in both x and y directions Equation (3).

$$Gx = \begin{bmatrix} -1 & 0 & 1 \\ -2 & 0 & 2 \\ -1 & 0 & 1 \end{bmatrix} \quad Gy = \begin{bmatrix} -1 & 2 & -1 \\ 0 & 0 & 0 \\ 1 & 2 & 1 \end{bmatrix} \tag{3}$$

Then, the following equations are applied in order to find the matrix's strength and slope:

$$G = \sqrt{Gx^2 + Gy^2} \tag{4}$$

$$\theta = \arctan \frac{Gy}{Gx} \tag{5}$$

(θ) Represents the direction and the orientation of the edge indicating possible color change. The calculated value subsiding in every color region will be fixed to a specific angle rate, for example θ in yellow region ($0°$ to $22.5°$ and $157.5°$ to $180°$) will be set to $0°$ Equations (4) and (5).

Suppression: This step is applied to narrow the edge and eliminate pixels that are not considered to be part of it. Thus, it can help to overturn all the gradient values to 0 excluding the local maximal, which designates position of the piercing change of concentration rate. Compare the strength of the recent pixel and the adjacent pixel in the both directions. If the intensity of the current pixel is the largest compared to the other pixels in the mask with the same direction the value will be conserved. Else, the value will be replaced.

Double threshold: Once suppression is over, the edge pixels are exact to signify the real edge. Nevertheless, at this step there would still be some errors due to color disparity. In order to dispose of them, it is vital to filter out the edge pixel with the minimal gradient value and reserve the edge with the maximal gradient value. Therefore, two threshold values are assigned to elucidate pixels, one is called upper threshold value and the other is called the lower threshold value.

The two threshold values are not simply calculated or assigned. They are specified by the "by trial and error" method. Countless values are applied until the exact one could be determined.

Hysteresis: Hysteresis is the phenomenon in which the values of the physical assets break behind the variations triggering it. To do so, Canny will use the two assigned thresholds (upper and lower) determined in the step above:

- If the pixel's intensity gradient is greater than the upper threshold, the pixel is recognized as an edge.
- If a pixel intensity gradient is less than the lower threshold, then it is excluded.
- If the pixel gradient is between the two thresholds and is adjacent to an edge pixel, it will also be considered to be part of the edge.

This step really makes a big difference in the size of the edge (**Figure 14**).

The figure above clearly shows the dissimilarity in the boundaries' size though the image is binary, which implies that it only has edges when the pixel changes from logical 1 (white) to logical 0 (black).

Finally, and for even more accuracy, a third level of matching is applied.

Matching via method 3 (data Histogram): (Imhist) is an algorithm used to analyze the histogram for the intensity of an image and demonstrates the results in the form of histogram scheme. The quantity of silos in the histogram is itemized by the image form. If the image is grayscale, (imhist) uses a default rate of 256 silos. If it is binary, (imhist) uses two silos.

For concentrated images, each of the n silos of the histogram consists of a half-open interval of width equal to A. $(n − 1)^{-1}$ (**Figure 15**).

Finally and after combining the three matching algorithms, the matching results in the unique letters reached 100%, and reached up to 80% in letters that where 0% in other similar systems.

6. Recognizing the Letter

Once running the Matching algorithms, the maximum resemblance percentage between the input image and

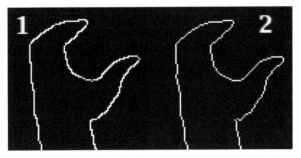

Figure 14. Edge difference between Canny (1) and Sobel (2) in a binary image.

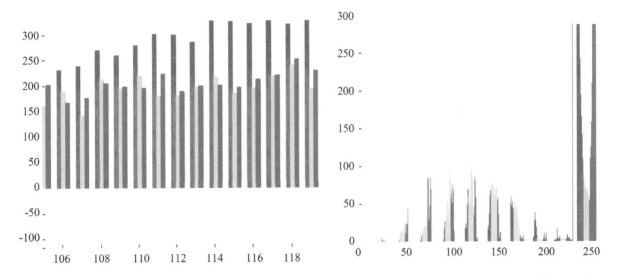

Figure 15. Data histograms of the input image in (RB G) format.

images in the database will be saved and displayed. To realize to which specific image in the database this percentage belongs to, we use the "Find" function which is a built I function used to determine the indices and values of the nonzero elements in the database. After recognizing the index, we need to relate it to a certain letter. For this step, another algorithm is used. For instance, input images that match with the database's image having index "1" will represent the letter "A".

Words containing multiple letters and sentences containing spaces are verified using the same method but after passing through the extraction step which separates each letter and identify empty images as spaces.

7. Text to Speech

A Text-To-Speech (TTS) synthesizer is a computer based system that should be able to read any text aloud, when it is directly introduced in the computer by an operator. It is more suitable to define Text-To-Speech or speech synthesis as an automatic production of speech, by "grapheme to phoneme" transcription. A grapheme is the smallest distinguishing unit in a written language. It does not carry meaning by itself. Graphemes include alphabetic letters, numerical digits, punctuation marks, and the individual symbols of any of the world's writing systems. A phoneme is "the smallest segmental unit of sound employed to form meaningful utterances" [14]. TTS creates speech from a string of characters, and states it. The audio layout is mono, 16 bit, 16 kHz by default. This function requires the Microsoft Win32 Speech API (SAPI).

8. System Results and Advantages

The overall matching result is 85% - 90% recognition for words and letters. It is important to mention that though the system contains up to 1200 images as a database, and about 200 sample images, the system's size doesn't exceed 4 MB. Running software with such a small size is unique and successful. Another advantage is the speed of the system. Matching a letter with 1200 images using 3 different methods means that the database is processed 1200 × 3 times. However the results are out within few seconds, which means that the system is fast and real-time.

9. Conclusion

Nowadays, hand gesture recognition had been implemented into many forms of bids and in several. This is a proof of the importance and improvement of this research title over the past few years. Hand gestures are at the heart of vision collaboration and machinery control. This paper principally dedicated to the ASL system. Though the equipment supply where is humble and standard, the final results live up to our expectations, we are simply proud of our work. The collection of detailed algorithm for data extracting and matching depends on the request desired. Description of gesture recognition topics and detail debate of used schemes are given as well.

References

[1] Kurtenbach, G. and Hulteen, E.A. (1990) Gestures in Human-Computer Communication. In: Laurel, B., Ed., *The Art of Human-Computer Interface Design*, Addison-Wesley Publishing Company, Inc., New York.

[2] Ibraheem, N.A. and Khan, R.Z. (2012) Vision Based Gesture Recognition Using Neural Networks Approaches: A Review. *International Journal of Human Computer Interaction (IJHCI)*, **3**, 1-14.

[3] Ferdousi, Z. (2008) Design and Development of a Real-Time Gesture Recognition System. U.M.I. Publishers.

[4] Kendon, A. (2004) Gesture: Visible Action as Utterance. Cambridge University Press, Cambridge.

[5] Yang, M.-H. and Narendra, A.(2001) Face Detection and Gesture Recognition for Human-Computer Interaction. Springer, US. http://dx.doi.org/10.1007/978-1-4615-1423-7

[6] Khan, R.Z. and Ibraheem, N.A. (2012) Hand Gesture Recognition, a Literature Review. *International Journal of Artificial Intelligence & Applications (IJAIA)*, **3**, 161.

[7] Rokade, U.S., Doye, D. and Kokare, M. (2009) Hand Gesture Recognition Using Object Based Key Fram Selection. *Proceedings of the* 2009 *International Conference on Digital Image Processing*, Bangkok, 7-9 March 2009, 288-291.

[8] Nachamai, M. (2013) Alphabet Recognition of American Sign Language a Hand Gesture Recognition Approach Using Sift Algorithm. *International Journal of Artificial Intelligence & Applications (IJAIA)*, **4**, 105-115.

[9] Castelli, V. and Bergman, L.D. (2002) Image Databases: Search and Retrieval of Digital Imagery. John Wiley & Sons, Hoboken.

[10] Szmurlo, M. (1995) A Comparative Study of Statistically Classifiable Features Used within the Field of Optical Character Recognition. Master's Thesis, Image Processing Laboratory, Oslo.

[11] Mohamad, H.S. and Mahmood, F. (2008) Real-Time Background Modeling Subtraction Using Two-Layer Codebook Model. *Proceedings of the International Multi Conference of Engineers and Computer Scientists*, Hong Kong, 19 March 2008, 978-988.

[12] Bauer, B. and Hienz, H. (2000) Relevant Features for Video-Based Continuous Sign Language Recognition. *Proceedings of the* 4*th IEEE International Conference on Automatic Face and Gesture Recognition*, Washington DC, 26-30 March 2000, 440. http://dx.doi.org/10.1109/afgr.2000.840672

[13] Moeslund, T. (2009) Canny Edge Detection.

[14] Wright, O. and Wright, W. (2013) Flying-Machine. *International Journal of Advanced Trends in Computer Science and Engineering*, **2**, 269-278.

7

The Optimization and Improvement of MapReduce in Web Data Mining

Jun Qu, Chang-Qing Yin, Shangwei Song

[1]Logistics Department, Tongji University, Shanghai, China
[2]School of Software Engineering, Tongji University, Shanghai, China
[3]College of Design and Innovation, Tongji University, Shanghai, China
Email: yinchangqing@tongji.edu.cn

Abstract

Extracting and mining social networks information from massive Web data is of both theoretical and practical significance. However, one of definite features of this task was a large scale data processing, which remained to be a great challenge that would be addressed. MapReduce is a kind of distributed programming model. Just through the implementation of map and reduce those two functions, the distributed tasks can work well. Nevertheless, this model does not directly support heterogeneous datasets processing, while heterogeneous datasets are common in Web. This article proposes a new framework which improves original MapReduce framework into a new one called Map-Reduce-Merge. It adds merge phase that can efficiently solve the problems of heterogeneous data processing. At the same time, some works of optimization and improvement are done based on the features of Web data.

Keywords

Cloud Computing, Web Data, MapReduce, Map-Reduce-Merge

1. Introduction

Social network consists of several categories of social entities and the relationship among them. Social Network Analysis (SNA) is an important tool to understand the behavior of human and analyze the social architecture. Social Network Analysis can not only be applied in sociology, but also in the informatics, information retrieval, information behavior and information metrology. In addition, Social Network Analysis has a significant effect on network knowledge mining, scientific evaluation, network information behavior research and knowledge management.

However, the theoretical and practical value of SNA depends on the quality and reliability of social network data. If the data itself is low in quality, the analysis result from that would be nonsense. Traditional sociology mainly acquires data via social investigation and group sampling. As the research in social network analysis develops, traditional method for acquiring social network data cannot meet the requirement of large scale social network analysis in many aspects. In the recent years, the appearance of various web platforms with social feature, such as online forum, twitter, SNS, makes it possible to extract and mining large quantity of high reliable and quality social network information from huge web data source via computer.

Web data sources usually contain massive entity, the number of relationships between these entities is the square of the number of entities, and massive computing provides challenges for research on this issue. In recent years, with the rapid growth of information and data in the age of the Internet, the concept of cloud computing was proposed. Cloud computing is an emerging model of business computing which is the further development of distributed computing, parallel processing and grid computing. It is able to provide a wide variety of Internet applications hardware services, infrastructure services, platform services, software services and storage service system. The sophistication of cloud computing platform provides new parallel computing framework for massive data, especially for Web data source large-scale data acquisition and an effective way for massive scale data processing.

But how to implement a Web mining based on the core computing model MapReduce of cloud computing is still a problem to be solved. As we all know, MapReduce is efficient when deals with isomorphic data, but the performance faced with heterogeneous data is often less than ideal. However, there are always heterogeneous data sets with no fixed format in the Web. In order to solve this problem in the existing MapReduce framework, developers need to write additional code, which is not what we expect.

In Web data mining, processing relational data is very common, especially for the user characteristic extraction and analysis. Like Facebook and Twitter have a large amount of user information to do extraction and mining these two sites combined information would be better than process only one site, so we need to do an effective integration on the heterogeneous information obtained from the two sites.

In this paper, the general concepts and definitions of MapReduce are provided, and introduce an improved model in Web data mining named Map-Reduce-Merge, merge the heterogeneous data produced by Reduce end effectively by increasing the Merge stage. In the meantime, it enhances the efficiency of Web data mining through optimizing the scheduling strategy, Map and Reduce tasks.

2. Map-Reduce

2.1. Overview

MapReduce is a programming model proposed by Google [1], it combines file system GFS [2] to implement parallel computing for large data set on massive scale distributed servers system. The concepts of "Map" and "Reduce", and their basic thoughts come from the features of functional program language and vector program language. MapReduce makes it greatly available for developers to deploy their programs on distributed system without knowledge of parallel programming.

MapReduce model consists of map function and reduce function. After input data processed by map function, it will produce a local intermediate result of key/value pairs. Reduce function remotely use the key/value pairs produced by map function as input to process under the schedule of Master. In order to take the independence and correlation of distributed data processing into consideration, it will then combine the result with same key value to get the final output. Doug Cutting used Java developed open source project Hadoop to implement MapReduce mechanism [3], and HDFS distributed file system [4], which allows the enterprises all over the world have a chance to utilize MapReduce to implement large scale distributed data processing.

MapReduce is not simply divided into Map and Reduce operations. On the one hand it has a more detailed division of operation, such as Combine, Shuffle and Sort. On the other hand in order to achieve large-scale data parallel and distributed processing it does a compact capsulation. The whole architecture help users to finish much hard work and solve problems like data partitioning, scheduling, data and code co-located, the process synchronous communication, fault tolerance and failure handling, load balancing and other issues [5] and make these functions transparent to the developers. Developers only need to implement the Map and Reduce interface, without concentrating on the underlying system-level problems, to complete the development of parallel programs on distributed clusters.

Certainly MapReduce has its own drawbacks [5].

1) High start consumption, when starting the cluster it visited all nodes in the network.

2) Low efficiency of random disk access. The MapReduce distributed file system is sequentially read and blocks access.

3) Synchronization mechanism is the hardest problem, the MapReduce tasks do not support the sharing of global data.

Besides, Mappers and Reducers run independently, they cannot interact through some other mechanism. But under the background of large-scale data, these disadvantages are related to applications and tolerant compared with their advantages. And they can also be alleviated or eliminated through a variety of optimization.

2.2. Programming Model

MapReduce is a simple programming model for data processing. A MapReduce program can be applied to a data set, which means a job. One job generally consists of several or even hundreds of tasks. The control machine responsible for assigning tasks in MapReduce is called master, the machine for executing task is called worker (core multi-thread, multi-core, multi-processor can also be regarded as worker). They are called master and slave in Hadoop respectively. From the view of storage they are divided into NameNode and DataNode. Namenode recorded the location and status information of distributed file block storage, whereas DataNode is responsible for the storage of real data, and under normal circumstances, DataNode is also the Task executor. Under the default setting of MapReduce, files are stored as blocks in a distributed file system [6].

The standard workflow of MapReduce is shown as **Figure 1**.

1) When a job is submitted, according to the distribution of file blocks in distributed systems, jobs are divided into several sub-tasks and processed by Mappers (the worker execute Map tasks). Generally tasks will be assigned to the machine contains data or the machine in the same rack to improve the processing speed, which is so-called "code find data" mode.

2) Each Mapper executes on different file block, according to the Map execution program, to transform data into key/value pairs. And as for each key/value pair, it executes the Map function provided by users to process. This stage is the massive parallel execution stage.

3) When Map task is completed, there will be Shuffle and Sort stage in the framework. It will distribute and sort the data produced by the Mappers and write them into local file system for the next stage, which improve the efficiency of Reduce.

4) Reduce tasks obtain their own data from the output of Map tasks, download to the local and merge them.

The mapping relationship of key/value can be illustrated by the following two formulas.

$$\text{map} \left(k1, v1 \right) \rightarrow \text{list} \left(k2, v2 \right)$$

$$\text{reduce} \left(k2, \text{list} \left(v2 \right) \right) \rightarrow \text{list} \left(v2 \right)$$

In the entire process, the user can assure the framework running by only implementing Map and Reduce functions, Which means only the two functions used in 2) 4) stages require the user to specify, whereas other stages are completed by the framework.

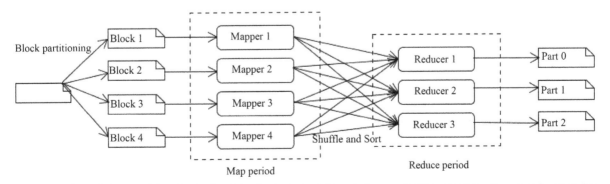

Figure 1. The standard workflow of MapReduce.

2.3. Schedule Execution Process

In Hadoop, there are two kinds of nodes to control the execution process of jobs: one JobTracker and several TaskTracker. JobTracker executes tasks by schedule TaskTracker, to coordinate all jobs on the platform. TaskTracker execute tasks and report the execution progress to JobTracker. As a result, every job has all corresponding records in a execution process. If any task fails, JobTracker will schedule another TaskTraker to execute the same task [7].

The job is initially generated in the user node, which communicate (RPC) through JobClient object and Job-Tracker. At first, ID of the job is got from the JobTracker. Then, job resources are submitted, including job data, job configuration information and MapReduce applications to the shared file system HDFS. Finally, job is submitted to JobTracker. The JobTracker firstly initialize the job, and then divide the data into the input split. The process is performed at logic level, rather than the actual data manipulation. TaskTracker periodically sent heartbeat to the JobTracker for the task. According to their own scheduling policy, JobTracker selects the appropriate task for TaskTracker and return to the TaskTracker by heartbeat. TaskTracker launches a separate virtual machine and perform task for an individual Map or Reduce task [8].

3. Map-Reduce-Merge

3.1. Programming Model

Map-Reduce-Merge model can handle multiple heterogeneous data sets, and its basic characteristics are as follows (α, β, γ represent different data set, k represent key and v represent value entity):

In this model, the map function will convert a key/value input (k1, v1) to an intermediate key/value pairs [(k2, v2)]. Reduce function will make value of [v2] whose key is k2 gathered together, to produce a value of [v3], which is associated with k2. Noted here, the input and output of the two functions are in the same data set α. Another pair of map and reduce functions produce intermediate output (K3 [v4]) from another dataset beta. Based on the keys: K2 and K3, merge function can merged into a key/value results (k4, v5) from the two output of Reduced function by different data sets. This ultimately results generate a new data set γ (**Figure 2**). If $\alpha = \beta$, then the merge function will do a self-merge, similar to the self-join in relational algebra.

The characteristics of Map and Reduce in new model are almost the same as its original MapReduce. The only difference is that here Reduce output is a key/value pairs, not just values. This change is introduced because the merge function needs the input of data set consisting of key/value. In the Google MapReduce, the result of Reduce is the final result, users can package any required data into [V3], and there is no need to pas k2 to the next stage.

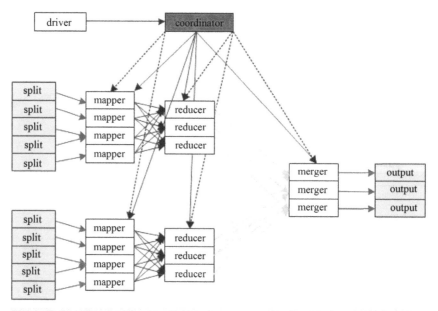

Figure 2. Map-Reduce-Merge model.

In order to build the merge function to read data from multiple data sets, design emphasizes to pass the key: k2 from the Map to Reduce, and then to the merge function. This can ensure that the data is divided into the areas and classified by keys before the Merge.

3.2. Example of SinaWeibo

In this section, a simple example of SinaWeibo will be proposed to illustrate how Map, Reduce and Merge module work together. Here we have two data sets, User and Friend Relationship. The key property of User is user_id, other information is included in user_info "value". The key property of Friend Relationship is user_id, other information is included in friend_info "value". Here the data processing is a combination of the two data sets and calculates the number of Weibo users "followers".

The left part of **Figure 3** is the table of every entity tag produced by Mapper processing User entity. Then Reducer merges the tag of every user and classifies them based on user_id. The right part is the table of every entity tag produced by Mapper processing Friend Relationship entity. Then Reducer merges the tag of every user and classifies them based on user_id. Finally Merge obtains output from two Renders and merge based on user_id and algorithm.

The code of Mappers and Reducers are as follows:

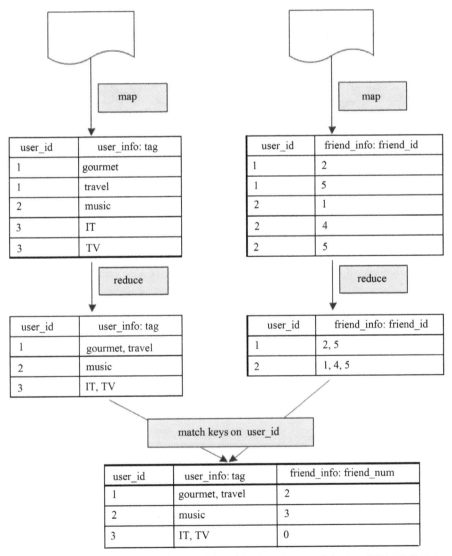

Figure 3. Combine and calculate number of "followers".

```
/* Algorithm 1 Map function for the User dataset. */
Map(const Key& key,/* user id */
    const Value& value /* user info */){
    user_id= key;
    tag=value.tag;
    /* compute tag using user info */
    output key =(user_id);
    output value =(tag);
    Emit(output key, output value);
}
/* Algorithm 2 Map function for the FriendRelationship dataset. */
Map(const Key& key,/* user id */
const Value& value /* firend info */){
user_id= key;
friend_id=value.firend_info:user_id;
Emit((user_id),(friend_id));
}
/* Algorithm 3 Reduce function for the User dataset. */
Reduce(const Key& key,/* user id */
    constValueIterator& value
    /* an iterator for a tags collection */){
    tag sum =/* sum up tags for each user id */
    Emit(key,(tag sum));
}
/* Algorithm 4 Reduce function for the FriendRelationship dataset. */
Reduce(const Key& key,/* (user id) */
constValueIterator& value
    /* an iterator on a friends collection */) {
    /* aggregate friends and compute friend_num */
Emit(key, (friend_num));
}
```

3.3. Model Implementation

So far has already implemented a Map-Reduce-Merge framework, whose Map and Reduce module has some trivial changes from MapReduce of Google. Merge is similar to Map and Reduce, developers can implement the user-defined logic of data processing. Calling mapper will produce one key/value pair. Calling Reducer will produce a set of value classified by key. Merger will process two key/value pairs which come from different sources.

At the Merge stage, users would adopt different data processing logic according to data resource. After the mission of Map and Reduce is completed, the Coordinator of Map-Reduce-Merge will start Mergers on a cluster of Nodes. When Merger starts, a Merger ID will be assigned to it. With this ID, Partition Selector can decide from which Render can Merge get input data. Similarly, Mappers and Reducers are also assigned an ID. As for Mappers, this ID stands for Input File Split. As for Reducers, this ID stands for Input Bucket. Mappers split and store their output. For the users of MapReduce, there IDs is the detail of system implementation. In Map-Reduce-Merge, users associate these IDs with the output and input between Mergers and Reducers.

4. Optimization

Aim at the features of Web data extraction and mining, such as small single data, large total amount of data, the existence of network latency, this chapter will provide some mechanism about model optimization, especially for the new Merge stage, it will provide specialized strategies to reduce consumption of resources (like number of network connection and disk bandwidth).

4.1. Schedule Strategy

The scheduler is the decision-makers which is running on the JobTracker and responsible for scheduling the jobs submitted by users. Users will submit jobs to the job queue to wait to be scheduled, the scheduler firstly select the job in the job queue and initialize it, then depending on the scheduling strategy, assign the tasks included in the job to the slot on TaskTracker to execute [9] (TaskTracker will periodically send heartbeat request to Job-Tracker to acquire tasks).

Because schedule strategy has significant impact on the efficient use of the cluster, load balancing, job execution efficiency [10], it has a great significance to provide an efficient scheduling execution environment to Map-Reduce-Merge programming model framework. Recently, the most influential scheduling strategies include the Capacity scheduler, Fair scheduler and LATE scheduler. They make improvements for the original FIFO scheduling algorithm, parallel scheduling in multi-user management, and cluster support for heterogeneous environments respectively.

FIFO scheduler is a Hadoop default task scheduler, it simply schedule the jobs submitted by users via a job queue. But it has a poor performance for multi-user and for the efficient use of the cluster.

Capacity scheduler can support multiple organizations to share the same large clusters, and ensure that each organization have the smallest computing power. But Capacity scheduler allocate resources equally, tend to regard the resources of jobs submitted by users is relatively equally, it does not take the diversity of job requirements into consideration.

Fair scheduling ensure small job has response time as short as possible through fair resource scheduling strategy, and provides service level assurance for product operations [11]. However as for the data analysis job which consume large computing resource, its prior schedule will result in life cycle delay of up to a task. This will have a great influence on the subsequent execution of jobs.

The LATE scheduler is the default scheduler in a heterogeneous environment which has a "try to execute" improvement on strategy [10]. But the determination of task execution time is based on the premise that all tasks are carried out in accordance with the constant rate of execution. With the change of use of joint resources, such as memory consumption, the rate of task execution is not constant. In addition, the idea of Reduce divide the execution process into 3 equal parts for copy, merge and reduce is not accurate.

Can be found, for the special case of Web data, there are certain limitation for existing scheduler. In order to better fulfill the requirement of Web data, the schedule strategy should be improved as follows:

1) Using the multi-queue to process jobs submitted by users. Like Capacity scheduler, every queue correspond to a user group, administrator can manage the users and their queue. Queue has priority according to that of user group. The group of the queue can submit jobs with different priority, which correspond to the urgency of the task, such as real-time operating can have higher job priority data whereas analysis jobs correspond to a lower priority, multi-queue scheduling support preemption.

2) Classify the type of tasks. Job type is the result of refinement for requirement of job resource. So far job type is divided into CPU-intensive and disk-intensive which is similar to three queue scheduler. Allocate a certain amount of computing resource for different job type and compute parallel can enhance the utilization of cluster. The multi-type of job scheduling policy is a best-effort scheduling under the premise of ensuring the multi-queue scheduling. Finally, introduce competition mechanism for resources among multi-user queue.

4.2. Map

In the process of Map task, the intermediate key/value pair <k2, v2> outputted by map function is written to a circular cache in logic, rather than immediately written to the local file system. When the circular cache is full, it will continue to receive the output from map function while write intermediate file to disk at the same time [12].

The output file is as follows: do partition and sort operation to the key/value pair in cache. Then spill file to disk.

If there are much the intermediate data in a Map task, it need spill several times to disk. Every Spill will get a file, so multiple operations will result in multiple file which is after segmentation and sort. At the end of Map task execution, it will merge all spill file. Under the guarantee of the order of split and sort is unchanged, merge all the intermediate files into one file.

Obviously this intermediate file organization is not compact enough, so it can be optimized. Increase one thread to merge the output of multiple Map tasks. This thread is started by the TaskTracker and will periodically check the number of Map output files of each task on the node. When the number of map output files of a certain task reaches the default size of configuration, the files will be merged. The file merge is the same way as the merge of multiple spill file, which is a merge on the disk to save the memory consumption of the node.

By this merge operation, reduce the number of intermediate files can be reduced, which makes the output data of the same the Map task on a node more compact. This compact organizational structure has two advantages:

1) The less output file can reduce the overhead of establishing a network connection in the Reduce task Shuffle stage, to improve the speed of data transmission on the network.

2) The merge operation of Map end reduces the workload of the Reduce task merge phase. In the download and merge stage of Reduce task, it will merge the Map intermediate data several times until get a complete Reduce input and then call reduce function. Merge in the node contains Map can reduce the number of intermediate files , and then reduce the round of merge, finally reduce the execution time.

4.3. Reduce

Reduce end can be improved in the following two aspects.

1) Unbalance of Reduce tasks

The reasons for unbalanced data can be summarized into two categories [13] [14]:

a) Intermediate results are key dispersed, while after partition too is aggregation. Although the number of different key is large, but after mapping, too many key gathered in the same Reduce task.

b) Intermediate results are key single, while result is diverse. The type of key number is relatively small, but the number of records corresponding to the key is large. According to the principle that the records with same key is mapping to the same Reduce, one Reduce can process all the records of one key.

Aim at the unbalance in the data, the improvement target is to make the data be evenly distributed to each Reduce task to ensure that each amount of Reduce task can be roughly equal. To avoid some nodes to deal with too much data "exhausting", while others node have no data processing "starve to death".

Improvement program will start twice MapReduce Job. Firstly, use the Reduce in first MapReduce to merge locally, to ensure Reduce operation data in the second reduce operation is balanced and the records with same key can be processed in the same Reduce task.

For the first input of the Reduce stage, it is not necessary to ensure that each key corresponding to the record must be mapped to the same Reduce. On the contrary, each record should be randomly mapped to a reduce records having the same key which is uniformly dispersed, but need to ensure that the amount of calculation in each Reduce should be substantially equal. Reduce operating merged the records with same key record into one, after the local polymerization data is greatly reduced, and there is only one record corresponding to one key in each Reduce output. At this point the data as the second input of MapReduce, map function have nothing to do, directly regard the input data as output, the data is mapped to Reduce task in accordance with the original partition. Reduce do one operation, the same data is combined to give the final output of each key corresponding to a result.

Figure 4 shows the data processing flow for improved Map-Reduce-Merge.

However this does not mean that all the calculations need local polymerization, if Map output can reach Reduce equilibrium requirements, this program will be executed. So need to develop a strategy to determine under what circumstances local data aggregation should be operated. At the beginning of Map firstly attempts to do Hash mapping, if the mapping of the different number of records/Try to certain records the number of records is greater than a given threshold, then it means the Map output data and input to the Reduce task is balanced, so just execute the original MapReduce process. Otherwise launch another MapReduce Job and operate local polymerization in the first Reduce.

2) The I/O problem in shuffle phase of Reduce

During the execution of the Reduce task, the Shuffle stage of I/O is often a performance bottleneck. In this stage, Reduce task will periodically inquiry the Map job information completed by JobTracker. For the completed Map task, the download threads will establish an HTTP connection between its nodes and download the intermediate data. When the output of the Map task download is complete, the connection is disconnected. Therefore, for a Reduce task in the Shuffle stage, at least creates the download connection with the same number of the Map tasks.

The average overhead for establishment of connection in less complex cluster of a network topology is the tens to hundreds of milliseconds, which is very short. But for the relatively small amount of output data of each Map, the overhead of establishment cannot be underestimated. Especially for Web data, this situation is particularly evident, most of the Map output is obtained from each of the sub-page jobs with small the amount of data.

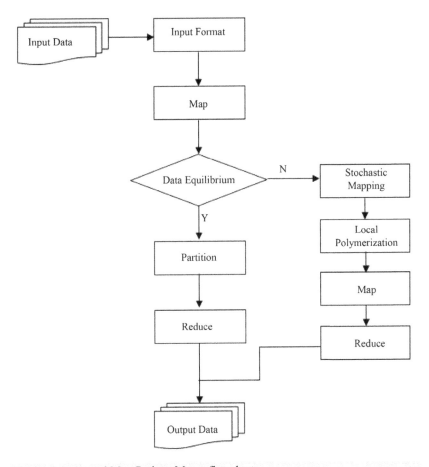

Figure 4. Improved Map-Reduce-Merge flowchart.

To optimize I/O in shuffle phase, firstly reduce the number of connections to establish, for each download thread in its life cycle, only to establish a long connection to the same node. When the output of the MAP can be downloaded, then download it from this link, after all output complete downloading, then close the connection. This is effective for jobs with many maps.

Because http is based on the TCP connection to transfer files, TCP slow start-up characteristics determine the data transfer rate cannot immediately reach the network bandwidth. The proposed method to merge Map output file can increase the amount of once data transmitted, which can improve the transmission rate [15].

Map output merger changed the organizational form of the intermediate data. Shuffle download thread will not necessarily be able to directly download a Map output file according to file information get from JobTracker It may get the output file, which may be obtained by combined Map output file. In this regard, solution is to keep the original Map task progress reporting mode and Shuffle stage download access to information the same way. Only make minor modifications in the implementation process of the download, as far as possible through the merger of the intermediate output file, making a large amount of data transferred.

For example, the map A task execution is complete and report to the JobTracker. Then Reduce tasks query to JobTracker for the completion of Map A, and try to communicate to the node contains map A and download the output data of Map A. At the same time, Map B is completed in the same node as Map A, and the output of Map A and Map B has been merged into an output file. The node will send combined output to the Reduce node, and inform that the transferred data is a result of the merger of A and B tasks. After Reduce tasks have received the data, it will mark Map A and MAP B as received, and do not further access to the node for the output data of the task B.

For a special case, the completion information of Map A and Map B has been acquired by Reduce separately, downloaded by two download threads. The nodes will receive one of the download requests, and send the merge of A and B. Reduce take retreat, does not immediately re-attempt when the download request of connection to the same node is refused, the download will not restart until all the threads connected to the node are completed and not able to obtain the desired output data .

4.4. Workflow

The MapReduce program strictly abides by the two-stage process, the first Map and the second Reduce. The user can change the default configuration. However, some basic operations, such as Partition and Sort are built-in, and must be executed. It is a little troublesome for the users just want to perform Map or Reduce tasks. Although such restrictions make MapReduce simple, but it cannot meet the needs of advanced users, who more often want to customize the entire workflow. So it should be possible to optimize the interface of the framework to allow advanced users to have greater freedom to define the workflow to meet their own requirements.

Because MapReduce has only two stages, the customization is relatively simple. After add Merge stage, there can be a combination of more kinds of processes to meet the specific data processing tasks (see **Figure 5**).

The left is the typical 2-pass MapReduce workflow. The entire process only contains a Map and Reduce.

The middle is the 3-pass Map-Reduce-Merge workflow. The whole process consists of two Map and Reduce a Merge.

The right is a multi-pass hierarchical workflow. The entire process contains multiple Map Reduce and merge.

4.5. Load Balancing

Load balancing helps to evenly dispersed load to the junction point of the idle when the load exceeds the threshold level in a junction point. Even though load balancing is not obvious enough when executing Map-Reduce-Merge algorithm, however, in processing large file, and hardware resources [16] utilization is critical the advantage is very obvious. A significant role in the tight resource situation is to increase hardware utilization, improve performance. To balance some of the data node which is full or new, empty node joins the cluster, implement a module to balance disk space usage on the cluster of distributed file system. If for each data point, the junction space and the ratio of the total capacity (Junction Point utilization) is different from the used space and total space ratio (Clusters utilization) on the cluster and does not exceed the threshold value, then the cluster is regarded as balanced.

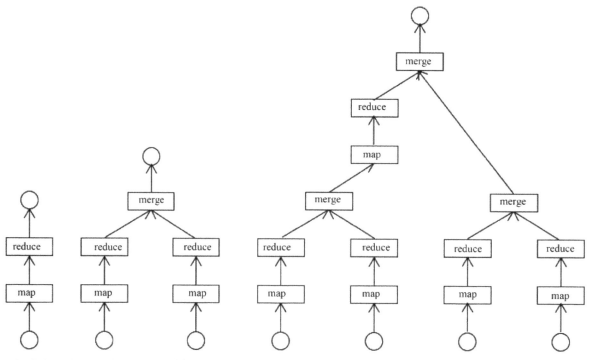

Figure 5. Workflow of Map-Reduce-Merge.

The module interactively moves data block in the node of high utilization to the point of the low utilization rate. In each iteration, the amount of move or receive of one point does not exceed the capacity threshold proportion. In this implementation, the node is classified as the high utilization, the average utilization and underutilized. According to the amount of use of each node, transfer the load among nodes to balance the cluster.

Load balancing module works as follows:

1) To obtain detailed information of the neighboring nodes. When the the DataNode load is added to the threshold level, will send a request to the NameNode and Namenode will get load level information in the neighboring nodes of specific the DataNode. Then NameNode compare the load information, and then send the details of the idlest adjacent nodes to a specific DataNode.

2) The DataNode start work. Each DataNode compare its load to its nearest node. If its load level is higher than its neighboring nodes, it will randomly select its neighbors and send the request to the destination node.

5. Conclusions

Firstly, this paper simply introduces the concept and programming model of MapReduce. The MapReduce has many important features, such as high-throughput, high-performance, fault tolerance and ease of manageability [17] [18]. Among them, the most important features is the parallel programming abstraction for two simple primitives, Map and Reduce, so developers can easily work in the real-world data processing converted into parallel programs.

However, MapReduce cannot directly support the handling of heterogeneous data sets, this is a fatal flaw for the non-standardization of Web data processing. It can be solved effectively by Adding Merge stage on the basis of the original model. And the new programming framework of the Map-Reduce-Merge inherited the the original MapReduce characteristics. Finally, for some of the features for Web data, do further optimization and improvement on the part of the Map-Reduce-Merge model scheduling policy, workflow, and load balancing to enhance the framework operating efficiency while also expanded its versatility.

References

[1]   Dean, R. and Ghemawat, A. (2004) MapReduce: Implified Data Processing on Large Cluster. *SDI*, 137-149.

[2]   Ghemawat, N., Gobioff, H. and Leung, S.T. (2003) The Google File System. *Proceedings of the SOSP'03*, Bolton Landing, 19-22 October 2003, 29-43.

[3]   DOUG CUTTING (2005) Scalable Computing with MapReduce. OSCON.

[4]   Borthankur, D. (2007) The Hadoop Distributed File System: Architecture and Design. Apache Software Foundation. 5-14.

[5]   Daniel Abadi, M., DeWitt, D.J., *et al.* (2010) MapReduce and Parallel DBMSs: Friends or Foes. *Communications of the ACM*, **53**.

[6]   Hadoop, T.W. (2009) The Definitive Guide. O'Reilly Media, 153-174.

[7]   Zaharia, M., Konwinski, A. and Joseph, A.D. (2008) Improving MapReduce Performance in Heterogeneous Environment. *Proceedings of the 8th USENIX Conference on Operating Systems Design and Implementation*, San Diego, 8-10 December 2008, 9-15.

[8]   Becerra, Y., Beltran, V., Carrera, D., Gonzalez, M., Torres, J. and Ayguade, E. (2009) Speeding Up Distributed MapReduce Applications Using Hardware Accelerators. *Proceedings of the* 2009 *International Conference on Parallel Processing*, Vienna, 22-25 September 2009, 42-49. http://dx.doi.org/10.1109/ICPP.2009.59

[9]   Fei, X., Lu, S. and Lin, C. (2009) A MapReduce-Enabled Scientific Workflow Composition Framework. *Proceedings of the IEEE International Conference on Web Services*, Los Angeles, 6-10 July 2009, 663-670.

[10]   Hadoop 0.20 Documentation, Capacity Scheduler.

[11]   Hadoop 0.20 Documentation, Fair Scheduler.

[12]   Tian, C., Zhou, H., He, Y. and Zha, L. (2009) A Dynamic MapReduce Scheduler for Heterogeneous Workloads. *Proceedings of the 8th International Conference on Grid and Cooperative Computing*, Lanzhou, 27-29 August 2009, 218-224.

[13]   Dean, J. and Ghemawat, S. (2004) MapReduce: Simplified Data Processing on Large Clusters. *Proceedings of OSDI'04*, San Francisco, 5 December 2004, 137-150.

[14]   Pike, R., Dorward, S., Griesemer, R., *et al.* (2005) Interpreting the Data: Parallel Analysis with Sawzall. *Scientific Programming*, **13**, 227-298. http://dx.doi.org/10.1155/2005/962135

[15] Lammel, R. (2006) Google's MapReduce Programming Model—Revisited. Draft, 26 p.

[16] Tian, F. and Chen, K. (2011) Towards Optimal Resource Provisioning for Running MapReduce Programs in Public Clouds. *Proceedings of the* 2011 *IEEE International Conference on Cloud Computing* (*CLOUD*), Washington DC, 4-9 July 2011, 155-162.

[17] Kim, K., Jeon, K., Han, H., Kim, S., Jung, H., Yeom, H.Y. and Bench, M.R. (2008) A Benchmark for MapReduce Framework. Proceedings of the 2008 14th IEEE International Conference on Parallel and Distributed Systems, Victoria, 8-10 December 2008, 11-18. http://dx.doi.org/10.1109/ICPADS.2008.70

[18] Kim, K., Jeon, K., Han, H., Kim, S., Jung, H. and Yeom, H.Y. (2008) Mrbench: A Benchmark for MapReduce Framework. *Proceedings of the* 2008 14*th IEEE International Conference on Parallel and Distributed Systems*, Melbourne, 8-10 December 2008, 11-18.

8

A Framework for Software Defect Prediction Using Neural Networks

Vipul Vashisht[1], Manohar Lal[1], G. S. Sureshchandar[2]

[1]SOCIS, IGNOU, New Delhi, India
[2]ASQ India Pvt Ltd., Chennai, India
Email: vipulvashisht@gmail.com, prof.manohar.lal@gmail.com, suresh.gettala@gmail.com,

Abstract

Despite the fact that a number of approaches have been proposed for effective and accurate prediction of software defects, yet most of these have not found widespread applicability. Our objective in this communication is to provide a framework which is expected to be more effective and acceptable for predicting the defects in multiple phases across software development lifecycle. The proposed framework is based on the use of neural networks for predicting defects in software development life cycle. Further, in order to facilitate the easy use of the framework by project managers, a software graphical user interface has been developed that allows input data (including effort and defect) to be fed easily for predicting defects. The proposed framework provides a probabilistic defect prediction approach where instead of a definite number, a defect range (minimum, maximum, and mean) is predicted. The claim of efficacy and superiority of proposed framework is established through results of a comparative study, involving the proposed framework and some well-known models for software defect prediction.

Keywords

Software Defect, Software Defect Prediction Model, Neural Network, Quality Management

1. Introduction

Software quality concerns require our gradually increasing attention, especially in view of our ever increasing dependency on software to conduct routine business of life. In particular, business goals of most organizations, being targeted towards customer satisfaction and profitable growth, are being met through increasing use of software. A minor defect, or even inefficiency, in the software may lead to not only loss of millions of dollars, but loss of customer base. In view of the potentially harmful consequences of defect leakage for the reputation of the product and to the supplier, its reduction in the production environment is extremely vital to achieve such goals of business.

As per IEEE definition [1], fault is an incorrect step, process, or data definition in a computer program. Throughout this paper, the terms defect and fault are used interchangeably. These terms refer to the manifestation of an error in source code, where an error is an erroneous action made by a developer [2]. Faults can be the cause of failures which occur when users experience undesirable system behavior at any point in time.

In the software development life cycle (SDLC), early prediction of defects has always been, though highly desirable yet, a challenging task for the project managers. Developing fault-free reliable software is a daunting task in the current context, when software is being developed for problems with increasing difficulty with more and more complex problem domains that involve constantly increasing constraints like requirement ambiguity and complex development processes. In spite of meticulous planning and well documented processes, occurrences of certain defects are inevitable. These software defects may lead to degradation of the product quality which may lead to failures leading to customer dissatisfaction. In today's cutting edge competition, it is necessary to make conscious efforts to control and minimize defects in software engineering processes. However, these efforts require organizations not only to spend large amount of money, time and resources but also defect prediction software based on appropriate model [3]. These efforts could help the project manager to take preventive actions, thereby saving time and cost apart from delivering high quality software. Also, the development and use of a Process Performance Model (PPM) that includes defect prediction model has been identified as one of the high maturity practices in SEI CMMI model. This falls under the process areas of Organizational Process Performance (OPP) and Quantitative Project Management (QPM). Organizations attempting for CMMI L5 appraisal have to mandatorily showcase the process improvements by making use of such prediction models [4].

In respect of software, apart from the quality consideration, the time of delivery is also an important factor. Implementing Quality reviews are time-consuming and if unplanned, they could delay the delivery of a software system. Automated tools are used to accelerate the review process. The assessments, through reviews, check whether the software has reached the required quality threshold or not and also highlight areas which still need attention [5]. This is the task of software defect predictors that are used as tools for the purpose of 1) identifying parts of a software system requiring further examination before release and 2) finding relative priorities among these parts.

In most projects, information collected during testing and defect detection phases is analyzed to help predict defects for similar types of projects. However, since it is found that so far, each of the models of defect prediction has areas where it does not function satisfactorily; the search for one model that can predict defects satisfactorily in a wide range of projects is still on. This justifies the investigations reported through this communication.

The paper is organized as follows. Section II provides a brief overview of Neural Networks, Section III reviews the existing literature on the subject, Section IV describes the proposed framework, Section V discusses the results as obtained through use of the proposed defect prediction framework vis-à-vis some other relevant models/frameworks and finally Section VI concludes the presented work.

Our investigations are based on statistical pattern classification of defects. Recent advances in learning algorithms using artificial neural networks and parallel computation have led to renewed research in the area of statistical pattern classification. Artificial neural networks, simply called ANNs or neural networks, have been applied both to time varying patterns as well as static patterns. In this respect, in the next section we briefly discuss some basic concepts, the structure and functions of a Neural Network.

2. Neural Networks

Artificial Neural Network (ANN) is a sort of an approach to computation or is a model of processor/computer based on human brain. Prevalent view of human brain is that it is a sort of neural network: A networks of about 100 billion neurons, each neuron being connected, on the average, to about 1000 other neurons. A neuron is the basic constituent of brain, a sort of elementary processor having small local memory and capable of localized information processing. To a connection between a pair of neurons, called interconnection, is associated an adjustable weight indicating the strength of the connection. The terminology of neuron and interconnection etc is used in the similar sense in ANN. In **Figure 1**, a circle denotes a neuron, and a straight line denotes interconnection. Generally, group of neurons are arranged in layers—as shown in **Figure 1** in the form of vertically arranged set

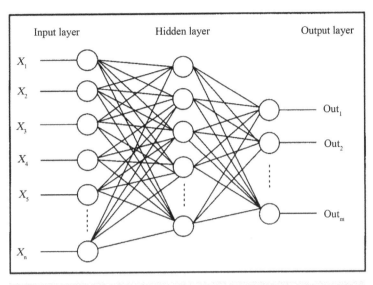

Figure 1. Neural network.

of neurons.

There is one layer for the input variables, and one for the output. There can be one or several layers between these two which are referred to as hidden layers. The signal or input given to one neuron is passed to all the neurons to which it is connected in fractions equivalent to the weight between these neurons. Each neuron calculates its output based on a function which can be sigmoid, step or some such suitable function. The strength of neural networks is their capability to learn from patterns. A neural network learns patterns by adjusting its weights. When the neural network is properly trained, it can give correct, or nearly correct, answers for not only the sample patterns, but also for new similar patterns [6] [7].

During the previous decades, neural network approach has emerged as a promising technology in applications which require generalization, abstraction adaptation and learning. The application of neural networks is to diverse fields range from autonomous vehicle control [8], financial risk analysis to handwriting recognition [9]. Therefore, it is only natural that the neural network technology can be exploited to solve different software engineering problems. For example, neural networks have been earlier applied in dynamic software reliability modeling [10].

The decision about using Neural network based framework for modeling defect prediction, was taken after diligent literature review of success of neural networks regarding software metrics models [11]-[15], and also, in view of the fact that neural networks have been found effective in situations where data relationships may not be known, as normally happens in the case of defect prediction. Also, there is sufficient evidence in support of applying neural networks in software effort estimation [16] [17]. Next, we give an over view of the relevant literature.

3. Review of Literature

In view of the fact that each model of defect prediction has its own set of advantages and disadvantages, it is hard to decide which model should be used for a particular type of project scenario, specially, as every project tends to be unique.

For the reasons mentioned earlier, software defect prediction is a very active research area in software engineering. Researchers have proposed new defect prediction algorithms and/or new metrics to effectively predict defects. The historical data of software systems is a valuable asset used for research ranging from software design to software development, software maintenance, software testing, etc.

Recently, there has been an increase in the use of computational intelligence in the field of software engineering. Computational Intelligence (CI) includes technologies of fuzzy logic, neural networks, genetic algorithms, genetic programming, and rough sets. Only a very small fraction of the activities involved in software design and development can be automated using software tools; most of the activities necessarily require human involvement. However, the human involvement, especially in view of the human judgment being imprecise and uncertain, characterizes many of the challenges including those observed in software defect prediction. Incorporation of computational intelligence into the various phases of software development and analysis helps in addressing the problems arising due to imprecise measurement and uncertainty of information [18] [19].

General principles/approaches/steps which have been found useful so far in handling the difficult task of software defect prediction, along with the relevant literature, are summarized below:

A defect prediction model based on an enhanced Multilayer Perceptron Neural Network technique using data mining is proposed and explored in [20], in which comparative analysis of modeling of defect proneness predictions using dataset of different metrics from NASA MDP (Metrics Data Program) was performed. The proposed MLP neural network model gave better results, when compared with the existing techniques like Random Tree, classification and regression trees (CART) algorithm, and Bayesian logistic regression.

Levenberg-Marquardt (LM) algorithm based on neural network tool for the prediction of software defects at an early stage of the SDLC is described in [21]. This study uses data gathered from the PROMISE repository of empirical software engineering dataset. The dataset uses the CKOO (Chidamber and Kemerer Object-Oriented) metrics. The study concludes that for predicting the software defects, the Levenberg-Marquardt (LM) neural network based algorithm provides better accuracy (88.09%) as compared to each of polynomial function-based neural networks (pF-NNs), linear function-based neural network (lf-NN) and quadratic function-based neural network (qf-NN) respectively.

In [22], it is suggested that an under development module with same or similar metrics properties of a defective module developed in the same environment, would have the same level of defect proneness. For the purpose of defect-prediction in software programs, the authors have designed Adaptive Resonance Neural Network having 29 input nodes and two output nodes. The network is trained with data extracted from PROMISE dataset. The network improves the recall (true positive) rate in predicting whether a module is defective or not [23].

In [24] an approach is described for static reliability modeling, and for modeling of software reliability from software complexity in terms of the predictive quality and the quality of fit. The performance of a model based on the approach is compared with more traditional regression modeling techniques. For the purpose, the data have been taken from an Ada development environment for the command and control of a military data link communication system (CCCS), in which neural and regression analysis techniques were employed. It was found that the neural network model is superior to traditional regression based techniques and also had a smaller standard error.

This paper describes a framework, for applying neural networks, for formulating models for defect prediction early in the software life cycle. A series of empirical experiments are conducted based on input and output measures extracted from "real world" project subsystems. The experiments establish the efficacy and superiority of the approach. Next section describes the proposed framework.

4. The Proposed Framework

As mentioned earlier, the objective in our study is to develop prediction framework based on Neural Network for forecasting the defects. In this section, first we explain the assumptions made about the proposed framework. Then we describe the structure of the proposed framework and functions of major components of the framework. The results and other related issues are discussed in the next section.

For this purpose we use the actual runtime historical data set that is fed into the system during training of the proposed network as shown in **Figure 2**. The historical data of software systems is a valuable asset used for research in all phases of SDLC ranging from requirement gathering, analysis, software design, coding, to system testing and maintenance. The experiments reported here involve data set taken from 45 real projects from a software organization. The actual defect data is taken from completed projects based on Java technology and waterfall life cycle model.

This historical data has served as a training data to build the proposed framework and then the neural network so obtained is used to predict the defects for all new projects. As waterfall model is the oldest among the models used for software development and which is still widely practiced, it tends to be the standard against which other development approaches are compared.

We have considered along with the production effort, the prevention effort, review effort and rework effort as

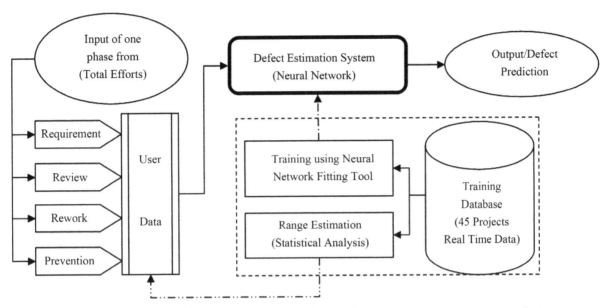

Figure 2. Model framework design.

components of input in our neural network based defect prediction framework in view of support for the fact that as voluntary costs of defect prevention are increased, the involuntary costs of rework decrease by much more than the increase in prevention costs [22] [25], thus leading to overall lower total costs, and better quality.

The proposed framework as shown in **Figure 3** requires user to enter the planned effort data of five SDLC phases, namely, Requirement Gathering, Analysis, Design, Coding and System integration testing (SIT). The data is provided with breakup of planned effort allocated to production effort, review effort, rework effort and prevention effort. If the data provided by the user matches with eligibility criteria of given range then defects are estimated using Defect Estimation System by Neural Network Technique.

4.1. Structure of the Proposed Neural Network

A feed-forward network with sigmoid (hidden and linear output neurons) is used to formulate the system. The network is trained with scaled conjugate gradient back-propagation (training).

Defect prediction system consists of five parallel neural networks with different configurations and parameters for each sub phase. Only first phase that is for Requirement Gathering is having 5 hidden layers & remaining phases have 10 hidden layers in their architecture. The architectural view of Neural Network for requirement gathering phase is shown in **Figure 4**. The selection of number of hidden layers is done in order to optimize the regression value for attaining the best performance. Although more neurons require more computation, and also have a tendency to over fit the data when the number is set too high, but at the same time, they allow the network to solve more complicated problems [26]. Input data of 45 real time projects is divided randomly in three parts before training with it is initiated: Training (70%), Validation (15%) and Testing (15%).

Levenberg Marquardt back-propagation optimization method is used for training the network. It is the fastest among methods available for the current scenario of Supervised Learning. It also requires less memory. Like the quasi-Newton methods, the Levenberg-Marquardt algorithm was designed to approach second-order training speed without having to compute the Hessian matrix. When the performance function has the form of a sum of squares (as is typical in training feedforward networks), then the Hessian matrix can be approximated as:

$$H = J^T J$$

and the gradient can be computed as: $g = J^T e$,

where J is the Jacobian matrix that contains first derivatives of the network errors with respect to the weights and biases, and e is a vector of network errors. Regression R Values measure the correlation between outputs and targets. **Figure 5** represents the relationship for all five SDLC phases.

Software Defect Prediction

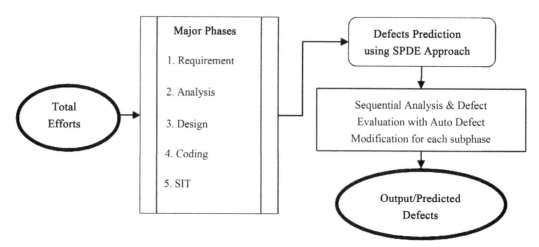

Figure 3. Software prediction model.

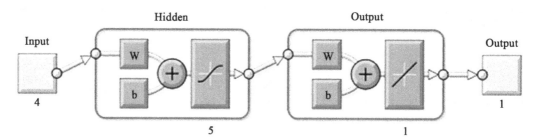

Figure 4. Architectural view of network for requirement gathering phase.

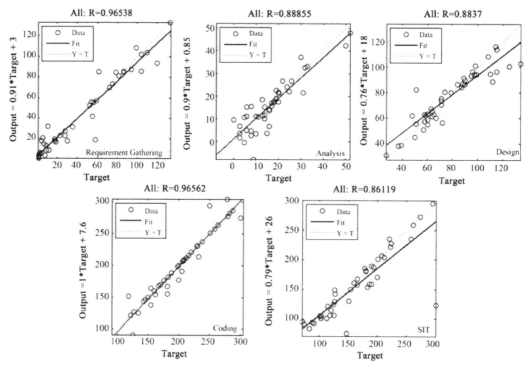

Figure 5. Representation of R value for SDLC phases.

4.2. User Interface for Testing the Framework with New Projects

One of the primary goals of our project is to present the prediction information to project managers in the most user friendly manner. Project Managers should not be required to understand the mathematics behind the prediction model. To make the predictions easily accessible to its users, a GUI based tool has been designed and implemented that asks for only the most basic information from users, and returns a straightforward output of the defect predictions.

A user interface tool (refer to **Figure 6**) has been developed using Matlab to help in testing the framework design.

NN Model Defect prediction

Total Efforts are:

	Requirement	Analysis	Design	Coding	SIT
R Gathering	140	139	168	556	208
Review	4	7	4	17	6
Rework	2	4	4	13	4
Prevention	10	6	12	13	5

Range Eligiblity Criteria for Min & Max Ranges of Efforts in Percentage:

	R Min	R Max	A Min	A Max	D Min	D Max	C Min	C Max	S Min	S Max
R Gathering	80	88	82	93	80	98	85	98	86	99
Review	2	4	0	3	2	3	2	3	2	3
Rework	2	4	0	2	1	2	1	2	1	3
Prevention	6	13	7	13	1	12	0	6	0	5

Hint as per Min & Max Ranges of Efforts in Percentage

	R Min	R Max	A Min	A Max	D Min	D Max	C Min	C Max	S Min	S Max
R Gathering	124	137	127	145	150	184	509	587	191	220
Review	3	6	0	4	3	6	3	21	4	7
Rework	3	6	0	3	1	4	7	14	2	6
Prevention	9	20	10	20	2	22	0	35	0	11

Defect Estimation

	Predicted Defects	Actual Defect	Modified Defect
Requirement	86	85	
Analysis	11	15	12
Design	66	63	63
Coding	164	162	164
SIT	131	130	133
Total	459	455	

Load Efforts	Defect Prediction	Reset

Figure 6. Defect prediction system UI.

The predictions thus achieved can be used to prioritize testing efforts, to plan code or design reviews, to allocate human and infrastructure resources, and to plan for risk mitigation strategy.

4.3. Working of Defect Prediction User Interface

- For any new project, the software project manager will provide the inputs required to the UI.
- The inputs would be the phase wise efforts planned for the project
- Apart from production effort, the planned review effort, planned prevention effort and the planned rework effort are also required as a feed to the framework.
- Framework provides graphical analysis for each sub phase to analyze the input eligibility (refer to **Figure 7**). Based on historical data the framework would also provide a warning message to the project manager if planned effort is less for review, rework or engineering activity for a particular phase. There could be specific scenarios where project manager might want to go ahead and ignore the warning. Example of such cases could be planning for a higher prevention effort for projects based on lesson learned from past projects or cases which might need a higher review effort since requirements from previous vendor could be incomplete or unavailable.
- Based on these inputs, the framework will forecast the number of defects that the project manager could expect to be discovered in various SDLC phases in the project.
- The defects are forecast in a range based manner. The framework would provide the minimum, maximum and the mean number of defects.
- The forecast would enable the project manager to plan prevention activities for the phase where the framework is projecting higher number of defects.
- The project manager can plan multiple preventive actions, like multiple review gates, usage of tools, increasing review effort etc to mitigate the higher probability of defect leakage.
- The framework is designed to autocorrect itself. After phase completion, user feeds the actual count of defect data. If actual defects are lower than predicted then defects leaked to the subsequent sub phase are auto corrected.
- For example, it may happen that there is higher amount of defects predicted in design phase but due to multiple preventive actions taken by the project manager, the actual defects count identified is less. As soon as the project manager enters the actual defects into the proposed framework based prediction model, the model corrects the predictions of future phases accordingly.

5. Result and Discussions

In this paper, proposed defect prediction framework has been validated on 15 real time projects of the same kind (based on Java technology and waterfall life cycle) and found that actual defects lie inside the range of predicted defects. Although there is a small deviation in some projects but that is well within the tolerance band of 2% to 5%. It is being evident from **Figure 8** that the actual defects are in line with the predicted defects. For the test results of pilot conducted on 15 projects, our proposed framework has accuracy of close to 90% .The regression value from **Figure 5** depicts a closer relationship between the predicted and actual defects.

In our experiments, the data sets with different network architectures have been used. The actual defects data from 45 completed projects was taken and used as a training data. Later, the framework was also tested for prediction of defects for newly started projects.

The quality of fit and the predictive quality found for each of the data sets have given very optimistic results. The prediction results indicate that the net (based on the proposed framework) tries to track the behavior of the full data set and sometimes its predicted value is more than the actual and sometimes less. The data set itself is an instance of random behavior. But what the net predicts is the number of faults that should occur, given the input variables based on the pattern it recognizes in the training data. The training data is the only data for the net to base its conclusions on, since that is the only information the net receives from the outer world.

Framework Comparison

The results of accuracy of close to 90% obtained by the proposed framework are comparable with, and even

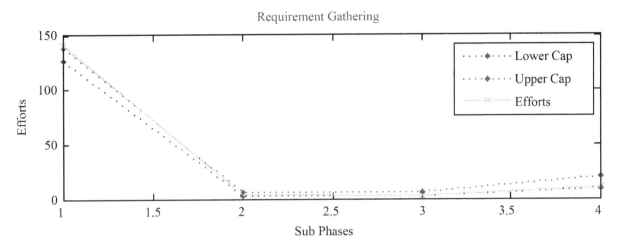

Figure 7. Input eligibility of requirement gathering phase.

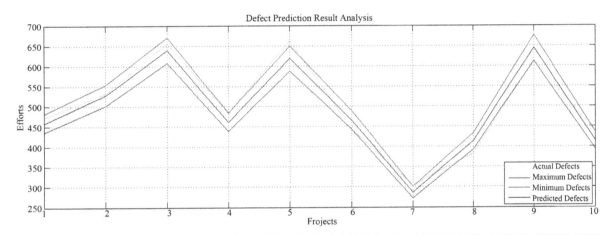

Figure 8. Defect prediction result analysis.

better than, the results with accuracy of 88.09% as obtained in [21], using public PROMISE library and Levenberg-Marquardt (LM) algorithm based neural network for predicting the software defects. Also, the data set used in our proposed framework is quite recent (year 2015) and the chosen technology (Java) is the widely used one in most software development scenarios.

Results were also compared with the ones obtained in [27], where evolutionary neural network (ENN) has been used to predict fault prone modules taken from a large software development project for which uniform crossover was used. The results even from best ENN Classifications were found to be close to only 75% of accuracy.

The same data set has also been compared with the linear regression based prediction model used in one of the large software development organization (refer to **Figure 9**). Linear regression based defect prediction model revealed an accuracy of 66% and only 10 projects from the sample of 15 were able to meet the predictions, where, as mentioned earlier, the proposed neural based framework has an accuracy of close to 90%.

6. Conclusion

Results from our experiments suggest that the proposed framework based on neural network approach possesses good properties from the standpoint of model quality of fit and predictive capability. Our conclusions are based on investigations of software development projects using java programming language and following waterfall life cycle model. It is expected that the proposed framework can be customized to suit other software development life cycle models like iterative and incremental development, agile etc. The investigation in those respects

DEFECTS	Project	Requirment	Analysis	Design	Coding	SIT	Total Defects	Variation from Predicted
Predicted Defects	P1	65	24	54	181	172	496	4.84%
Actual Defects		62	20	52	174	164	472	
Predicted Defects	P2	75	26	63	230	200	594	13.13%
Actual Defects		88	15	28	180	205	516	
Predicted Defects	P3	62	15	54	146	173	450	-18.22%
Actual Defects		74	11	71	172	204	532	
Predicted Defects	P4	68	16	59	180	189	512	-5.47%
Actual Defects		81	20	74	165	200	540	
Predicted Defects	P5	124	28	50	199	222	623	-5.30%
Actual Defects		137	26	60	204	229	656	
Predicted Defects	P6	48	21	60	198	150	477	-1.26%
Actual Defects		56	18	52	187	170	483	
Predicted Defects	P7	88	33	90	198	225	634	-4.57%
Actual Defects		108	20	95	225	215	663	
Predicted Defects	P8	16	5	85	150	175	431	-2.55%
Actual Defects		20	8	93	162	159	442	
Predicted Defects	P9	8	0	42	122	89	261	-16.86%
Actual Defects		13	3	54	130	105	305	
Predicted Defects	P10	2	2	88	199	79	370	-3.51%
Actual Defects		4	0	67	216	96	383	
Predicted Defects	P11	25	5	138	202	230	600	-2.17%
Actual Defects		30	11	120	233	219	613	
Predicted Defects	P12	15	11	43	132	184	384	-13.80%
Actual Defects		19	7	60	158	193	437	
Predicted Defects	P13	11	19	79	250	122	481	-5.20%
Actual Defects		7	15	95	295	94	506	
Predicted Defects	P14	51	4	148	198	278	679	-11.05%
Actual Defects		62	7	122	245	318	745	
Predicted Defects	P15	1	16	111	213	73	414	-5.80%
Actual Defects		2	17	119	221	79	438	

Figure 9. Defect prediction results from linear regression based model.

will be reported in subsequent communications.

References

[1]   (1990) IEEE Standard Glossary of Software Engineering Terminology. IEEE Std 610.12-1990, 1, 84.

[2]   Fenton, N.E. and Neil, M. (1999) A Critique of Software Defect Prediction Models. *IEEE Transactions on Software Engineering*, **25**, 675-689. http://dx.doi.org/10.1109/32.815326

[3]   Levinson, M. (2001) Let's Stop Wasting $78 Billion per Year. CIO Magazine.

[4]   Tamura, S. (2009) Integrating CMMI and TSP/PSP: Using TSP Data to Create Process Performance Models. Carnegie Mellon University, Pittsburgh.

[5]   Sommerville, I. (2006) Software Engineering. Addison-Wesley, Harlow, England.

[6]   Sivanandam, S.N. and Deepa, S.N. (2009) Principles of Soft Computing. 2nd Edition, John Wiley & Sons, Inc., Hoboken.

[7]   Munakata, T., Ed. (2007) Fundamentals of the New Artificial Intelligence. Texts in Computer Science. Springer, London. http://dx.doi.org/10.1007/978-1-84628-839-5

[8]   Narula, S.C. and Wellington, J.F. (1977) Prediction, Linear Regression and the Minimum Sum of Relative Errors. *Technometrics*, **19**, 185-190. http://dx.doi.org/10.1080/00401706.1977.10489526

[9]   Gafhey Jr., J.E. (1984) Estimating the Number of Faults in Code. *IEEE Transactions on Software Engineering*, **SE10**, 459-464.

[10]   Karunanithi, N., Malaiya, Y.K. and Whitley, D. (1991) Prediction of Software Reliability Using Neural Networks. *Proceedings of the International Symposium on Software Reliability Engineering*, Austin, 17-18 May 1991, 124-130. http://dx.doi.org/10.1109/issre.1991.145366

[11]   Boetticher, G., Srinivas, K. and Eichmann, D. (1993) A Neural Net-Based Approach to Software Metrics. *Proceedings*

of the 5th International Conference on Software Engineering and Knowledge Engineering, San Francisco, 16-18 June 1993, 271-274.

[12] Boetticher, G. and Eichmann, D. (1993) A Neural Net Paradigm for Characterizing Reusable Software. *Proceedings of the 1st Australian Conference on Software Metrics*, University of Houston, 18-19 November 1993, 41-49.

[13] Boetticher, G. (1995) Characterizing Object-Oriented Software for Reusability in a Commercial Environment. Reuse' 95 Making Reuse Happen—Factors for Success, Morgantown, August 1995.

[14] Boetticher, G. (2001) An Assessment of Metric Contribution in the Construction of a Neural Network-Based Effort Estimator. *2nd International Workshop on Soft Computing Applied to Software Engineering*, Enschede, 8-9 February 2001, 234-235.

[15] Boetticher, G. (2001) Using Machine Learning to Predict Project Effort: Empirical Case Studies in Data-Starved Domains. *Workshop on Model-Based Requirements Engineering*, San Diego, 30 November 2001, 17-24.

[16] Kumar, S., Krishna, B.A. and Satsangi, P.J. (1994) Fuzzy Systems and Neural Networks in Software Engineering Project Management. *Journal of Applied Intelligence*, **4**, 31-52. http://dx.doi.org/10.1007/BF00872054

[17] Srinivasan, K. and Fisher, D. (1995) Machine Learning Approaches to Estimating Software Development Effort. *IEEE Transactions on Software Engineering*, **21**, 126-137. http://dx.doi.org/10.1109/32.345828

[18] Boetticher, G.D. (2003) Applying Machine Learners to GUI Specifications in Formulating Early Life Cycle Project Estimations. In: Khoshgoftaar, T.M., Ed., *Software Engineering with Computational Intelligence*, Springer, New York, 1-16. http://dx.doi.org/10.1007/978-1-4615-0429-0_1

[19] Khoshgoftaar, T.M., Ed. (2003) Software Engineering with Computational Intelligence. Springer, New York. http://dx.doi.org/10.1007/978-1-4615-0429-0

[20] Gayathri, M. and Sudha, A. (2014) Software Defect Prediction System using Multilayer Perceptron Neural Network with Data Mining. *International Journal of Recent Technology and Engineering*, **3**, 54-59.

[21] Singh, M. and Salaria, D.S. (2013) Software Defect Prediction Tool based on Neural Network. *International Journal of Computer Applications*, **70**, 22-28. http://dx.doi.org/10.5120/12200-8368

[22] Crosby, P. (1979) Quality Is Free: The Art of Making Quality Certain. McGraw-Hill, New York.

[23] Singh, S. and Singh, M. (2012) Software Defect Prediction using Adaptive Neural Networks. *International Journal of Applied Information Systems*, **4**, 29-33. http://dx.doi.org/10.5120/ijais12-450612

[24] Katiyar, N. and Singh, R. (2011) Prediction of Software Development Faults Using Neural Network. *VSRD-IJCSIT*, **1**, 556-566.

[25] Juran, J. and Gryna, F. (1988) Quality Control Handbook. 4th Edition, McGraw-Hill, New York.

[26] Neural Network Toolbox™ User's Guide, 2015.

[27] Hochman, R., Khoshgoftaar, T.M., Allen, E.B. and Hudepohl, J.P. (2003) Improved Fault-Prone Detection Analysis of Software Modules Using an Evolutionary Neural Network Approach. In: Khoshgoftaar, T.M., Ed., *Software Engineering with Computational Intelligence*, Springer, New York, 69-100. http://dx.doi.org/10.1007/978-1-4615-0429-0_4

9

Why Formal Methods Are Considered for Safety Critical Systems?

Monika Singh[1], Ashok Kumar Sharma[1], Ruhi Saxena[2]

[1]Faculty of Engineering & Technology (FET), Mody University of Science & Technology, Sikar, India
[2]Computer Science & Engineering, Thapar University, Patiala, India
Email: Dhariwal.monika@gmail.com

Abstract

Formal methods are the mathematically techniques and tools which are used at early stages of software development lifecycle processes. The utter need of using formal methods in safety critical system leads to accuracy, consistency and correctness in proposed system. In safety critical real time application, requirements should be unambiguous and very accurate which can be achieved by using mathematical theorems. There is utter need to focus on the requirement phase which is the most critical phase of SDLC. This paper focuses on the use of Z notation for incorporating the accuracy, consistency, and eliminates ambiguity in safety critical system: Road Traffic Management System as a case study. The syntax, semantics, type checking and domain checking are further verified by using Z/EVES: a Z notation type checker tool.

Keywords

Formal Methods, Safety Critical System, Z Notation, Z/EVES, Syntax & Type Checking, Domain Checking

1. Introduction

Formal specification languages are mathematically based on languages which are adequately used for construction of accurate, consistent and unambiguous systems and software. As formal methods are equipped with tool, which can be used for both the prospective *i.e.* describing a system and later on for analyzing their functionalities. The major obstacles behind formal methods to be used in practices frequently are the time spent on specification [1] [2]. Nevertheless, formal methods do not guarantee correctness, but their use emphasize to increase the understanding of a system by divulging errors or facets of incompleteness that may be expensive to correct them at any later point of time. However, formal methods play a critical role in safety critical system as they focus on refinement of requirements in the early stage of development which consequently increase the system's accuracy and consistency. Various formal languages are used for this purpose like VDM, B-Methods, Petri Net, and Z notation etc. Z notation is a model based on formal specification language which uses the set theory and first order predicates [3].

A lot of work has been done in this area of formal analysis of UML diagrams with formal approaches [4]-[8]. In article 8, UML based framework is presented to develop web applications. [5] represents the verification properties by HOL theorem prover. A formalization approach is developed for UML class diagrams in [6]. The paper [7] advocates how the formal methods can be used for safety properties of real time critical application such as railways. [8] explains an integrated approach of Z notation and Pertinet for analysis of safety critical properties.

In this article, Z notation is used for formal analysis of safety critical system *i.e.* Road Traffic Management System which is further verified by using the Z/EVES tool.

2. Proposed Approach & Methodology

In the first part of this section, the proposed approach is discussed. Then the tool and methodology used are discussed in section.

2.1. Proposed Approach

Figure 1 defines the proposed approach for designing the safety critical system using the formal methods.

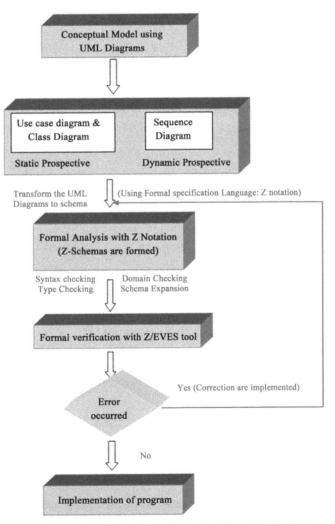

Figure 1. The proposed approach for formal analysis of safety critical application.

2.2. Z/EVES

This tool is used for verifying the specification written in Z notation language. This verification includes syntax, semantics, type checking, and domain checking of the given system's specification. Z/EVES present two type of interface: graphical user interface and the command line interface [3] [9]. In this paper, we used the graphical user interface for verifying and composing the specification which were written in Z notation language. Moreover, Z/EVES propose two mode of operations *i.e.* "Eager" and "Lazy". In our article we use the "Eager" mode since in this mode a paragraph is checked if and only if all the previous ones are checked which is highly recommended for safety critical real time application. By using Z/EVES, following can be done:

- syntax and type checking;
- schema expansion;
- precondition calculation;
- domain checking;
- general theorem proving.

2.3. UML

Unified Modeling language is in fact the blue prints for the system to be developed. It provides a better way to understands the requirements of the propose system. UML consists of nine diagrams which are used for capturing the both aspects of the system *i.e.* static and dynamic [10]-[12]. This paper aims at the static behaviour by composing the use case diagram of RTMS system which is further verified by using Z/EVES type checker tool. The conceptual model of Road Traffic Management System (RTMS) is given in **Figure 2**.

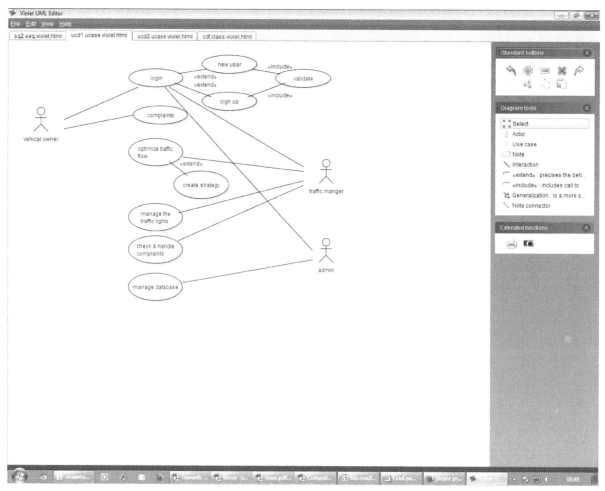

Figure 2. Use case diagrams of vehicle owner.

3. Formalization of Use Case Diagram Using Z/EVES

Z schema is the notion for structuring the specification including the pre, post condition and the list of invariant & variables. Z schema has two parts *i.e.* declaration part and predicate part. The Z schema has both declaration as well as predicate part that is shown in **Figure 3**.

The above part of central line consists of variables declaration and the below part of line describes the relationship the variable's various values. This paper emphasis on three main characteristics of formal analysis of safety critical system which are:

1) Syntax & Type checking; 2) Schema Expansion; and 3) Domain checking.

1) Syntax & Type Checking

The syntax and type checking facility is provided by the Z/EVES tool. The syntax & type checking facility enables that the syntax used in Z specification is correct which is automatically done by Z/EVES tool. In case of road traffic management system, the schema of Vehicle Owner is considered for syntax & type checking which is consists of two variables:

- *Vowner* is the set of names with RTMS registered.
- *Regist Vowner* is the function which when implemented on a particular Vehicle Owner name, provides the unique registration number associated with the person.

In **Figure 4**, the schema for Vehicle Owner with basic data type is given: [Name, Seqchar].

In Vehicle Owner schema, a partial function named "*Regist Vowner*" is defined which maps the corresponding vehicle owner with a registration number *i.e.*

Regist Vowner: *Name* ↛ *Seqchar*

Moreover, "*Regist Vowner*" is a one-to-one function which maps Vehicle Owner name with registration number. Since it is a one-to-one function, therefore every Vehicle Owner has a unique registration number and consequently, would be no ambiguity. The schema of Vehicle Owner is further verified by Z/EVES tool for syntax & type checking in **Figure 5**. The left most columns' value "Y" shows that the schema is implemented using correct syntax. If there would be any syntax error, it shows "N" instead of "Y" in syntax column [9].

2) Schema Expansion

The schema expansion facility enables to extend the functionality of system and helps in understanding the complex schema structure in detail. Initially, the list of registered vehicle owner in RTMS is empty which is depicted by the "Init Vehicle Owner" schema in **Figure 6**.

Since the lower part of the schema explain the relation between the variables, the function *Regist Vowner* is assigned a value "∅", and means initially there is no registered vehicle owner in RTMS. **Figure 7** shows the Z/EVES result of "Init Vehicle Owner".

Now, the Vehicle Owner may perform a list of tasks like: Login. If the Vehicle Owner is Login first time, he/she has to register him/her; otherwise he/she will sign in. In **Figure 8**, the schemas of Login operation is implemented.

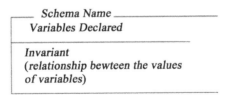

Figure 3. State space of schema.

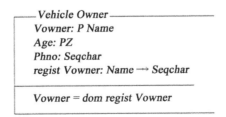

Figure 4. Vehicle Owner schema with invariants.

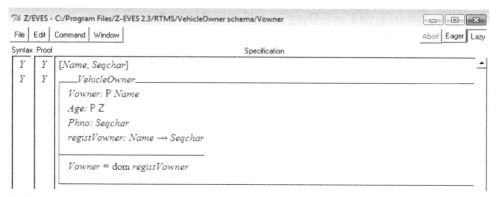

Figure 5. Syntax checking of Vehicle Owner schema by Z/EVES.

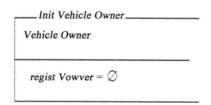

Figure 6. Initial state space of schema Vehicle Owner.

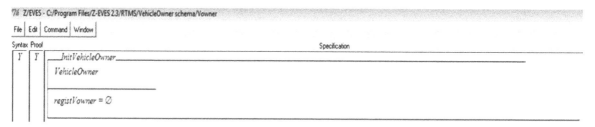

Figure 7. Initial Vehicle Owner schema.

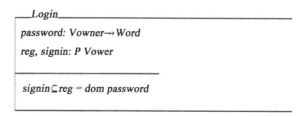

Figure 8. State space of schema Login.

In this schema:

Password: _Vowner↠Word_

"Password" is a function which associates a username to password. Nevertheless, it is a one-to-one function which in turn provides accuracy and correctness to system. Now Signin set and registered set both is the member of power set of Vehicle Owner which is mathematically shown by using set theory as following.

Signin, Reg: ℙ _Vowner_

Also the Signin set is a subset of registered set and the registered set having the values which are there in domain of "password" function _i.e._

Signin ⊆ _Reg_ = _Dom Password_

Initially, Login schema is empty which is here explained by assigning a value "φ" to both the set whether it's a registers one or a new one _i.e._

Reg = _φ_; _Signin_ = _φ_

This is called schema expansion which is one of the key features of Z/EVES tool _i.e._ from "Init Login" schema to "Login" schema.

In **Figure 9**, the schema expansion is shown and verified by Z/EVES as follow.

3) Domain Checking

Domain checking feature of Z/EVES tool enables us to write the statements which are meaningful and in finding the domain errors. However, it has been found that as compared to syntax & type checking, domain checking is more crucial because where syntax and type checking is done automatically, one needs to work together with theorem prover to accomplish the domain checking. We also observed that proof "by reduce" in the proof window of the tool was sufficient for our formal specifications for domain checking. Now if you are already registered, you will opt for the sigin option. By investigating **Figure 10**, the value for syntax column is "Y", means no error, but the value in proof column is "N". This is related to domain checking. The proof can be initiated by selecting the theorem in the *Specification window*, right clicking, and selecting "*Show proof*" which is shown in **Figure 9**.

The proof can be done by various mean in Z/EVES by choosing "Action Point" by Reduction, Cases, Quantifiers, Normal Norms and Equality. In our case, we use the option "**prove by reduction**". **Figure 11** describes the proof by reduce action point in case of "Signin" schema.

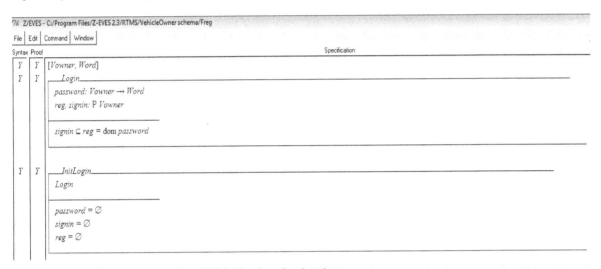

Figure 9. Z/EVES Schema expansion of Initial Login to Login schema.

Figure 10. Domain checking with Z/EVES.

4. Result Analysis

Any proposed model is incomplete without tool support. Nevertheless, use of formal language adequately increases the accuracy and completeness but, the use of computer tool indeed increases the level of confidence significantly for the system to be developed by fingering out the potential errors in syntax and semantics of formal narration. **Table 1** depicts the result of formal analysis of proposed schemas of road traffic management system using Z/EVES. The attributes in the table are name of the schema followed by syntax & type checking, domain checking, proof and reduction. The second row in table, having status Y for all columns indicating that the schema named "Vehicle Owner" is correct with respect to syntax & type check errors, domain check and having correct proof by performing reduction on the set of predicates for making specification meaningful. The Y[1] symbol shows that the action point in proof window is chosen as "**prove by reduce**".

5. Conclusion

The use of formal methods in safety critical application increases quality in terms of accuracy, consistency, and

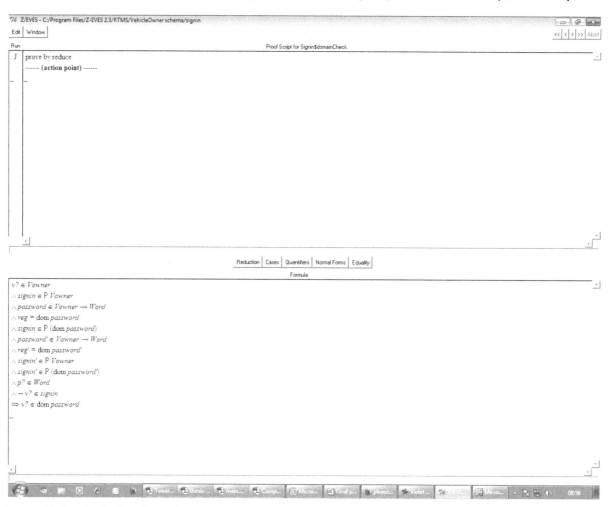

Figure 11. Proof script by using action point "**proof by reduce**" for "Signin" schema.

Table 1. Result analysis by Z/EVES.

Schema Name	Syntax & Type Checking	Domain Checking	Schema Expansion	Proof by Reduction
Vehicle Owner	Y	Y	Y	Y[1]
Login	Y	Y	Y	Y[1]
Signin	Y	Y	Y	Y[1]

in completeness. This paper describes the use of Z notation, a formal method for Vehicle Owner, an actor of Road Traffic Management System; which will be further verified by Z/EVES, a typechecker tool for Z notation specification. In Future, the schema of Traffic Police, Admin, and Traffic Manager will be implemented and verified by Z/EVES theorem prover.

Acknowledgements

Authors are thankful to faculty of Engineering & Technology (FET), Mody University of Science & Technology for providing the facility to carry out the research work.

References

[1]   Woodcock, J.C.P. (1989) Structuring Specifications in Z. *IEE/BCS Software Engineering Journal*, **4**, 51-66. http://dx.doi.org/10.1049/sej.1989.0007

[2]   Hall, A. (2002) Correctness by Construction: Integrating Formality into a Commercial Development Process. *Proceedings of International Symposium of Formal Methods Europe*, **2391**, 139-157. http://dx.doi.org/10.1007/3-540-45614-7_13

[3]   Spivey, J.M. (1989) The Z Notation: A Reference Manual. Prentice-Hall, Englewood Cliffs.

[4]   Hamdy, K.E., Elsoud, M.A. and El-Halawany, A.M. (2011) UML-Based Web Engineering Framework for Modeling Web Application. *Journal of Software Engineering*, **5**, 49-63. http://dx.doi.org/10.3923/jse.2011.49.63

[5]   Hasan, O. and Tahar, S. (2007) Verification of Probabilistic Properties in the HOL Theorem Prover. *Proceedings of the Integrated Formal Methods*, **4591**, 333-352. http://dx.doi.org/10.1007/978-3-540-73210-5_18

[6]   He, X. (2000) Formalizing UML Class Diagrams: A Hierarchical Predicate Transition Net Approach. *Proceedings of 24th Annual International Computer Software and Applications Conference*, Taipei, 25-28 October 2000, 217-222.

[7]   Zafar, N.A., Khan, S.A. and Araki, K. (2012) Towards the Safety Properties of Moving Block Railway Interlocking System. *International Journal of Innovative Computing, Information and Control* (*ICIC International*), 5677-5690.

[8]   Heiner, M. and Heisel, M. (1999) Modeling Safety Critical Systems with Z and Petri-Nets. *Proceedings of International Conference on Computer Safety, Reliability and Security*, London, 26-28 October 1999, 361-374. http://dx.doi.org/10.1007/3-540-48249-0_31

[9]   The Z/EVES 2.0 User's Guide: Mark Saaltink. October 1999 ORA Canada.

[10] Mostafa, A.M., Manal, A.I., Hatem, E.B. and Saad, E.M. (2007) Toward a Formalization of UML2.0 Meta-Model Using Z Specifications. *Proceedings of 8th ACIS International Conference on Software Engineering, Artificial Intelligence, Networking and Parallel/Distributed Computing*, **3**, 694-701. http://dx.doi.org/10.1109/SNPD.2007.508

[11] Jacobson, R.I. and Booch, G. (2006) The Unified Modeling Language Reference Manual. 2nd Edition.

[12] Selic, B. and Rumbaugh, J. (1998) UML for Modeling Complex Real-Time Systems. Technical Report, Object Time.

10

Evaluating Enterprise Content Management Tools in a Real Context

M. J. Escalona*, F. J. Domínguez-Mayo, J. A. García-García, N. Sánchez, J. Ponce

Web Engineering and Early Testing Research Group, IWT2, University of Seville, Seville, Spain
Email: *mjescalona@us.es, fjdominguez@us.es, josepg@us.es, julian.garcia@iwt2.org,
nicolas.sanchez@iwt2.org

Abstract

Managing documentation in a suitable way has become a critical issue for any organization. Organizations depend on the information they store and they are required to have appropriate mechanisms to support the functional needs of information storage, management and retrieval. Currently, there are several tools in the market, both free software and proprietary license, normally named Enterprise Content Management (ECM) tools, which offer relevant solutions in this context. This paper presents a comparative study among several of the most commonly used ECM tools. It starts with a systematic review of the literature to analyze possible solutions and then it defines a characterization schema instantiated in a particular case, the Regional Government of Andalusia.

Keywords

Software Engineering, Standards, Methodologies, Enterprise Content Management, Quality Analysis and Evaluation

1. Introduction

Nowadays, one of the most important assets for any organization is the information available at the staff's disposal. A suitable management of information is essential, therefore, document management is a key aspect [1]. Besides, in the current digital era, the right administration of digital documentation is crucial and handling the vast amount of digital documentation involves a hard task for many organizations, since lacking the proper mechanisms to manage documentation provide timely results.

Enterprise Content Management (ECM) [2] tools are tools solutions offering support mechanisms to assist

---
*Corresponding author.

this task. However, today's variability makes it difficult to know which of them the best for a concrete environment is.

This paper presents a comparative study among five of these tools as part of three main objectives:

- Find out which ECM tools the market offers at present.
- Compare them under homogenous criteria.
- Illustrate how this study can be adapted to a concrete environment.

A systematic literature review will be conducted in order to cope with the first aim. The paper shows that this line of work is not enough to analyze the current situation, thus it must be complemented with some other resources, which together with the former, will provide five tools for our study. The second aim is to define a characterization schema that will be instantiated in the paper for each approach under study.

Once finished, this work illustrates how the global comparative study can be customized in a concrete environment. For the third aim, the practical case of THOT Project will be used [3]. The Agencia de Obra Pública of Junta de Andalucía, Spain, is developing the project in liaison with the University of Seville, Spain, as it is further detailed.

The paper is structured as follows so as to cover the three aforementioned objectives. Firstly, Section 2 presents a related work section with a global view of ECM. Then, Section 3 introduces the mechanism used to get the two first goals, based on SLR and characterization schema. Later, Section 4 explains the detailed application of this mechanism and Section 5 presents THOT project and the study performance in its context. The paper finishes stating relevant conclusions and future lines of work.

2. Related Work

As regards reviews related to ECM systems, Scott [4] assesses the factors that lead to the user acceptance of an ECM system. Findings reveal the importance of cognitive engagement with technology. It mainly shows how a document perspective provides insights on the surprising results and highlights the importance of including the cognitive engagement construct in technology acceptance studies. Alalwan and Weistroffer [2] providea comprehensive literature review of ECM research. It proposes a conceptual framework of areas of concern regarding ECM and shows an agenda for future research on ECM, based on review and conceptual frameworks. After revising and classifying 91 ECM publications, it was concluded that ECM involved several sophisticated and interacting technical, social, organizational and business aspects. The authors suggested that today's literature concerning ECM could be grouped into three main pillars: the first pillar consists of the four ECM component dimensions (tools, strategy, process and people). The second pillar deals with the enterprise system lifecycle (adoption, acquisition, evolution and evaluation) and the final pillar is the strategic managerial aspect (change management and management commitment). An agenda for future research around the aforementioned pillars, in terms of review and suggested conceptual framework, is recommended.

As far as ECM implementations are concerned, Haug [5] includes a definition of a process model for ECM implementation in SMEs. This author identifies success factors related to ECM system implementation and proposes a definition of a new pattern for ECM technology development, compared to existing case studies. Thus, it contributes to the sparse literature on ECM implementation. In fact, the case seems to be the first longitudinal study regarding ECM implementations in SMEs.

In [6], Van Rooij explains that lessons learned from the implementation of ERP reveal that such implementations may be compromised by a large number of legacy issues. The author argues that the same issues may similarly affect the implementation of ECMs. Therefore, it is advised, with due adaptation, to take these issues into account when devising implementation strategies for ECMs.

In relation to ISO standards, many industry associations publish their own lists of particular document control standards that are used in their particular fields. ISO 2709:2008 [7] specifies the requirements for a generalized exchange format that will hold records describing all forms of material capable of providing bibliographic description as well as other types of records. It neither defines the length or the content of individual records nor assigns any meaning to tags, indicators or identifiers, being these specifications the functions of an implementation format. This ISO standard describes a generalized structure, a framework especially designed to enhance communication between data processing systems and not to be used as a processing format within systems. ISO 15836:2009 [8] establishes a standard for cross-domain resource description, known as Dublin Core Metadata Element Set. Similarly to RFC 3986, ISO 15836:2009 does not limit what might be a resource. This ISO standard defines the elements typically used in the context of an application profile, which constrains or specifies their use in accordance with local or community-based requirements and policies. However, it does not add implementation details, since it is out of its scope.

Another ISO standard to consider is ISO 15489 part 1 and part 2 [9]. This standard focuses on the principles of records management and establishes the basic requirements that allow organizations to establish a best practices framework that improves, in a systematic and effective manner, the creation and maintenance of its records, supporting in this way the organizational policy and objectives.

As regards capabilities about information retrieval services, ISO 23950 [10] defines the Information Retrieval Application Service and specifies the Information Retrieval Application Protocol. The service definition describes services that support capabilities within an application; these services are in turn supported by Z39.50 protocol. This description neither specifies nor constrains the implementation within a computer system. The protocol specification includes the definition of the protocol control information, the rules for exchanging this information and the conformance requirements to be met by the implementation of this protocol. This standard addresses connection-oriented and program-to-program communication intended for systems supporting information retrieval services and organizations such as information services, universities, libraries and union catalog centers. It does not address information exchange among terminals or via other physical media.

ISO 10244:2010 [11] gives detailed information associated with the activities organizations perform when documenting existing work or business processes (business process baselining), defining the level of information required to be gathered, methods of documentation for work or business processes, and procedures used when evaluating or analyzing work-business processes. This ISO standard provides organizations with tools to identify relevant aspects of work-business processes and document them in a standardized format, thus permitting a detailed analysis and identification of relevant technology, so that the processes can improve.

3. Our Mechanism for the Study

As it was introduced, our general study is divided in two different parts. The first one deals with looking for approaches and tools that will be considered in the study and the second one will compare them under a concrete set of criteria. For the former, we will use a Systematic Literature Review (SLR) and for the latter, we will define a characterization schema.

A Systematic Literature Review (SLR) is mainly carried out in order to find and develop innovative ideas for further research. In [12], authors conceive SLRs as the means of completing processes based on identifying, evaluating and interpreting all available documents focused on particular research questions or a specific investigation area. However, this process is not only associated with scientific environments, but also with any domain or environment (such as research, enterprise or engineering, among others), as it is not exclusively related to research work. In addition, it is normally used as a method for carrying out comparative studies on software tools or technology proposals.

Therefore, SLR aims to provide an exhaustive summary of the literature relevant to a research, technological or technical question.

The use of SLRs is relatively recent in the Software Engineering (SE) context, but it has gained significant importance in this area as a means to identify, evaluate and interpret all available data to answer research questions on a particular topic in SE. It has been growing in importance as a systematic and structured approach regarding literature reviews since 2004, when Barbara Kitchenham [13] proposed special guidelines that were adapted to cope with specific problems in the SE area. These guidelines have been used and evaluated in many contexts [14]-[17]. Last year, Kitchenham's proposal was updated again [18] in order to be implemented, taking into account recent results published by software engineering researchers concerning their experiences when performing SLRs, as well as their advices for improving the SLR process.

Moreover, there are other ideas or views to conduct systematic reviews. For instance, in [19], authors introduce different perspectives of SLRs. They issue their proposals after systematically selecting and analytically studying a large number of papers (SLRs) in order to understand the state-of-the-practice of search strategies in evidence-based SE.

In consequence, these SLRs proposals are highly directed towards answering research questions on some scientific knowledge. Nevertheless, SLR is not enough for a study led to compare technologies or tools solutions. For this reason, we will complement SRL with the two points below to carry out our study:

1) We will try to look for responses to our research questions not only in the research environment, but also in the context of a common search engine for enterprises, like Google.
2) We will analyze enterprise tendencies, like Gartner.

Apart from offering a SLR, we aim to provide a comparative study. For this purpose, we propose a characterization schema, based on SEG approaches [20]. This schema will allow us to offer a homogenous evaluation of each approach under study that, at the end of the process, will be essential for stating final conclusions and learned lessons.

4. Applying the Study

4.1. Finding the Approaches

As introduced, the guidelines for the systematic review stated in this work follow the protocol defined by Kitchenmham [15], which is one of the most acknowledged in SE. In addition, we take into consideration Wohlin and Prikladnicki's conclusions [21] about SLRs in SE. They consider that the search strategy is key to ensure a good starting point for the identification of studies and ultimately for the actual outcome of a particular study.

Nevertheless, this proposal initially centers on systematic reviews of research studies. In light of this, we have adapted this proposal to focus on ECM systems studies and all those related fields. A SLR essentially involves three phases: 1) planning the review; 2) conducting the review and 3) reporting the review.

- The stages associated with planning the review are: identification of reviewer needs, specification of the research question(s), development a review protocol and evaluation of that protocol.
- The stages associated with conducting the review are: identification of research, selection of primary studies, study of quality assessment, data extraction and monitoring, and data synthesis.
- The stages associated with reporting the review are: specification of dissemination mechanisms, formatting the main report and evaluation of that report.

The planning phase has two main goals; on the one hand, deciding which method will be used to conduct the review and on the other hand, identifying and formulating the thesis that the systematic review will prove. Regarding the first goal, this work aims to answer the next questions:

- Question 1: What ECM systems currently exist in the market and what do they offer?
- Question 2: How ECM systems can be adapted to the general guidelines of the Andalusian Public Administration?
- Question 3: What is the most appropriate ECM system the Andalusian Public Administration, and more specifically, the Contracting Services for Transport and Infrastructure Constructions must use?
- Question 4: What areas of improvement are needed for the selected ECM system?

A large number of identified search keywords picked up from these questions will be used in the review process, as **Table 1** summarizes.

The following databases have been considered in the systematic literature review: ACM Digital Library, EI Compendex, IEEE Xplore, ISI Web of Knowledge, Science Direct, SCOPUS, Springer Link and Wiley Inter Science Journal Finder. **Table 2** shows the fields where the defined search keywords have been applied in each database. Besides, this table represents the logical relationship among these fields.

Once all planning phase goals have been achieved, the review process enters in the review phase, which consists in finding and evaluating the adequacy and relevance of many primary studies associated with the research question as possible sources for further analysis. Primary studies are searched through the aforementioned databases by means of the keywords represented in **Table 1** together with the search fields shown in **Table 2**. Then, a strategic definition for evaluating the adequacy and relevance of the studies is needed after the search.

Firstly, keywords of **Table 1** are searched for each logical criterion in the search field included in **Table 2**. Secondly, the set with the previous primary studies is reduced according to the following inclusion criteria:

1) The primary study must have been published in the last four years, that is, from 2010 to 2013 (both included). This exclusion criterion is considered realistic and acceptable in the context of this work, because the number of ECM systems and versions has increased in the last years. Therefore, the considered primary study must be recent in order to infer useful conclusions.
2) The paper must focus on Computing Science.
3) The paper must have been published in any influential magazine (for instance, Journal Citation Reports indexed).

Table 1. Search keywords.

Abbreviation	Search Keywords
SMEC	Solutions for Managing Enterprise Contents
SMDP	Software for Managing Document Processes
EMCRE	ECM in Real Environment

Table 2. Logical criteria for fields used in each database.

Database	Logical Relationship of Search Fields
ACM Digital Library	"Title & Abstract"
Ei Compendex	"Title & Abstract"
IEEE Xplore	"Abstract" or "Publication Title" or "Index Terms"
ISI Web of Knowledge	"Title & Abstract"
Science Direct	"Abstract, Title, Keywords"
SCOPUS	"Title & Abstract"
Springer Link	"Title & Abstract"
Wiley Inter Science Journal Finder	"Title & Abstract"

Thirdly, a new discrimination is conducted through a fast reading of each primary study. First of all, the title theme of the primary study must be linked to the topic of this work. For example: "ECM", "Enterprise Contents Management" or "Document Process". The introduction and abstract must mention the goals of the research questions posed in this section, once that condition is satisfied and this primary study is catalogued as promising.

Finally, after carrying out this review, we neither find concrete solutions for ECM systems nor studies on them. We have found some work associated with theoretical proposals in the context of ECM systems. Therefore, classic search engines and those running on the Internet have been selected in order to conduct a specific survey of this type of systems. In addition, we have considered the last Gartner's analysis concerning Enterprise Content Management [22], which is popularly known as Magic Quadrant and was presented in October 2012. Gartner [23] is an international research and consulting company dealing with Information Technology (esta última frase quizá debería ser una nota al pie, una aclaración).

It follows the criteria below among the pre-selection ones:

- Basic functionality (core components). It takes into account the capabilities and/or applications to manage the content life cycle:
o Document Management. It refers to basic skills such as locking and unlocking documents (check-in/check-out), change control and versioning, full-text indexing, security, library cataloging and document types, and advanced capabilities such as support for document composition, association life cycles, taxonomy and content replication.
o Records Management. It is used for long-term retention of content through automation and implementing policies that ensure legal compliance and regulatory framework. The minimum requirement is the ability to enforce retention of business critical documents, based on a records retention program. Higher ratings are given for compliance with certification standards and the requirements model for electronic document management.
o BPM (Workflow/Business Process Management). It deals with supporting business processes, routing content, assigning work tasks and states, and creating audit trails. The minimum requirement is the document review and approval workflow. Higher scores are given to graphics-capable solutions to define routing processes in series and in parallel.
o Document Imaging/Image-processing. They are applications for capturing, processing and managing images of paper documents. There are two possibilities for these component solutions: 1) Document Capture (scanning hardware and software, character recognition technologies and forms processing technology), either using native capabilities or through a formal partnership with a third provider, for example Knowledge Lake,

Kofax, EMC (Captiva) or IBM (Datacap) and 2) the ability to store images of scanned documents as "other" type of content in the repository, both in a folder or through an electronic process route.

o   Interoperability functions/extended components. They deal with the ability to share data and enable the exchange of information and/or digital assets and the ability to generate electronic forms and integrate them into email and packaged applications.

o   WCM (Web Content Management). It controls the content and interactions with Web solutions. This includes content creation features, such as templates, workflows and change management, and content distribution functions that offer packaged or on-demand content to Web servers. The minimum requirement is a formal partnership with a WCM provider.

o   Social content/collaboration. It refers to collaboration, knowledge management and shared documents, such as blogs, wikis and online support between users. Social content, including videos, is the fastest growing category of new content in organizations. This feature is becoming increasingly important due to the incorporation of social networks in today's society.

•   Market positioning of ECM solution taking a strategic approach, that is, how they can help these solutions for businesses and organizations to take control of their content and, consequently, increase efficiency, enhance collaboration, and facilitate information sharing.

According to this criterion, firstly the analysis conducted in 2012 by Gartner ® on Enterprise Content Management tools is taken into account and secondly, the study of global Internet searches trendlines conducted on certain key words is considered.

On the one hand, we integrate Gartner's analysis into ECM based on the evaluation of different weighted criteria whose overall results are represented by means of a two-dimensional matrix that assesses suppliers in terms of their expectation for future performance and tools execution capacity.

The weighting established by Gartner for basic functionalities is listed below:

•   Document Management: 15%
•   Document Imaging/Image-processing Applications: 18%
•   Workflow/BPM: 22%
•   Records Management: 13%
•   Web Content Management (WCM): 7%
•   Social Content/Collaboration: 15%
•   Interoperability/Extended components: 10%

Figure 1 shows the result obtained through Gartner Magic Quadrant for ECM solutions ®.

On the other hand, a study on the Internet searching habits regarding ECM solutions has been recently conducted in Spain. This study has been carried out through Google Inc. Insights for Search. This tool generates trendlines in Google from certain keywords historical search.

Figure 2 shows the result of this study:

These trendlines have allowed us to corroborate the importance of various ECM solutions, showing high activity in Alfresco solution.

Therefore, the following ECM solutions (in alphabetical order) have been pre-selected attending to preliminary analyses: Alfresco [24], Docu Ware [25], EMC Documentum [26], IBM File Net [27], Knowledge Tree [28] Nuxeo [29], Open Text [30] and MS Sharepoint [31].

4.2. Defining the Characterization Schema

The characterization schema checklist is composed of a set of attributes and qualities assessed in each ECM solution.

This schema enables applying a brief and homogeneouse valuation of each approach under study. It is described in parts to facilitate reading and initial presentation, although, as noticed, the instantiation of the evaluation of each tool is presented as a whole.

Functional modules: The following functionalities are included natively and minimally in this group of items. They are described in the previous section so, in this case, **Table 3** only enumerates the possible values that each of them can take. ✓ represents that the feature is completely covered by the approach, × means that the feature is not supported by the approach and ⊘ represents that the feature is partially supported by the approach.

For the next groups of items, features can take a value between 1 and 4. 1 represents that the approach does not cover the feature and 4 is the best value given. Values 2 and 3 are obviously intermediate values depending

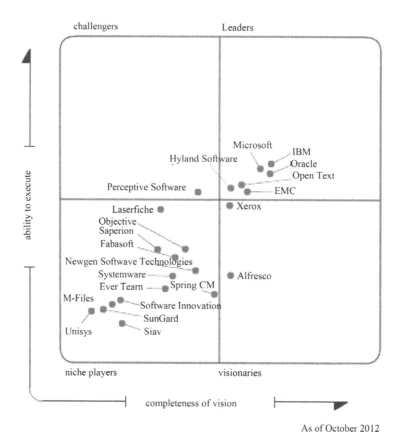

Figure 1. Gartner comparative results.

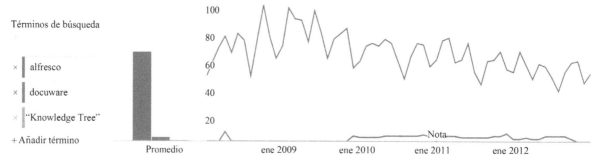

Figure 2. Google Inc. results.

Table 3. Functional modules.

Group	Features	Values
	Document Management	$\{\checkmark, \times, \oslash\}$
	Records Management	$\{\checkmark, \times, \oslash\}$
Functional Modules	BPM (Workflow/Business Process Management)	$\{\checkmark, \times, \oslash\}$
	Document Imaging/Image-processing	$\{\checkmark, \times, \oslash\}$
	Interoperability functions/extended components.	$\{\checkmark, \times, \oslash\}$
	WCM (Web Content Management)	$\{\checkmark, \times, \oslash\}$
	Social content/collaboration.	$\{\checkmark, \times, \oslash\}$

on their coverage.

a) User Orientation. Although ECM systems offer standard solutions on its orientation towards the end user, many companies need using easy and versatile systems because not all their employees have the same user profile to handle computer tools. Next, the Sub-features of this feature are described below:

- Usability compliance. It measures whether the system is user-friendly for non-expert employees in ICT tools.
- Accessibility. It analyses the accessibility level of the system based on the UNE 139803:2012, which is based, in turn, on WCAG 2.0.
- Document preview. It evaluates whether the system provides a suitable interface for previewing and resizing documents.
- Drag & Drop. It reviews whether the system provides visual utilities of drag & drop.
- Bulk uploads. It facilitates massive uploads of documents and evaluates whether the system allows users to upload a large amount of documents in a single operation.
- Undo. It assesses whether the system allows the user to undo an operation.
- WYSIWYG Editor (What You See Is What You Get). It evaluates whether the system has a user-friendly WYSIWYG editor for creating workflows or forms, for example.
- Customization. It measures the customization degree of GUI (Graphical User Interface) the ECM system provides.
- Groups and Social networks. They help a business gain contacts, clients and increase public conscience. Even entrepreneurs who run small businesses from their homes can take advantage of this resource to set up a global presence. Consequently, we have considered this aspect to be essential. This Sub-feature evaluates whether the system provides an integration mechanism for sharing documents and information through different social networks such as Facebook, Twitter and LinkedIn, among others.
- Multilanguage. This Sub-feature evaluates whether the system provides a GUI multilanguage and allows both, managing information and documents in different languages and integrating the ECM system with translation software.

b) Functionality to capture, access, retrieve and view documents. The ability to capture, access, retrieve and display, within the group, includes those features that let anyone customize the system according to the preferences of users or the organization being implemented. Next, we describe the Sub-features of this feature:

- Degree of Cataloging. It assesses whether the system allows complete and flexible cataloging folders and documents, *i.e.*, the system provides default metadata and allows creating new metadata. In addition, this Sub-feature evaluates the ability to index metadata and create semantic relationships among documents.
- Agrupation. This Sub-feature evaluates whether the system allows grouping documents according to their content type in order to present them as a single content.
- Thesaurus Support. It appraises whether the system can be integrated with some kind of thesaurus.
- Digitalization. It controls that the system can scan documents without using third-party software component.
- Bulk Upload. It reviews whether the system provides functionality to upload documents massively within digitization or importation processes.
- Content Generation. It monitors that the system can generate new content (in different formats) from a document.
- Office Integration. It assesses whether the system allows its integration with office IT such as Microsoft Office, Google Docs and Open Office, among others.
- Forms and Templates. It tests whether the system can create forms and templates in order to store content homogeneously.
- Integration Forms Managers. It evaluates whether the system allows its integration with forms manager (e.g. formul@) in order to store content homogeneously.
- Advanced Search Methods. It measures whether the system provides agile methods to find documents, e.g., using search patterns or describing relevance criteria of results and metadata patterns, among others.
- Search Algorithms. It evaluates whether the system can configure the search algorithm, *i.e.*, places to look for, customizations of search syntaxes, accents tolerance and case sensitivity, among others.
- Display Formats. It guarantees that the system allows displaying contents of documents in different formats electronically.

c) Documental Life Cycle. This feature enables us to assess the level or degree of support the system offers to the document cycle. Next, we describe the Sub-features of this feature:

- Check-in Check-out. It evaluates whether the system allows locking (using check-in and check-out operations) a document when a user is modifying it.
- Life cycle. It evaluates whether the system supports the document life cycle: creation, revision, classification, search, management, distribution, archiving and destruction.
- Versioning Support. It assesses whether the ECM system provides mechanism to control versions.
- Actions traceability. It tests whether the system allows auditing and monitoring actions on documents.
- Inconsistencies management. It evaluates whether the ECM system provides mechanism to control inconsistencies and conflicts between related documents.
- Dissemination management. It controls that the system can support the content dissemination based on user subscriptions.
- Conservation. It evaluates whether the ECM system allows defining retention periods on documents. This aspect ensures the integrity of electronic documents throughout their life cycle.
- Destruction. It lets users know whether the ECM system allows physical destruction of documentation. The destruction operation must be registered by the ECM system.
- Physical actions. It evaluates whether the ECM system allows carrying out physical operations on documents, for instance, to compose/decompose documents, to seal, to add notes or to append text, among others operations.

d) Workflows. This feature, can assess whether the tool supports management with business processes. Below, we describe the Sub-features of this feature:

- Supported standards. It evaluates the supporting degree of standards such as XML-RDF, Wf-XML and WARIA.
- Management support. It controls that the system can support the definition and maintenance of processes and procedures.
- Available options. It tests whether the system provides additional functionality to create workflows (for instance, alternative flows, sequential flows or collaborative flows).
- Motorization. It evaluates whether the ECM system allows process monitoring.
- Simulation and modeling. It lets us know whether the system provides simulation and modeling utilities.
- Graphical utilities. It points out whether the system provides graphical utilities to design workflows.
- Task management. It evaluates whether the system provides mechanism to manage tasks, deadlines and alerts.

e) E-Government. Measuring the support and features involving e-Government is essential, given the context in which this project is developed. This group of features evaluates the degree of support this context offers. Therefore, we can evaluate whether the system allows accessing and using valid electronic documents according to the guidelines of the Spanish National Interoperability Scheme. The Sub-features of this feature are described below:

- Electronic documents. It evaluates whether accessing to services, data and electronic documents and using them is admitted (according to the guidelines of the Spanish National Interoperability Scheme).
- Digital signature. It enables us to test whether the system allows signing online documents, as well as validating electronic signatures according to a signature policy shown in the electronic document signature.
- Accreditation and representation. It confirms whether the ECM system is able to use accreditation mechanisms and identify every citizen by recognizing his/her electronic signature.
- Indexes support. It lets us evaluate whether the system generates signed electronic indexes for each electronic record that have been processed.
- Unique identification. It confirms whether the system identifies each document exclusively.
- Minimum metadata. It assesses whether the system allows allocating mandatory minimum metadata to every electronic document according to the guidelines of the Spanish National Interoperability Scheme.
- Classification plan support. It evaluates whether the ECM system allows classifying electronic documents in accordance with the classification schema of the Spanish Public Administration.
- Official time synchronization. It lets us know whether the system allows synchronization with the official time.

f) Interoperability Compliance. A specific section dealing with interoperability has been included: Integration with tools. This sub-feature evaluates whether the ECM system provides mechanisms (e.g. APIs) to integrate with third-party tools. The Sub-features of this feature are described as follows:

- Connection. It examines whether and to what degree APIs that enable integration with third-party systems are provided.
- ERPs. It confirms whether the system supports direct access to documents from ERP systems and allows creating transactions and exchanging data in both directions.
- Capture tools. It lets us know whether the system supports integration with capture tools.
- Email. It evaluates whether the ECM system supports integration with email solutions.
- CMIS repository. It controls that the ECM system can be integrated with any repository (for instance, web portals and virtual offices) that implements the CMIS standard.
- Web services. It confirms whether the system provides integration mechanisms based on Web services using XML (eXtensible Markup Language) and MetaData.
- Single window. It guarantees that the ECM system can be integrated with the main single window platforms (for instance, Solicit@ and Present@).
- Electronic record. It confirms whether the ECM system can be integrated with the main electronic record platforms (for instance, @riesand SIGEM).
- Records manager. It tests whether the ECM system can be integrated with the main records management platforms (for instance, Trew@).
- Electronic files. It evaluates whether the ECM system can be integrated with the main electronic file platforms and custody of documents (for instance, Archiv@).
- Digital signature. It assesses whether the ECM system can be integrated with the main digital signature platforms (for instance, @firma, viafirm@).
- EAI. It asserts whether the ECM system can be integrated with EAI tools (Enterprise Application Integration).
- Streaming. It analyzes whether the system can be natively integrated with streaming servers in order to see and/or listen to online audiovisual content.

g) Security and Control. One of the major objectives of document management solutions is to ensure information security, by controlling accessing the system from inside and outside the organization and managing the documents including such information either to archive or destruct them. As a result, these solutions must provide services that ensure that the information stored is secure. It evaluates whether the system is functional enough to analyze data, or otherwise, whether the system allows using third-party tools. Next, we describe the Sub-features of this feature:

- Data Analysis. It studies whether the data analysis system is allowed, or otherwise, third-party tools to perform data extraction system can be used.
- Exportation. It evaluates whether the system is functional enough to export data, or otherwise, it allows using third-party tools.
- Activity indicators. It confirms whether the system provides indicators to measure each user's activity in the system.
- Granularity. It assesses whether the system provides security utilities to control the access to a specific document or some parts of it.
- LOPD. It evaluates that the system allows switching between HTTPS and HTTP protocols according to the system module to which the user is accessing or encrypting contents and documents traceability, among others aspects.
- Logs. It controls whether the system allows audits (activity log) and issues reports on all actions taken.
- SSO. It reviews whether the system supports different kind of authentication: Single Sign ON, LDAP or Kerberos.
- Notifications. It specifies whether the system reports any security problem to the administrators.

h) Architecture. Open architecture. It evaluates whether the system has an open architecture (*i.e.*, the system allows adding, upgrading and changing its components) or a closed architecture (*i.e.*, the software manufacturer chooses the components, and the end user does not intend to upgrade them). Next, we describe the Sub-features of this feature:

- Open architecture. It evaluates whether the system has an open (to add, upgrade and change its components) or a proprietary architecture.
- Browsers. It assesses whether the system interacts successfully with popular Web browsers such as Internet

Explorer, Mozilla or Chrome, among others.

- Mobility. It lets us know whether the system provides a mobile interface for Smart Phone and Tablets.
- Development kit. It reviews whether the system offers a self-development kit (SDK, API or Web services).
- Cloud solution. It confirms that the system can provide a cloud solution.
- Administrative capabilities. It analyzes whether the system allows managing, monitoring and optimizing its architectural resources.
- Programming language. It studies the implementation degree of the programming language.
- Version. It revises the policy deployment and version management of the ECM solution, *i.e.*, update procedure and pre-upgrade tasks.
- Multiplatform. It evaluates whether the system supports multiple technological platforms (operating systems, Web servers, application servers and DBMS, among others).
- Extensibility. It studies whether the system has a modular platform and is easily extended using plugins, modules or extensions.
- Volumes. It tests whether the system successfully manages a large amount of information.
- High availability. It evaluates whether the system allows high availability configurations, *i.e.*, active-active or active-passive clusters and automatic recovery, among others.
- Scalability. It evaluates whether the ECM system can be automatically adapted (without losing quality) to increase workflows and system requests.

i) Cost. Cost (both initial and long-term by maintenance) is one of the most important factors any organization must take into account when choosing an ECM solution. The Sub-features of this feature are described below:

- Licenses. It evaluates the type of license and its cost.
- Infrastructure. It analyses the total cost (software and hardware) of the minimum necessary infrastructure.
- Open source. It assesses the existence of an active community development.
- Maintenance and support. It calculates the cost of multi-year support and maintenance of the solution.

j) Assistance and RM (Roadmap) Support. This last feature listed in the latter group includes aspects for the evaluation of the Characteristics support, assistance and roadmap provided by the ECM solution. Next, we describe the Sub-features of this feature:

- Certification program. It evaluates whether the ECM solution designer provides a recognized and complete certification program.
- User Manuals. It lets us know whether the manufacturer provides enough online manuals regarding the system operation.
- Service support. It confirms whether the designer offers a 24-hour support.
- Formation service. It revises whether the designer promotes classroom training.
- Roadmap. It assesses the roadmap of the system, *i.e.* a plan with short-term and long-term goals.

4.3. Applying the Characterization Schema

Once characterization schema is defined, it is time to instantiate every approach under study and evaluate them according to our criteria. The first analysis excludes four of our initial approaches: Docu Ware, Knowledge Tree, Nuxeo and MS SharePoint. They are discarded due to the fact that basic functional features are not supported by these approaches. Thus, in our view, these approaches are not considered suitable ECM tools. However, Nuxeo is an exception. ECM alone does not cover the basic functional features, therefore it is supported by a commercial solution, named Athento [32] that is a proprietary solution that enriches Nuxeo. In terms of these considerations, we will instantiate our characterization schema only in Alfresco, Athento + Nuxeo, ECM Documentum, IBM Filenet and Opentext.

Besides, it is necessary to consider three important aspects before presenting the final instantiation:

1) Multiple evaluation: The numerical value of each feature was calculated according to three evaluations:
a) We asked each company that works with these approaches for its own evaluation of each approach.
b) The group of researchers of this paper makes our own evaluation, based on our expertise. As we worked in different projects related to ECM, we installed each tool to test it.
c) We selected a group of 3 students pursuing a PhD in computer sciences without any expertise in ECM tools

and asked them to assess each feature individually.

The results shown were merged and discussed, and the points on which the three groups disagreed were studied in detail. Thus, although our evaluation was subjective, it mixed a set of tests from different levels.

2) Multiobjective optimization: Although it is out of the scope of this paper, we have to mention multiobjective optimization [33]. After revising the results obtained and shown below, the problem that has arisen in this comparative study can be classified as a multiobjective optimization problem. The comparative study that has been executed comprises a large number of desirable characteristics for the tools to develop (this is detailed in the classification schema) and the relative weight of each of these multiple features depends largely on the particular work environment.

Therefore, and attending to the principles established in multiobjective optimization problems [34], this section will cope with the instantiation of the classification chart according to each characteristic specific values, that means that each studied characteristic is posed as a simple optimization problem. That is, each feature is independently studied without taking into account other characteristics. Thus, tables presented in Section 5 do not take into account the multiobjective approach.

3) Preference composition: The preference theory is framed in the theory of specific methods of assessing preferences to quantify changes in people's welfare [35], caused by a change in the quantity or quality of a good or service, which, in turn, is grounded in neoclassical welfare theory methods.

If we considered the comparative proposal under this theory, it would be necessary to assess the preferences of every feature marked in each of the three groups of evaluation given (companies, researcher and students). Thus, the assessment issues an appraisal which varies from 1 to 4, where 4 represents the highest score and 1 the worst solution. It is reminded that the allowable values shown in the classification could range from 1..99, therefore at the end, it was decided to reduce this range to facilitate results understanding. This will allow us to have an order of preference for each of the characteristics of the classification. With regard to subjective criteria, proposals will be sorted from lowest to highest in terms of group provisions, leaving the possibility of being ranked only in the case of factors that can be objectively measured.

After these remarks, we present the results of our study.

Table 4 shows the first set of concepts: Functional modules. As the coverage of these functional characteristics is an obligatory constraint for our approaches, all of them are well valued in this group of items. However, we have to stick out Athento/Nuxeo solution, which currently does not support the record management module completely. Designers promise to include it in the new version of the solution.

Table 5 values user orientation characteristics. This section highlights Alfresco side for its native ability to preview a lot of formats. It also includes capabilities for streaming video and audio (the display is supported on a Flash Document previewer). An additional advantage is how easily Alfresco customize user interface using

Table 4. Characterization schema instantiation: Functional modules.

Group	Features	Alfresco	Athento / Nuxeo	EMC Documentum	IBM Filenet	OpenText
Functional Modules	Document Management	✓	✓	✓	✓	✓
	Records Management	✓	⊘	✓	✓	✓
	BPM (Workflow/Business Process Management)	✓	✓	✓	✓	✓
	Document Imaging/Image-processing	✓	✓	✓	✓	✓
	Interoperability functions/extended components	✓	✓	✓	✓	✓
	WCM (Web Content Management)	✓	✓	✓	✓	✓
	Social content/collaboration	✓	✓	✓	✓	✓
	Features	✓	✓	✓	✓	✓

Table 5. Characterization schema instantiation: User orientation.

Group	Features	Alfresco	Athento/ Nuxeo	EMD Dcoumentum	IBM Filenet	Open Text
	Usability compliance	1	1	1	1	1
	Accessibility	1	1	1	1	1
	Document preview	4	1	2	2	2
	Drag & Drop	1	1	1	1	1
User orientation	Bulk uploads	1	2	1	1	1
	Undo	1	1	1	1	1
	WYSIWYG Editor	2	1	4	4	3
	Customization	3	2	2	2	1
	Groups and Social networks	3	1	2	2	2
	Multilanguage	2	1	4	3	3
	TOTAL	19	13	19	18	16

Spring Surf and languages, like Javascript, as well as SDK to design components dashlets.

In contrast, EMC Documentum platform manages users and geographically distributed locations contents adapted to every language, culture and currency, as well as stores multilingual content in shared repositories.

This platform can provide a single virtual repository that encompasses multiple geographic locations under the shape of either a single distributed repository or federations of repositories, which are groups of repositories that work together. The virtual repository allows users to access content regardless of language or geography. Multilingual presentation management is the unique feature that binds versions of the same content in different languages so that users can choose the language they will use for communication.

In addition, EMC Documentum provides a platform for developing and deploying advanced business solutions and case management, cloud-based optimized, including EMC on Demand deployments. This solution, called xCP elaborates applications working on four different levels: data model, processes/services, user interface and reporting (BAM).

Tabla 6 values functionality to capture, access, retrieve and view documents. IBM Filenet, EMC Documentum and Opentext provide good answers to this set of features. On the one hand, IBM Filenet is notable for the addition of two search engines, Content Search Services, based on Lucene, and Content Search Engine, based on Autonomy K2.On the other hand, EMC Documentum platform incorporates FAST index server, an enterprise search technology leading the industry. The search capability is modular and entails alternative engines for Documentum specific market offerings. For example, the publication of the original manufacture of Documentum is developed for software suppliers incorporate it into their products. Documentum platform offers open-source Lucene alternative as the default engine. However, the FAST search engine for all the standard offerings to business customers is built into the repository.

Table 7 shows the instances for the treatment of documental life cycle in each tool. There are no tangible differences between EMC Documentum, IBM FiletNet and Opentext solutions in this set of features, highlighting very slightly that both, EMC Documentum and IBM FileNet incorporate tools that facilitate screening, traceability and possible inconsistencies and conflicts solutions, as well as implement automatic content rules.

Table 8 instances aspects related with workflows. This section points out EMC Documentum and IBM FiletNet to provide extended functionality in the workflow engine. However, IBM Filen Net is vaguely better positioned to deliver a powerful console for process simulation.

In **Table 9**, aspects related with e-Government are presented. Here, the case of Nuxeo/Athento solution is different since it is a management solution in charge of adding more electronic records to document management utilities.

Table 6. Characterization schema instantiation: Functionality to capture, access, retrieve and view documents.

Group	Features	Alfresco	Athento/ Nuxeo	EMC Documentum	IBM Filenet	Open Text
Functionality to capture, access, retrieve and view documents	Degree of Cataloging	2	1	3	3	2
	Agrupation	2	1	3	3	3
	Thesaurus Support	1	1	2	2	2
	Digitalization	1	3	1	1	1
	Bulk Upload	1	2	1	1	1
	Content Generation	2	1	3	3	3
	Office Integration	2	1	3	3	3
	Forms and Templates	2	1	3	4	3
	Integration Forms Managers	1	1	2	2	1
	Advanced Search Methods	2	1	4	3	4
	Search Algorithms	2	1	4	4	3
	Display Formats	3	1	2	2	2
	TOTAL	21	15	31	31	28

Table 7. Characterization schema instantiation: Documental life cycle.

Group	Features	Alfresco	Athento/ Nuxeo	EMC Documentum	IBM Filenet	Open Text
Documental Life Cycle	Check-in/check-out	1	1	1	1	1
	Life cycle	2	1	3	3	3
	Versioning Support	2	1	3	3	3
	Actions traceability	2	1	4	4	3
	Inconsistencies management	2	1	4	4	3
	Dissemination management	2	1	3	3	4
	Conservation	2	1	3	3	3
	Destruction	2	1	3	3	3
	Physical actions	1	1	1	1	1
	TOTAL	16	9	25	25	24

Aspects related with interoperability are presented in **Table 10**. These features are well supported in general by the different ECM solutions. However, Alfresco Enterprise vaguely stands because of its large implementation in Public Administration. This has led to integration works developed in liaison with the staff responsible for the electronic issue of e-Government in Andalusia and SIGEM [36] in Extremadura.

Table 11 includes the three solutions that longer have stayed in the market: Dcoumentum EMC, IBM File Net and Open Text. Nevertheless, IBM Filenet receives a higher score because it has proper and specific tools to analyze data and identify activity indicators: File Net Business Activity Monitor.

In characteristics related with architecture refer in **Table 12**, we would like to highlight once again the three solutions that longer have stayed in the market. There is a relevant difference especially with Athento/Nuxeo,

Table 8. Characterization schema instantiation: Workflows.

Group	Features	Alfresco	Athento/ Nuxeo	EMC Documentum	IBM Filenet	Open Text
Workflows	Supported standards	4	1	3	3	2
	Management support	2	1	3	3	3
	Available options	2	1	4	4	3
	Motorization	2	1	4	4	3
	Simulation and modeling	2	1	3	4	3
	Graphical utilities	2	1	3	3	3
	Task management	2	1	4	4	3
	TOTAL	15	7	24	25	20

Table 9. Characterization schema instantiation: e-Government.

Group	Features	Alfresco	Athento/ Nuxeo	EMC Documentum	IBM Filenet	Open Text
e-Goverment	Electronic documents	1	3	1	1	1
	Digital signature	1	2	1	1	1
	Accreditation and representation	1	2	1	1	1
	Indexes support	1	1	1	1	1
	Unique identification	1	1	1	1	1
	Minimum metadata	1	3	1	1	1
	Classification plan support	1	2	1	1	1
	Official time synchronization	1	1	1	1	1
	TOTAL	8	15	8	8	8

Table 10. Characterization schema instantiation: Interoperability compliance.

Group	Features	Alfresco	Athento/ Nuxeo	EMC Documentum	IBM Filenet	Open Text
Interoperability Compliance	Connection	2	2	1	1	1
	ERPs	2	1	3	3	4
	Capture tools	1	3	1	1	1
	Email	1	1	3	3	4
	CMIS repository	4	3	2	2	2
	Web services	1	1	1	1	1
	Single window	2	1	1	1	1
	Electronic record	1	1	1	1	1
	Records manager	2	1	2	1	1
	Electronic files	2	1	1	1	1
	Digital signature	1	2	1	1	1
	EAI	1	1	1	1	1
	Streaming	2	1	1	1	1
	TOTAL	22	19	19	18	20

Table 11. Characterization schema instantiation: security and control.

Group	Features	Alfresco	Athento/ Nuxeo	EMC Documentm	IBM Filenet	Open Text
Security and Control	Data Analysis	2	1	3	4	3
	Exportation	1	1	2	2	2
	Activity indicators	2	1	3	4	3
	Granularity	2	1	3	3	3
	LOPD	1	1	2	2	2
	Logs	2	1	3	3	3
	SSO	2	1	3	3	3
	Notifications	1	1	2	3	2
	TOTAL	13	8	21	23	21

Table 12. Characterization schema instantiation: Architecture.

Group	Features	Alfresco	Athento/ Nuxeo	EMC Documenum	IBM Filenet	Open Text
Architecture	Open architecture	1	1	1	1	1
	Browsers	2	1	3	3	3
	Mobility	2	1	2	2	2
	Development kit	2	1	4	4	3
	Cloud solution	3	1	3	2	2
	Administrative capabilities	1	1	2	2	2
	Programming language	2	1	2	2	2
	Version	2	1	3	3	3
	Multiplatform	3	2	3	3	3
	Extensibility	2	1	3	3	3
	Volumes	2	1	3	3	3
	High availability	2	1	4	4	4
	Scalability	3	1	4	4	4
	TOTAL	27	14	37	36	35

because this solution neither focuses on providing cloud service, nor a high-availability good solution for large volumes of information.

Table 13 analyses aspects related with cost. Athento/Nuxeo is very well valued in this comparative solution as the cost of licensing and support is low in comparison to the other standard solutions. It is followed by Alfresco Enterprise thanks to the large community of developers who currently covers.

In the area of software licensing, it should be indicated that suppliers' offer for non-free tools concerns named users (or named users bags, such as IBM Filenet). This would imply a high cost for large deployments, if compared to Alfresco Enterprise or Athento/Nuxeocosts. Besides, IBM FileNet licensing costs include DB2 and WebSphere Application Server licenses.

Finally, in **Table 14**, assistance and RM support are instantiated. EMC and IBM FiletNet Documentum area little better rated in this group of features since they have an extensive program of certification, a lengthy roadmap, as well as a broad presence in the market, apart from providing a wide range of training and online support options.

Table 13. Characterization schema instantiation: Cost.

Group	Features	Alfresco	Athento/ Nuxeo	EMC Documentum	IBM Filenet	Open Text
Cost	Licenses	2	4	1	1	1
	Infrastructure	3	3	1	2	1
	Open source	4	2	1	1	1
	Maintenance and support	1	3	2	2	2
	TOTAL	10	12	5	6	5

Table 14. Characterization schema instantiation: Assistance and RM support.

Group	Features	Alfresco	Athento/ Nuxeo	EMC Documentum	IBM Filenet	Open Text
Assistance and RM Support	Certification program	3	1	4	4	3
	User Manuals	2	1	3	3	3
	Service support	3	1	3	3	3
	Formation service	2	1	4	4	3
	Roadmap	2	1	3	3	3
	TOTAL	12	5	17	17	15

4.4. Conclusions from the General Evaluation

In order to obtain conclusions to develop the Document Management System from these ECM tools within the THOT Project, it is very important to take into account not only the value that all these ECM tools offer to us but also other important factors when these tools are used like the costs, risks or incertitude of these tools.

As regards the value, the most valuable ECM tool depends on the project scope. So, each ECM tool has its strength and weakness points and the relevance of each tool feature depends on the project scope. So, just with the context we could say which ECM tool is the most suitable one to be used in the development of the final Document Management System.

As regards costs, there are several ECM tools in the market, both free software and proprietary license, which offer appropriate solutions in this context. We must consider that we just going to pay a fee for the licenses of these ECM tools if it is sure that we are going to receive the value we need for the THOT Project but with minimal costs, risks and incertitude in the development of the final solution and its deployment in the Andalusian agency. Thus, we try to make the Andalusian agency more competitive using the Document Management system.

But not only is important the costs of a license but the risks and incertitude that organizations assume with the implementation of this Document Management system. For instance, these can be measured by different aspects like an existing community of developers about the tool, the quantity of existing documentation, existing forums and tutorials about the tool among other things.

So, we have evaluated these tools by solving a multiobjective optimization problem. Multiobjective optimization is an area of multiple criteria decision making, which is concerned with mathematical optimization problems involving more than one objective function to be optimized simultaneously. For a nontrivial multiobjective optimization problem, there does not exist a single solution that simultaneously optimizes each objective. The multiobjective study has taken into account the cost of5 years, risks and competitiveness based on previous values to state the following conclusions:

- According to cost

Establishing a 5 year period as the framework for this comparison, Alfresco Enterprise solution has involved higher costs than other solutions evaluated, although the discharge, as in the case of Athento/Nuxeo package does not increase significantly in the functional aspect as it depends on the named user number.

Furthermore, ECM Documentum, IBM Filenet and Opentext tools are aligned in terms of cost/value where IBM File Net and Documentum ECM are offering greater functional scope than Nuxeo/Athento package which is on the other side of the scale.

Regarding cost, Nuxeo/Athentois located just below ECM Documentum, IBM Filenet or Opentext solution in the framework of this comparison, therefore this multiobjective relationship Nuxeo/Athento should be discarded for it offers a lower functional scope. **Figure 3** graphically represents the results:

- According to risk

IBM File Net, EMC Documentum, Open Text and Alfresco Enterprise are distinguished by their position in the market (see Gartner Inc. Google and outcome) and therefore they assume less risk and uncertainty. Regarding value, IBM File Net is best positioned at a reasonable cost compared to other solutions. **Figure 4** shows the relationship between Risk and Value whereas **Figure 5** represents the relationship between Risk and Cost.

- Finally, according to competitive (**Figure 6**).

IBM File Net has a slightly better position than EMC Documentum and Open Text. Despite the three solutions are highly competitive in the context of this comparison, they are far from other solutions evaluated.

5. Customizing Our Study in a Real Project

This section presents a concrete use of the study, after analysing our work in general. We introduce a view of a real project named THOT to cover the three objectives of our work. We ponder on each characteristic for the concrete necessity of the project.

5.1. A Global View of Thot Project

Nowadays, the Andalusian Public Administration has already implemented or is currently implementing different initiatives, which are driving the need for a deep change in document management systems:

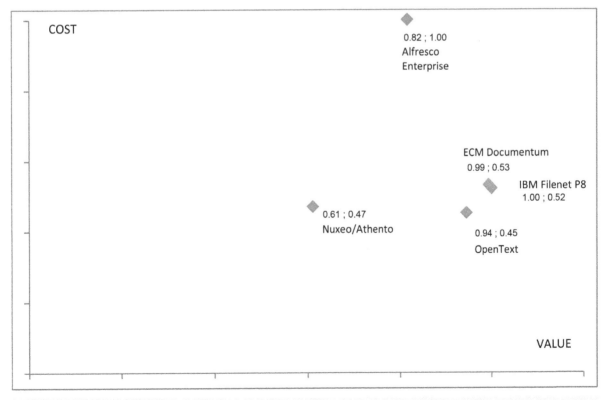

Figure 3. Diagram according to cost.

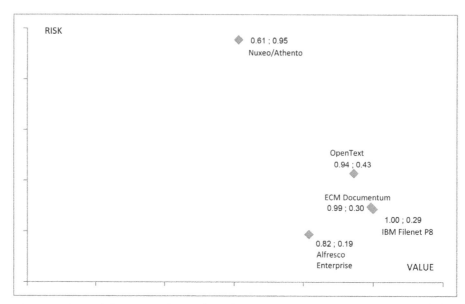

Figure 4. Risk vs Value.

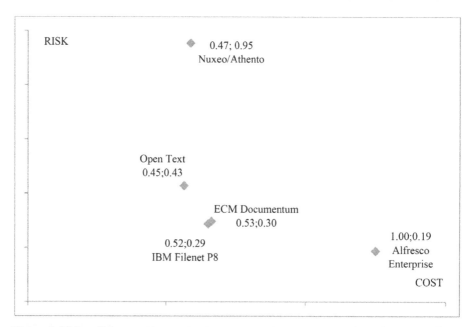

Figure 5. Risk vs Cost.

- The financial management of records is now being supported by JUPITER [37] Information System, although this situation will change because the Ministry of Finance and Public Administration of the Regional Government of Andalusia has launched an initiative to migrate the current JUPITER System to an ERP technology platform. In fact, there are already some institutions in Andalusia where this technology has been implemented, such as the Public Agency of Contracting Services for Transport and Infrastructure Constructions.
- In July 2011, the Andalusian Parliament approved a new law concerning establishing ERIS-G3 [38] system, which is an e-Government system to manage electronic procedures to process public records in each public agency.
- @rchivA [39] Information System that facilitates proper management of the Patrimony Documentation of Andalusia is providing researchers and the general public with the necessary tools to consult and distribute such Patrimony through new technologies.

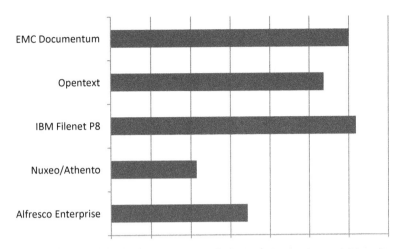

Figure 6. Competitive.

Therefore, in the near future we will witness a general scenario in the Regional Government of Andalusia Administration compiling:
- A clear objective to improve the efficiency and effectiveness of strategic, tactical and financial resources,
- A high level of automation of management and business processes, and
- A technology that integrates data and processes and also enables integrating document management.

This increases the opportunity (and also the need) to propose innovations in document management, in this case related to public infrastructure and services. Then, we propose the implementation of a document management model to be applied to this context. THOT project is an e-Government project aiming at implementing an ECM system in the Public Administration of the Regional Government of Andalusia (Spain). The project has been granted for a total of 621,250 Euros. It tends to define an environment for managing agile documentary records, framed within the existing real world, to be implemented by appropriate technological solution aligned with guidelines and the current context. The specific objectives of this research project are:
- Objective 1: Create a document management solutions model integrated with ERP (Enterprise Resource Planning).
- Objective 2: Optimize resource investment in Andalusia for the development of the new ERP technology platform, providing new adjacent functionality as document management model.
- Objective 3: Develop such a model applied to records of procurement of services and transport infrastructure projects of the Public Works Agency of Andalusia, responding to specific casuistry project technical documents and favoring the existing need to exploit the spatial reference information (such as support for planning and sectoral processes).
- Objective 4: Apply European recommendations and e-Government principles to promote the format conversion, from printed papers to online versions, in written communications between management and contractors as well as facilitate compliance with current regulations related to e-Government.
- Objective 5: Achieve a large number of digital documents instead of paper in order to be able to save and keep them.
- Objective 6: Standardize and structure information in order to encourage the development and applicability of information technology and communication in the public works sector.
- Objective 7: Apply standards in the document management system that allows a secure interoperability with other systems.

This project aims to make a qualitative leap covering different disciplines of research and innovation, such as document management policies, e-Government policies, dissemination and integration policies in Web environments (aspects that are treated and profusely investigated by different groups and research fora, both national and international). That enables organizations to provide a common framework for document management and cover the need to have a comprehensive management to complement business processes from beginning to end. The project offers, with innovation and research jobs, a solution that not only permits organizations to manage documents intelligently, but also to distribute, maintain and custody them.

5.2. Customization of Our Study

We held a set of meetings with functional users in order to adjust our study to the concrete case of THOT Project. At theses meeting, we studied each group of features depending on its relevance in THOT context. Results are presented in **Table 15**.

5.3. Conclusions from THOT Project

As can be realized along this paper, non-free comparative tools have clear advantages in opposition to other tools. Particularly, IBM Filenet has obtained best weighted overall result just for a minimum difference. This result can be justified from the fact that both IBM Filenet and EMC Documentum are solutions with extensive experience and worldwide deep implementation.

They have a better performance in more general characteristics of ECM tools such as ability to capture, access, retrieve and display document management life cycle or workflow, security, access control and activity or support issues, manual and roadmap.

However, as expected, the lowest score is framed in specific aspects of the context of this study such as e-Government, and aspects related to cost, such as license regarding number of named users.

Finally, we would like to remark the case of Athento/Nuxeo solution because, as previously commented, Nuxeo solution does not achieve an initial value in the functional coverage that justifies its introduction in this study (it has been incorporated due to the studied experiences aroused the interest of improving Athento solution). We have also observed that the resulting package is quite far from the highest values because this study is focused exclusively on document management tools, whereas Nuxeo solution is centered on aspects more related to administration files management.

6. Conclusions and Future Work

This paper presents a comparative study of five different ECM tools. The work uses an enriched systematic literature review in order to decide which tools are included. After carrying out this review, this paper presents a characterization schema that allows comparing each approach under study in a similar way.

The schema is applied to each approach and a set of global results are obtained and commented. Moreover,

Table 15. Characterization schema instantiation for THOT project.

Group of items	Weigth	Alfresco	Athento/ Nuxeo	EMC Documenum	IBM Filenet	Open Text
1. User Orientation	0.5	19	12	19	18	16
2. Functionality to capture, access, retrieve and view documents	1.0	21	15	31	31	28
3. Documental Life Cycle	1.0	16	7	24	25	20
4. Workflows	0.2	16	7	24	25	20
5. e-Government	1.0	8	15	8	8	8
6. Interoperability Compliance	1.1	22	19	19	18	20
7. Security and Control	1.1	13	8	21	23	21
8. Architecture	1.3	27	14	37	36	35
9. Cost	1.8	10	12	5	6	5
10. Assistance and RM	1.0	12	5	17	17	15
RESULT...		164	116	206	207	192
Pondered Result...		16.13	12.09	19.64	19.77	18.66

the paper illustrates how this study can be customized to a concrete environment with its real application to THOT Project. Thus, the three aims that are cited on the introduction are achieved.

As a final conclusion, we would like to add that it is a very active environment and there are continuous changes in tools and versions. This study was finished in February 2014, taking into consideration the current situation of the analyzed tools at this moment.

For this reason, in terms of future work, we would conclude that the evaluated tools presented a constant process of change and evolution. In fact, the lines that seem most promising and empower these tools can be clearly aligned with strategic Action Digital Economy and Society, specifically with the following subject priorities:

- Future Internet (networks, services, things or people).
- Cloud computing: development, innovation and selection of technologies and solutions.
- Mobility: technology-based services and mobility, networking and mobile systems products.
- Safety in the use of applications, especially in e-ID.
- Cyber-security and digital trust, protecting particularly vulnerable groups.
- Open/Linked/Big Data: re-use of public sector information and knowledge to create value.
- Social Media for their business-generating potential and provided services.
- Digital content: systems, platforms, services and processes that facilitate design, production and packaging.
- Systems, platforms, services and processes for new solutions and audio-visual broadcasting.

Acknowledgements

This research has been partially supported by MeGus (TIN2013-46928-C3-3-R) project of the Ministerio de Educación y Ciencia, Spain, and FEDER of European Union for financial support via the project "THOT. Proyecto de innovación de la gestión documental aplicada a expedientes de contratación de servicios y obras de infraestructuras de transporte" of the "Programa Operativo FEDER de Andalucía 2007-2013". We would also like to thank all the staff and researches of Agency of Public Works of the Regional Government of Andalusia for their support and professionalism.

References

[1] AIIM (2013) The Global Community of Information Professionals. http://www.aiim.org/

[2] Alalwan, J.A. and Weistroffer, H.R. (2012) Enterprise Content Management Research: A Comprehensive Review. *Journal of Enterprise Information Management*, **25**, 441-461. http://dx.doi.org/10.1108/17410391211265133

[3] THOT Project. http://www.aopandalucia.es/inetfiles/agencia_innovacion_estructura/14122012112320.pdf

[4] Scott, J.E. (2011) User Perceptions of an Enterprise Content Management System. *Proceedings of the 44th Hawaii International Conference on Systems Science (HICSS-44 2011)*, Koloa, 4-7 January 2011, 1, 9, 4-7.

[5] Haug, A. (2012) The Implementation of Enterprise Content Management Systems in SMEs. *Journal of Enterprise Information Management*, **25**, 349-372. http://dx.doi.org/10.1108/17410391211245838

[6] Van Rooij, J.C. (2013) Legacy Issues in the Implementation of Enterprise Content Management (ECM). *International Journal of Information*, **3**, 120-123.

[7] ISO 2709:2008, Information and Documentation—Format for Information Exchange. http://www.iso.org/iso/iso_catalogue/catalogue_tc/catalogue_detail.htm?csnumber=41319

[8] ISO 15836:2009, Information and Documentation—The Dublin Core Metadata Element Set. http://www.iso.org/iso/catalogue_detail.htm?csnumber=52142

[9] ISO 15489-1:2001, Information and Documentation—Records Management—Part 1: General. http://www.iso.org/iso/catalogue_detail?csnumber=31908

[10] ISO 23950:1998, Information and Documentation—Information Retrieval (Z39.50)—Application Service Definition and Protocol Specification. http://www.iso.org/iso/catalogue_detail.htm?csnumber=27446

[11] ISO 10244:2010, Document Management—Business Process Baselining and Analysis. http://www.iso.org/iso/home/store/catalogue_tc/catalogue_detail.htm?csnumber=45935

[12] Zhang, H. and Babar, M.A. (2013) Systematic Reviews in Software Engineering: An Empirical Investigation. *Information and Software Technology*, **55**, 1341-1354.

[13] Kitchenham, B. (2004) Procedures for Performing Systematic Reviews. Keele University, Keele, 33.

[14] Brereton, P., Kitchenham, B.A., Budgen, D., Turner, M. and Khalil, M. (2007) Lessons from Applying the Systematic Literature Review Process within the Software Engineering Domain. *Journal of Systems and Software*, **80**, 571-583. http://dx.doi.org/10.1016/j.jss.2006.07.009

[15] Kitchenham, B. and Brereton, P. (2007) Introduction to Special Section on Evaluation and Assessment in Software Engineering EASE06. *Journal of Systems and Software*, **80**, 1423-1424. http://dx.doi.org/10.1016/j.jss.2006.10.031

[16] Staples, M. and Niazi, M. (2007) Experiences Using Systematic Review Guidelines. *Journal of Systems and Software*, **80**, 1425-1437. http://dx.doi.org/10.1016/j.jss.2006.09.046

[17] Kitchenham, B. and Charters, S. (2007) Guidelines for Performing Systematic Literature Reviews in Software Engineering, Technical Report EBSE 2007-001, Keele University and Durham University Joint Report.

[18] Kitchenham, B. and Brereton, P. (2013) A Systematic Review of Systematic Review Process Research in Software Engineering. *Information and Software Technology*, **55**, 2049-2075.

[19] Zhang, H., Babar, M.A. and Tell, P. (2011) Identifying Relevant Studies in Software Engineering. *Information and Software Technology*, **53**, 625-637.

[20] SEG (Software Enginnering Group) (2007) Guidelines for Performing Systematic Literature Reviews in Software Engineering Version 2.3. EBSE Technical Report. EBSE-2007-01. School of Computer Science and Mathematics. Keel University and Department of Computer Science. University of Durham. United Kingdom.

[21] Wohlin, C. and Prikladnicki, R. (2013) Systematic Literature Reviews in Software Engineering. *Information and Software Technology*, **55**, 919-920.

[22] Gilbert, M.R., Shegda, K.M., Chin, K., Tay, G. and Koehler-Kruener, H. (2012) Magic Quadrant for Enterprise Content Management. Article ID: G00237781.

[23] Gartner Company Is Based in Stamford, Connecticut, USA. http://www.gartner.com

[24] Alfresco. http://www.alfresco.com

[25] DocuWare. www.docuware.com

[26] Documentum. http://www.emc.com/domains/documentum/index.htm

[27] IBM FileNet. http://www-03.ibm.com/software/products/us/en/filecontmana/

[28] KnowledgeTree.www.knowledgetree.com

[29] Nuxeo/Athento. http://www.athento.com/nuxeo/

[30] OpenText. http://www.opentext.es/

[31] MS Sharepoint. http://office.microsoft.com/es-es/sharepoint-server-help/introduccion-a-sharepoint-HA102772778.aspx?CTT=5&origin=HA010378184

[32] Athento. http://www.athento.com/

[33] Afshin-Mansouri, S., Gallear, D. and Askariazad, M.H. (2012) Decision Support for Build-to-Order Supply Chain Management through Multiobjective Optimization. *International Journal of Production Economics*, **135**, 24-36. http://dx.doi.org/10.1016/j.ijpe.2010.11.016

[34] Renaud, J.E. (2012) Interactive Multiobjective Optimization Procedure.

[35] Espinosa, O. (2012) Método de Valoración de Preferencias' Análisis Conjunto': Una Revisión de Literatura (Method of Preference Valuation'Conjoint Analysis': A Review of the Literature). Econografos Escuela de Economía. http://dx.doi.org/10.2139/ssrn.2194963

[36] SIGEM. https://www.planavanza.es/avanzalocal/soluciones/paginas/sigem.aspx

[37] JUPITER Project, Junta de Andalucía. http://www.juntadeandalucia.es/repositorio/usuario/listado/fichacompleta.jsf?idProyecto=19

[38] ERIS-G3 Project, Junta de Andalucía. http://www.juntadeandalucia.es/repositorio/usuario/listado/fichacompleta.jsf?idProyecto=680

[39] Archiva (@rchiva), Junta de Andalucía. https://ws024.juntadeandalucia.es/ae/adminelec/areatecnica/archiva

11

A Quantitative Analysis of Collision Resolution Protocol for Wireless Sensor Network

Reema Patel, Dhiren Patel

Computer Engineering Department, NIT, Surat, India
Email: reema.mtech@gmail.com, dhiren29p@gmail.com

Abstract

In this paper, we present formal analysis of 2CS-WSN collision resolution protocol for wireless sensor networks using probabilistic model checking. The 2CS-WSN protocol is designed to be used during the contention phase of IEEE 802.15.4. In previous work on 2CS-WSN analysis, authors formalized protocol description at abstract level by defining counters to represent number of nodes in specific local state. On abstract model, the properties specifying individual node behavior cannot be analyzed. We formalize collision resolution protocol as a Markov Decision Process to express each node behavior and perform quantitative analysis using probabilistic model checker PRISM. The identical nodes induce symmetry in the reachable state space which leads to redundant search over equivalent areas of the state space during model checking. We use "Explicit-PRISMSymm" on-the-fly symmetry reduction approach to prevent the state space explosion and thus accommodate large number of nodes for analysis.

Keywords

Wireless Sensor Network, Collision Resolution Protocol, Probabilistic Model Checking, Symmetry Reduction

1. Introduction

In last few years, our lives have been greatly influenced by a wireless communication technology that promotes the development of low cost tiny sensor devices which are capable of sensing, processing and communicating. These tiny sensor devices are collaborated to form an ad hoc and self-configurable network, generally referred as the Wireless Sensor Network (WSN) [1]. These tiny sensor devices have been used in a wide array of applications such as battlefield surveillance, home automation, target tracking, traffic monitoring, health-care monitoring, etc. Although WSN supports a wide array of applications, it has severe resource limitations [2]. The tiny sensor devices are composed of very limited resources such as memory, bandwidth, processor, and energy [3]. In WSN, the data collected by tiny sensor devices have to be transmitted from source to sink node with maximum accuracy and least resource utilization.

To communicate with each other, each node initiates neighbor discovery process which collects the neighbor nodes information by receiving packets from them. If two or more nodes send their packets at the same time, a collision may occur at the receiving node. A key challenge for successful neighbor discovery is to resolve the collisions that occur at the receiving node. Here, we focus onto *two cells sorted wireless sensor network* (2CS-WSN) collision resolution protocol [4] designed to be used during the contention phase of IEEE 802.15.4 [5].

In this paper, we consider formal verification of 2CS-WSN collision resolution protocol using probabilistic model checker PRISM [6]. Given a probabilistic model, expressed as a stochastic process such as Markov Decision Process (MDP) [7], and a property specification, such as "node 1 has delivered a data packet with probability 1", the probabilistic model checking verifies whether model satisfies the given specification or not.

José A. Mateo *et al.* have also presented formal analysis of 2CS-WSN protocol using PRISM in [8]. They formalize protocol description at very abstract level using counter abstraction based approach. In counter abstraction approach, the abstract state contains a counter for each possible local state that a process can be in. For example, for 2CS-WSN model, authors defined counters like TC (Transmission Cell) and WC (Waiting Cell) which denote the number of nodes currently in TC and WC. As a limitation of this approach, we cannot analyze the behavior of individual node *i.e.* whether node 1 has performed successful transmission or not.

We use Markov Decision Process (MDP) as formalization to capture the complete behavior of each node in 2CS-WSN protocol. We evaluate quantitative properties such as "probability of node 1 to transmit successfully within 10 seconds". Major constraint of our modeling approach is the verification of protocol model with large number of nodes. As the number of nodes increases, states will grow exponentially which is known as state space explosion problem. State explosion prevents the analysis of protocol with large number of nodes. To prevent the state space explosion, we use "ExplicitPRISMSymm" on-the-fly symmetry reduction technique [9], thus making it feasible to analyze protocol with large number of nodes.

We can perform modifications in our modeling approach according to the situations occur in the protocol. For example, we can assign priority to any node like cluster head, so any message from higher priority node will be transmitted before all other messages.

The paper proceeds with the informal description of 2CS-WSN collision resolution protocol in next section. In section 3, we discuss the protocol modeling using counter abstraction based approach and its limitations. Section 4 explains protocol formalization using MDP. Experimental results are explained in section 5 followed by conclusion in section 6.

2. Background

In this section, we give brief introduction of probabilistic model checking and symmetry reduction. Symmetry reduction is a well-known abstraction technique to prevent the state space explosion in concurrent system analysis.

2.1. Probabilistic Model Checking

Probabilistic model checking integrates automated verification techniques aim to quantitatively analyze the probabilistic systems. Calculating likelihood of the occurrence of certain events during the system execution is referred as quantitative analysis.

PRISM is a widely used probabilistic model checker, has been developed at the University of Birmingham [6]. It has been used to model and analyze a wide range of applications such as distributed randomized algorithms, wireless communication protocols, game theory, quantum computing etc. [10]. PRISM supports a range of probabilistic models and property specification languages based on temporal logic, and have been extended with costs and rewards [11].

The system to be analyzed is described in a high-level PRISM specification language then transformed into an internal representation, such as symbolic [12] or explicit [11]. Symbolic uses Multi Terminal Binary Decision Diagram (MTBDD) [13] mathematical data structure for compact representation of state space. Whereas explicit enumerate complete state space in memory. Properties are expressed as temporal logical formulas, enriched with probabilistic operators, and may include additional features such as time bounds or rewards depending on the model [11].

The probabilistic model checker exhaustively search entire reachable state space associated with the system model, and generate two types of outputs, either true/false which indicate whether the specification holds in model or not, or the numerical value, for example, the probability or expected time to reach a state satisfying the specification [11].

2.2. Symmetry Reduction

One of the major problems associated with probabilistic model checking is the state space explosion. This problem is more severe with concurrent system analysis as it contains non-distinguishable components [14]. We can consider 2CS-WSN protocol as a concurrent system consisting identical nodes where behavior of each node is similar. As the number of nodes increases in the protocol, the reachable state space grows exponentially. The identical nodes induce symmetry in the reachable state space which leads to redundant search over equivalent areas of the state space during model checking [15].

Symmetry reduction discovers the equivalence classes of symmetrical states to prevent the state explosion in concurrent system analysis. Symmetry reduction reduces the size of system model by choosing only one state as a representative from each equivalence class of states [16]. This smaller model referred as quotient model, which is yet similar in function to its original model.

PRISM has built-in symmetry reduction technique "PRISMSymm" [17] works with symbolic representation of probabilistic models. In [9], authors have proposed symmetry reduction technique "ExplicitPRISMSymm" for explicitly represented probabilistic models.

Model building task is much faster using symbolic compare to explicit. But explicit performs better in property evaluation compare to symbolic. For verification of any system, model building is one time task only, where property evaluation can be performed frequently on built model [9]. Thus, we have used "ExplicitPRISMSymm" symmetry reduction technique for analysis of 2CS-WSN protocol.

2.3. 2CS-WSN Collision Resolution Protocol

2CS-WSN protocol is originally adapted from 2C (two cell) algorithm introduced in [4] for wired network. Here, time is slotted and nodes can transmit at the beginning of a given time slot. The main issue in collision resolution protocol is how to detect a collision. The collision detection method in both the wired 2CS protocol and wireless 2CS-WSN protocol is as follows:

- Collision detection in 2CS: In a given time slot, node transmits a packet and receives a feedback message from the central station. The feedback message represents C if collision takes place otherwise represents NC.
- Collision detection in 2CS-WSN: In 2C, it is assumed that, there is a central station which continuously monitors the channel and provides the feedback message. However, this assumption is unrealistic in self-configuring wireless ad hoc network. For instance, a wireless node may infer that its transmission has collided if the reply to its request does not arrive.

Figure 1 shows the working of 2CS-WSN protocol [8]. If a node wants to send a message, it is consider into Transmission Cell (TC). The transmission is successful if node receives an acknowledgment of a sent message. If acknowledgment does not receive, the node will randomly choose whether to retransmit or join waiting cell for later transmission. This aspect is model using probabilities. Let's denote P_{TC} the probability to remain in TC and $P_{WC} = 1 - P_{TC}$ probability to join the waiting cell (WC). When the transmission cell becomes empty, nodes move from WC to TC [18].

In next slot, if TC contains more than one node, then nodes again redistribute in TC and WC with the help of probabilities. This process repeat until only one node remains in TC and transmit successfully.

2.4. Example

Figure 2 demonstrate how collision resolves between 3 nodes with the help of two waiting cells WC1 and WC2. Initially each node stays into TC, then each node randomly decides either to stay in TC or to move into WC1 with respective probabilities P_{TC} and P_{WC}.

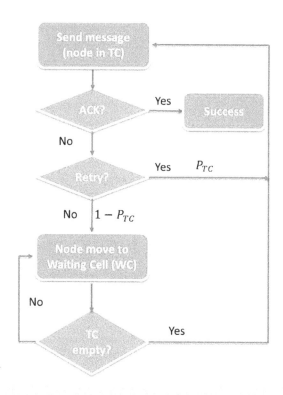

Figure 1. 2CS-WSN protocol.

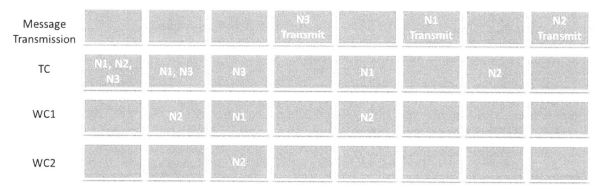

Figure 2. Example of 2CS-WSN protocol.

In this example, node $N1$ and $N3$ choose to stay in TC, whereas $N2$ decide to move into WC1. Further $N1$ and $N3$ attempt to retransmit, and collide again. In next slot, $N1$ move to WC1, at the same time $N2$ shift to WC2. Now there is only one node $N3$ in TC, thus achieve successful transmission. Now TC becomes empty and $N1$ and $N2$ move to TC and WC1 respectively. This process repeats until all nodes achieve successful transmission.

3. Abstract Model of 2CS-WSN Protocol Based on Counter Abstraction Approach

José A. Mateo et. al have also presented formal analysis of 2CS-WSN collision resolution protocol using probabilistic model checking [8]. They formalize protocol description based on counter abstraction approach.

3.1. Counter Abstraction

Counter abstraction is a well-known abstraction method [19] for concurrent system consisting n number of identical processes.

Let's consider a probabilistic model of a concurrent system consisting n finite number of concurrently executing processes. Let $I = \{1, 2, \cdots, n\}$ be the set of process identifiers. For some $k > 0$, let $L = \{1, 2, \cdots, k\}$

denote the possible local variables of a single process. A system state s can be represented in form of $s = (l_1, l_2, \cdots, l_n)$ where l_i represents the values of all local variables of process i.

Let $Unique\_possible\_local\_state : \{upl_1, upl_2, upl_{N_{up}}\}$ be the set of possible unique local states that a process can be in. Here, N_{up} denotes the number of possible unique local states.

In counter abstraction method, the abstract state contains a counter for each possible local state that a process can be in. An abstract state $abs(s)$ can be represented as $abs(s) : \left(c_{upl_1}, c_{upl_2}, \cdots, c_{upl_{N_{up}}}\right)$ where counter c_{upl_i} denotes the number of processes currently in local state upl_i.

3.2. 2CS-WSN Protocol Model as Counter Abstraction

Authors of [8] formalize abstract model of 2CS-WSN protocol as Discrete Time Markov Chain. According to the protocol description, the node can be in one of two conditions, *i.e.* TC or WC.

In formalization, they maintain different counters for transmission cell and waiting cells. Let's consider a protocol configured with 2 waiting cells. Then representation of system state can be: (TC, WC1, WC2) where TC represents the number of nodes collide in TC and WC1, WC2 represents the number of nodes waiting in each respective cell. For example, state $s : (4, 2, 1)$ represents that 4 nodes collide in TC and 2 and 1 nodes are waiting to into WC1 and WC2 respectively.

Here, major restriction of counter abstraction is that the model cannot capture the behavior of individual node. We cannot analyze the performance of a single node behavior. For example, we cannot measure collision resolution time for individual node.

4. Formalization of 2CS-WSN Protocol as Markov Decision Process

The MDP model for the 2CS-WSN protocol will be obtained by composing MDPs for each node. **Figure 3** shows the control-flow diagram of MDP formalizing the operational behavior of the ith node. The model of the ith node consists of four locations TC, WC1, WC2 or FIN. Initially the ith node is in the state TC.

An integer variable Ntc, $Nwc1$ and $Nwc2$ keeps track of the number of nodes that are currently in the local state TC, WC1 or WC2. The edges in the control-flow diagram refer to the conditions that must be satisfied to move into the next state. For synchronization of all the nodes, we use notation like ? to represent that all nodes in current state will simultaneously transit into the next state if condition satisfy.

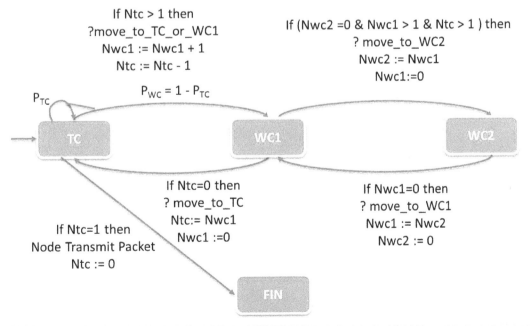

Figure 3. Conceptual MDP model of ith node of 2CS-WSN protocol.

Initially all nodes collide into TC, then they choose to move into state TC or WC1 with P_{TC} or P_{WC} probability, which is indicated by the synchronize action *?move_to_TC_or_WC1*. At the same time, nodes waiting into WC1 moves to WC2 with *?move_to_WC2*.

Node can transmit a packet if collision does not occur into local state TC, and node moves from TC to FIN. whenever counter *Ntc* reaches to zero, nodes from local states WC2 and WC1 move to WC1 and TC respectively. This process repeats until all nodes transmit successfully.

Let's consider 2CS-WSN protocol configured with one waiting cell WC1 and transmission probability $P_{TC} = 0.5$. Here, we consider two nodes which are colliding with each other in TC. The state space generated for two such nodes is shown in **Figure 4** with probability distribution. In general, for any system consisting n number of nodes with k possible local states will have maximum k^n total number of reachable states. In 2CS-WSN, nodes can be in one of three possible local states(TC, WC1 or FIN) $k = 3$, thus MDP model of two nodes will consist maximum 3^2 states. State space of such model tends to grow exponentially large with increasing number of nodes. Due to this state space explosion problem, verification of protocol with large number of nodes is not feasible. A model of such system frequently contains the symmetrical components in form of nodes where behavior of all nodes is indistinguishable.

For example, symmetrical components exist in 2CS-WSN protocol model, e.g. two states $s1$: (TC,WC1) and $s2$: (WC1,TC) are symmetric to each other in **Figure 4**. There is a transition from state $s1$: (TC,WC1) to $s4$: (FIN,WC1). After applying permutation $(1,2)$ on source $s1$ and destination $s4$, we will get states $s2$: (WC1,TC) and $s5$: (WC1,FIN) respectively. **Figure 4** shows that the transition between $s2$ to $s5$ also exists. Here, two states $s1$ and $s2$ represent same situation, where one node is into transmission cell and another into waiting cell. Hence, both the states $(s1, s5)$ belong to a same equivalence class. Same way, both destination states $(s4, s5)$ also represent the same situation.

In formal verification, all states belonging to the same equivalence class indicate the same event in the system. Therefore, considering only one state instead of all from each equivalence class will not affect the results. Symmetry reduction exploits this fact and reduces the state space: only one representative from each equivalence class of states is chosen.

5. Quantitative Analysis

We now proceed to quantitative analysis of 2CS-WSN protocol. In [8] [18], authors conclude that $P_{TC} = 0.5$ and 5 waiting cells $(WC1, WC2, \cdots, WC5)$ are best configurations to achieve minimum collision resolution time. Thus, to evaluate the MDP model of protocol, we consider $P_{TC} = 0.5$ and 5 number of waiting cells with varying number of nodes. For experiments, we used virtual machine configured with Xeon Processor, 20 GB RAM and Linux Operating system.

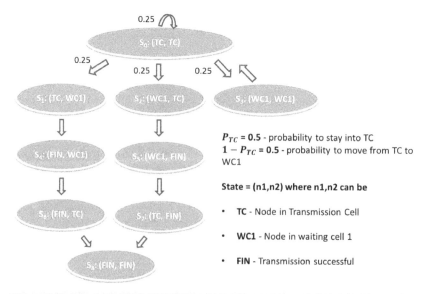

Figure 4. State space of 2CS-WSN protocol for 2 nodes.

5.1. Property Specifications

To analyze the protocol, significant properties are expressed using PCTL logical formulas. Specific properties for probabilistic model checking can be grouped into three different categories [20]:

1). Probabilistic Reachability: This type of property verifies that event will take place or not with defined probability at some point in the future during the system execution. Two probabilistic reachability properties for 2CS-WSN protocol are as follows:

First we want to verify that whether all nodes have performed successful transmission or not. This is computed by using the following formula:

$$\text{formula finish} = \left(n1 = \text{FIN} \ \& \ n2 = \text{FIN} \ \& \ \cdots \ \& \ nz = \text{FIN} \right)$$

where z = number of nodes.

- **P1**: *"Eventually with probability at least 1, all nodes successfully transmit"*

$$\left[P = 1 \ \left[F \ \left(\text{finish} = \text{FIN} \right) \right] \right]$$

If the property evaluate to *true* then it ensures that the protocol eventually terminates successfully.

- **P2**: *"Eventually with probability at least 1, node 1 successfully transmit"*

$$\left[P = 1 \ \left[F \ \left(n1 = \text{FIN} \right) \right] \right]$$

This property ensures that whether node n1 has performed successful transmission or not.

2). Time Bounded Probabilistic Reachability: These properties allow to evaluating the specific event within bounded time deadline.

- **T1**: *Minimum probability of protocol termination within time T.*

$$\left[P\min = ? \ \left[F \leq T \ \left(\text{finish} = \text{FIN} \right) \right] \right]$$

- **T2**: *Minimum probability that node 1 correctly transmit its packet within time T.*

$$\left[P\min = ? \ \left[F \leq T \ \left(n1 = \text{FIN} \right) \right] \right]$$

3). Expected Reachability: Reachability reward properties can be analyzed by associating rewards/costs to PRISM model. For evaluation, tool accumulates expected reward values along a path until a certain point is reached.

According to the original protocol description [8] [18], time required by single node to move from one cell to another is 1.6 ms. We associate reward named as *"time"* of 1.6 to our MDP model. Thus, each transition of system model is associated with 1.6 reward value. Following properties allow to calculating expected time required by the specific event.

- **R1**: *Maximum expected time taken by protocol to resolve all the conflicts*

$$\left[R\{\text{"time"}\} = ? \ \left[F \ \left(\text{finish} = \text{FIN} \right) \right] \right]$$

- **R2**: *Maximum expected time taken by node 1 to successfully transmit its packet*

$$\left[R\{\text{"time"}\} = ? \ \left[F \ \left(n1 = \text{FIN} \right) \right] \right]$$

5.2. Evaluation

We built an MDP model of 2CS-WSN protocol using PRISM's explicit representation. We first analyze property **P1**, that evaluate to *true*, which ensures that protocol has successfully resolved all the collisions.

Time bounded probabilistic property **T1** calculates the probability of protocol termination within given time. As the time deadline **T** increases, probability of protocol termination is also increase.

We validate our MDP model by comparing "Expected reachability value of property **R1**" for different number of nodes with the results given in [8]. Collision resolution time required for specific number of nodes using our model is same as results given in [8].

In 2CS-WSN protocol verification, as the number of node increases, reachable states also increase. Thus, the full MDP model with large number of nodes cannot build using explicit representation. Therefore, we have applied "ExplicitPRISMSymm" on-the-fly symmetry reduction technique [9] to build a quotient explicit MDP model of protocol with large number of nodes. On-the-fly symmetry reduction reduces symmetrical states at the time of exploration of reachable states. Thus, it saves time from exploring symmetrical states and also free storage space by only storing representative state from each equivalence class of states. The reduced model built by choosing representative states and their corresponding transitions known as quotient model.

In **Figure 5**, graph shows the comparison between full explicit model and quotient explicit model. We observe that full explicit model cannot build with more than 6 numbers of nodes. Whereas using on-the-fly symmetry reduction we are able to build a model up to 21 numbers of nodes.

Properties **P2**, **T2** and **R2** cannot analyze using counter abstraction based approach. But using our MDP formalization, we can analyze properties related to individual node as it represents information of each node.

PRISM gives facility to define symmetry parameters as *NBS* and *NFS*, in which we can specify number of non-symmetric nodes. Here *NBS* represents number of non-symmetric nodes before symmetric nodes and *NFS* defines number of non-symmetric nodes after symmetric nodes. That means, all symmetric nodes must be defined in a consecutive manner.

For example, we want to verify that what is the probability that node *n*1 will successfully transmit its packet within given deadline. For that, we can specify symmetry reduction parameters as 1.0 which perform the symmetry reduction on all nodes except node 1.

We have evaluated property **T2** against node 1 with varying the time deadline and number of nodes. **Table 1** shows the probability of successful transmission by node 1 with different time deadlines. We observe that as the number of node increases, probability of node 1 transmission is decreases for short deadlines.

We have also evaluated property **R2**, "expected collision resolution time" for *n*1 with different P_{TC} values range from 0.1 to 0.9. We have taken the results of property **R2** with different number of nodes.

Figure 6 shows the graph for experimental results of property *R2*. From experimental results, we infer that as the number of node increases, time required for successful transmission by node 1 also increases. Experimental results show that $P_{TC} = 0.4$ or $P_{TC} = 0.5$ is best choice as the parameter for retransmission probability, which minimize the collision resolution time.

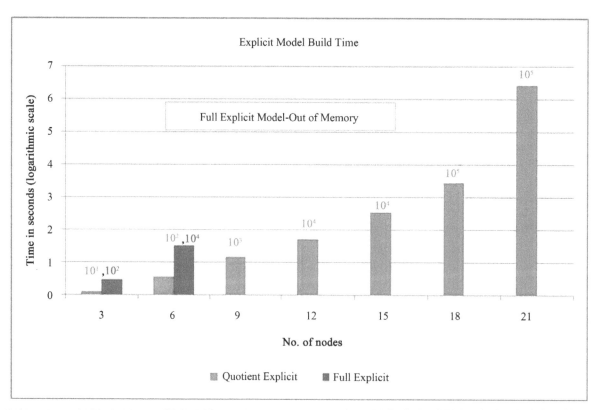

Figure 5. Model building time using full explicit model Vs. Quotient explicit model.

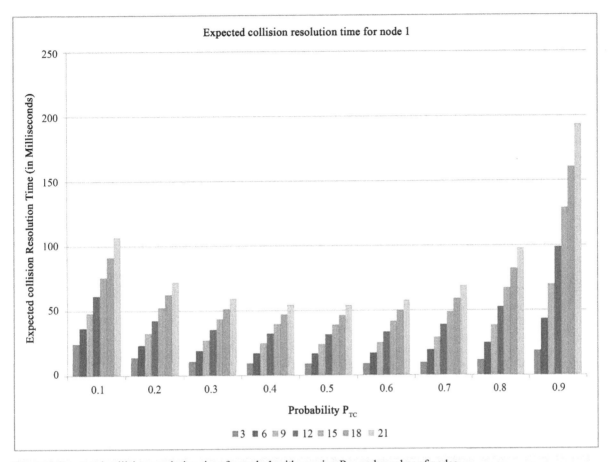

Figure 6. Expected collision resolution time for node 1 with varying P_{TC} and number of nodes.

Table 1. Probability of successful transmission by node $n1$ with varying the time deadline and number of nodes.

Finish Time T (ms)	N = 3	N = 6	N = 9	N = 12	N = 15	N = 18	N = 21
10	0.93	0.53	0.32	0.23	0.17	0.14	0.11
15	0.99	0.83	0.52	0.38	0.32	0.25	0.21
20	0.99	0.95	0.74	0.53	0.41	0.34	0.28
25	0.99	0.98	0.89	0.68	0.53	0.43	0.37
30	0.99	0.99	0.96	0.83	0.65	0.53	0.45
35	0.99	0.99	0.99	0.92	0.78	0.63	0.53
40	0.99	0.99	0.99	0.97	0.88	0.73	0.62
45	0.99	0.99	0.99	0.99	0.94	0.83	0.71
50	0.99	0.99	0.99	0.99	0.98	0.91	0.79
60	0.99	0.99	0.99	0.99	0.99	0.98	0.92
70	0.99	0.99	0.99	0.99	0.99	0.99	0.98
80	0.99	0.99	0.99	0.99	0.99	0.99	0.99

6. Conclusions

We formalized 2CS-WSN collision resolution protocol as Markov Decision Process and performed quantitative analysis using probabilistic model checking techniques implemented in the model checker PRISM. We have analyzed quantitative properties such as "probability of node 1 to transmit successfully within 20 seconds". From experimental results, we infer that probability of transmission $P_{TC} \simeq 0.4$ or 0.5 and waiting cells $\simeq 5$ can be considered as a best configuration option to minimize collision resolution time.

In collision resolution protocol, all nodes are identical; behavior of all nodes is similar. In protocol model, as the number of node increases, state space explosion problem arises. We have successfully applied "Explicit-PRISMSymm" on-the-fly symmetry reduction technique to prevent the state explosion in probabilistic model checking and make the protocol analysis with large number of nodes feasible.

References

[1]   Yick, J., Mukherjee, B. and Ghosal, D. (2008) Wireless Sensor Network Survey. *Computer Networks, Science Direct,* **52**, 2292-2330. http://dx.doi.org/10.1016/j.comnet.2008.04.002

[2]   Akyildiz, I.F., Weilian, S., Sankarasubramaniam, Y. and Cayirci, E. (2002) A Survey on Sensor Networks. *IEEE Communications Magazine*, **40**, 102-114. http://dx.doi.org/10.1109/MCOM.2002.1024422

[3]   Rawat, P., Singh, K., Chaouchi, H. and Bonnin, J. (2014) Wireless Sensor Networks: A Survey on Recent Developments and Potential Synergies. *The Journal of Supercomputing*, **68**, 1-48.
       http://dx.doi.org/10.1007/s11227-013-1021-9

[4]   Paterakis, M. and Papantoni-Kazakos, P. (1988) A Simple Window Random Access Algorithm with Advantageous Properties. *Proceedings of the 7th Annual Joint Conference of the IEEE Computer and Communications Societies, Networks: Evolution or Revolution (INFOCOM'88)*, New Orleans, 27-31 March 1988, 907-915.
       http://dx.doi.org/10.1109/infcom.1988.13006

[5]   (2006) IEEE Standard for Information Technology—Local and Metropolitan Area Networks—Specific Requirements—Part 15.4: Wireless Medium Access Control (MAC) and Physical Layer (PHY) Specifications for Low Rate Wireless Personal Area Networks (WPANs). IEEE Std 802.15.4-2006 (Revision of IEEE Std 802.15.4-2003), 1-320.
       http://dx.doi.org/10.1109/IEEESTD.2006.232110

[6]   Hinton, A., Kwiatkowska, M., Norman, G. and Parker, D. (2006) PRISM: A Tool for Automatic Verification of Probabilistic Systems. *Proceedings of the 12th International Conference on Tools and Algorithms for the Construction and Analysis of Systems* (TACAS'06), Vienna, 25 March-2 April 2006, 441-444. http://dx.doi.org/10.1007/11691372_29

[7]   Rutten, J.J.M.M., Kwiatkowska, M., Norman, G. and Parker, D. (2004) Mathematical Techniques for Analyzing Concurrent and Probabilistic Systems. CRM Monograph Series, American Mathematical Society, 23.
       http://qav.comlab.ox.ac.uk/bibitem.php?key=KNP04a

[8]   Mateo, J.A., Macià, H., Ruiz, M.C., Calleja, J. and Royo, F. (2015) Probabilistic Model Checking: One Step Forward in Wireless Sensor Networks Simulation. *International Journal of Distributed Sensor Networks*, **2015**, Article ID: 285396. http://dx.doi.org/10.1155/2015/285396

[9]   Patel, R., Patel, K. and Patel, D. (2015) ExplicitPRISMSymm: Symmetry Reduction Technique for Explicit Models in PRISM. *Proceedings of the 12th Annual Conference on Theory and Applications of Models of Computation* (TAMC'15), Singapore, 18-20 May 2015, 400-412. http://dx.doi.org/10.1007/978-3-319-17142-5_34

[10]   Dave Parker, G.N. and Kwiatkowska, M. PRISM Case Studies.
       http://www.prismmodelchecker.org/casestudies/index.php

[11]   Katoen, J.P. (2010) Advances in Probabilistic Model Checking. *Proceedings of the 11th International Conference on Verification, Model Checking, and Abstract Interpretation* (VMCAI'10), Madrid, 17-19 January 2010, 25-25.
       http://dx.doi.org/10.1007/978-3-642-11319-2_5

[12]   Kwiatkowska, M., Norman, G. and Parker, D. (2002) PRISM: Probabilistic Symbolic Model Checker. *Proceedings of the 12th International Conference on Computer Performance Evaluation: Modelling Techniques and Tools* (TOOLS'02), London, 14-17 April 2002, 200-204. http://dx.doi.org/10.1007/3-540-46029-2_13

[13]   Fujita, M., McGeer, P.C. and Yang, J.C.Y. (1997) Multi-Terminal Binary Decision Diagrams: An Efficient Data Structure for Matrix Representation. *Formal Methods in System Design*, **10**, 149-169.
       http://dx.doi.org/10.1023/A:1008647823331

[14]   Sistla, P. (2004) Employing Symmetry Reductions in Model Checking. *Computer Languages, Systems and Structures*, **30**, 99-137. http://dx.doi.org/10.1016/j.cl.2004.02.002

[15]   Miller, A., Donaldson, A. and Calder, M. (2006) Symmetry in Temporal Logic Model Checking. *ACM Computing*

Surveys, **38**, Article No. 8. http://dx.doi.org/10.1145/1132960.1132962

[16] Wahl, T., and Donaldson, A.F. (2010) Replication and Abstraction: Symmetry in Automated Formal Verification. *Symmetry*, **2**, 799-847. http://dx.doi.org/10.3390/sym2020799

[17] Kwiatkowska, M., Norman, G. and Parker, D. (2006) Symmetry Reduction for Probabilistic Model Checking. *Proceedings of the 18th International Conference on Computer Aided Verification (CAV'06)*, Seattle, 17-20 August 2006, 234-248. http://dx.doi.org/10.1007/11817963_23

[18] Royo, F., Lopez-Guerrero, M., Orozco-Barbosa, L. and Olivares, T. (2009) 2C-WSN: A Configuration Protocol Based on TDMA Communications over WSN. *Proceedings of the 28th IEEE Conference on Global Telecommunications (GLOBECOM'09)*, Honolulu, 30 November-4 December 2009, 4057-4062. http://dx.doi.org/10.1109/glocom.2009.5425742

[19] Pnueli, A., Xu, J. and Zuck, L.D. (2002) Liveness with (0, 1, Infty)-Counter Abstraction. *Proceedings of the 14th International Conference on Computer Aided Verification (CAV'02)*, Denmark, July 27-31 2002, 107-122. http://dx.doi.org/10.1007/3-540-45657-0_9

[20] Ballarini, P. and Miller, A. (2006) Model Checking Medium Access Control for Sensor Networks. *Proceedings of the 2nd International Symposium on Leveraging Applications of Formal Methods, Verification and Validation (ISoLA)*, Paphos, 15-19 November 2006, 255-262. http://dx.doi.org/10.1109/isola.2006.16

12

Data Modeling and Data Analytics: A Survey from a Big Data Perspective

André Ribeiro, Afonso Silva, Alberto Rodrigues da Silva

INESC-ID/Instituto Superior Técnico, Lisbon, Portugal

Email: andre.ribeiro@tecnico.ulisboa.pt, afonso.silva@tecnico.ulisboa.pt, alberto.silva@tecnico.ulisboa.pt

Abstract

These last years we have been witnessing a tremendous growth in the volume and availability of data. This fact results primarily from the emergence of a multitude of sources (e.g. computers, mobile devices, sensors or social networks) that are continuously producing either structured, semi-structured or unstructured data. Database Management Systems and Data Warehouses are no longer the only technologies used to store and analyze datasets, namely due to the volume and complex structure of nowadays data that degrade their performance and scalability. Big Data is one of the recent challenges, since it implies new requirements in terms of data storage, processing and visualization. Despite that, analyzing properly Big Data can constitute great advantages because it allows discovering patterns and correlations in datasets. Users can use this processed information to gain deeper insights and to get business advantages. Thus, data modeling and data analytics are evolved in a way that we are able to process huge amounts of data without compromising performance and availability, but instead by "relaxing" the usual ACID properties. This paper provides a broad view and discussion of the current state of this subject with a particular focus on data modeling and data analytics, describing and clarifying the main differences between the three main approaches in what concerns these aspects, namely: operational databases, decision support databases and Big Data technologies.

Keywords

Data Modeling, Data Analytics, Modeling Language, Big Data

1. Introduction

We have been witnessing to an exponential growth of the volume of data produced and stored. This can be explained by the evolution of the technology that results in the proliferation of data with different formats from the most various domains (e.g. health care, banking, government or logistics) and sources (e.g. sensors, social networks or mobile devices). We have assisted a paradigm shift from simple books to sophisticated databases that keep being populated every second at an immensely fast rate. Internet and social media also highly contribute to the worsening of this situation [1]. Facebook, for example, has an average of 4.75 billion pieces of content shared among friends every day [2]. Traditional Relational Database Management Systems (RDBMSs) and Data Warehouses (DWs) are designed to handle a certain amount of data, typically structured, which is completely different from the reality that we are facing nowadays. Business is generating enormous quantities of data that are too big to be processed and analyzed by the traditional RDBMSs and DWs technologies, which are struggling to meet the performance and scalability requirements.

Therefore, in the recent years, a new approach that aims to mitigate these limitations has emerged. Companies like Facebook, Google, Yahoo and Amazon are the pioneers in creating solutions to deal with these "Big Data" scenarios, namely recurring to technologies like Hadoop [3] [4] and MapReduce [5]. Big Data is a generic term used to refer to massive and complex datasets, which are made of a variety of data structures (structured, semi-structured and unstructured data) from a multitude of sources [6]. Big Data can be characterized by three Vs: volume (amount of data), velocity (speed of data in and out) and variety (kinds of data types and sources) [7]. Still, there are added some other Vs for variability, veracity and value [8].

Adopting Big Data-based technologies not only mitigates the problems presented above, but also opens new perspectives that allow extracting value from Big Data. Big Data-based technologies are being applied with success in multiple scenarios [1] [9] [10] like in: (1) e-commerce and marketing, where count the clicks that the crowds do on the web allow identifying trends that improve campaigns, evaluate personal profiles of a user, so that the content shown is the one he will most likely enjoy; (2) government and public health, allowing the detection and tracking of disease outbreaks via social media or detect frauds; (3) transportation, industry and surveillance, with real-time improved estimated times of arrival and smart use of resources.

This paper provides a broad view of the current state of this area based on two dimensions or perspectives: Data Modeling and Data Analytics. **Table 1** summarizes the focus of this paper, namely by identifying three representative approaches considered to explain the evolution of Data Modeling and Data Analytics. These approaches are: Operational databases, Decision Support databases and Big Data technologies.

This research work has been conducted in the scope of the DataStorm project [11], led by our research group, which focuses on addressing the design, implementation and operation of the current problems with Big Data-based applications. More specifically, the goal of our team in this project is to identify the main concepts and patterns that characterize such applications, in order to define and apply suitable domain-specific languages (DSLs). Then these DSLs will be used in a Model-Driven Engineering (MDE) [12]-[14] approach aiming to ease the design, implementation and operation of such data-intensive applications.

To ease the explanation and better support the discussion throughout the paper, we use a very simple case study based on a fictions academic management system described below:

Case Study—Academic Management System (AMS):

The Academic Management System (AMS) should support two types of end-users: students and professors. Each person has a name, gender, date of birth, ID card, place of origin and country. Students are enrolled in a given academic program, which is composed of many courses. Professors have an academic degree, are associated to a given department and lecture one or more courses. Each course has a name, academic term and can have one or more locations and academic programs associated. Additionally, a course is associated to a schedule composed of many class periods determining its duration and the day it occurs.

The outline of this paper is as follows: Section 2 describes Data Modeling and some representative types of data models used in operational databases, decision support databases and Big Data technologies. Section 3 details the type of operations performed in terms of Data Analytics for these three approaches. Section 4 compares and discusses each approach in terms of the Data Modeling and Data Analytics perspectives. Section 5 discusses our research in comparison with the related work. Finally, Section 6 concludes the paper by summarizing its key points and identifying future work.

2. Data Modeling

This section gives an in-depth look of the most popular data models used to define and support Operational Databases, Data Warehouses and Big Data technologies.

Table 1. Approaches and perspectives of the survey.

Approaches	Operational	Decision Support	Big Data
Data Modeling Perspective	ER and Relational Models	Star Schema and OLAP Cube Models	Key-Value, Document, Wide-Column and Graph
	RDBMS	DW	Big Data-Based Systems
Data Analytics Perspective	OLTP	OLAP	Multiple Classes (Batch-oriented processing, stream-processing, OLTP and Interactive ad-hoc queries)

Databases are widely used either for personal or enterprise use, namely due to their strong ACID guarantees (atomicity, consistency, isolation and durability) guarantees and the maturity level of Database Management Systems (DBMSs) that support them [15].

The data modeling process may involve the definition of three data models (or schemas) defined at different abstraction levels, namely Conceptual, Logical and Physical data models [15] [16]. **Figure 1** shows part of the three data models for the AMS case study. All these models define three entities (Person, Student and Professor) and their main relationships (teach and supervise associations).

Conceptual Data Model. A conceptual data model is used to define, at a very high and platform-independent level of abstraction, the entities or concepts, which represent the data of the problem domain, and their relationships. It leaves further details about the entities (such as their attributes, types or primary keys) for the next steps. This model is typically used to explore domain concepts with the stakeholders and can be omitted or used instead of the logical data model.

Logical Data Model. A logical data model is a refinement of the previous conceptual model. It details the domain entities and their relationships, but standing also at a platform-independent level. It depicts all the attributes that characterize each entity (possibly also including its unique identifier, the primary key) and all the relationships between the entities (possibly including the keys identifying those relationships, the foreign keys). Despite being independent of any DBMS, this model can easily be mapped on to a physical data model thanks to the details it provides.

Physical Data Model. A physical data model visually represents the structure of the data as implemented by a given class of DBMS. Therefore, entities are represented as tables, attributes are represented as table columns and have a given data type that can vary according to the chosen DBMS, and the relationships between each table are identified through foreign keys. Unlike the previous models, this model tends to be platform-specific, because it reflects the database schema and, consequently, some platform-specific aspects (e.g. database-specific data types or query language extensions).

Summarizing, the complexity and detail increase from a conceptual to a physical data model. First, it is important to perceive at a higher level of abstraction, the data entities and their relationships using a Conceptual Data Model. Then, the focus is on detailing those entities without worrying about implementation details using a Logical Data Model. Finally, a Physical Data Model allows to represent how data is supported by a given DBMS [15] [16].

2.1. Operational Databases

Databases had a great boost with the popularity of the Relational Model [17] proposed by E. F. Codd in 1970. The Relational Model overcame the problems of predecessors data models (namely the Hierarchical Model and the Navigational Model [18]). The Relational Model caused the emergence of Relational Database Management Systems (RDBMSs), which are the most used and popular DBMSs, as well as the definition of the Structured Query Language (SQL) [19] as the standard language for defining and manipulating data in RDBMSs. RDBMSs are widely used for maintaining data of daily operations. Considering the data modeling of operational databases there are two main models: the Relational and the Entity-Relationship (ER) models.

Relational Model. The Relational Model is based on the mathematical concept of relation. A relation is defined as a set (in mathematics terminology) and is represented as a table, which is a matrix of columns and rows, holding information about the domain entities and the relationships among them. Each column of the table corresponds to an entity attribute and specifies the attribute's name and its type (known as domain). Each row of

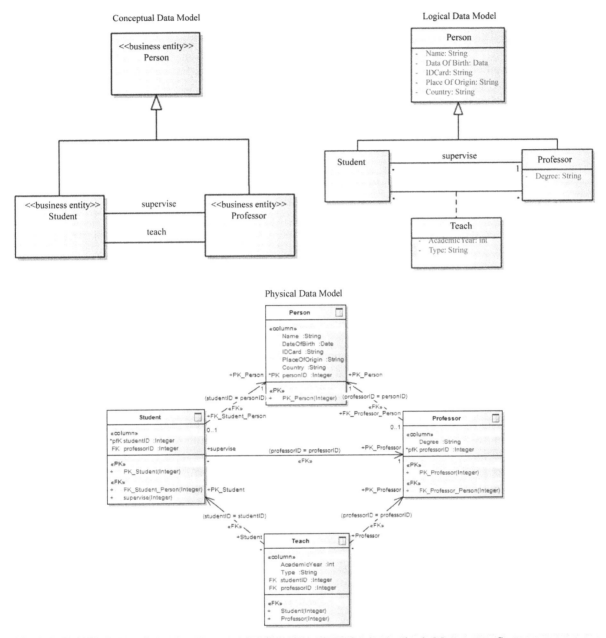

Figure 1. Example of three data models (at different abstraction levels) for the Academic Management System.

the table (known as tuple) corresponds to a single element of the represented domain entity. In the Relational Model each row is unique and therefore a table has an attribute or set of attributes known as **primary key**, used to univocally identify those rows. Tables are related with each other by sharing one or more common attributes. These attributes correspond to a primary key in the referenced (parent) table and are known as **foreign keys** in the referencing (child) table. In **one-to-many relationships**, the referenced table corresponds to the entity of the "one" side of the relationship and the referencing table corresponds to the entity of the "many" side. In **many-to-many relationships**, it is used an additional association table that associates the entities involved through their respective primary keys. The Relational Model also features the concept of **View**, which is like a table whose rows are not explicitly stored in the database, but are computed as needed from a view definition. Instead, a view is defined as a query on one or more base tables or other views [17].

  Entity-Relationship (ER) Model. The Entity Relationship (ER) Model [20], proposed by Chen in 1976, appeared as an alternative to the Relational Model in order to provide more expressiveness and semantics into the database design from the user's point of view. The ER model is a semantic data model, *i.e.* aims to represent the meaning of the data involved on some specific domain. This model was originally defined by three main concepts: entities, relationships and attributes. An **entity** corresponds to an object in the real world that is distinguishable from all other objects and is characterized by a set of attributes. Each **attribute** has a range of possible values, known as its domain, and each entity has its own value for each attribute. Similarly to the Relational Model, the set of attributes that identify an entity is known as its primary key.

Entities can be though as **nouns** and correspond to the tables of the Relational Model. In turn, a **relationship** is an association established among two or more entities. A relationship can be thought as a *verb* and includes the roles of each participating entities with multiplicity constraints, and their cardinality. For instance, a relationship can be of one-to-one (1:1), one-to-many (1:M) or many-to-many (M:N). In an ER diagram, entities are usually represented as rectangles, attributes as circles connected to entities or relationships through a line, and relationships as diamonds connected to the intervening entities through a line.

The Enhanced ER Model [21] provided additional concepts to represent more complex requirements, such as generalization, specialization, aggregation and composition. Other popular variants of ER diagram notations are Crow's foot, Bachman, Barker's, IDEF1X and UML Profile for Data Modeling [22].

2.2. Decision Support Databases

The evolution of relational databases to decision support databases, hereinafter indistinctly referred as "**Data Warehouses**" **(DWs)**, occurred with the need of storing operational but also historical data, and the need of analyzing that data in complex dashboards and reports. Even though a DW seems to be a relational database, it is different in the sense that DWs are more suitable for supporting query and analysis operations (fast reads) instead of transaction processing (fast reads and writes) operations. DWs contain historical data that come from transactional data, but they also might include other data sources [23]. DWs are mainly used for **OLAP (online analytical processing)** operations. OLAP is the approach to provide report data from DW through multi-dimensional queries and it is required to create a multi-dimensional database [24].

Usually, DWs include a framework that allows extracting data from multiple data sources and transform it before loading to the repository, which is known as ETL (Extract Transform Load) framework [23].

Data modeling in DW consists in defining fact tables with several dimension tables, suggesting **star or snowflake schema** data models [23]. A star schema has a central **fact table** linked with **dimension tables**. Usually, a fact table has a large number of attributes (in many cases in a denormalized way), with many foreign keys that are the primary keys to the dimension tables. The dimension tables represent characteristics that describe the fact table. When star schemas become too complex to be queried efficiently they are transformed into multi-dimensional arrays of data called **OLAP cubes** (for more information on how this transformation is performed the reader can consult the following references [24] [25]).

A star schema is transformed to a cube by putting the fact table on the front face that we are facing and the dimensions on the other faces of the cube [24]. For this reason, cubes can be equivalent to star schemas in content, but they are accessed with more platform-specific languages than SQL that have more analytic capabilities (e.g. MDX or XMLA). A cube with three dimensions is conceptually easier to visualize and understand, but the OLAP cube model supports more than three dimensions, and is called a hypercube.

Figure 2 shows two examples of star schemas regarding the case study AMS. The star schema on the left represents the data model for the Student's fact, while the data model on the right represents the Professor's fact. Both of them have a central fact table that contains specific attributes of the entity in analysis and also foreign keys to the dimension tables. For example, a Student has a place of origin (DIM_PLACEOFORIGIN) that is described by a city and associated to a country (DIM_COUNTRY) that has a name and an ISO code. On the other hand, **Figure 3** shows a cube model with three dimensions for the Student. These dimensions are represented by sides of the cube (Student, Country and Date). This cube is useful to execute queries such as: the students by country enrolled for the first time in a given year.

A challenge that DWs face is the growth of data, since it affects the number of dimensions and levels in either the star schema or the cube hierarchies. The increasing number of dimensions over time makes the management of such systems often impracticable; this problem becomes even more serious when dealing with Big Data scenarios, where data is continuously being generated [23].

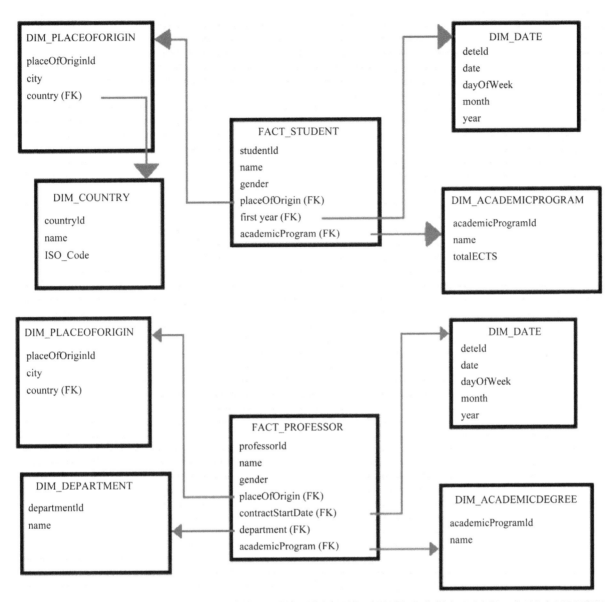

Figure 2. Example of two star schema models for the Academic Management System.

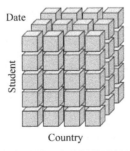

Figure 3. Example of a cube model for the
Academic Management System.

2.3. Big Data Technologies

The volume of data has been exponentially increasing over the last years, namely due to the simultaneous growth of the number of sources (e.g. users, systems or sensors) that are continuously producing data. These data sources produce huge amounts of data with variable representations that make their management by the traditional RDBMSs and DWs often impracticable. Therefore, there is a need to devise new data models and technologies that can handle such Big Data.

NoSQL (Not Only SQL) [26] is one of the most popular approaches to deal with this problem. It consists in a group of non-relational DBMSs that consequently do not represent databases using tables and usually do not use SQL for data manipulation. NoSQL systems allow managing and storing large-scale denormalized datasets, and are designed to scale horizontally. They achieve that by compromising consistency in favor of availability and partition-tolerance, according to Brewer's CAP theorem [27]. Therefore, NoSQL systems are "eventually consistent", *i.e.* assume that writes on the data are eventually propagated over time, but there are limited guarantees that different users will read the same value at the same time. NoSQL provides BASE guarantees (Basically Available, Soft state and Eventually consistent) instead of the traditional ACID guarantees, in order to greatly improve performance and scalability [28].

NoSQL databases can be classified in four categories [29]: Key-value stores, (2) Document-oriented databases, (3) Wide-column stores, and (4) Graph databases.

Key-value Stores. A Key-Value store represents data as a collection (known as dictionary or map) of key-value pairs. Every *key* consists in a unique alphanumeric identifier that works like an index, which is used to access a corresponding value. *Values* can be simple text strings or more complex structures like arrays. The Key-value model can be extended to an ordered model whose keys are stored in lexicographical order. The fact of being a simple data model makes Key-value stores ideally suited to retrieve information in a very fast, available and scalable way. For instance, Amazon makes extensive use of a Key-value store system, named Dynamo, to manage the products in its shopping cart [30]. Amazon's Dynamo and Voldemort, which is used by Linkedin, are two examples of systems that apply this data model with success. An example of a key-value store for both students and professors of the Academic Managements System is shown in **Figure 4**.

Document-oriented Databases. Document-oriented databases (or document stores) were originally created to store traditional documents, like a notepad text file or Microsoft Word document. However, their concept of document goes beyond that, and a document can be any kind of domain object [26]. Documents contain encoded data in a standard format like XML, YAML, JSON or BSON (Binary JSON) and are univocally identified in the database by a unique key. Documents contain semi-structured data represented as name-value pairs, which can vary according to the row and can nest other documents. Unlike key-value stores, these systems support secondary indexes and allow fully searching either by keys or values. Document databases are well suited for storing and managing huge collections of textual documents (e.g. text files or email messages), as well as semi-structured or denormalized data that would require an extensive use of "nulls" in an RDBMS [30]. MongoDB and CouchDB are two of the most popular Document-oriented database systems. **Figure 5** illustrates two collections of documents for both students and professors of the Academic Management System.

Students	
Key	Value
1	Name: Jean Grey DateOfBirth: 19-05-1963 IDCard: 1234567 PlaceOfOrigin: Austin Country: USA AcademicProgram_ID:1

2	Name: Scott Summers
	DateOfBirth: 12-10-1968
	IDCard: 765414A
	Supervisor: {
	  Name: Emma Frost
	  DateOfBirth: 1-1-1936
	  IDCard: 222222
	}

Professors	
Key	Value
1	Name: Charles Xavier DateOfBirth: 13-07-1940 IDCard: 111111 PlaceOfOrigin: Mirfield Country: UK
2	Name: Emma Frost DateOfBirth: 1-1-1936 IDCard: 222222

Figure 4. Example of a key-value store for the Academic Management System.

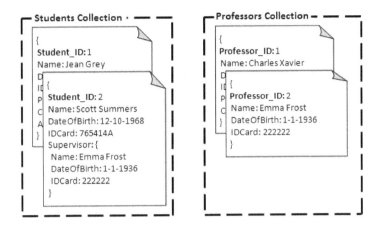

Figure 5. Example of a documents-oriented database for the Academic
Management System.

Wide-column Stores. Wide-column stores (also known as column-family stores, extensible record stores or column-oriented databases) represent and manage data as sections of columns rather than rows (like in RDBMS). Each section is composed of key-value pairs, where the keys are rows and the values are sets of columns, known as column families. Each row is identified by a primary key and can have column families different of the other rows. Each column family also acts as a primary key of the set of columns it contains. In turn each column of column family consists in a name-value pair. Column families can even be grouped in super column families [29]. This data model was highly inspired by Google's BigTable [31]. Wide-column stores are suited for scenarios like: (1) Distributed data storage; (2) Large-scale and batch-oriented data processing, using the famous MapReduce method for tasks like sorting, parsing, querying or conversion and; (3) Exploratory and predictive analytics. Cassandra and Hadoop HBase are two popular frameworks of such data management systems [29]. **Figure 6** depicts an example of a wide-column store for the entity "person" of the Academic Managements System.

Graph Databases. Graph databases represent data as a network of nodes (representing the domain entities) that are connected by edges (representing the relationships among them) and are characterized by properties expressed as key-value pairs. Graph databases are quite useful when the focus is on exploring the relationships between data, such as traversing social networks, detecting patterns or infer recommendations. Due to their visual representation, they are more user-friendly than the aforementioned types of NoSQL databases. Neo4j and Allegro Graph are two examples of such systems.

3. Data Analytics

This section presents and discusses the types of operations that can be performed over the data models described in the previous section and also establishes comparisons between them. A complementary discussion is provided in Section 4.

3.1. Operational Databases

Systems using operational databases are designed to handle a high number of transactions that usually perform changes to the operational data, *i.e.* the data an organization needs to assure its everyday normal operation. These systems are called **Online Transaction Processing (OLTP)** systems and they are the reason why RDBMSs are so essential nowadays. RDBMSs have increasingly been optimized to perform well in OLTP systems, namely providing reliable and efficient data processing [16].

The set of operations supported by RDBMSs is derived from the relational algebra and calculus underlying the Relational Model [15]. As mentioned before, SQL is the standard language to perform these operations. SQL can be divided in two parts involving different types of operations: Data Definition Language (SQL-DDL) and Data Manipulation Language (SQL-DML).

SQL-DDL allows performing the creation (CREATE), update (UPDATE) and deletion (DROP) of the vari-

Column Family: Students					
Key				Columns	
1	Name	DateOfBirth	IDCard	PlaceOfOrigin	Country
	Jean Grey	19-05-1963	1234567	Austin	USA
2	Name	DateOfBirth	IDCard	Supervisor	
	Scott Summers	12-10-1968	765414A	Name	DateOfBirth	IDCard
				Emma Frost	1-1-1936	222222

Column Family: Professors					
Key				Columns	
1	Name	DateOfBirth	IDCard	PlaceOfOrigin	Country
	Charles Xavier	13-07-1940	111111	Mirfield	UK
2	Name	DateOfBirth	IDCard		
	Emma Frost	1-1-1936	222222		

Figure 6. Example of a wide-column store for the Academic Management System.

ous database objects. First it allows managing schemas, which are named collections of all the database objects that are related to one another. Then inside a schema, it is possible to manage tables specifying their columns and types, primary keys, foreign keys and constraints. It is also possible to manage views, domains and indexes. An index is a structure that speeds up the process of accessing to one or more columns of a given table, possibly improving the performance of queries [15] [16].

For example, considering the Academic Management System, a system manager could create a table for storing information of a student by executing the following SQL-DDL command:

```
CREATE TABLE Student (
    Student ID NOT NULL IDENTITY,
    Name VARCHAR(255) NOT NULL,
    Date of Birth DATE NOT NULL,
    ID Card VARCHAR(255) NOT NULL,
    Place of Origin VARCHAR(255),
    Country VARCHAR(255),
    PRIMARY KEY (Student ID))
```

On the other hand, **SQL-DML** is the language that enables to manipulate database objects and particularly to extract valuable information from the database. The most commonly used and complex operation is the SELECT operation, which allows users to query data from the various tables of a database. It is a powerful operation because it is capable of performing in a single query the equivalent of the relational algebra's selection, projection and join operations. The SELECT operation returns as output a table with the results. With the SELECT operation is simultaneously possible to: define which tables the user wants to query (through the FROM clause), which rows satisfy a particular condition (through the WHERE clause), which columns should appear in the result (through the SELECT clause), order the result (in ascending or descending order) by one or more columns (through the ORDER BY clause), group rows with the same column values (through the GROUP BY clause) and filter those groups based on some condition (through the HAVING clause). The SELECT operation also allows using aggregation functions, which perform arithmetic computation or aggregation of data (e.g. counting or summing the values of one or more columns).

Many times there is the need to combine columns of more than one table in the result. To do that, the user can use the JOIN operation in the query. This operation performs a subset of the Cartesian product between the involved tables, *i.e.* returns the row pairs where the matching columns in each table have the same value. The most common queries that use joins involve tables that have one-to-many relationships. If the user wants to include in the result the rows that did not satisfied the join condition, then he can use the outer joins operations (left, right and full outer join). Besides specifying queries, DML allows modifying the data stored in a database. Namely, it allows adding new rows to a table (through the INSERT statement), modifying the content of a given table's rows (through the UPDATE statement) and deleting rows from a table (through the DELETE statement) [16].

SQL-DML also allows combining the results of two or more queries into a single result table by applying the Union, Intersect and Except operations, based on the Set Theory [15].

For example, considering the Academic Management System, a system manager could get a list of all students who are from G8 countries by entering the following SQL-DML query:

SELECT Name, Country
FROM Student
WHERE Country in ("Canada", "France", "Germany", "Italy", "Japan", "Russia", "UK", "USA")
ORDER BY Country

3.2. Decision Support Databases

The most common data model used in DW is the OLAP cube, which offers a set of operations to analyze the cube model [23]. Since data is conceptualized as a cube with hierarchical dimensions, its operations have familiar names when manipulating a cube, such as slice, dice, drill and pivot. **Figure 7** depicts these operations considering the Student's facts of the AMS case study (see **Figure 2**).

The **slice** operation begins by selecting one of the dimensions (or faces) of the cube. This dimension is the one we want to consult and it is followed by "slicing" the cube to a specific depth of interest. The slice operation leaves us with a more restricted selection of the cube, namely the dimension we wanted (front face) and the layer of that dimension (the sliced section). In the example of **Figure 7** (top-left), the cube was sliced to consider only data of the year 2004.

Dice is the operation that allows restricting the front face of the cube by reducing its size to a smaller targeted domain. This means that the user produces a smaller "front face" than the one he had at the start. **Figure 7** (top-right) shows that the set of students has decreased after the dice operation.

Drill is the operation that allows to navigate by specifying different levels of the dimensions, ranging from the most detailed ones (**drill down**) to the most summarized ones (**drill up**). **Figure 7** (bottom-left) shows the drill down so the user can see the cities from where the students of the country Portugal come from.

The **pivot** operation allows changing the dimension that is being faced (change the current front face) to one that is adjacent to it by rotating the cube. By doing this, the user obtains another perspective of the data, which requires the queries to have a different structure but can be more beneficial for specific queries. For instance, he can slice and dice the cube away to get the results he needed, but sometimes with a pivot most of those operations can be avoided by perceiving a common structure on future queries and pivoting the cube in the correct fashion [23] [24]. **Figure 7** (bottom-right) shows a pivot operation where years are arranged vertically and countries horizontally.

The usual operations issued over the OLAP cube are about just querying historical events stored in it. So,

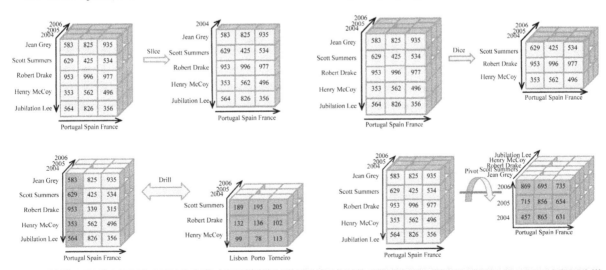

Figure 7. Representation of cube operations for the Academic Management System: slice (top-left), dice (top-right), drill up/down (bottom-left) and pivot (bottom-right).

a common dimension is a dimension associated to time. The most popular language for manipulating OLAP cubes is MDX (Multidimensional Expressions) [32], which is a query language for OLAP databases that supports all the operations mentioned above. MDX is exclusively used to analyze and read data since it was not designed with SQL-DML in mind. The star schema and the OLAP cube are designed *a priori* with a specific purpose in mind and cannot accept queries that differentiate much from the ones they were design to respond too. The benefit in this, is that queries are much simpler and faster, and by using a cube it is even quicker to detect patterns, find trends and navigate around the data while "slicing and dicing" with it [23] [25].

Again considering the Academic Management System example, the following query represents an MDX select statement. The SELECT clause sets the query axes as the name and the gender of the Student dimension and the year 2015 of the Date dimension. The FROM clause indicates the data source, here being the Students cube, and the WHERE clause defines the slicer axis as the "Computer Science" value of the Academic Program dimension. This query returns the students (by names and gender) that have enrolled in Computer Science in the year 2015.

```
SELECT
    { [Student].[Name],
      [Student].[Gender]} ON COLUMNS
    { [Date].[Academic Year] &[2015] } ON ROWS
FROM [Students Cube]
WHERE ([Academic Program].[Name] &[Computer Science])
```

3.3. Big Data Technologies

Big Data Analytics consists in the process of discovering and extracting potentially useful information hidden in huge amounts of data (e.g. discover unknown patterns and correlations). Big Data Analytics can be separated in the following categories: (1) Batch-oriented processing; (2) Stream processing; (3) OLTP and; (4) Interactive ad-hoc queries and analysis.

Batch-oriented processing is a paradigm where a large volume of data is firstly stored and only then analyzed, as opposed to Stream processing. This paradigm is very common to perform large-scale recurring tasks in parallel like parsing, sorting or counting. The most popular batch-oriented processing model is MapReduce [5], and more specifically its open-source implementation in Hadoop[1]. MapReduce is based on the divide and conquer (D&C) paradigm to break down complex Big Data problems into small sub-problems and process them in parallel. MapReduce, as its name hints, comprises two major functions: Map and Reduce. First, data is divided into small chunks and distributed over a network of nodes. Then, the Map function, which performs operations like filtering or sorting, is applied simultaneously to each chunk of data generating intermediate results. After that, those intermediate results are aggregated through the Reduce function in order to compute the final result. **Figure 8** illustrates an example of the application of MapReduce in order to calculate the number of students enrolled in a given academic program by year. This model schedules computation resources close to data location, which avoids the communication overhead of data transmission. It is simple and widely applied in bioinformatics, web mining and machine learning. Also related to Hadoop's environment, Pig[2] and Hive[3] are two frameworks used to express tasks for Big Data sets analysis in MapReduce programs. Pig is suitable for data flow tasks and can produce sequences of MapReduce programs, whereas Hive is more suitable for data summarization, queries and analysis. Both of them use their own SQL-like languages, Pig Latin and Hive QL, respectively [33]. These languages use both CRUD and ETL operations.

Streaming processing is a paradigm where data is continuously arriving in a stream, at real-time, and is analyzed as soon as possible in order to derive approximate results. It relies in the assumption that the potential value of data depends on its freshness. Due to its volume, only a portion of the stream is stored in memory [33]. Streaming processing paradigm is used in online applications that need real-time precision (e.g. dashboards of production lines in a factory, calculation of costs depending on usage and available resources). It is supported by Data Stream Management Systems (DSMS) that allow performing SQL-like queries (e.g. select, join, group, count) within a given window of data. This window establishes the period of time (based on time) or number of events (based on length) [34]. Storm and S4 are two examples of such systems.

---

[1] https://hadoop.apache.org
[2] https://pig.apache.org
[3] https://hive.apache.org

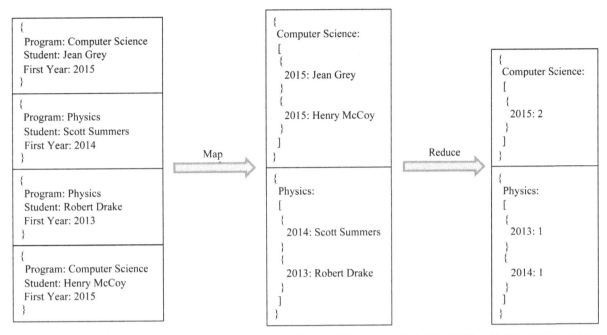

Figure 8. Example of Map Reduce applied to the Academic Management System.

OLTP, as we have seen before, is mainly used in the traditional RDBMS. However, these systems cannot assure an acceptable performance when the volume of data and requests is huge, like in Facebook or Twitter. Therefore, it was necessary to adopt NoSQL databases that allow achieving very high performances in systems with such large loads. Systems like Cassandra[4], HBase[5] or MongoDB[6] are effective solutions currently used. All of them provide their own query languages with equivalent CRUD operations to the ones provided by SQL. For example, in Cassandra is possible to create Column Families using CQL, in HBase is possible to delete a column using Java, and in MongoDB insert a document into a collection using JavaScript. Below there is a query in JavaScript for a MongoDB database equivalent to the SQL-DML query presented previously.

db.students.find({ country: ["Canada", "France", "Germany", "Italy", "Japan", "Russia", "UK", "USA"] }, { name: 1, country: 1 }).
sort({ country: 1 })

At last, **Interactive ad-hoc queries and analysis** consists in a paradigm that allows querying different large-scale data sources and query interfaces with a very low latency. This type of systems argue that queries should not need more then few seconds to execute even in a Big Data scale, so that users are able to react to changes if needed. The most popular of these systems is Drill[7]. Drill works as a query layer that transforms a query written in a human-readable syntax (e.g. SQL) into a logical plan (query written in a platform-independent way). Then, the logical plan is transformed into a physical plan (query written in a platform-specific way) that is executed in the desired data sources (e.g. Cassandra, HBase or MongoDB) [35].

4. Discussion

In this section we compare and discuss the approaches presented in the previous sections in terms of the two perspectives that guide this survey: Data Modeling and Data Analytics. Each perspective defines a set of features used to compare Operational Databases, DWs and Big Data approaches among themselves.

Regarding the ***Data Modeling Perspective***, **Table 2** considers the following features of analysis: (1) the data model; (2) the abstraction level in which the data model resides, according to the abstraction levels (Conceptual, Logical and Physical) of the database design process; (3) the concepts or constructs that compose the data model;

---

[4] http://cassandra.apache.org
[5] https://hbase.apache.org
[6] https://www.mongodb.org
[7] https://drill.apache.org

Table 2. Comparison of the approaches from the Data Modeling Perspective.

Approaches / Features	Data Model	Abstraction Level	Concepts	Concrete Languages	Modeling Tools	DB Tools Support
Operational	Entity-Relationship Model	Conceptual, Logical	Entity Relationship Attribute Primary Key Foreign Key	Chen's, Crow's foot, Bachman's, Barker's, IDEF1X	Sparx Enterprise Architect, Visual Paradigm, Oracle Designer, MySQL Workbench, ER/Studio	
	Relational Model	Logical, Physical	Table Row Attribute Primary Key Foreign Key, View, Index	SQL-DDL, UML Data Profile	Sparx Enterprise Architect, Visual Paradigm, Oracle Designer, MySQL Workbench, ER/Studio	Microsoft SQL Server, Oracle, MySQL, PostgreSQL, IBM DB2
Decision Support	OLAP Cube	Conceptual, Logical	Dimensions, Levels, Cube faces, Time dimension, Local dimension	Common Warehouse Metamodel	Essbase Studio Tool, Enterprise Architect, Visual Paradigm	Oracle Warehouse Builder, Essbase Studio Tool, Microsoft Analysis Services
	Star Schema	Logical, Physical	Fact table, Attributes table, Dimensions, Foreign Key	SQL-DDL, DML, UML Data Model Profile, UML Profile for Modeling Data Warehouse Usage	Enterprise Architect, Visual Paradigm, Oracle SQL Data Modeler	Microsoft SQL Server, Oracle, MySQL, PostgreSQL, IBM DB2
Big Data	Key-Value	Logical, Physical	Key, Value	SQL-DDL, Dynamo Query Language		Dynamo, Voldemort
	Document	Logical, Physical	Document, Primary Key	SQL-DDL, Javascript		MongoDB, CouchDB
	Wide-Column	Logical, Physical	Keyspace, Table, Column, Column Family, Super Column, Primary Key, Index	CQL, Groovy		Cassandra, HBase
	Graph	Logical, Physical	Node, Edge, Property	Cypher Query Language, SPARQL		Neo4j, AllegroGraph

(4) the concrete languages used to produce the data models and that apply the previous concepts; (5) the modeling tools that allow specifying diagrams using those languages and; (6) the database tools that support the data model. **Table 2** presents the values of each feature for each approach. It is possible to verify that the majority of the data models are at a logical and physical level, with the exception of the ER model and the OLAP cube model, which are more abstract and defined at conceptual and logical levels. It is also possible to verify that Big Data has more data models than the other approaches, what can explain the work and proposals that have been conducted over the last years, as well as the absence of a *de facto* data model. In terms of concepts, again Big Data-related data models have a more variety of concepts than the other approaches, ranging from key-value pairs or documents to nodes and edges. Concerning concrete languages, it is concluded that every data model presented in this survey is supported by a SQL-DDL-like language. However, we found that only the operational databases and DWs have concrete languages to express their data models in a graphical way, like Chen's notation for ER model, UML Data Profile for Relational model or CWM [36] for multidimensional DW models. Also, related to that point, there are none modeling tools to express Big Data models. Thus, defining such a modeling language and respective supporting tool for Big Data models constitute an interesting research direction that fills this lack. At last, all approaches have database tools that support the development based on their

data models, with the exception of the ER model that is not directly used by DBMSs.

On the other hand, in terms of the *Data Analytics Perspective*, **Table 3** considers six features of analysis: (1) the class of application domains, which characterizes the approach suitability; (2) the common operations used in the approach, which can be reads and/or writes; (3) the operations types most typically used in the approach; (4) the concrete languages used to specify those operations; (5) the abstraction level of these concrete languages (Conceptual, Logical and Physical); and (6) the technology support of these languages and operations.

Table 3 shows that Big Data is used in more classes of application domains than the operational databases and DWs, which are used for OLTP and OLAP domains, respectively. It is also possible to observe that operational databases are commonly used for reads and writes of small operations (using transactions), because they need to handle fresh and critical data in a daily basis. On the other hand, DWs are mostly suited for read operations, since they perform analysis and data mining mostly with historical data. Big Data performs both reads and writes, but in a different way and at a different scale from the other approaches. Big Data applications are built to perform a huge amount of reads, and if a huge amount of writes is needed, like for OLTP, they sacrifice consistency (using "eventually consistency") in order to achieve great availability and horizontal scalability. Operational databases support their data manipulation operations (e.g. select, insert or delete) using SQL-ML, which has slight variations according to the technology used. DWs also use SQL-ML through the select statement, because their operations (e.g. slice, dice or drill down/up) are mostly reads. DWs also use SQL-based languages, like MDX and XMLA (XML for Analysis) [37], for specifying their operations. On the other hand, regarding Big Data technologies, there is a great variety of languages to manipulate data according to the different class application domains. All of these languages provide equivalent operations to the ones offered by SQL-ML and add new constructs for supporting both ETL, data stream processing (e.g. create stream, window) [34] and MapReduce operations. It is important to note that concrete languages used in the different approaches reside at logical and physical levels, because they are directly used by the supporting software tools.

5. Related Work

As mentioned in Section 1, the main goal of this paper is to present and discuss the concepts surrounding data

Table 3. Comparison of the approaches from the Data Analytics perspective.

Features \ Approaches	Class of Application Domains	Common Operations	Operations	Concrete Languages	Abstraction Level	Technology Support
Operational	OLTP	Read/Write	Select, Insert, Update, Delete, Join, OrderBy, GroupBy	SQL-DML	Logical, Physical	Microsoft SQL Server, Oracle, MySQL, PostgreSQL, IBM DB2
Decision Support	OLAP	Read	Slice, Dice, Drill down, Drill up, Pivot	SQL-DML, MDX, XMLA	Logical, Physical	Microsoft SQL Server, Oracle, MySQL, PostgreSQL, IBM DB2, Microsoft OLAP Provider, Microsoft Analysis Services
Big Data	Batch-oriented processing	Read/Write	Map-Reduce, Select, Insert, Update, Delete, Load, Import, Export, OrderBy, GroupBy	Hive QL, Pig Latin	Logical, Physical	Hadoop, Hive Pig
	Stream processing	Read/Write	Aggregate, Partition, Merge, Join,	SQL stream	Logical, Physical	Storm, S4, Spark
	OLTP	Read/Write	Select, Insert, Update, Delete, Batch, Get, OrderBy, GroupBy	CQL, Java, JavaScript	Logical, Physical	Cassandra, HBase
	Interactive ad-hoc queries and analysis	Read	Select, Insert, Update, Delete, OrderBy, GroupBy	SQL-DML	Logical, Physical	Drill

modeling and data analytics, and their evolution for three representative approaches: operational databases, decision support databases and Big Data technologies. In our survey we have researched related works that also explore and compare these approaches from the data modeling or data analytics point of view.

J.H. ter Bekke provides a comparative study between the Relational, Semantic, ER and Binary data models based on an examination session results [38]. In that session participants had to create a model of a case study, similar to the Academic Management System used in this paper. The purpose was to discover relationships between the modeling approach in use and the resulting quality. Therefore, this study just addresses the data modeling topic, and more specifically only considers data models associated to the database design process.

Several works focus on highlighting the differences between operational databases and data warehouses. For example, R. Hou provides an analysis between operational databases and data warehouses distinguishing them according to their related theory and technologies, and also establishing common points where combining both systems can bring benefits [39]. C. Thomsen and T.B. Pedersen compare open source ETL tools, OLAP clients and servers, and DBMSs, in order to build a Business Intelligence (BI) solution [40].

P. Vassiliadis and T. Sellis conducted a survey that focuses only on OLAP databases and compare various proposals for the logical models behind them. They group the various proposals in just two categories: commercial tools and academic efforts, which in turn are subcategorized in relational model extensions and cube-oriented approaches [41]. However, unlike our survey they do not cover the subject of Big Data technologies.

Several papers discuss the state of the art of the types of data stores, technologies and data analytics used in Big Data scenarios [29] [30] [33] [42], however they do not compare them with other approaches. Recently, P. Chandarana and M. Vijayalakshmi focus on Big Data analytics frameworks and provide a comparative study according to their suitability [35].

Summarizing, none of the following mentioned work provides such a broad analysis like we did in this paper, namely, as far as we know, we did not find any paper that compares simultaneously operational databases, decision support databases and Big Data technologies. Instead, they focused on describing more thoroughly one or two of these approaches

6. Conclusions

In recent years, the term Big Data has appeared to classify the huge datasets that are continuously being produced from various sources and that are represented in a variety of structures. Handling this kind of data represents new challenges, because the traditional RDBMSs and DWs reveal serious limitations in terms of performance and scalability when dealing with such a volume and variety of data. Therefore, it is needed to reinvent the ways in which data is represented and analyzed, in order to be able to extract value from it.

This paper presents a survey focused on both these two perspectives: data modeling and data analytics, which are reviewed in terms of the three representative approaches nowadays: operational databases, decision support databases and Big Data technologies. First, concerning data modeling, this paper discusses the most common data models, namely: relational model and ER model for operational databases; star schema model and OLAP cube model for decision support databases; and key-value store, document-oriented database, wide-column store and graph database for Big Data-based technologies. Second, regarding data analytics, this paper discusses the common operations used for each approach. Namely, it observes that operational databases are more suitable for OLTP applications, decision support databases are more suited for OLAP applications, and Big Data technologies are more appropriate for scenarios like batch-oriented processing, stream processing, OLTP and interactive ad-hoc queries and analysis.

Third, it compares these approaches in terms of the two perspectives and based on some features of analysis. From the data modeling perspective, there are considered features like the data model, its abstraction level, its concepts, the concrete languages used to described, as well as the modeling and database tools that support it. On the other hand, from the data analytics perspective, there are taken into account features like the class of application domains, the most common operations and the concrete languages used to specify those operations. From this analysis, it is possible to verify that there are several data models for Big Data, but none of them is represented by any modeling language, neither supported by a respective modeling tool. This issue constitutes an open research area that can improve the development process of Big Data targeted applications, namely applying a Model-Driven Engineering approach [12]-[14]. Finally, this paper also presents some related work on the data modeling and data analytics areas.

As future work, we consider that this survey may be extended to capture additional aspects and comparison features that are not included in our analysis. It will be also interesting to survey concrete scenarios where Big Data technologies prove to be an asset [43]. Furthermore, this survey constitutes a starting point for our ongoing research goals in the context of the Data Storm and MDD Lingo initiatives. Specifically, we intend to extend existing domain-specific modeling languages, like XIS [44] and XIS-Mobile [45] [46], and their MDE-based framework to support both the data modeling and data analytics of data-intensive applications, such as those researched in the scope of the Data Storm initiative [47]-[50].

Acknowledgements

This work was partially supported by national funds through FCT—Fundação para a Ciência e a Tecnologia, under the projects POSC/EIA/57642/2004, CMUP-EPB/TIC/0053/2013, UID/CEC/50021/2013 and Data Storm Research Line of Excellency funding (EXCL/EEI-ESS/0257/2012).

References

[1]   Mayer-Schönberger, V. and Cukier, K. (2014) Big Data: A Revolution That Will Transform How We Live, Work, and Think. Houghton Mifflin Harcourt, New York.

[2]   Noyes, D. (2015) The Top 20 Valuable Facebook Statistics. https://zephoria.com/top-15-valuable-facebook-statistics

[3]   Shvachko, K., Hairong Kuang, K., Radia, S. and Chansler, R. (2010) The Hadoop Distributed File System. *26th Symposium on Mass Storage Systems and Technologies (MSST)*, Incline Village, 3-7 May 2010, 1-10. http://dx.doi.org/10.1109/msst.2010.5496972

[4]   White, T. (2012) Hadoop: The Definitive Guide. 3rd Edition, O'Reilly Media, Inc., Sebastopol.

[5]   Dean, J. and Ghemawat, S. (2008) MapReduce: Simplified Data Processing on Large Clusters. *Communications*, **51**, 107-113. http://dx.doi.org/10.1145/1327452.1327492

[6]   Hurwitz, J., Nugent, A., Halper, F. and Kaufman, M. (2013) Big Data for Dummies. John Wiley & Sons, Hoboken.

[7]   Beyer, M.A. and Laney, D. (2012) The Importance of "Big Data": A Definition. Gartner. https://www.gartner.com/doc/2057415

[8]   Duncan, A.D. (2014) Focus on the "Three Vs" of Big Data Analytics: Variability, Veracity and Value. Gartner. https://www.gartner.com/doc/2921417/focus-vs-big-data-analytics

[9]   Agrawal, D., Das, S. and El Abbadi, A. (2011) Big Data and Cloud Computing: Current State and Future Opportunities. *Proceedings of the 14th International Conference on Extending Database Technology*, Uppsala, 21-24 March, 530-533. http://dx.doi.org/10.1145/1951365.1951432

[10]   McAfee, A. and Brynjolfsson, E. (2012) Big Data: The Management Revolution. Harvard Business Review.

[11]   DataStorm Project Website. http://dmir.inesc-id.pt/project/DataStorm.

[12]   Stahl, T., Voelter, M. and Czarnecki, K. (2006) Model-Driven Software Development: Technology, Engineering, Management. John Wiley & Sons, Inc., New York.

[13]   Schmidt, D.C. (2006) Guest Editor's Introduction: Model-Driven Engineering. *IEEE Computer*, **39**, 25-31. http://dx.doi.org/10.1109/MC.2006.58

[14]   Silva, A.R. (2015) Model-Driven Engineering: A Survey Supported by the Unified Conceptual Model. *Computer Languages, Systems & Structures*, **43**, 139-155.

[15]   Ramakrishnan, R. and Gehrke, J. (2012) Database Management Systems. 3rd Edition, McGraw-Hill, Inc., New York.

[16]   Connolly, T.M. and Begg, C.E. (2005) Database Systems: A Practical Approach to Design, Implementation, and Management. 4th Edition, Pearson Education, Harlow.

[17]   Codd, E.F. (1970) A Relational Model of Data for Large Shared Data Banks. *Communications of the ACM*, **13**, 377-387. http://dx.doi.org/10.1145/362384.362685

[18]   Bachman, C.W. (1969) Data Structure Diagrams. *ACM SIGMIS Database*, **1**, 4-10. http://dx.doi.org/10.1145/1017466.1017467

[19]   Chamberlin, D.D. and Boyce, R.F. (1974) SEQUEL: A Structured English Query Language. In: *Proceedings of the 1974 ACM SIGFIDET (Now SIGMOD) Workshop on Data Description, Access and Control (SIGFIDET' 74)*, ACM Press, Ann Harbor, 249-264.

[20]   Chen, P.P.S. (1976) The Entity-Relationship Model—Toward a Unified View of Data. *ACM Transactions on Database Systems*, **1**, 9-36. http://dx.doi.org/10.1145/320434.320440

[21] Tanaka, A.K., Navathe, S.B., Chakravarthy, S. and Karlapalem, K. (1991) ER-R, an Enhanced ER Model with Situation-Action Rules to Capture Application Semantics. *Proceedings of the* 10*th International Conference on Entity-Relationship Approach*, San Mateo, 23-25 October 1991, 59-75.

[22] Merson, P. (2009) Data Model as an Architectural View. Technical Note CMU/SEI-2009-TN-024, Software Engineering Institute, Carnegie Mellon.

[23] Kimball, R. and Ross, M. (2013) The Data Warehouse Toolkit: The Complete Guide to Dimensional Modeling. 3rd Edition, John Wiley & Sons, Inc., Indianapolis.

[24] Zhang, D., Zhai, C., Han, J., Srivastava, A. and Oza, N. (2009) Topic Modeling for OLAP on Multidimensional Text Databases: Topic Cube and Its Applications. *Statistical Analysis and Data Mininig*, **2**, 378-395. http://dx.doi.org/10.1002/sam.10059

[25] Gray, J., *et al.* (1997) Data Cube: A Relational Aggregation Operator Generalizing Group-By, Cross-Tab, and Sub-Totals. *Data Mining and Knowledge Discovery*, **1**, 29-53. http://dx.doi.org/10.1023/A:1009726021843

[26] Cattell, R. (2011) Scalable SQL and NoSQL Data Stores. *ACM SIGMOD Record*, **39**, 12-27. http://dx.doi.org/10.1145/1978915.1978919

[27] Gilbert, S. and Lynch, N. (2002) Brewer's Conjecture and the Feasibility of Consistent, Available, Partition-Tolerant Web Services. *ACM SIGACT News*, **33**, 51-59.

[28] Vogels, W. (2009) Eventually Consistent. *Communications of the ACM*, **52**, 40-44. http://dx.doi.org/10.1145/1435417.1435432

[29] Grolinger, K., Higashino, W.A., Tiwari, A. and Capretz, M.A.M. (2013) Data Management in Cloud Environments: NoSQL and NewSQL Data Stores. *Journal of Cloud Computing*: *Advances, Systems and Applications*, **2**, 22. http://dx.doi.org/10.1186/2192-113x-2-22

[30] Moniruzzaman, A.B.M. and Hossain, S.A. (2013) NoSQL Database: New Era of Databases for Big data Analytics-Classification, Characteristics and Comparison. *International Journal of Database Theory and Application*, **6**, 1-14.

[31] Chang, F., *et al.* (2006) Bigtable: A Distributed Storage System for Structured Data. *Proceedings of the 7th Symposium on Operating Systems Design and Implementation* (*OSDI*' 06), Seattle, 6-8 November 2006, 205-218.

[32] Spofford, G., Harinath, S., Webb, C. and Civardi, F. (2005) MDX Solutions: With Microsoft SQL Server Analysis Services 2005 and Hyperion Essbase. John Wiley & Sons, Inc., Indianapolis.

[33] Hu, H., Wen, Y., Chua, T.S. and Li, X. (2014) Toward Scalable Systems for Big Data Analytics: A Technology Tutorial. *IEEE Access*, **2**, 652-687. http://dx.doi.org/10.1109/ACCESS.2014.2332453

[34] Golab, L. and Özsu, M.T. (2003) Issues in Data Stream Management. *ACM SIGMOD Record*, **32**, 5-14. http://dx.doi.org/10.1145/776985.776986

[35] Chandarana, P. and Vijayalakshmi, M. (2014) Big Data Analytics Frameworks. *Proceedings of the International Conference on Circuits, Systems, Communication and Information Technology Applications* (*CSCITA*), Mumbai, 4-5 April 2014, 430-434. http://dx.doi.org/10.1109/cscita.2014.6839299

[36] Poole, J., Chang, D., Tolbert, D. and Mellor, D. (2002) Common Warehouse Metamodel. John Wiley & Sons, Inc., New York.

[37] XML for Analysis (XMLA) Specification. https://msdn.microsoft.com/en-us/library/ms977626.aspx.

[38] ter Bekke, J.H. (1997) Comparative Study of Four Data Modeling Approaches. *Proceedings of the* 2*nd EMMSAD Workshop*, Barcelona, 16-17 June 1997, 1-12.

[39] Hou, R. (2011) Analysis and Research on the Difference between Data Warehouse and Database. *Proceedings of the International Conference on Computer Science and Network Technology* (*ICCSNT*), Harbin, 24-26 December 2011, 2636-2639.

[40] Thomsen, C. and Pedersen, T.B. (2005) A Survey of Open Source Tools for Business Intelligence. *Proceedings of the* 7*th International Conference on Data Warehousing and Knowledge Discovery* (*DaWaK*'05), Copenhagen, 22-26 August 2005, 74-84. http://dx.doi.org/10.1007/11546849_8

[41] Vassiliadis, P. and Sellis, T. (1999) A Survey of Logical Models for OLAP Databases. *ACM SIGMOD Record*, **28**, 64-69. http://dx.doi.org/10.1145/344816.344869

[42] Chen, M., Mao, S. and Liu, Y. (2014) Big Data: A Survey. *Mobile Networks and Applications*, **19**, 171-209. http://dx.doi.org/10.1007/978-3-319-06245-7

[43] Chen, H., Hsinchun, R., Chiang, R.H.L. and Storey, V.C. (2012) Business Intelligence and Analytics: From Big Data to Big Impact. *MIS Quarterly*, **36**, 1165-1188.

[44] Silva, A.R., Saraiva, J., Silva, R. and Martins, C. (2007) XIS-UML Profile for Extreme Modeling Interactive Systems. *Proceedings of the* 4*th International Workshop on Model-Based Methodologies for Pervasive and Embedded Software*

(*MOMPES*'07), Braga, 31-31 March 2007, 55-66. http://dx.doi.org/10.1109/MOMPES.2007.19

[45] Ribeiro, A. and Silva, A.R. (2014) XIS-Mobile: A DSL for Mobile Applications. *Proceedings of the* 29*th Symposium on Applied Computing* (*SAC* 2014), Gyeongju, 24-28 March 2014, 1316-1323. http://dx.doi.org/10.1145/2554850.2554926

[46] Ribeiro, A. and Silva, A.R. (2014) Evaluation of XIS-Mobile, a Domain Specific Language for Mobile Application Development. *Journal of Software Engineering and Applications*, 7, 906-919. http://dx.doi.org/10.4236/jsea.2014.711081

[47] Silva, M.J., Rijo, P. and Francisco, A. (2014). Evaluating the Impact of Anonymization on Large Interaction Network Datasets. In: *Proceedings of the* 1*st International Workshop on Privacy and Security of Big Data*, ACM Press, New York, 3-10. http://dx.doi.org/10.1145/2663715.2669610

[48] Anjos, D., Carreira, P. and Francisco, A.P. (2014) Real-Time Integration of Building Energy Data. *Proceedings of the IEEE International Congress on Big Data*, Anchorage, 27 June-2 July 2014, 250-257. http://dx.doi.org/10.1109/BigData.Congress.2014.44

[49] Machado, C.M., Rebholz-Schuhmann, D., Freitas, A.T. and Couto, F.M. (2015) The Semantic Web in Translational Medicine: Current Applications and Future Directions. *Briefings in Bioinformatics*, **16**, 89-103. http://dx.doi.org/10.1093/bib/bbt079

[50] Henriques, R. and Madeira, S.C. (2015) Towards Robust Performance Guarantees for Models Learned from High-Dimensional Data. In: Hassanien, A.E., Azar, A.T., Snasael, V., Kacprzyk, J. and Abawajy, J.H., Eds., *Big Data in Complex Systems*, Springer, Berlin, 71-104. http://dx.doi.org/10.1007/978-3-319-11056-1_3

13

A Well-Built Hybrid Recommender System for Agricultural Products in Benue State of Nigeria

Agaji Iorshase, Onyeke Idoko Charles

Department of Mathematics/Statistics/Computer Science, Federal University of Agriculture, Makurdi, Nigeria
Email: sasemiks@gmail.com, ior.agaji@uam.edu.ng

Abstract

Benue State of Nigeria is tagged the Food Basket of the country due to its heavy production of many classes of food. Situated in the North Central Geo-Political area of the country, its food production ranges from root crops, fruits to cereals. Recommender systems (RSs) allow users to access products of interest, given a plethora of interest on the Internet. Recommendation techniques are content-based and collaborative filtering. Recommender systems based on collaborative filtering outshines content-based systems in the quality of their recommendations, but suffers from the cold start problem, *i.e.*, not being able to recommend items that have few or no ratings. On the other hand, content-based recommender systems are able to recommend both old and new items but with low recommendation quality in relation to the user's preference. This work combines collaborative filtering and content based recommendation into one system and presents experimental results obtained from a web and mobile application used in the simulation. The work solves the problem of serendipity associated with content based (RS) as well as the problem of ramp-up associated with collaborative filtering. The results indicate that the quality of recommendation is promising and is competitive with collaborative technique recommending items that have been seen before and also effective at recommending cold-start products.

Keywords

Preference, Rating, Filtering, Serendipity, Ramp-Up, Cold-Start, Skip Gram

1. Introduction

Recommender systems (RSs) are systems that filter out information. They also serve as decision support tools.

They provide product and service recommendations tailored to the user's needs and preferences. Recommender systems are intelligent personalized applications that suggest products or services, or more generally speaking information "items", which best suit the user's needs and preferences, in a given situation and context [1] [2]. The major task of an RS is to predict the evaluation a user will give to an item using a number of predictive models. These models exploit the ratings provided by user(s) for previously viewed or purchased items and generate recommendations.

Major recommendation techniques are collaborative filtering and content based filtering. Collaborative-based systems predict product ratings for the current user based on the ratings provided by other users, who have preferences highly correlated to the current user [3] Content-based systems predict ratings for an unseen item based on how much its description (content) is similar to items which the user has highly rated in the past [4].

Many problems are associated with the use of the various RS techniques. The most common problems are serendipity associated with content based RS, ratio diffusion associated with content and collaborative RS and ramp-up associated with collaborative recommender systems.

Serendipity is a problem that arises when users are offered items similar to the ones they have seen before while taking for granted new ones that they may like. The problem of ratio diffusion arises when the current user rations do not match with other users ratios. Ramp-up arises either because there are no enough rank ratios for a new user or there is no enough ranking on an item.

To address these problems, it is desirable to combine the RS techniques to leverage on the advantage(s) provided by individual techniques in order to improve recommendation accuracy; hence the need for a hybrid approach which is the basis of this work

2. Review of Related Literature

An efficient technique of hybrid web recommendation based on association rule mining algorithm using weighted association rule mining algorithm and text mining was presented and investigated by [5]. This improvement in their algorithm not only adds semantic knowledge to the result but is more efficient, gives better quality and performance approaches. Bloomjoin algorithm was used by [6]. The algorithm filtered out redundant intermediate records. Their system reduced the number of intermediate results and improved the join performance. A context-based recommender system that supported medical imaging diagnosis was presented by [7]. Their system relied on data mining and context retrieval methods to automatically hook up for relevant information that helped physicians in diagnosis. A context-aware commendation technique as a clarification to address the information overload problem for smart device users in the mobile cloud atmosphere was proposed by [8]. Their system used Smartphone sensors to enhance unified and automatic recognition of the operator context information in real time derived of using additional bound devices. Architecture for course recommender system was proposed by [9]. Their architecture indicated how data flowed through their system. Their method predicted the best combination of subjects in which students were more interested in. A recommender System based on semantic relatedness of concepts computed by texts from digital publishing resources was presented by [10]. Their method involved the extraction of concepts from encyclopaedias and reorganisation of digital publishing resources by concepts. The method generates concept vectors using skip gram model. The method did not require historical date for recommendation A framework that takes a user centric approach to recommender system evaluation by linking objective system aspects to objective user behaviours using a series of perceptual and evaluation constructs was proposed by [11] An intelligent recommender system to generate more justifiable estimate to evaluate the long term policies was developed by [12]. Their system also integrates trend impact analysis, RT Delphi, knowledge-based explanation and mathematical forecasting models to generate participatory approach that helped decision makers for long term strategic planning

3. Methodology

The new system utilizes both user and item based approaches. In the user-based approach, the users perform the main role. If majority of the users have the same taste then they joined into one group. Recommendations are given to users based on evaluation of items by other users from the same group, with whom he or she shares common preferences.

In Item-based approach, taste of users may remain constant or change very slightly. Similar items build neighbourhoods based on appreciations of users. Afterwards the system generates recommendations with items in the neighbourhood that a user would prefer. The system is a hybrid system which combines both content based and collaborative filtering methods of recommendation. This is done to take care of the problem of serendipity in content based recommender systems as well as the problem of ram-up in collaborative recommender systems. The architecture of the system is as shown in **Figure 1**. It has two types of user, those accessing the system via the web front and those accessing from mobile devices. Requests from both interfaces are routed via a common host running a web server, compatible to both interfaces. Inputs are gotten from the user as well as the database, the hybrid recommender system makes the appropriate recommendation in the form of response through the web server back to the respective mobile and web clients all modules of this work have been developed using open-source java platform and are organized in a client-server structure. The most relevant aspect of the system is the meticulous combination of different technologies (JAVA SE, JAVA EE and ANDROID). Users can access the system through any of the interfaces. The web front was built up with Java Server Pages together with state of the art container managed security.

The heart of the architecture is the recommender system developed in Java, which will be responsible for the interaction between all the functional modules.

Core java classes which will drive the hybrid recommender system are presented as class diagrams in **Figure 2**. The classes are DataSet, Ratings, HybridRecommender and RatingCountMatrix. Dataset provides the input to the HybridRecommender system. The data for the dataset class are instances of UserProfile, Rating and Product. The behaviour of the dataset class is specified by the getRatingsCount, getUserCount, getItemList and getUser. Ratings hold the ratings on products by user with userid, productid and rating as class members. Methods of Rating are getUserId and getRating. The agreements of the ratings are stored in a sparse matrix created in the RatingCountMatrix class. HybridRecommender class provides recommendations for the system. Data for the hybridRecommender class are instances of user profile and Product alongside a character flag, rectype which specifies the type of recommendation to be performed.

The primary data repository for this system is a MySQL database with four tables. The tables are presented in **Appendix A**.

The rating table contains a listing of all the users on the system together with the items they have rated as well as the ratings and the date the information was captured.

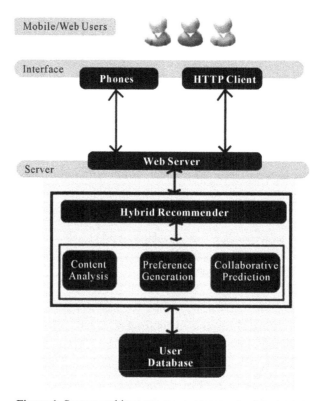

Figure 1. System architecture.

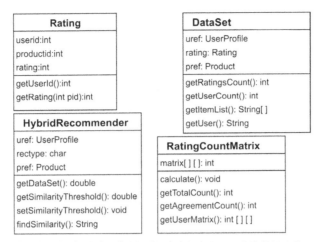

Figure 2. Java classes for the hybrid recommender system.

The product table is a repository of agricultural products from Benue State. Information captured in the table are the item Id which is the primary key to the table and will be auto generated, name of the item and production date.

Userprofile table stores the profile of users and the fields held in the table are userid age, gender, occupation, email and phone. Userid is a unique identification assigned each user.

Userroletable is a utility table and is employed when implementing the java authentication and authorization service for the system. It holds a reference to the roles of each user in the system. The various relationships between the tables are as shown in the ERD shown in **Figure 3**.

System Sequence Diagram

Figure 4 shows the sequence of events from the user interface through the web server to the database and then back to user. User profiles can be created on the system. The system can also get user preferences by passing a reference to the user object as parameter to that module. initProduct() module will help in initializing the product database by passing a reference to the product details object as parameter to the module. The initRatings() module initializes user ratings with the help of the rating file object sent to it as parameter. getRecommendations() will return recommendations to users based on their preferences, locations and user profile reference. With the user profile reference sent as parameter to the getRecommendations method, the system efficiently combine both collaborative and contents approaches for classical recommendations. Inner workings of the getRecommendations module use a character flag to switch between user and item approach to recommendation.

4. Results and Discussions

A functional web application as well as a functional mobile application was developed to test the concepts presented in this work. The program language used in development is Java and the results obtained are presented as follows. The Userprofile table was initialized with 23 hypothetical users who have rated 19 products in Benue state held on the Product table. The rating values for the products by the user are on a scale of 1 to 5, with 1 to 3 for poor rating and 4 and 5 for good ratings.

4.1. Experiment 1

In this experiment, a user called Babatunde was randomly selected among the hypothetical users and his similarity with other users as well as products recommended for him are seen in **Table 1**. **Table 1** showed the number of users with similar taste as Babatunde under Social Network for Babatunde alongside their similarity values captured under Level of Agreement.

Similarity enables us to compare how closely related two users are in their taste. The range of allowable values for similarity is 0 to 1. 1 is the maximum value for similarity and it comes from the fact that most similarity techniques are based on distances. In **Table 1** also are the recommended products for Babatunde. The result

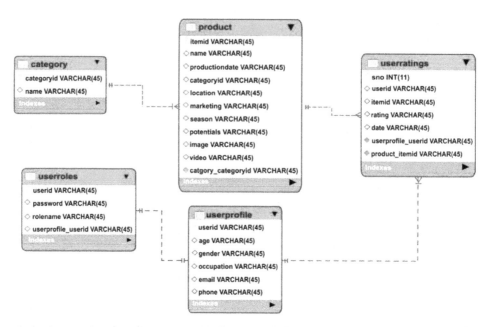

Figure 3. ERD for the database.

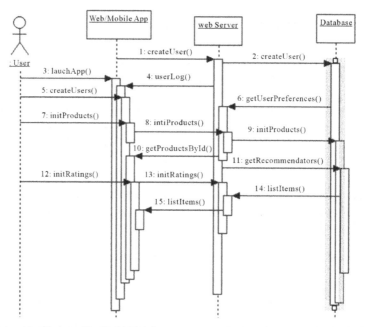

Figure 4. Sequence diagram for the system.

showed the products as well as the average ratings on the products by the users with similar taste as Babatunde. The rating values for the recommended products ranged from 4 to 5 showing that all the similar users rated the products to the same extent.

4.2. Experiment 2

Another user Goja was randomly selected from the list of hypothetical users and a list of users with similar taste as Goja was rendered under Social Network For: Goja in **Table 2**. Notice that the similarity values of these users with Goja is between 0.3 and 0.5 which depicts poor level of agreement in taste. The recommended product for Goja has been presented under Recommended Products for: GOJA in **Table 2**.

Table 1. Experimental result for recommendations based on users for Babatunde.

Social Network for: Babatunde	
Name	Level of Agreement
Cole	0.7272727272727273
Comfort	0.6363636363636364
Agana	0.5833333333333334
Catherine	0.5454545454545454
Daniel	0.5384615384615384
Recommended Products for: Babatunde	
Products	Ratings
Groundnuts	4.5906
Rice	4.5109
Makurdi Juice Plant	4.389
Aliade Oranges	4.3355

Table 2. Experimental results for recommendations based on contents for user Goja.

Social Network for: Goja	
Name	Level of Agreement
Maria	0.5
James	0.4545454545454543
Eric	0.3636363636363635
Luper	0.3636363636363635
Ene	0.3333333333333333
Recommended Products for: Goja	
Products	Ratings
Agro Millers	2.2627
Soy Bean Hub Agan	2.0967
Otukpo Oil Palm	2.0014
Ikpayongo Mango Depot	1.9485

The average ratings for these products by the users in the group ranges from 1 to 2 showing a poor rating status from our rating scale of 1 to 5. The method of recommendation used in the experiment for Goja is the content based approach of our hybrid technique.

4.3. Experiment 3

User Bello was also randomly selected and the collaborative item based approach of our hybrid technique was used in recommending four items with an average rating ranging from 4.3 to 4.5 showing a good rating. **Table 3** is the presentation of output from a java server page showing recommendations for a user Bello. The Item Based approach to collaborative filtering was used here to recommend agricultural products for this current user since items cannot also form neighbourhood for recommendation.

Table 3. Experimental results for recommendations based on content for Bello.

Recommended Products for: Bello	
Products	Ratings
Oju Millets	4.5717
Makurdi Abbatoir	4.4923
California Fresh Oranges	4.4044
Animal Farm UAM	4.3401

For users who are new to the system and have not rated an agricultural product before, our hybrid system uses a reference to the profile they created upon entry from the login page to generate recommendations for them.

5. Conclusion and Recommendation

This work proposed a hybrid technique for recommendation. The system was used in the recommendation of agricultural products from Benue state of Nigeria to various buyers. Results show that the proposed method provides better recommendation quality. Results of this work can also be extended to recommend agricultural product to new users based on extended preferences. In the future, this work can be extended to solve problems such as how our system can give feedback on its reasoning to users, the minimum amount of ratings or profile information required to return accurate recommendations and a more correct way of adding product information.

References

[1]   Adomavicius, G. and Tuzhilin, A. (2005) Toward the Next Generation of Recommender Systems: A Survey of the State-of-the-Art and Possible Extensions. *IEEE Transactions on Knowledge and Data Engineering*, **17**, 734-749. http://dx.doi.org/10.1109/TKDE.2005.99

[2]   Burke, R. (2002) Hybrid Recommender Systems: Survey and Experiments. *User Modelling and User-Adapted Interaction*, **12**, 331-370. http://dx.doi.org/10.1023/A:1021240730564

[3]   Herlocker, J.L., Konstan, J.A., Borchers, A. and Riedl, J. (1999) An Algorithmic Framework for Performing Collaborative Filtering. *Proceedings of the 22nd Annual International ACM SIGIR Conference on Research and Development in Information Retrieval*, 230-237.

[4]   Pazzani, M. and Billsus, D. (1997) Learning and Revising User Profiles: The Identification of Interesting Web Sites. *Machine Learning: Special Issue on Multistrategy Learning*, **27**, 313-331.

[5]   Ujwala, H.W., Sheetal, R.V. and Debajyoti, M. (2013) A Hybrid Web Recommendation System Based on the Improved Association Rule Mining Algorithm. *Journal of Software Engineering and Applications*, **6**, 396-404. www.scirp.org/journal/jsea

[6]   Pagare, R. and Shinde, A. (2013) Recommendation System Using Bloom Filter in Map Reduce. *International Journal of Data Mining and Knowledge Management Process (IJDKP)*, **3**, 127-134. https://doaj.org/article/72be16a4732148ccaa346fbdfead3bf7

[7]   Monteiro, E., Valante, F., Costa, C. and Oliveira, J.L. (2015) A Recommendation System for Medical Imaging Diagnostic. *Studies in Health Technology and Informatics*, **210**, 461-463. http://person.hst.aau.dk/ska/MIE2015/Papers/SHTI210-0461.pdf

[8]   Jayshri, M.S. and Gurav, Y.B. (2014) Cloud-Based Mobile Multinedia recommendation System with User Behavior Information. *International Journal of Innovative Research in Computer Science and Communication*, **2**, 6830-6834.

[9]   Aher, S.B and Labo, L.M.R.J. (2012) Course Recommender System in E-Learning. *International Journal of Computer Science and Communication*, **3**, 159-164. http://csjournals.com/IJCSC/PDF3-1/Article_35.pdf

[10]   Ye, M., Tang, Z., Xu, J.B. and Jin, L.F. (2015) Recommender System for E-Learning Based on Semantic Relatedness of Concepts. *Information*, **6**, 443-453. http://www.mdpi.com/2078-2489/6/3/443

[11]   Bart, P.K., Martijn, C.W., Zeno, G., Hakan, S. and Chris, W. (2012) Explaining the User Experience of Recommender Systems. *User Modeling and User-Adapted Interaction*, **22**, 441-504. http://dx.doi.org/10.1007/s11257-011-9118-4

[12]   Ahmed, M.O. and Motaz, K. (2013) An Intelligent Recommender System for Long View of Egypt's Livestock Production. *AASRI Procedia*, **6**, 103-110. http://www.sciencedirect.com/science/article/pii/S221267161400016x

Appendix A: Database Tables for the System

Product Table

Item ID	Name	Production Date	Category ID	Location
p001	Oju Millets	NA	Cereals	Oju
p002	Soy Bean Hub Agan	NA	Grains	Makurdi
p003	Aliade Oranges	NA	Fruits	ALiade
p004	Agro Millers	NA	Processing	MAkurdi
p005	Yams	NA	Roots and Tubers	Logo
p006	Yandev Cassava Farm	NA	Roots and Tubers	Gboko
p007	Ground nuts	NA	Ground nuts	Oju
p008	California Fresh Oranges	na	fRUITS	Gboko
p009	Animal Farm UAM	NA	Farms	MAkurdi
p010	Makurdi Abbatoir	NA	Processing	Makurdi
p011	Otukpa Oil Palm	NA	Oil Plant	Ogbadibo
p012	Ikpayongo Mango Depot	NA	Fruit	Makurdi

User Profile Table

User ID	Gender	Occupation
Agana	M	Lecturer
Ahmed	M	Trader
Angbera	M	Lecturer
Ashezua	M	Lecturer
Babatunde	M	Trader
Bello	M	Trader
Bill	M	Trader
Catherine	F	Farmer
Charles	M	Farmer
Cole	F	Farmer
Comfort	F	Marketer
Daniel	M	Marketer
Ene	F	Marketer
Eric	F	Marketer
Frank	M	Farmer
Goja	M	Farmer
James	M	Farmer
John	M	Trader
Luper	F	Trader
Maria	F	Trader
Nicky	F	Trader
Terry	M	Farmer
Terver	M	Lecturer

Ratings Table			
S No.	User ID	Item ID	Rating
1	Angbera	P001	4
2	Bello	p002	5
3	Ashezua	p001	2
4	Maria'	p005	4
6	Babatunde	p006	3
7	Eric	p002	1
8	Cole	p006	3

Category Table	
Category ID	Name
001	Fruit
002	Cereals
003	Roots and Tubers
004	Oil Plants
005	Processing
006	Spices

14

Software Project's Complexity Measurement: A Case Study

Panos Fitsilis*, Vyron Damasiotis

Technological Educational Institute of Thessaly, Larissa, Greece
Email: *fitsilis@teilar.gr, bdama@teilar.gr

Abstract

Project management is a well understood management method, widely adopted today, in order to give predictable results to complex problems. However, quite often projects fail to satisfy their initial objectives. This is why studying the factors that affect the complexity of projects is quite important. In this paper, we will present the complexity factors that are related to project time, cost and quality management and then we will apply them to a number of selected projects, in order to compare the acquired results. The projects have been chosen in a way that results can be easily compared.

Keywords

Software Project Management, Project Complexity, AHP

1. Introduction

Research studies have shown that very often projects fail to meet their requirements in terms of quality, time and cost restrictions. It is widely accepted that amongst the main reasons for these failures is the increased complexity of modern projects due to their special characteristics. There is a lack of consensus in defining what project complexity is. This fact resulted in the development of different approaches for classifying project management complexity. However many researchers agree that complexity is "consisting of many varied and interrelated parts" [1].

Software projects are among the most complex ones. Many studies on various types of software project have proven that their outcomes are far from the complete fulfilment of the initial requirements [2]. Most studies measure complexity either by measuring the software project product based on its attributes such as size, quality, reliability or the characteristics of software project process using attributes such as performance, stability, im-

---

*Corresponding author.

provement [3]. As such the need to establish a systematic way to evaluate the software project complexity is important.

Project complexity is a common concept recognized in a number of different ways. It is given a number of different interpretations based on the reference context or on each individual's experience. In many cases project complexity is used as a replacement for project size, or alternatively to project difficulty; or it is perplexed with project's product complexity [4]. In most cases, the complexity of projects is measured either by measuring the attributes of project products or by measuring the characteristics of project processes. In our approach, it is suggested that the complexity of projects should be studied by applying structured project management techniques [5].

The purpose of this paper is to study how factors are contributing to the complexity of projects. These factors are related with project time, cost and quality management and they have been identified in [6] [7]. Based on these factors a complexity model is built. Subsequently, this model has been validated with a number of projects. Finally, the results and the future work are presented.

2. Background

Complexity is part of our environment and appears in different domains. Many scientific fields have dealt with complex systems and have attempted to define the term complexity according to their domain. This implies that there is a different definition of complexity in computational theory, in information theory, in business, in software engineering etc. and many times there are different definitions inside the same domain. Schlidwein and Ison [8] states that are two major approaches of complexity. The first one describes the complexity as a property of a system, called descriptive complexity. The other approach describes complexity as perceived complexity and translates it as the subjective complexity that someone experiences through the interaction with the system.

This lack of consensus in defining what project complexity is has resulted in a variety of approaches on classifying project management complexity. One of the first researches that deal with the concept of complexity was Baccarini [9]. He considers complexity as something "consisting of many varied and interrelated parts" and operationalized them in terms of "differentiation" the number of varied elements (e.g. tasks, components) and "interdependency" the degree of interrelatedness between these elements. Finally he describes four types of complexity: 1) organizational complexity by differentiation and 2) organizational complexity by interdependency 3) technological complexity by differentiation and 4) technological complexity by interdependency.

Extending the work of Baccarinni, Williams [10] added the dimensions of uncertainty in projects and the multi-objectivity and multiplicity of stakeholders. The definition of project complexity according to Williams is divided in structural complexity sourcing from number and interdependence of elements and uncertainty sourcing from uncertainty in goals and methods.

Geraldi and Adlbrecht [11] and Geraldi [12] [13] based on structural complexity and uncertainty defined three types of complexity, the complexity of faith (CoFaith), Complexity of Fact (CoFact) and Complexity of Interaction (CoInt).

Maylor *et al.* [14] focused on perceived managerial complexity under two dimensions structural and dynamic and identified five aspects of complexity. They defined a complexity model that is based on Mission, Organization, Delivery, Stakeholders and Team (MODeST).

According to our previous work [6] in order to assess complexity we need a holistic framework that will take into account all areas of PM as they are defined in PMBOK [15]. This framework should define factors that affect complexity and metrics associated with each factor. Subsequently, these metrics will be evaluated by experts for their contribution in total project complexity and as such a model shall be developed. It should be noted that the developed model is not unique, neither the same for all projects. Simply, each developed model represents the consensus of each group of experts, of each company, etc. The final outcome is a parametric model that gives a quantitative indication of the expected complexity of the project (**Figure 1**). The numerical

Figure 1. Project evaluation according to their complexity.

representation of the project complexity makes easier the relative comparison of projects complexity as well as the complexity of the project itself. In addition, this approach allows the implementation of thresholds in project complexity that will allow the projects classification into categories according to the level of complexity. Also relative comparison of complexity will allow the comparison of different management and implementation approaches of projects and selection of the one with the lowest complexity. The main problem of this approach was, that building such models requires laborious work since the number of subject areas as they have been defined in PMBOK are ten (www.pmi.org), resulting to hundreds of factors and metrics.

The same problem has been faced by other researchers that attempted to limit the number of complexity categories and dimensions (factors) to a minimum number. For example, Vidal *et al.* [4], studied project complexity under the organizational and technological dimensions and identified four aspects for studying project complexity: project size, project variety, project interdependence and project context. For this reason, in our model it was decided to limit the number of subject areas and instead of using PMBOK's ten subject areas, to use three subject areas namely: time, cost and quality [15]. This constitutes the well know project management iron triangle that according to all scholars and practitioners defined the most influential factors for project success. A number of potential complexity factors have been identified as a result of an extensive literature review.

3. Presentation of the Case Study

After adopting the proposed factors that were found most frequently in the literature review, this initial set of factors was evaluated using the multi-criteria decision-making method, Analytical Hierarchy Process (AHP) [16] for defining the relative weight of each factor. The application of AHP method was done by using online AHP system that facilitated the whole process (http://bpmsg.com/academic/ahp.php).

The primary objective of AHP is to classify a number of alternatives (e.g., a set of quality determinants) by considering a given set of qualitative and/or quantitative criteria, according to pair wise comparisons/judgments provided by the decision makers. AHP results in a hierarchical levelling of the quality determinants, where the upper hierarchy level is the goal of the decision process, the next level defines the selection criteria which can be further subdivided into sub criteria at lower hierarchy levels and, finally, the bottom level presents the alternative decisions to be evaluated.

The main advantages of applying the AHP method are: it is capable to provide a hierarchical decomposition of a decision problem that helps in better understanding of the overall decision making process, it handles both quantitative and qualitative criteria, it is based on relative, pair wise comparisons of all decision elements; instead of arbitrarily defining a percentage score and a weight for each decision element, AHP allows the decision maker to focus on the comparison of two criteria/alternatives, at a time, thus it decreases the possibility of defining ratings based only on personal perceptions of the evaluators or other external influences.

Three are the basic concepts that AHP is based on (see **Figure 2**):

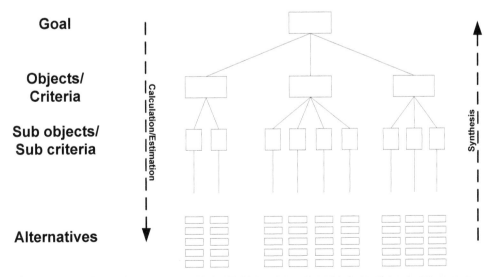

Figure 2. AHP structure.

- Complexity Analysis: A hierarchical tree is created with criteria, sub-criteria and alternative solutions as the leaves.
- Calculation/Estimation is executed in every tree level based on a 1 to 9 scale in order to measure priorities. More specifically, a pair wise comparison takes place in every tree level with regards to the parent node. The goal node in the hierarchical tree exists only to highlight the top-down analysis of the methodology.
- Synthesis with ultimate goal to extract the final priorities of the alternatives.

As it was mentioned, AHP is a method that orders the priorities in a given situation, incorporating the element of subjectivity and intuition so that a final decision can be reached by making decisions for part-issues in a consistent way and gradually move up levels to deal with the given situation having a clear view of what it entails. In AHP, alternatives are paired and decisions makers are called to note their preference between the two alternatives for a variety of issues (see **Figure 2**), in a scale of 1-9, assigning relative levels of priority to these judgments as they go along. Each element in compared to all other elements, using the scale presented, for defining their relative importance. These judgments are quantified and calculated so that when synthesized, they reveal the best alternative. AHP is relatively simple and logical and given that a certain consistency in the part-decisions is maintained, AHP can help decision makers deal with complicated issues where often not only tangible but also intangible parameters affect their decision. It should be noted briefly at this point that AHP is as effective as its design in each individual case and that analysts should exercise care and precision in capturing the true sub-elements and requirements of the case in question.

A small number of project managers have evaluated these factors and the ranking produced is presented in **Table 1**.

Table 1. Complexity factors.

Time related factors		
Factor	**%**	**Rank**
Large number of deliverables	26.10%	1
Lack/insufficient resources, especially rare	23.40%	2
Large number of dependencies between activities	10.70%	3
Large number of project activities	8.40%	4
Long project duration	7.40%	5
Number of critical activities	7.00%	6
Lack/insufficient time management experience	6.50%	7
Lack/insufficient time management tools	4.50%	8
Other time related factors	3.70%	9
Long duration activities	2.30%	10
Cost related factors		
Factor	**%**	**Rank**
Budget changes and budget cuts	28.60%	1
Insufficient project planning	16.30%	2
Financing from various sources	12.70%	3
Time consuming approval mechanisms	10.10%	4
Lack/insufficient of costing data for the specific project	6.60%	5
Project duration and timeframe	6.50%	6
Other costing factors	5.30%	7
Team know-how and experience	5.30%	8
Lack/insufficient of cost management tools	4.40%	9
Lack/insufficient of historical costing data	4.20%	10
Quality related factors		
Factor	**%**	**Rank**
Lack of QA department	41.40%	1
Insufficient definition and communication of quality objectives for project	21.10%	2
Lack/insufficient of responsible personnel on quality procedures	19.10%	3
Lack/insufficient quality management tools	12.50%	4
Not well known quality procedures and mechanisms	5.90%	5

The above factors lead to the decision tree presented in **Figure 3**. We have done the assumption that all top level factors: cost, time and quality contribute to the complexity with the same weight, 33.33% since all factors are considered equivalent for project success.

In order to evaluate the above model we have defined three projects. The reasons that we have decided to define these projects and not to evaluate real projects was simply for better demonstrating the validity of the proposed model, at least at this level. The characteristics of these projects are the following:

Project A: It is a project offering IT services to third parties. As such it is a long duration project, with many of diverse type of activities, having many dependencies since it has many stakeholders and large number of deliverables. However, this is a well-planned project and therefore the number of critical activated is quite limited. Since this is a service project we might have additional service requests leading usually to budget increase. Project A is financed by a number of companies that are sharing the same building infrastructure. A QA department is used to ensure the quality of the services delivered and since it is a long duration project all procedures followed are documented in detail.

Project B: Project B is totally different case than project A, since this is an IT services consultancy projects. This is a short duration (three months) with few tasks. However, the required resources are rare since this project requires high-end technical profiles. Project B's budget may vary significantly, in relation to the findings of the preliminary problem analysis. If a quick solution can be found, project B will finish successfully and quickly. However, if technical problems still persist it might be needed to be extended in duration, considerably. Project B is financed by a single source, the company that ordered the consultancy services and since project B was the result of urgent request due to technical problems, the project was not planned and it started without any actual planning. Quality procedures have not been foreseen.

Project C: It is a software development project requiring complex software development. The duration of the project is average (one year), with average number of dependencies between the activities and average number of deliverables. Project C is a fixed price project and it is foreseen a regular and constant cash flow. Project C is financed by a single source, a public organization that is solely funded by the State. Since the project is funded by a public organization, there are bureaucratic procedures involved in all project management activities. All quality procedures are well documented, known and the quality assurance positions are fully staffed.

Since, all projects are run from the same company we consider that factors related to experience and tools are influencing with the same weight the complexity of all three projects.

In **Figure 4**, we present the evaluation of the time related factors, according to a small group of experts. As we can observe according to project time management complexity, the most complex project is A, that it is really a large project (see project profile above), followed by project B that is a project starving for resources. According to the classification of the time factors, the factor "Lack/Insufficient resources, especially rare" influences heavily Project B. The result is that project B is perceived as more complex that project C.

The same analysis (pairwise comparisons) has been done for cost (see **Figure 5**) and quality (see **Figure 6**) factors. In relation, to the cost management project B is the most complex, since the project started without any initial planning and the budget may change considerably. The less complex is project C that is funded by a public organisation, the funding is secured and it is a fixed price contract. Similarly, if we evaluate the quality complexity factors we see that the fact that project B does not apply any quality procedure makes this project the most difficult to handle. The other two projects according to their profile exhibit similar complexity.

The final step is to combine, time, cost and quality complexity scores into one score. As we have already explained we make the assumption that all these three factors have equal weight, since their contribution to project success is valued equally The end results are presented in **Table 2** which demonstrates that even if project B is considered smaller, with less tasks, etc. it has been evaluated as more complex.

The above presented results give a logical and valid representation of project complexity. However, in order, for this model to be used in reality, it has to be validated with real projects and possibly to make adaptions to the influencing factors and on its weights.

4. Conclusions

The need to measure complexity is well understood and sufficiently justified. Obviously, software project complexity is an area that needs to be studied further, and in detail.

We have presented a simple and straight forward model for the measurement of project complexity. Project complexity is a useful measure on how much attention, we should put on a project taking into account not only the size but also the budget value of the project. It may be used together with other metrics for lowering the risk undertaken in various projects. Of course, a lot of work remains to be done.

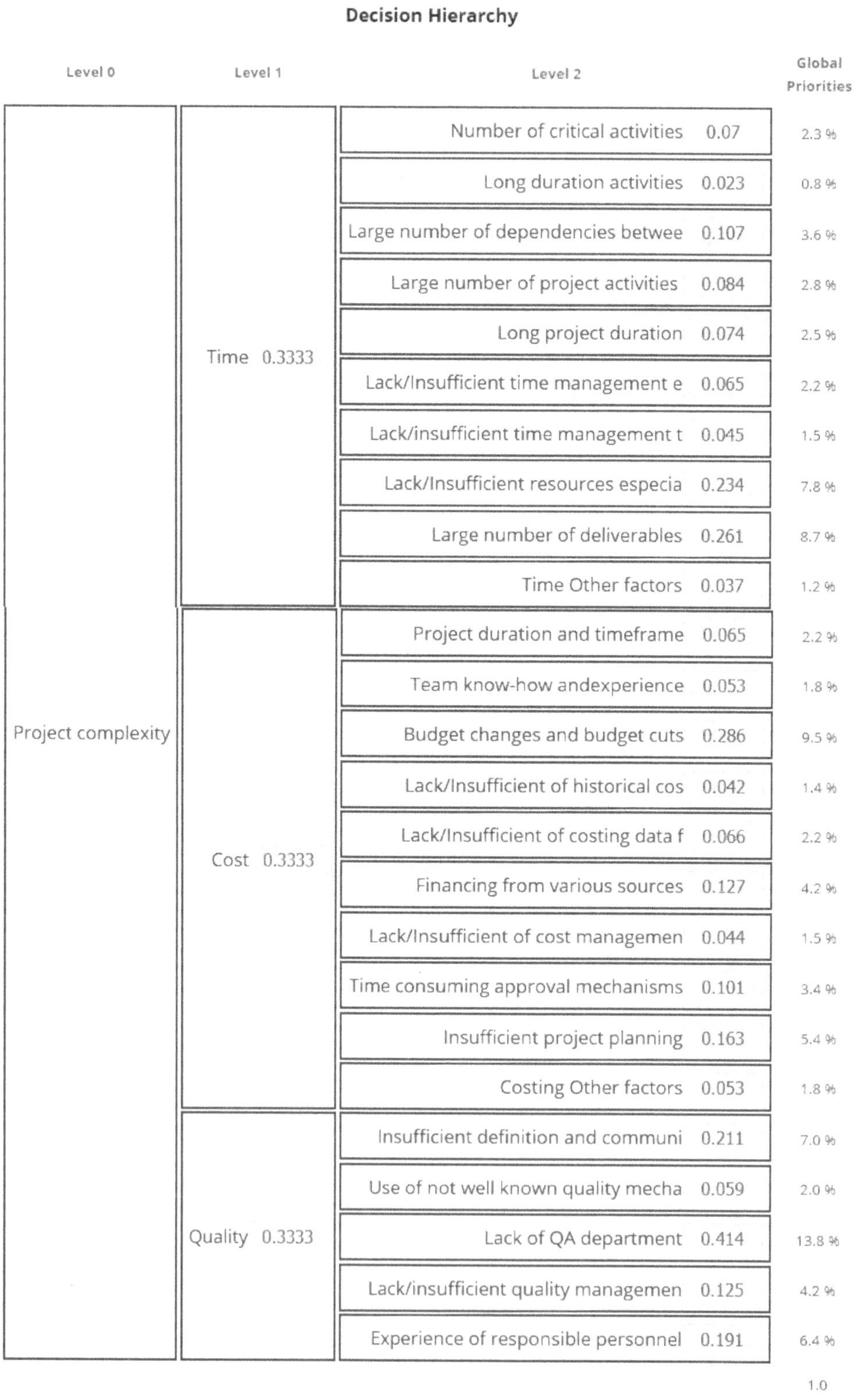

Decision Hierarchy

Level 0	Level 1	Level 2		Global Priorities
Project complexity	Time 0.3333	Number of critical activities	0.07	2.3 %
		Long duration activities	0.023	0.8 %
		Large number of dependencies betwee	0.107	3.6 %
		Large number of project activities	0.084	2.8 %
		Long project duration	0.074	2.5 %
		Lack/Insufficient time management e	0.065	2.2 %
		Lack/insufficient time management t	0.045	1.5 %
		Lack/Insufficient resources especia	0.234	7.8 %
		Large number of deliverables	0.261	8.7 %
		Time Other factors	0.037	1.2 %
	Cost 0.3333	Project duration and timeframe	0.065	2.2 %
		Team know-how andexperience	0.053	1.8 %
		Budget changes and budget cuts	0.286	9.5 %
		Lack/Insufficient of historical cos	0.042	1.4 %
		Lack/Insufficient of costing data f	0.066	2.2 %
		Financing from various sources	0.127	4.2 %
		Lack/Insufficient of cost managemen	0.044	1.5 %
		Time consuming approval mechanisms	0.101	3.4 %
		Insufficient project planning	0.163	5.4 %
		Costing Other factors	0.053	1.8 %
	Quality 0.3333	Insufficient definition and communi	0.211	7.0 %
		Use of not well known quality mecha	0.059	2.0 %
		Lack of QA department	0.414	13.8 %
		Lack/insufficient quality managemen	0.125	4.2 %
		Experience of responsible personnel	0.191	6.4 %
				1.0

Figure 3. Complexity decision tree.

	Criterion	Node	Glb Priorities	Compare	Project A	Project B	Project C
1.	Number of critical activities	Time	7%	AHP	0.101	0.255	0.643
2.	Long duration activities	Time	2.3%	AHP	0.667	0.167	0.167
3.	Large number of dependencies betwee	Time	10.7%	AHP	0.655	0.095	0.25
4.	Large number of project activities	Time	8.4%	AHP	0.571	0.143	0.286
5.	Long project duration	Time	7.4%	AHP	0.571	0.143	0.286
6.	Lack/Insufficient time management e	Time	6.5%	AHP	0.333	0.333	0.333
7.	Lack/insufficient time management t	Time	4.5%	AHP	0.333	0.333	0.333
8.	Lack/Insufficient resources especia	Time	23.4%	AHP	0.156	0.745	0.099
9.	Large number of deliverables	Time	26.1%	AHP	0.682	0.082	0.236
10.	Time Other factors	Time	3.7%	AHP	0.333	0.333	0.333
				Total weight of alternatives:	0.446	0.299	0.254

Figure 4. Evaluation of time related complexity factors.

	Criterion	Node	Glb Priorities	Compare	Project A	Project B	Project C
1.	Project duration and timeframe	Cost	6.5%	AHP	0.661	0.208	0.131
2.	Team know-how andexperience	Cost	5.3%	AHP	0.333	0.333	0.333
3.	Budget changes and budget cuts	Cost	28.6%	AHP	0.345	0.547	0.109
4.	Lack/Insufficient of historical cos	Cost	4.2%	AHP	0.333	0.333	0.333
5.	Lack/Insufficient of costing data f	Cost	6.6%	AHP	0.167	0.667	0.167
6.	Financing from various sources	Cost	12.7%	AHP	0.707	0.07	0.223
7.	Lack/Insufficient of cost managemen	Cost	4.4%	AHP	0.333	0.333	0.333
8.	Time consuming approval mechanisms	Cost	10.1%	AHP	0.167	0.167	0.667
9.	Insufficient project planning	Cost	16.3%	AHP	0.167	0.667	0.167
10.	Costing Other factors	Cost	5.3%	AHP	0.333	0.333	0.333
				Total weight of alternatives:	0.35	0.412	0.237

Figure 5. Evaluation of cost related complexity factors.

	Criterion	Node	Glb Priorities	Compare	Project A	Project B	Project C
1.	Insufficient definition and communi	Quality	21.1%	AHP	0.444	0.111	0.444
2.	Use of not well known quality mecha	Quality	5.9%	AHP	0.1	0.8	0.1
3.	Lack of QA department	Quality	41.4%	AHP	0.091	0.818	0.091
4.	Lack/insufficient quality managemen	Quality	12.5%	AHP	0.091	0.818	0.091
5.	Experience of responsible personnel	Quality	19.1%	AHP	0.091	0.818	0.091
				Total weight of alternatives:	0.166	0.668	0.166

Figure 6. Evaluation of quality related complexity factors.

Table 2. Evaluating complexity.

	Project A	Project B	Project C
Time complexity	0.45	0.30	0.26
Cost complexity	0.35	0.41	0.24
Quality complexity	0.17	0.67	0.17
Total project complexity	0.32	0.46	0.22

Firstly, all presented elements have to be further analysed in order to produce a model that is able to calculate robustly project complexity by combining factual, dynamic and interaction elements. Secondly, we need to know how we can practically measure the evolution of project complexity over project duration and what interventions are necessary for managing and controlling the complexity. Finally, we need to validate the model, in order to see if measured and perceived complexity is similar.

Acknowledgements

This research has been co-financed by the European Union (European Social Fund—ESF) and Greek national funds through the Operational Program "Education and Lifelong Learning" of the National Strategic Reference Framework (NSRF)—Research Funding Program: ARCHIMEDES III. Investing in knowledge society through the European Social Fund.

References

[1]   Bertelsen, S. (2003) Complexity-Construction in a New Perspective. IGLC-11, Blacksburg, Virginia.

[2]   The Standish Group (2009) CHAOS Summary 2009. The 10 Laws of CHAOS, The Standish Group International. https://www.classes.cs.uchicago.edu/archive/2014/fall/51210-1/required.reading/Standish.Group.Chaos.2009.pdf

[3]   Laird, L. and Brennan, M. (2006) Software Measurement and Estimation. A Practical Approach. John Wiley and Sons, New York. http://dx.doi.org/10.1002/0471792535

[4]   Vidal, L.-A. and Marle, F. (2008) Understanding Project Complexity: Implications on Project Management. *Kybernetes*, **37**, 1094-1110. http://dx.doi.org/10.1108/03684920810884928

[5]   Damasiotis, V. and Fitsilis, P. (2015) Assessing Software Project Management Complexity: PMCAT Tool. New Trends in Networking, Computing, E-Learning, Systems Sciences, and Engineering. Springer International Publishing, 235-242. http://dx.doi.org/10.1007/978-3-319-06764-3_30

[6]   Damasiotis, V., O'Kane, J.F. and Panos, F. (2014) Scope Management Complexity in Software Projects: An Approach to Evaluate It. BAM 2014, British Academy of Management, UK.

[7]   Georgosopoulou, A. (2015) Measuring Construction Project Complexity. TEI Thessaly, School of Business and Economics.

[8]   Schlindwein, S.L. and Ison, R. (2004) Human Knowing and Perceived Complexity: Implications for Systems Practice. *Emergence: Complexity and Organization*, **6**, 27-32.

[9]   Baccarini, D. (1996) The Concept of Project Complexity—A Review. *International Journal of Project Management*, **14**, 201-204. http://dx.doi.org/10.1016/0263-7863(95)00093-3

[10]   Williams, T.M. (1999) The Need for New Paradigms for Complex Projects. *International Journal of Project Management*, **17**, 269-273. http://dx.doi.org/10.1016/S0263-7863(98)00047-7

[11]   Geraldi, J. and Adlbrecht, G. (2006) On Faith, Fact, and Interaction in Projects. *Project Management Journal*, **38**, 32-43.

[12]   Geraldi, J. (2008) Patterns of Complexity: The Thermometer of Complexity. *Project Perspectives, IPMA*, **29**, 4-9.

[13]   Geraldi, J. (2008) The Balance between Order and Chaos in Multi-Project Firms: A Conceptual Model. *International Journal of Project Management*, **26**, 348-356. http://dx.doi.org/10.1016/j.ijproman.2007.08.013

[14]   Maylor, H., Vidgen, R. and Carver, S. (2008) Managerial Complexity in Project Based Operations: A Grounded Model and Its Implications for Practice. *Project Management Journal*, **39**, S15-S26. http://dx.doi.org/10.1002/pmj.20057

[15]   Rose, K.H. (2013) A Guide to the Project Management Body of Knowledge (PMBOK® Guide)—Fifth Edition. *Project Management Journal*, **44**, e1.

[16]   Saaty, T.L. (1988) What Is the Analytic Hierarchy Process? Springer, Berlin Heidelberg. http://dx.doi.org/10.1007/978-3-642-83555-1_5

15

Automatic Test Data Generation for Java Card Applications Using Genetic Algorithm

Saher Manaseer[1], Warif Manasir[1], Mohammad Alshraideh[1], Nabil Abu Hashish[2], Omar Adwan[3]

[1]Department of Computer Science, The University of Jordan, Amman, Jordan
[2]Al Israa University, Amman, Jordan
[3]Department of Computer Information Systems, The University of Jordan, Amman, Jordan
Email: saher@ju.edu.jo, warefalmanaseer@gmail.com, mshridah@ju.edu.jo, nabil.mosa@iu.edu.jo, adwanoy@ju.edu.jo

Abstract

The main objective of software testing is to have the highest likelihood of finding the most faults with a minimum amount of time and effort. Genetic Algorithm (GA) has been successfully used by researchers in software testing to automatically generate test data. In this paper, a GA is applied using branch coverage criterion to generate the least possible set of test data to test JSC applications. Results show that applying GA achieves better performance in terms of average number of test data generations, execution time, and percentage of branch coverage.

Keywords

Software Testing, Genetic Algorithm, Java Smart Card

1. Introduction

In recent years, software testing is becoming more essential in the software development industry, and it is a vital component of software engineering. Indeed, software testing is a broad term encircling a variety of activities along the development cycle and beyond aimed at different goals. Software testing represents 40% of software development budget [1]. Software testing has become more difficult because of the vast array of programming languages, operating systems, and hardware platforms that have evolved in the last decades [2]. In practice, testing cannot be exhaustive and some approaches to test selection must be used [3].

Software testing is the process of executing a program with inputs and observing the results. The aim of software testing is to generate a minimal number of test data such that it detects as many faults as possible [4]. Test data generation techniques attempt to find a program input that will satisfy the testing requirement. The tester chooses test data inputs in order to achieve some given structural coverage criteria. The automation of test data generation is an important step in the reduction of the cost of software development and maintenance [5]. GA is a leading technique of evolutionary software testing for generating test data to examine branch, statement and path coverage [6].

GA is well applied in software testing but it has never been used in testing of JSC applications. Smart cards store and process information through electronic circuits embedded on board [7]. A smart card can be intelligent, *i.e.* offers reading, writing, and calculating capability, or a memory card which offers information storage; only Java-based smart cards are capable of running Java programs [8]. JSC programs are called applets. Multiple applets can reside on the same card at the same time, and can be updated dynamically [9]. However, due to limitation in memory resources and computing power in the smart card, not all the language features of the Java programming language are supported on the JSC [7].

In this paper, we will apply GA to automatically generate test data to test JSC applications. The goal is to test JSC applications to reveal as many faults as possible, with a least possible number of test data using GA according to branch coverage criterion.

The rest of the paper is organized as follows: Section 2 presents the fundamentals of GA. Section 3 gives an overview of JSC. Section 4 describes the literature review on JSC software testing. Section 5 presents the proposed methodology and experiments. Section 6 evaluates the results and concludes the paper. Section 7 gives an overview of our future work.

2. Genetic Algorithms

The GA created by John Holland in the 1970's at the University of Michigan (USA), is an evolutionary algorithms inspired by biological evolution principles such as natural selection and genetic inheritance [10]. Evolutionary computing techniques attempt to simulate the biological process on the computer in order to solve problems in many applications with great complexity.

Holland simulated the methods used when biological systems adapt to their environment in computer software models to solve optimization problems [11]. In the context of software testing, the basic idea is to search the search space for input that satisfies the testing criteria.

The possible solutions to a problem being solved are represented by a population of chromosomes. Each chromosome is made of genes, and the value of a gene can be represented in binary, numerical or string of characters depending on the problem to be solved. GA uses three operators on its population which are described below:

- **Selection**

The selection for reproduction is the first operator applied on the population. Here, the selection operator chooses two individuals from a generation to become parents for the reproduction process to produce an offspring for the next generation. Individuals are chosen based on their fitness; the fitness function measures the suitability of a chromosome to survive in an environment. Before being included in the next generation, the chromosome must undergo the crossover and mutation operations which will be discussed briefly. Selection is a key factor of affecting the performance of evolutionary algorithms [12].

- **Crossover**

This operator combines two chromosomes to produce a new offspring. With the idea that new individuals will be closer to a global optimum, the best genes of the parent chromosome are combined to produce an offspring that is better than the parent [13]. Crossover occurs during evolution according to a predefined crossover probability. Crossover is of different types. It can be at one point crossover, double point crossover, or uniform crossover.

- **Mutation**

The aim of this operator is to maintain diversity among generation of one population chromosomes to the next. In mutation, one or more gene values are altered, according to a predefined mutation probability, from its initial value, thus resulting in a new gene value added to the gene pool. As a result, the mutation avoids the solution to fall into local optima of the search space. De Jong showed that mutation rates can have a destructive characteristic. If the mutation rate is too high, search is like a random search, and if too low the search might get stuck at local minima [14].

3. Java Smart Card

Smart cards currently exist for a vast verity of applications. A smart card is a secure, efficient and cost effective computational device of an embedded system that comprises of a microprocessor, memory modules (RAM, ROM, and EEPROM), serial input/output interfaces and data bus. The operating system of the chip is contained in ROM and the applications are stored in the EEPROM [15].

JSC is an open standard from Sun Microsystems for a smart card development platform. JSC brings the benefits of the Java technology to the world of smart cards. Smart cards created using the JSC platform have Java applets stored on them. The applets can be added to or changed after the card is issued. Each applet has unique Applet Identification (AID).

Java-based smart cards store data on an integrated microprocessor chip. Applets are loaded into the memory of the microprocessor and run by the Java Card Virtual Machine (JCVM). JSC enables multiple application programs to be installed and coexist independently [9].

The JSC technology supports a limited subset of Java functionalities to develop applets that run on smart cards. JSC does not support long, double, character, string, and float data types, multi-dimensional arrays, and threads. The supported features include byte, short and Boolean data types in addition to one-dimensional arrays [16].

Smart cards are deployed in a wide range of industries to support access, identity, payment and other services. An example of JSC application is the electronic purse payment application. The smart card carries a monetary value to allow the card holder to issue transactions [1].

Another example of smart card application in the governmental field is the e-Passport issued by the United States Government Printing Office and the Department of Homeland Security. The e-passport contains a small embedded integrated circuit that stores the same data a regular passport hold digitally [17].

As in typical communications, data packages are interchanged following set of protocols, JSC uses data packages for communication. Data packages used in smart card communications are called Application Program Data Units (APDU). APDU allow communication between the card application and the client via commands and response messages [18].

4. Literature Review

Software testing has become more difficult because of the vast array of programming languages, operating systems, and hardware platforms that have evolved in the last decades [2]. Software quality is the central concern of software engineering. Testing is the single most widely used approach to ensuring software quality [8].

Most research concentration was on testing JSC applets using models. Model-based testing can be easily introduced to the development process of the smart card, automatic test generation process saves 30% of labor when modeling task is included compared with manual testing. However, model-based testing is limited to functional testing [19].

Martin and Bousquet (2001) proposed a solution for JSC applet validation. In order to perform applet validation, the authors used a conformance testing approach that is black box testing [20].

Automatic test data are generated from the specifications and test purposes of the application. The specifications are expressed with a UML model, and then automatically translated into a Labeled Transition System (LTS). After that, the authors used the Test Generation with Verification (TGV) tool to automatically produce test data from the LTS. The strategy followed here is to test each function for every normal use and every possible misuse. Results show that the proposed approach by the authors offer high confidence in the application conformity regarding its UML specification [20].

Van Weelden, et al. (2005) showed that automated, formal, specification-based testing of smart card applets is feasible, and that errors can be detected [21].

Bouquet, et al. (2005) focused on functional testing based on formal models of functional specifications of the software under test to automatically generate test data. Functional testing aims at ensuring the correctness of operations and their conformance to the functional requirements. Unfortunately, formal methods demand real effort in order to formalize the specifications of the smart card applications [19].

Most of the testing conducted for smart cards and automatic test case generation are model-based testing. Model-based testing requires additional cost to construct the model and the test case specifications [22]. None of the applied automatic test data generation tools used heuristic search techniques. Although, heuristic search techniques have proved their strength in the software testing field especially GA, but they were never introduced to the JSC world.

5. Methodology and Experiments

In this section, we will explain the details steps of applying GA to automatically generate test data for JSC applications to achieve branch coverage with minimal test data. This approach is considered the first to use GA to test JSC applets. JSC applets are used in vital areas in our lives so observing the execution of the applets to validate whether they behave as intended and identify faults is an essential process that must be considered, especially because the JSC applet structure is complex. As software systems become more complex and embedded in industries, the cost of failure becomes more severe [23]. Such challenges can be faced by GA due to its capabilities of testing complex software. GA has been successfully applied in the area of software testing.

5.1. Experimental Settings

The following sets of parameters were considered for test data generation using GA.

Fitness function: the fitness value for an individual solution is computed according to Korel's Local Distance (LD) function [24]. The predicate distance is calculated according to Korel's Local distance function in **Table 1**, and each branch predicate is transformed to the equivalent predicate provided in the table. A predicate has only two outcomes, either it evaluates to TRUE or FALSE. A branch is traversed only if the predicate is evaluated to TRUE and not traversed if the predicate is FALSE. Korel assumed that a FALSE branch is greater than zero and a TRUE branch is less than or equal zero [24]. K is the smallest positive constant in the domain (*i.e.* 1 in the case of integer domain).

- Coding: binary string.
- Selection method: tournament selection.
- Single point crossover.
- Mutation probability: 0.05.
- Stopping criteria: fitness value equals 0 or number of generation's equals 700.

5.2. Evaluation Parameters

The performance of the GA to automatically generate test data for JSC applets was assessed by test data generation time, average number of generations and coverage target that is branch coverage. The average values were calculated after running the algorithm ten times for every program unit, this experiment was done for five times, every time with different population size. The populations sizes considered are 30, 50, 70, 90 and 110. After each execution, we recorded the average number of generations and the average execution time in addition to the coverage percentage achieved. It is useful to have the smallest average number of generations because it means that GA generates required test data with the small number of generations which is required.

Table 1. The Korel's Distance Function.

Branch Predicate	Branch Function
$A = B$	$ABS(A - B)$
$A \neq B$	$K - ABS(A - B)$
$A < B$	$(A - B) + K$
$A \leq B$	$(A - B)$
$A > B$	$(B - A) + K$
$A \geq B$	$(B - A)$
X OR Y	MIN (Distance(X), Distance(Y))
X AND Y	MAX (Distance(X), Distance(Y))

5.3. Programs under Test

We applied the algorithm to eight JSC programs, these programs are tested for the first time using GA, and these programs are described in **Table 2**, where LOC stands for lines of code in each program. The size of the programs is different from 59 lines to 4277 lines.

- **Passport Applet**

   The passport applet is an open source, card side implementation of the Java Machine Readable Travel Documents (JMRTD) that follows the International Civil Aviation Organization (ICAO) standards. The smart card chip holds the biometric information of the passport holder thus provides security and protection against identity theft [17].

   This program consists of 12 classes each class is responsible for a specific functionality such as processing APDU's, initializing the applet, encryption and decryption, scanning tags, and other instructions. The source code of the applets is available at (http://sourceforge.net/).

   The nature of the code was diverse; different data types, structures (simple and compound predicates) exist, as well as different nesting levels of conditional statements. For example, **Figure 1** shows calcLc From Padded Data ( ) method, this method computes the actual length of a data block as byte value.

- **CoolKey Applet**

   CoolKey Applet generates cryptographic keys on the card and allows external keys to be inserted onto the

Table 2. Programs under test.

Program Name	LOC	Number of Branches
Passport	3548	280
Network Connection Tracker	413	50
OATH	810	154
PKI	1738	220
RSACrypto	147	22
Calculator	182	48
CoolKey	4277	310
HelloWorld	59	6

```
public static byte calcLcFromPaddedData(short[]
apdu, short offset, short length){
        if(length>=0){
        if((apdu[(short)(offset + length)] & 0xff)!=
0x80){
                return (byte)(length & 0xff);
            }
            else{
                return (byte)(length & 0xff);
            }
        }
        return 0;
    }
```

Figure 1. CalcLc From Padded Data ( ) method.

card. These keys can be used in encryption and decryption operations after proper user authentication. When a new key is created and the user plugs it in for the first time, the key is automatically supported with certificates and unique PIN. The source code is available at (https://github.com).

In this applet there are five main classes with a total of 310 branches. The applet contains all combinations of nested if-statements, switch statements, for loops, do-while, and calls to other methods inside if-statements. In spite of the complexity of the branches, the test data generated by the algorithm achieved 100% coverage.

- **Network Connection Tracker Applet**

This applet keeps track of the account information for a wireless device connecting to a network service. The device has a local area network and can operate remotely. The applet provides a number of functionalities via specific commands such that you can add credits to the account and inquiry the amount of available credits. The source code of the applet is available at (https://kenai.com).

In this program there are 50 branches, where there are nested if-statements and switch statements, with simple and composite predicates. Although the structure of this program is not as complex as the previously discussed counterparts, full branch coverage was not achieved. Only 98% of the branches were covered at all population sizes specified.

Figure 2 below provides the code with the uncovered branch. The else branch of the if-statement on line 12 was not traversed because the algorithm could not find the test data that covers this branch. Unfortunately the algorithm reached the maximum number of generations without any improvement on the generated solutions. The main problem in this section of code was the incorrect handling of boundary values; a value out of range exception was thrown because the value of INACTIVE_AREA is out of the range of its data type (*i.e.* short) that allows it to traverse the else branch on line 12.

- **Calculator Applet**

This program is a JSC calculator, the instructions available by this calculator are the ASCII characters of the keypad keys: "0" – "9", * "-", * "x", ":", "=". The applet has a simple structure of if-statements and switch statements. Most of the conditions in this program used the "==" operator and logical "||" operator. The source code of the applet is available at (http://www.codeproject.com/).

- **RSACrypto Applet**

The RSA cryptosystem is the most widely-used public key cryptography algorithm invented by Ron Rivest, Adi Shamir, and Len Adleman [25]. The RSA algorithm can be used to encrypt messages and digital signatures.

The RSACrypto JSC applet encrypts and decrypts data blocks of at most 128 bytes long using RSA keys which are generated off-card and uploaded to the card. The source code of the applet is available at (https://www.cs.ru.nl).

```
1.    private void timeTick(APDU apdu) {

2.    byte[] buffer = apdu.getBuffer();

3.    byte numBytes = (buffer[ISO7816.OFFSET_LC]);

4.    byte byteRead = (byte) (apdu.setIncomingAndReceive());

5.    if ((numBytes != 2) || (byteRead != 2)) {

6.    ISOException.throwIt(ISO7816.SW_WRONG_LENGTH);

7.    }

8.    short newAreaCode=(short) (buffer[ISO7816.OFFSET_CDATA+1] &
0x00FF);

9.    if (newAreaCode != INACTIVE_AREA) {

10.   activeAreaCode[0] = newAreaCode;

11.   }

12.   else {

13.   resetConnection();

14.   ISOException.throwIt(SW_NO_NETWORK);

15.   }
```

Figure 2. Timetick () method.

- **HelloWorld Applet**

The JSC HelloWorld applet is the simplest applet that can be written, it outputs "HelloWorld" to the off-card application after receiving a specific APDU. This applet is the smallest applet tested by the algorithm, we wanted to test variety of programs that differ in functionality, structure and most important the number of branches. This program has six branches with combination of if-statements and switch statements. The applet source code is available at (https://kenai.com).

- **OATH Applet**

OATH (Open Authentication) is an open specification for One-Time-Passwords (OTP) developed by the Initiative for Open Authentication. It includes public, open specifications for event based authentication and time-based authentication using encryption techniques. OATH is capable of generating an event-based OTP that is triggered by a button press. In addition to event-based OTP, a time-based OTP is generated automatically every 30 seconds.

The OATH applet is designed for use on JSC to provide a one-time password generation service that conforms to the OATH specifications. The OATH applet implements a PIN user authentication, triple-DES encryption and decryption, and a secure hashing generation. This project implements the card functionality used on the YubiKey Neo device that is sold by Yubico [26]. The source code is available at (https://github.com).

In this program there are 154 branches in addition to a complex structure of nested if-statements and for loops as well as switch statement. Simple and complex predicates exist a lot in this program.

- **PKI Applet**

Public Key Infrastructure (PKI) is an architecture that supports secure digital communication by issuing digital certificates. PKI is based on public and private keys to encrypt and digitally sign information; it offers a high level of authentication for users.

As with web browsers, web servers, and many other types of hardware and software, PKI standards support smart cards [27].

This applet was one of the complex applets to test, it has 220 branches. The structure of the code was complex as well, there exists many nested if-statements, switch statements, while loops, do-while, and for loops all together. The source code is available at (http://sourceforge.net/).

5.4. Experimental Results

This section presents the results of the conducted experiments and provides a discussion of the results. **Figure 3**

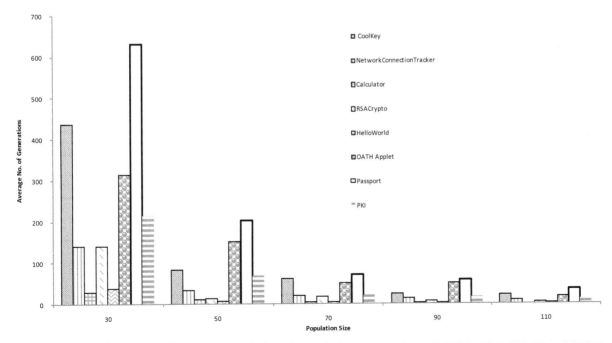

Figure 3. Average no. of generations for software under test.

presents the average number of generations generated for each applet as the population size increases. **Figure 4** presents the time consumed by the algorithm to generate the required test data.

It is clear from **Figure 3** that the average number of generation decreases as the population size increases same thing in **Figure 4** where the execution time decreases as the population size increases. This is due to the fact that the probability of finding optimal solution increases as the sample size of candidate solutions from the search space increases leading to a less number of generations and consequently execution time since the optimal solution would be near. Moreover, increasing the population size increases the accuracy of the GA because the greater the population size is the greater the chance that the population contains a chromosome representing the optimal solution [5]. The GA can generates the required test data with a small number of generations and less time since it selects the individuals with the best fitness such that it accelerates the process of searching and consequently reduces the time required to find the right individual.

5.5. Performance Evaluation

The experiments in this paper address eight different JSC programs to test the proposed algorithm, each program with different number of branches and unique characteristics.

Three evaluation parameters are used, average number of generations, execution time, and percentage of coverage that is branch coverage. The behavior of each parameter is monitored against the dynamic change of population size. Each parameter was used to study the behavior of the GA when applied to JSC programs.

Starting with the first parameter, the average number of generations, the general behavior of this parameter was decreasing as population size increases. This is justified by the fact that the greater the population size the greater the chance that the population will contain a chromosome representing the optimal solution, the probability of finding optimal solution increases as the sample size of candidate solutions from the search space increases. The GA can generate the required test data with a small number of generations to reach the test target in all programs under test as the population size increase. Therefore, this behavior is reflected on the time of searching for the optimal solution throughout the produced generations.

In terms of coverage, out of eight JSC programs under test, seven programs achieved 100% branch coverage at different population sizes. It can be noticed that the percentage of branch coverage increases as the population size increases. This is due to the fact that more numbers of candidate solutions increases the probability of traversing a new branch.

The experimental results were satisfactory; the GA was capable of automatically generating test data to achieve 100% branch coverage for most of the JSC programs under test. The algorithm was able to handle different code structures with simple and complex predicates; however some performance degradation occurred

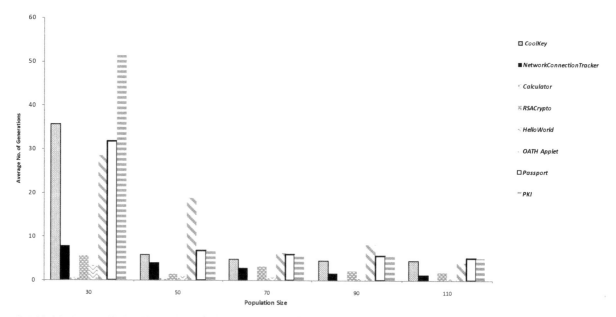

Figure 4. Execution time for software under test.

when dealing with complex predicates. In these cases, the performance of the algorithm was relatively different. For example, the execution time increased, and the average number of generations increased as well.

5.6. Java Card Applets Investigation

Testing JSC programs using GA revealed several aspects that must be considered when programming JSC programs.

One of the limitations is that JSC programs intensively use byte data type which limits the search space and throws an exception because the maximum value for byte data type is 127. This is an issue because the values of parameters specified are larger than 127 that is incorrect handling of boundary values. For example, in **Figure 5** the data type of p1p2 is byte but when it is compared to 0xdead an Input Mismatch Exception specifically "value out of range error" is thrown because the range of 0xdead exceeds 127. However, the test was performed on a modified version of the code.

Another limitation is that many variables are defined but not initialized, and they are used before initialization. For example, in **Figure 6** the Boolean variable found was used before initialization this led to an error and consequently the entire block of code is not reachable.

To sum up, many exceptions were thrown in the programs mostly Null Pointer Exceptions and Array Index out of Bound Exception, as well as different logical problems that were found similar to the ones we discussed above. This means that precise development and evaluation of JSC applets must be considered in order for it to function as expected. JSC applets must be tested using powerful testing techniques such as the GA that was successfully able to generate test data that revealed errors, forced exceptions to be thrown, and most importantly highlighted unreachable branches in the programs that were tested.

The test process used the following general flow shown in **Figure 7**. Moreover, a sample of the GA used is also presented in **Figure 8**.

6. Result Evaluation and Conclusion

In software development life cycle, software testing is considered as one of the most critical phases. The efficiency of a software test is directly related to code coverage. In turn, code coverage is greatly influenced by the test data, so providing efficient techniques to automatically generate test data is a key step.

A GA based on theory of natural selection is used to automatically generate test data to test JSC applets. The overall aim is to use the GA as search technique in order to find the required test data according to branch criteria to test JSC programs.

The experimental results show that branch coverage is achieved such that all test targets in all programs under test are reached, except for one program. The algorithm cannot find the test data that covers one of the branches of the Network Connection Tracker program. This means that the coverage percentage achieved is 99%.

In summary, we analyze the performance of the GA based on the average number of generations, execution time, and percentage of branch coverage. We measure the behavior of those parameters while changing the population's size, we start with initial population of size 30 then we increase it to 50, 70, 90 and 110. The GA shows good results in searching the search space for test data for every JSC program we tested.

The experiments show that the average number of generations decreases as the population size increases. It

```
byte ins = buf[ISO7816.OFFSET_INS];

byte p1p2= buffer[OFFSET_CLA];

if (ins == RESET_INS) {

        if (p1p2 == (byte)0xdead) {

handleReset();

            }

        }
```

Figure 5. Example of incorrect handling of boundary values.

```
public void destroyObject(short type, short id, booleansecure,shortcurr,shortprev)

  {boolean found;

       if(found) {

     short curr = obj_list_head;

      short prev = -1;

        found=false;

    if ( !found &&curr != -1 ) {

        if(mem.getShort(curr,(short)OBJ_H_CLASS)==type                        &&mem.getShort(curr,

(short)OBJ_H_ID)== id){

                   found = true;

            } else {

               prev = curr;

               curr = mem.getShort(curr, (short)0);

            }

         }

         if(found) {

            if(prev != -1)

   mem.setShort(prev, (short)0, mem.getShort(curr, (short)0));

            else

               obj_list_head = mem.getShort(curr, (short)0);

            if(secure) {

               Util.arrayFillNonAtomic(mem.getBuffer(),

                  (short)(curr + OBJ_H_DATA),

                  mem.getShort(curr, (short)OBJ_H_SIZE),

                  (byte)0);

            }

            mem.free(curr);

            }

   }
```

Figure 6. Example of uninitialized variables.

has been clarified that such behavior occurs because the probability of finding optimal solution increases as the sample size of candidate solutions from the search space increases. Accordingly the second parameter, the execution time is affected. The execution time decreases or increases as the average number of generations decreases or increases.

From the experiments, we conclude that JSC programs are complex and require being tested using powerful techniques such as GA because the power of using GAs lies in their ability to handle input data which may be of

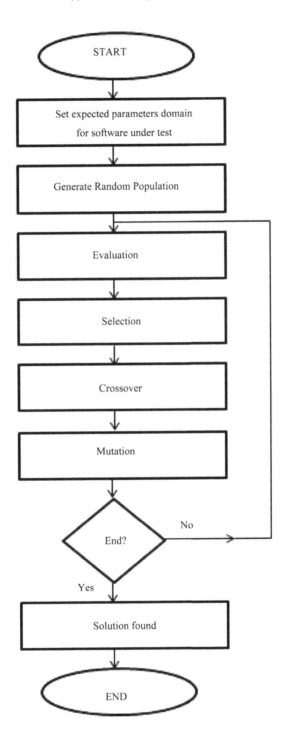

Figure 7. General test process.

complex structure, and predicates which may be complicated. As we have already mentioned, JSC applets are complex in structure and are implemented in important and highly demanding environments. Also, we highlight important issues that must be taken care of when implementing JSC programs; such as incorrect handling of boundary values.

The main advantage of using the GA as search technique is the strength of GAs; because the GA searches from a population of points rather than from a single point, thus reducing the probability of being stuck at a local

```
public class GA {

 private int NUM_CHROMOSOMES=30;

 private float MUTATE=(float)0.05;

 private Vector population;

int [] intArray= new int[NUM_CHROMOSOMES];

 double [] fitArray=new double [NUM_CHROMOSOMES];


 public GA(){

 generatePopulationRandomly();

 }

 private void generatePopulationRandomly(){

   population= new Vector();

   for(int i=0;i<NUM_CHROMOSOMES;i++){

 intrandomValue=(int)(Math.random()*MAX_NUMBER);

 population.add(new Chromosome(randomValue,MAX_POWER));

   }

 }

fitval= fitnessFuncofBranchData(intArray[t]);

         if(intNum==val){

             fitness=0;

           }


         else{

dest=(Math.abs(intNum-val));

         double k= Math.pow(1.001, dest);

         double k2=1/k;

         fitness=1-k2;

           }

 private Chromosome TournamentParentSelection(){

int index1= (int) (Math.random()*NUM_CHROMOSOMES);

int index2 = (int) (Math.random()*NUM_CHROMOSOMES);

intbestParentIndex;

       if(fitArray[index1]>fitArray[index2]){

 bestParentIndex=index1;

 }

 else{
```

Figure 8. GA example.

optimum, in addition to other advantages such as: it can be employed for a wide variety of optimization problems. GA is an effective global smart search method; it can solve efficiently the large space of complicated problems.

7. Future Work

The main aspect of the future work in this paper is to make a real-world prototyping of the algorithm on an actual JSC. Also, test JSC programs using different test coverage criteria such as path coverage in order to distinguish which is the most appropriate test coverage criterion for testing JSC.

References

[1] Stuber, G. (1996) The Electronic Purse: An Overview of Recent Developments and Policy Issues. Bank of Canada.

[2] Myers, G.J., Sandler, C. and Badgett, T. (2011) The Art of Software Testing. John Wiley & Sons, Hoboken.

[3] Sommerville, I. (2000) Software Engineering. Addison-Wesley, Harlow.

[4] Srivastava, P.R. and Kim, T.H. (2009) Application of Genetic Algorithm in Software Testing. *International Journal of Software Engineering and Its Applications*, **3**, 87-96.

[5] Pargas, R.P., Harrold, M.J. and Peck, R.R. (1999) Test-Data Generation Using Genetic Algorithms. *Software Testing Verification and Reliability*, **9**, 263-282.
http://dx.doi.org/10.1002/(SICI)1099-1689(199912)9:4<263::AID-STVR190>3.0.CO;2-Y

[6] McCart, J., Berndt, D. and Watkins, A. (2007) Using Genetic Algorithms for Software Testing: Performance Improvement Techniques. *Proceedings Americas Conference on Information Systems (AMCIS)*, Colorado, 2007, 222.

[7] Coglio, A. (2003) Code Generation for High-Assurance Java Card applets. *Proceedings of 3rd NSA Conference on High Confidence Software and Systems*, Gold Coast, April 2003, 85-93.

[8] Tuteja, M. and Dubey, G. (2012) A Research Study on Importance of Testing and Quality Assurance in Software Development Life Cycle (SDLC) Models. *International Journal of Soft Computing*, **2**, 251

[9] Giorgio, Z. (2015) Understanding Java Card 2.0.
http://www.javaworld.com/article/2076617/embedded-java/understanding-java-card-2-0.html

[10] Mitchell, M. (1996) An Introduction to Genetic Algorithms. MIT Press, Cambridge.

[11] Hermawanto, D. (2013) Genetic Algorithm for Solving Simple Mathematical Equality Problem. Cornell University Library, Computer Science, Neural and Evolutionary Computing, Indonesia, 1-10.

[12] Xie, H. and Zhang, M. (2009) Sampling Issues of Tournament Selection in Genetic Programming. School of Engineering and Computer Science, Victoria University of Wellington, Wellington.

[13] Spears, W.M. and Anand, V. (1991) A Study of Crossover Operators in Genetic Programming. Springer, Berlin Heidelberg, 409-418. http://dx.doi.org/10.1007/3-540-54563-8_104

[14] DeJong, K.A. (1975) Analysis of the Behavior of a Class of Genetic Adaptive Systems. Department of Computer and Communication Sciences, University of Michigan, Ann Arbor.

[15] El Farissi, I., Azizi, M., Lanet, J.L. and Moussaoui, M. (2013) Neural Network vs. Bayesian Network to Detect Java Card Mutants. *Agriculture and Agricultural Science Procedia*, **4**, 132-137.
http://dx.doi.org/10.1016/j.aasri.2013.10.021

[16] Kindermann, R. (2009) Testing a Java Card Applet Using the LIME Interface Test Bench: A Case Study. Technical Report TKK-ICS-R18, Helsinki University of Technology, Department of Information and Computer Science, Espoo.

[17] Mostowski, W. and Poll, E. (2010) Electronic Passports in a Nutshell. Technical Report ICIS-R10004, Radboud University, Nijmegen. https://pms.cs.ru.nl/iris-diglib/src/getContent.php

[18] Vandewalle, J.J. and Vetillard, E. (1998) Developing Smart Card Based Applications Using Java Card. *Proceedings of the Third Smartcard Research and Advanced Application Conference*, Louvain-la-Neuve, 14-16 September 1998, 105-124.

[19] Bouquet, F., Legeard, B., Peureux, F. and Torreborre, E. (2005) Mastering Test Generation from Smart Card Software Formal Models. In: *Construction and Analysis of Safe, Secure, and Interoperable Smart Devices*, Springer, Berlin Heidelberg, 70-85. http://dx.doi.org/10.1007/978-3-540-30569-9_4

[20] Martin, H. and du Bousquet, L. (2001) Automatic Test Generation for Java Card Applets. In: *Java on Smart Cards: Programming and Security*, Springer, Berlin Heidelberg, 121-136. http://dx.doi.org/10.1007/3-540-45165-X_10

[21] VanWeelden, A., Oostdijk, M., Frantzen, L., Koopman, P. and Tretmans, J. (2005) On-the-Fly Formal Testing of a Smart Card Applet. In: *Security and Privacy in the Age of Ubiquitous Computing*, Springer, New York, 565-576.
http://dx.doi.org/10.1007/0-387-25660-1_37

[22] Philipps, J., Pretschner, A., Slotosch, O., Aiglstorfer, E., Kriebel, S. and Scholl, K. (2003) Model-Based Test Case Generation for Smart Cards. *Electronic Notes in Theoretical Computer Science*, **80**, 170-184.
http://dx.doi.org/10.1016/S1571-0661(04)80817-X

[23] Berndt, D.J. and Watkins, A. (2005) High Volume Software Testing Using Genetic Algorithms. *Proceedings of the 38th Annual Hawaii International Conference on System Sciences*, Big Island, 3-6 January 2005, 318b. http://dx.doi.org/10.1109/hicss.2005.296

[24] Korel, B. (1990) Automated Software Test Data Generation. *IEEE Transactions on Software Engineering*, **16**, 870-879. http://dx.doi.org/10.1109/32.57624

[25] Boneh, D. (1999) Twenty Years of Attacks on the RSA Cryptosystem. *Notices of the AMS*, **46**, 203-213.

[26] Willis, N. (2014) Smart Card Features on the YubiKey NEO. https://lwn.net/Articles/618888/

[27] Al-Khouri, A.M. (2012) PKI in Government Digital Identity Management Systems. *European Journal of ePractice*, **4**, 4-21.

16

An Expert System Oriented towards the Detection of Influenza and Dengue Developed on Mobile Platforms

Raúl Beltrán Ramírez[1], Rocío Maciel Arellano[1], Carlos González Sandoval[2], Adauto Casas Flores[1]

[1]Departamento de Sistemas de Información, Universidad de Guadalajara Periférico Norte, Zapopan, México
[2]Centro de Enseñanza Técnica Industrial, Guadalajara, México
Email: jrbeltran@cucea.udg.mx, rmaciel@cucea.udg.mx, carlos.augusto.gs@hotmail.com, adauto.casas@gmail.com

Abstract

Nowadays, mobile technology makes it possible for us to realize processes in a relatively short amount of time, showing the user friendly and efficient interfaces that any person is capable of adapting to. Continuing this trend, we develop a mobile application that aids in giving an early diagnosis of Influenza and Dengue, two diseases that affect approximately 5% of the world population (in the case of Dengue) and 5% - 15% of the northern hemisphere (in the case of influenza). Our application consists of an expert system based on fuzzy logic that analyzes symptoms introduced by the user and formulates a diagnosis in approximately 2 - 4 minutes. This system considerably reduced the diagnostic time, improving the recuperation process from these diseases due to their early detection.

Keywords

Mobile Technology, Mobile Applications, Dengue, Influenza, Expert System

1. Introduction

In Mexico, two of the diseases that have most caused health problems in the society are Dengue and Influenza H1N1, whose symptoms can be confused amongst themselves or other simple sicknesses which in many cases can lead to a late diagnosis.

Influenza is an acute, contagious viral respiratory disease whose typical manifestations are fever, myalgia, coryza, throat pains and coughing. The influenza virus usually attacks the superior respiratory tract. However, in more extreme cases, it can affect the lower respiratory tract (lungs and bronchioles) [1]. In the past 100 years, there have been 4 pandemics: one in 1918 caused by the Influenza Virus A (H1N1), in 1957 by the type A (H2N2), in 1968 by A (H3N2), and in 2009 A (H1N1). The last pandemic led to a severe health problem due to the similitude of its symptoms with those of a common cold [2] [3].

The epidemiological vigilance is the key to an early detection of the first cases of this disease, helping the patient increase their recovery expectations and simultaneously fire an alarm and start response actions to avoid another pandemic [4].

Dengue disease is the most prevalent arthropod-borne viral disease in humans. It is caused by four serotypes of single-strand RNA flavivirus (dengue virus [DENV]-1, -2, -3, and -4), which are transmitted by blood-feeding mosquitos—mainly *Aedesaegypti* (Linnaeus) [5] [6].

It's one of the most important re-emerging diseases in the world [7]. There are between 50 - 100 million cases annually in over 100 countries and in the majority of those cases it is manifested as flu syndrome and causes approximately 24,000 deaths per year. Around 2.5% of the infected cases result to be fatal due to lack of adequate treatment. Access to capacitated professionals or intelligent systems that recognize symptoms for a rapid diagnosis is of utmost importance [8].

In the present day, the rapid development of technology and telecommunications has offered humanity the opportunity to improve areas such as education, industrial productivity and productivity in general for that matter, and of course video game development, pressuring technological evolution worldwide. Some examples of the implementation of this technology can be observed in applications that carry out image analysis and three-dimensional reconstruction utilizing specific information. These diagnoses would have been impossible without the aid of experts. However once developed, this project would be useful in places where mentioned experts would not be of disposition, for example, accidents where muscular or bone damage is present.

In this case, our developed application (BioDnX) is focused on the diagnosis of diseases such as Influenza and Dengue, which have taken many lives on a global scale every year. Commonly, when people suffer of the first symptoms, they wait 1 to 3 days before consulting a physician and as more time goes by, the probabilities of recover are slimmer. BioDnX directly impacts this aspect, reducing the diagnostic time for all people with access to mobile platforms, enabling better recovery times, treatment and possibly saving the patient's life. Apart from the simple and friendly environment, the available assistant (Dr. DnX), in every stage of the application, converts someone of any age into a potential user without presenting any difficulty in its use or operation.

2. Material and Methods

Many electronic devices have been employed, such as a personal computer capable of running the developing software "Adobe Flash CS6", a mobile device "Smart Phone" (Motorola G2) for testing and many others such as tablets, iPads and other Android operating system devices.

2.1. Hardware

Computer: CPU: Intel Core i5-3210M 2.5 GHz, RAM: 6 GB, OS: Windows 8.1 Single Language 64 bits.
   Testing Devices: Android Operating System Lg L5x, Moto G2 and Samsung Galaxy S3 mini.

2.2. Software

Adobe Flash Professional CS6, Animation Software for app development, Adobe Air Version 15.00.249 (programming language converter for iOS and Android Systems), Adobe Photoshop CS6 Version 13.0 (photo and image editor), CorelDraw Graphics Suite X6 64bits Version 16.0.707 (image designer).

2.3. Fuzzy Logic

Fuzzy logic is an alternative logic as opposed to classical logic which introduces a level of uncertainty in what it evaluates, in the world that we live in there exists many ambiguous or imprecise concepts of nature. Fuzzy logic was designed precisely to imitate human behavior.

A diagnostic can be obtained due to the evaluation of the symptoms implementing fuzzy logic, we cannot determine exactly when a patient is actually suffering of these diseases or not, however we can calculate the probability of the user being victim to these diseases.

The program calculates every symptom, paying close attention to the slightest of details, (this is where expert knowledge comes into play), the user selects the symptoms presented and the system calculates the probability of the user possessing each disease. Finally, the diagnosis is determined based on the inputted symptoms.

2.4. Differentiation of Diseases

The similitude between the symptoms of these two diseases is quite high, thus there is a probability of confusion between the two diseases upon their diagnosis, to resolve this confusion the system proceeds to ask the user if he/she has certain symptoms that they might have overlooked upon inputting data in the main menu, helping the system calculate the probabilities of their diagnosis as accurately as possible.

3. Project Development

An expert system which implements fuzzy logic to give an approximate diagnosis of Influenza and Dengue utilizing a friendly interface based on images, where the user selects his/her gender and parts of the body where he/she feels pain with a simple tap, taking into consideration the patient's age as the first parameter.

After inputting all of the user's symptoms, the consultation is finalized by tapping the "OK" button from the main menu. The system also contains an assistant, Dr. DnX that makes the user experience much more comfortable.

In order to proceed with the development process and to create a knowledge database that contains all the symptoms and their values, it was necessary to consult information from medical experts in the Virology area at the University of Guadalajara.

3.1. Knowledge Database

Table 1 shows us the database created during the investigation process, completed from the expert knowledge in virology from the University of Guadalajara. We investigated the symptoms presented in both diseases and assigned a numeric value based on the impact caused by each disease. The assigned values were corroborated and accepted by the earlier mentioned medical experts.

3.2. Operations

Equation (1) and Equation (2), describe each disease operation, adding each value of the symptoms corresponding to index (i).

$$\sum_{i=0}^{i=10} \text{Influenza} = \text{Influenza} + \text{Symptom}[i] \tag{1}$$

$$\sum_{i=8}^{i=20} \text{Dengue} = \text{Dengue} + \text{Symptom}[i] \tag{2}$$

At the final stage of the application in the diagnosis window, the algorithm compares the values of both disease variables and shows the higher result to the user.

4. Research Procedure

In **Figure 1** our algorithm is represented by a flow diagram to analyze the information from each user's diagnosis. This procedure simulates the behavior of a medical consultation, taking into account symptoms, their relation, and differentiating between Influenza and Dengue. If the quantity of Dengue symptoms is equivalent to that of Influenza symptoms, the system reminds the users of symptoms that they may not have inputted at the beginning of the simulated consultation to correctly diagnose said user.

5. Experiment Results

In this development we implemented mobile technology to improve the pre-diagnostic times in case of the need for efficient and accurate recognition of the symptoms pertaining to said diseases. The development of BioDnX

Table 1. Knowledge database (information obtained by medical experts).

Disease	Symptoms and values			
	Symptom	Index	Value	Impact
Influenza	Nasal irritation	0	8	High
Influenza	Loss of appetite	1	5	Moderate
Influenza	Red eyes	2	10	High
Influenza	Watery eyes	3	7	High
Influenza	Cough	4	5	Moderate
Influenza	Nasal congestion	5	7	High
Influenza	Breathing difficulties	6	3	Low
Influenza	Sore throat	7	15	High
Influenza/dengue	Fever (temperature > 99°F)	8	40	High
Influenza/dengue	High temperature to touch	9	20	High
Influenza/dengue	Diarrhea	10	2	Low
Dengue	Vomit	11	1	Low
Dengue	Drowsiness	12	8	High
Dengue	Joint-aches	13	7	High
Dengue	Skin Problems	14	6	Moderate
Dengue	Headaches	15	7	Moderate
Dengue	Eye-aches	16	6	High
Dengue	Chills	17	3	Low
Dengue	Chest pressure	18	2	Low
Dengue	Body pain	19	15	High
Dengue	Dizziness	20	3	Low

[a]Knowledge database implemented on BioDnX (*supervised by medical experts*).

showed satisfactory results regarding the detection time of these two diseases, due to what granted the patients a pre-diagnosis within 2 - 4 minutes. It is common for people with the first symptoms to wait days while scheduling a physician's appointment before being able to receive a reliable diagnosis. BioDnX considerably reduced the time of uncertainty concerning these diseases by allowing the patients to have access to a tool permitting reliable diagnoses.

Table 2 shows us the duration of the disease and the diagnosis time. Data of the evolution of the disease was collected from different people at different times to recognize the early symptoms which are generally presented, when the patient was first diagnosed with the disease, its progress and his/her recovery time. These same people were offered to try BioDnX, simulating the same early symptoms, and the pre-diagnosis showed results after approximately 2 - 4 minutes.

Application's Environment

Figure 2 and **Figure 3**, show the appearance of the system and the environment that the user will experience. We utilized a Motorola G2 cellular device and the testing was done with the Android KitKat 4.4 operating system.

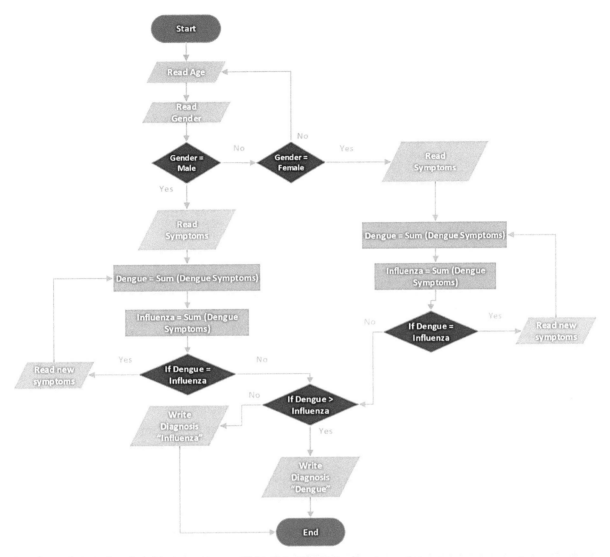

Figure 1. BioDnX flowchart (shows every step of the diagnosis process).

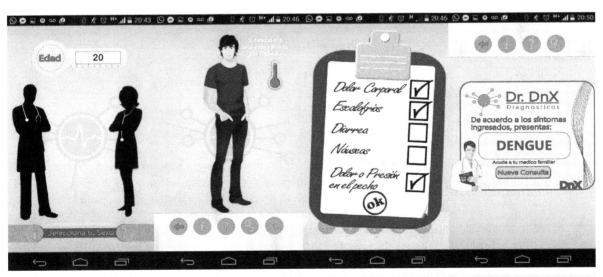

Figure 2. BioDnX environment (designed for easy, quick and accurate use).

Figure 3. BioDnX fully functional (available only on android mobile devices).

Table 2. Experiment results (with real and simulated cases).

Situation	Diagnosis data				
	Name	Diagnosis	1st symptom date	Diagnosis date	Recovery time
Without BioDnx	Marisela Fernandez Serrano	Dengue	27/04/2010 Body pain	29/04/2010	12 days
With BioDnx		High probabilities of dengue	14/05/2015 5:07 pm	14/05/2015 5:09 pm	-
Without BioDnx	Nicole Muñoz Filippetti	Dengue	09/10/2012 Joints-aches	12/10/2012	15 days
With BioDnx		Dengue	14/05/2015 11:18 pm	14/05/2015 11:21 pm	-
Without BioDnx	Carlos Gonzalez Ávila	Dengue	20/08/1998 Eye-aches	24/08/1998	11 days
With BioDnx		High probabilities of dengue	15/05/2015 12:09 am	15/05/2015 12:12 am	-
Without BioDnx	Fernando Miguel Saucedo	Influenza	02/03/2013 10:00 am Simple Flu	02/03/2013 8:00 pm	3 days
With BioDnx		High probabilities of influenza	15/05/2015 12:55 am	15/05/2015 12:57 am	-
Without BioDnx	Jonathan Arredondo Macias	Dengue	27/05/2009 Fever	4/06/2009	21 days
With BioDnx		Dengue	15/05/2015 1:08 am	15/05/2015 1:11 am	-

[a]BioDnX was used for the recreation of the cases (*the procedure was executed with the same symptoms presented on the same day*).

6. Discussion

In this investigation we designed an Android based application utilizing human expertise to obtain an early diagnosis of Influenza and Dengue, whose symptoms are very similar, taking into account the growing use of mobile devices in the Mexican population. Given that both diseases have impacted the population and due to the time consuming diagnoses, many lives have been lost. We hope that with an application of this nature, the society can have a tool to obtain information pertaining to their symptoms in a timely manner.

We utilized BioDnX to improve the response time of the diagnosis of diseases Influenza H1N1 and Dengue and even though this is just a pre-diagnosis, this will aid the physician. However, it is necessary to debug the diagnostic algorithm to add more diseases and symptoms to the database.

References

[1]   Neumann, G. and Kawaoka, Y. (2015) Transmission of Influenza A Viruses. *Virology*, **479-480**, 234-246.
      http://www.sciencedirect.com/science/article/pii/S0042682215001452
      http://dx.doi.org/10.1016/j.virol.2015.03.009

[2]   Scalera, N.M. and Mossad, S.B. (2009) The First Pandemic of the 21st Century: A Review of the 2009 Pandemic Variant Influenza A (H1N1) Virus. *Postgraduate Medicine*, **121**, 43-47. http://dx.doi.org/10.3810/pgm.2009.09.2051

[3]   Centers for Disease Control and Prevention (CDC) (2011) Self-Reported Influenza-Like Illness during the 2009 H1N1 Influenza Pandemic—United States, September 2009-March 2010. *Morbidity and Mortality Weekly Report*, **60**, 37.

[4]   Nucamendi Cervantes, G. (2014) Epidemiología de Influenza en México. Subsecretaría de Prevención y Promoción de la Salud, 32-36.

[5]   Gomez-Dantés, H., *et al.* (2011) La estrategia para la prevención y el control integrado del dengue en Mesoamérica. *Saludpública Méx*, **53**, s349-s357.

[6]   Gubler, D.J., Ooi, E.E., Vasudevan, S. and Farrar, J. (2014) Dengue and Dengue Hemorrhagic Fever. CABI.

[7]   Fajardo-Dolci, G., Meljem-Moctezuma, J., Vicente-González, E., Venegas-Páez, F.V., Mazón-González, B. and Aguirre-Gas, H.G. (2012) Dengue Fever in Mexico. Knowledge for Improving the Quality of Health. *Revista Médica del Instituto Mexicano del Seguro Social*, **50**, 631-639.

[8]   Guzman, M.G. and Harris, E. (2015) Dengue. *The Lancet*, **385**, 453-465.
      http://www.sciencedirect.com/science/article/pii/S0140673614605729
      http://dx.doi.org/10.1016/S0140-6736(14)60572-9

17

Ontology of Domains. Ontological Description Software Engineering Domain—The Standard Life Cycle

Ekaterina M. Lavrischeva

Moscow Physics-Technical Institute, Dolgoprudnuy, Russia
Email: lavryscheva@gmail.com

Abstract

Basic concepts and notions of ontological description of domains are implemented in the conceptual model being understandable to ordinary users of this domain. Ontological approach is used for the presentation of software engineering domain—Life Cycle (LC) ISO/IEC 12207 with the aim to automate LC processes and to generate different variants of LC for development systems. And the second aim of Conceptual Model must teach the student to standard process LC, which includes general, organizational and supported processes. These processes are presented in graphical terms of DSL, which are transformed to XML for processing systems in the modern environment (IBM, VS.Net, JAVA and so on). The testing process is given in ontology terms of Protégé systems, and semantics of tasks of this process is implemented in Ruby. Domain ontology LC is displayed by the several students of MIPT Russia and Kiev National University as laboratory practicum course "Software Engineering".

Keywords

Ontology, Life Cycle, Models, Processes, Actions, Tasks, Testing, DSL, XML, Protégé

1. Introduction

At the given work, new conception of automation in general processes of LC and generation of variants specialized are offered for their use in the modern programs, information systems and technologies and implementations in the distributed environments of Grid and Clouds processing, highly productive cluster systems and in web-semantic to the Internet.

This conception is formulated by the author for the students of MIPT and Kiev National University (KNU) at the basic course lections of "Software Engineering" (2010-2013). Standard LC ISO/IEC 12207-2007 is a general mechanism of construction of various program systems (PS) and program products (PP). The 17 processes enter into his composition, 74 under processes (actions) and 232 technological tasks. The automation of LC is a very thorny and heavy problem. Variants of the standard LC will be implemented by many companies in case of development of the different application systems. A submachine gun is absent. Offered by our conception of LC automation through the formal conceptual model LC is an attempt in development of the Case commons instruments for support LC to the future industry PP [1]-[5].

In addition, for implementation of this conception we use new languages of description in conceptual models of knowledge: OWL (Web Ontology Language), ODSD (Ontology-Driven Software Development), XML (Extensible Markup Language), MBPN (Modeling Biasness Process Notation) and others like that. There are systems of design of domains—ODM (Organizational Domain Modeling), FODA (Feature-Oriented Domain Analysis), DSSA (Domain-Specific Software Architectures), DSL (Domain Specific Language) Tools VS.Net, Eclipse-DSL, Protégé and others like that. That is terms are used for the formal specification of the LC processes and design from them of different PP. The ontological approach ODSD allows getting descriptions of classes from notions to the domain. Unlike previous, models to the domain can be used not only for the generation of code, but also can be "executable" artifacts.

An important aspect of design in different domains is the notion base and system of notions, by which all problems are formulated to the domain. The notion base is given by terminology, substantial relations between notions and their interpretations.

Among the relations the main are [1]:

–Concretization, as an union of notions in the new notion, the substantial signs of which can be a sum of signs of notions or substantially new;

–Association, that approves a presence of communication between notions without clarification of dependence of them from maintenance and volumes;

–Aggregation of terminology, notions, characters for their relations and paradigms of their interpretations in scopes to the domain is accepted to name the ontology of domain knowledge.

In the same general case, ontology is an agreement about the general use of notions, which includes facilities of subject knowledge and agreement about methods of reasoning representation.

The ontology appears by the semantic networks, knots of which are been by domain notion, and by arcs—copulas or relation, associations between them. On the given time the ontological approaches got the wide distribution in the decision of problems of knowledge, semantic integration of informative resources, informative searches and others like that representation. They allow getting descriptions of classes of objects domain, which are specific at notion and knowledge about them. Some ontology domains are given by knowledge, dictionaries of notions, concepts and relations between them. So, the XML become a standard language for marking of various data domains for their saving and exchange between different domains. It is a mean of automatic transformation of descriptions of model domains in the modern ontological languages to the charts, which are suitable for work in the different applied applications.

Offered conception ontology was considered in the different models of LC (spiral, interaction, incremental and so on) on student lections and on the scientific seminars of the Theory Programming and Information Systems departments of the Kiev National University (KNU), and also case of the discipline teaching the "Software engineering" [3]. Within the framework of this discipline the students learn modern methods and design facilities domains and PS constructions, and also learning standards of LC ISO/IEC 12207-2007 and General Data Types ISO/IEC 11404 GDT-2006. At the practical classes evaluation of facilities is conducted for general description and implementation of some experimental ontology on DSL Tools VS.Net and Protégé. For example of description of some fragments of science domains by the ontological facilities they built models PS with purpose of their use in case of PP construction [4] [5]. Some students of department of the IC and TP faculty of cybernetics defended diploma works on given topics with the use of ontological facilities and notions (classes, axioms, slots, facets and others like that) for description of calculable geometry, GDT and LC on the ITC of developing object and component and configuration them [6]. (http://sestudy.edu-ua.net)

Approach to LC automation and its evaluation by students in curriculum of the model LC and standard ISO/IEC 12207-2007, namely to study LC structure, processes and actions, and also use of ontology facilities for their description and implementation in the open ontological instruments are offered—DSL Tools VS.Net and Protégé. Students received ontological knowledge may apply them in the implementation of other application areas.

2. Ontology as a Basic Formal Description of Subject Areas

Ontology is a conceptual tool to describe base set of concepts and relations for some domains (or subject **area-SA**). The concept of the SA is classified and dictionary and thesaurus database schema knowledge is created. Domain Ontology—is a system of concepts or conceptual model which is supplied with a set of entities and relationships between them. Now, many anthologies for various scientific and applied areas are created. For example: ontology Census general knowledge of English natural concepts (70,000 more terms and their definitions); ontology concepts of e-commerce; global ontology products and services (UN); commercial ontology SCTG, Rosetta Net-traffic products from 400 companies. Medical ontology's: Galen-to determine the clinical condition; UMLS-US National Library of Medicine; ON9-famous for certification of health systems; chemical, biological ontology; all-Web portal mathematical resources; universal mathematical system Math Lab, Ret, etc.

A basic instrument of implementation of the subject description is the DSL Tools VS.Net and Eclipse-DSL [7]-[9], the result of the tools is described in the XML (Extensible Markup Language) language, which actually became a standard of data marking for their saving and exchange of information between different applications. XML serves to transformation of the domain ontology model in XML-charts, suitable for work of applied applications.

Using the properties ontology for description of processes LC was given the subject-oriented DSL (Domain Specific Language), and also language the BPMN description of semantics of these processes, the author offers approach of implementation of suggested conception. In the example implementation of the given conception we select the process of testing by the ontological facilities and semantics description by language of programming. At developments to the domain LC used ontological instrumental facilities, DSL Tools VS.Net, DSL Eclipse and Protégé. Set of different methodologies, facilities of language for description of domains are shown in **Figure 1**.

Ontology of LC is absent. We consider two means of implementing domain LC-language OWL and tools DSL for the overall presentation of the model standard ISO/IEC 12207 and basic concepts of the testing process LC in the standard system Protégé.

Ontology Means

The form of representation of ontology is a conceptual model (CM) on the reflecting system concepts with common properties (attributes), attitude and behavior rules. CM serves as a communication (between people, between computer systems), storage of information in a computer environment and the recycling of finished objects stored in libraries and repositories. To describe the use of ontology language OWL (Web Ontology Language) with a range of languages and markup languages RDF is to access and exchange ontological knowledge in the Internet. Description in ontology language OWL is a sequence of axioms and facts, information about classes, properties and resources for ID documents and Web imported URI in the form: <DatatypeID>:: = <URI reference> (see **Figure 2**).

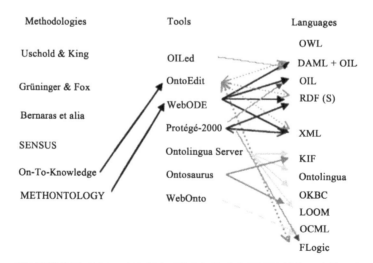

Figure 1. List of methodologies, facilities and the ontology language.

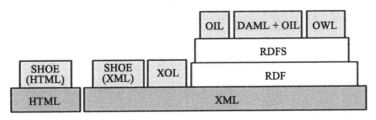

Figure 2. Languages definition of ontology.

Axiom class is a set of more general classes and restrictions on local properties of objects.

The class or a subset of the intersection of more general classes of constraints may be equivalent.

Axiom class in OWL is a set of specifications that can be in the form of generalized classes, restrictions, sets of resources, Boolean combinations of descriptions and more.

As ontology editor was used Protégé 3.4. It seems ontology classes, slots, facets and axioms. (http://protege.stanford.edu/)

Classes describe concepts of, and slots—properties (attributes) classes.

Facets describe the properties of slots (specific types and ranges of possible values).

The axioms define additional constraints (rules).

Classes can be abstract or concrete.

Abstract classes are classes and concrete containers may contain abstract attributes (which do not contain specific values).

Attributes of concepts in a domain called Protégé slots. Specific classes contain specific slots, which can be assigned a value (a copy attributes). To determine the types and limits on the value (like the rules of XML-Schema) used facets.

Protégé supports multiple inheritances but a class can have more than one superclass.

3. Life Cycles Ontology of Software Systems

LC received evolution from the beginning of programming, from simplified life cycle for each application models to spiral, iterative and so on. They formed a separation in group development of various types PS. As the result the standard ISO/IEC 1996 (first edition) was introduced, and in 2007 the second edition of its life cycle appeared, which reflects the overall structure of processes that may be involved in the development of the different PS. These standards should be studied by students who will participate in the joint development of various applications and commercial systems [3].

3.1. Presentation of Formal Specification of the LC Standard ISO/IEC-12207

The LC processes are given in standard by three categories (see **Table 1**).

In the each process it defines types of activity (actions-activity), tasks, aggregate of results (going out) of activity and decision of tasks design, testing, assembly and others, and also tracing some specific requirements. A list of works for the basic, organizational and support processes is led in standard, but method of their implementation and form of presentation not available. Next, we give a general description of the basic, organizational and support processes.

To the *basic processes* belong:

–Acquisition process determines actions of buyer at automated system or service. Actions are initiation and preparation of query, legalization of contract; monitoring and acceptance;

–Delivery process determines actions from the transmission of product or service to the buyer. It has preparation of suggestions, legalization of contract, planning, implementation and control of product, and also its estimation and delivery;

–Development process determines the processes and actions (development of requirements, planning, encoding, integration, testing, the system testing, and installation) for development of PP;

–Exploitation process (introduction, support of user, testing functions, exploitation of the system) determines actions of operator from maintenance of processes the system during its exploitation by users;

–Maintenance process (management by modifications, support of current status and functional fitness, PP installation in the operating environment, accompaniment and modification, development of system modification

Table 1. The process is of standard life cycle.

№ п/п	Process (subprocess)
1. Category the "Basic processes"	
1.1	Order (agreement)
1.1.1	Preparation of order, choice of supplier
1.1.2	Monitoring supplier activity, acceptance by user
1.2	Delivery (acquisition)
1.3	Development
1.3.1	Exposure of requirements
1.3.2	Analysis of system requirements
1.3.3	Planning system architecture
1.3.4	Analysis of system requirements
1.3.5	Planning the system
1.3.6	Constructing (code) the system
1.3.7	Integration of the system
1.3.8	Testing the system
1.3.9	System integration
1.3.1	System testing
1.3.1	Installation of the system
1.4	Exploitation
1.4.1	Functional application
1.4.2	Support of user
1.5	Accompaniment
2. The support "Processes category"	
2.1	Documenting
2.2	Management by configuration
2.3	Providing a quality guarantee
2.4	Verification
2.5	Validation
2.6	General review
2.7	Audit
2.8	Decision of problems
2.9	Providing product applicability
2.10	Evaluation of product
3. Category the "Organizational processes"	
3.1	Management
3.1.1	Management at level organization
3.1.2	Management by project
3.1.3	Management by quality
3.1.4	Management by the risk
3.1.5	Organizational providing
3.1.6	Measuring
3.1.7	Management by knowledge's
3.2	Improvement
3.2.1	Introduction of processes
3.2.2	Evaluation of processes
3.2.3	Improvement of processes

plans, PP migrations on other and others like that), which determines actions of organization, that development PP.

The LC standard contains description of the ancillary proceeding, that regulate the additional actions from verification of product, management by project and his quality.

The *support process* contains: documenting, management by versions, verification and validation, revisions, audits, evaluation of product and etch. To the *organizational processes* belong: management by project (development management) and perfection of processes.

The *management process* includes the processes of management by configuration, project, quality, risks, changes and others like that. The *perfection* process includes introduction, project estimation and his perfection.

Quantity of processes, actions and LC standard tasks are shown in **Table 2**.

Depending on the purpose of concrete project the main developer and project manager choose the processes, actions and tasks, line up the LC chart for application in the concrete project. Description of semantics of processes and methods of their implementation (objective, component, service and so on) written in kernel of SWEBOK knowledge and [3]. (www.swebok.com)

Theoretical, applied methods, quality standards, general and fundamental types of data (ISO/IEC 15404, ISO/IEC 9126, ISO/IEC 11404 and others), and also recommendations and methods of this standards are used at every technology of the PS programming with the use of the LC standard.

Task of automation of standard LC arose up in the students groups MIPT and KNU of course Software Engineering. Taking into account this task, the author discussed with the students the features of standards and machineries of their presentation in the modern operating environments. On the practical lessons the students learned LC processes and gave their description for DSL Tools VS.Net. The students executed LC ontology description in graphic (**Figure 3**) and the XML kinds within this framework. Then they used DSL Eclipse and Protégé.

XML description of general, support and organization processes are given on web-site ITC.

3.2. Formal Presentation of Conceptual Model Domain LC

Starting from **Table 2**, we give description to the conceptual model (CM) domain LC standard, described highly from terms: P—processes, A—actions and T—tasks.

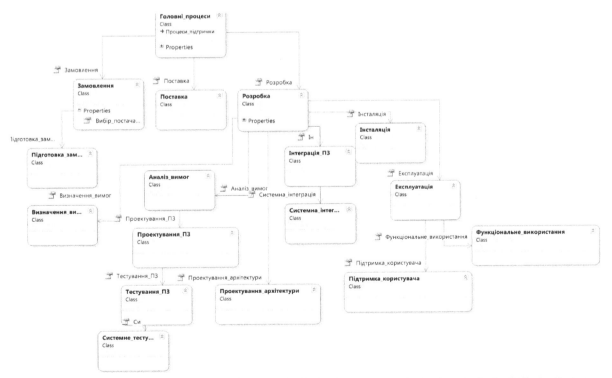

Figure 3. Graphical representation of the basic life cycle processes.

Table 2. Processes, under processes tasks and LC actions.

Classes	Process	Action	Task
Basic processes	5	35	135
Support processes	10	25	70
Organizational processes	2	14	27
All	17	74	232

The LC model has such kind:

$$M_{LC} = \left(P_\kappa, A_{_M}, T_n \right)$$

where $P\kappa = \left(P_{1\kappa}, P_{2\kappa 1}, P_{3\kappa 2} \right) - P_{1\kappa, \kappa =1-5}$ —basic processes of the LC first category,

$P_{2\kappa 1, \kappa 1=1-8}$ —processes of LC support of the second category;

$P_{3\kappa 2, \kappa 2=4}$ —organizational processes of the LC second category;

$$A_{_M} = \left(A_{\kappa r}, A_{\kappa 1l}, A_{\kappa 2j} \right)$$

where $A_{\kappa, r\; r=1-35}$ —action on the basic processes LC,

$A_{\kappa 1l, l=1-25}$ —Action on the LC support processes,

$A_{\kappa 2\, j=1-14}$ —action on the processes LC;

$T_n = \left(T_{n\kappa}, T_{nl}, T_{nj} \right)$

where $T_{n\kappa}$, $\kappa = 1$ - 135 —tasks of the basic processes LC;

$T_{nl, l=1-70}$ —tasks of LC support processes;

$T_{nj, j=1-27}$ —tasks of the organizational processes LC.

The goal processes, operations given is highly contained in essence, and description of maintenance of tasks on it is led them in standard. The tasks not formal and will be in the future at the first given description of their setting, then selection languages for the formal specification for realization to their semantics.

For presentation the structure of the CM LC is used graphic language DSL. This language has an expressive feature, directed on the reflection of the process specific LC, while languages of the general setting (Java, C++, C#, Ruby and others) oriented on description of actions of any programs of the data processing. The DSL contains general abstractions for the reflection of classes of objects domain type process, action, and also relations between them [2] [9]. On its maintenance this language near to the HTML, XML, WSDL and others like that.

Model LC it is described by one DSL, can be transformed in model by other DSL. It allows freely to integrate between itself different parts of system processes, written in the different DSL. That is domain LC can be described at one level of abstraction, and then regenerate with the additional going into detail on the more low level of abstraction, that allows complementing a model domain by the repeated components and objects. Main to the CM domain LC there is a model of general descriptions of processes as objects domain.

Processes of transformation of the LC models in the DSL at the different levels are given in **Figure 4**.

Transformation of description of the models LC in this language DSL is conducted by facilities of the model-guided development MDD (Model Driven Development). According to this model system architecture are designed at two levels—platform of level independent on the PIM (Platform Independent Model) model and platform of dependent level on the PSM model (Platform Specific Models).

The LC domain CM model can be automated with the use of specific languages, be tuned especially for processes and actions, which are in class language ontology. The models can contain information about the union of processes and actions, including artifacts, which participate in it, and also their dependence between itself. They can also contain information about the configuration structure of the programs of treatment of processes, vehicle and program resources, necessary in case of implementation of the programs of automation of processes and their development.

3.2.1. Ontology of Domain Characteristic Model

DSL development pre-condition is made by the detailed analysis and structured to the domain. Among the existent methodologies of domain analysis most knowing such: ODM (Organization Domain Modeling), FODA

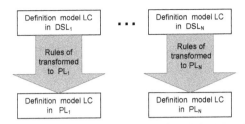

Figure 4. Transformation of description of models LC in DSL.

(Feature-Oriented Domain Analysis), characteristic analysis to the domain and DSSA (*Domain*-Specific Software Architectures) [9]-[11].

In case of analysis to the domain is created a model of characteristic. This model secures *generalization* and *disagreements of the PS* domain processes by the indication of general characteristic for all processes and excellent characteristic each of the LC processes.

A model of characteristic is given by *diagrams of characteristic* with description of relations between them. Conception of diagrams is inherited from the FODA method, which gives possibility briefly to describe all possible configurations of processes within the limits of different categories of the LC processes, which are considered as instances, selecting general and alternative characteristics, which can be excellent for each configuration of the LC processes.

For the given time notation of characteristic diagram is executed by the DSL language under the FDL (Feature Definition Language) name, as languages of description of characteristic of notions to the domain and formal definite operations for treatment of FDL expressions.

The diagrams of characteristic is given system characteristic the different domains. In case of creation of automated instruments, intended for construction of diagrams of characteristic and their treatment, text presentation is necessary. It inflicts all information, which exists in the graphic diagram. The determination consists of great number of characteristic (feature definitions), names of characteristic and *expression* (feature expression), that includes:

–Atomic characteristics;

–Composition characteristics: names of which determination elsewhere;

–Optional characteristics (*optional*) of expression, is it completed by the "character"?

–Obligatory characteristics (*mandatory*) of expressions, what reserved in construction of *all* ();

–Alternative characteristic (*exclusive*-choice): y expression of *one-of* ();

–Exceptional set of descriptions ("or-features") from the list of characteristic expressions of *more-of* () and their combination;

–Value of characteristic by default (default)—atomic to description;

–Other (indefinite) characteristic in the form of ".".

The specification of FDL characteristic gives formals for determination of syntax, which it is possible to compare to the BNF (P.Naur) form for conducting a lexical and semantic analysis of described characteristic of model domain, which is used for creation of the different variants PS.

3.2.2. About Machineries of Dependence of Characteristic

Offered approach is contained on principle of inherences characteristic with such terms:

– Every characteristic answers class;

–*Associations* (copulas) between classes are noticed to so call <stereotype>, which marks a type of characteristic dependence:

–Obligatory (*mandatory*) dependence between aggregations in classes;

–Optional (*optional*) dependence between association and range of cardinal numbers (by power of great number or quantity of elements of great number) from 0 до1;

–Obligatory list of *one-of* and *more-of* in specified class each of alternatives.

The result of translation of description of characteristic in FDL can be given by the XMI language, as a format of exchange by information of Meta data (the XML Meta data Information Exchange format). The XML–documents can be imported in the UML design instruments, such as Rational and UML, and also for the generation of the Java classes. After creation of the DSL language to the domain it is necessary to use the FDL language. Approach to description of model of domain it is used for developed the LC processes of variants PS by configuring different processes for automation the PS. On the given model LC are solved the task of providing a generation of special variants from necessary processes for realization of the set PS. Every variant will be addition of semantics of some tasks for included processes. For the receipt of the working variant LC PS a use of Java facilities is planned [6] [7].

3.3. Standard Life Cycle Ontology in DSL Eclipse

For description of ontology of domains there is other approach of Eclipse DSL [3] [6]. This development environment is used for presentation of the graphic models LC because it has effective instruments for description the object of this domain. On beginning it is necessary to develop a visual model of domain LC. Than it make description of classes of sections processes LC domain and relations between them (**Figure 5** and **Figure 6**).

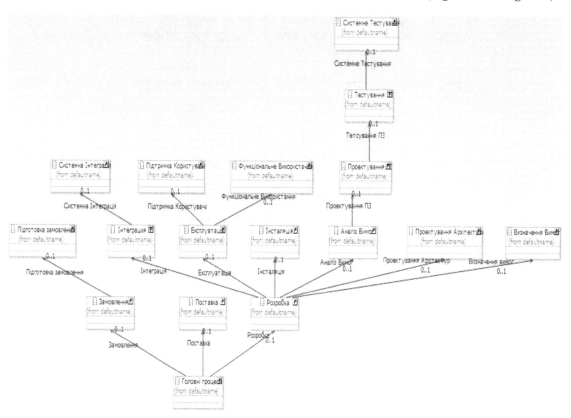

Figure 5. Structure organization process LC in DSL.

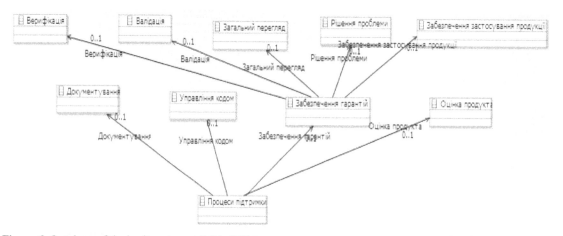

Figure 6. Ontology of the basic processes LC in DSL.

The types of relations allow realizing basic logic of project. Present methods and fields necessary are described in every class for functioning a project. The support processes contain all processes that are executed after the domain construction and support his capacity and actuality. Their ontological structure answers a structure of basic processes and is pointed it will not be.

A next step is been by the generation of text presentation of present graphic models, and then generation in XML. A process of the LC testing is annotated by facilities of knowledge domain notion and their relation in Protégé representation.

Text description of the LC processes by XML

Given graphic presentation of the CL processes was used for the receipt of text in the XML.

Errors in the graphic description, which were found by designer and correction by, correspond to the editor. After it a result of every process is given in XML. An example is below led to the description fragment to the fragment of the main processes LC in the XML.

```
<? Xml version="1.0" encoding="utf-8"?>
    <Association Line Name="Determination of requirements" Type="Main. Determination of requirements"
Manually Routed = "true" FixedFromPoint = "true"   </Association Line>
    <AssociationLine Name = "Integration PS" Type = "Main. Integration PS"
    <AssociationLine Name = "Installetion" Type = "Main. Installetion"
    <AssociationLine Name = "Exploatation" Type = "Main. Exploatation"
     <Property Name = " Integration PS" />
     <Property Name = " Installetion" />
     <Property Name = " Requirements Analyses" />
     <Property Name = "Exploitation" />...
```

For receipt descriptions of the LC processes in XML is given their semantic description. Annotating is executed on example of the LC testing processes by Protégé facilities [10] [11].

Facilities of the Protégé for Description Ontology

To the basic facilities of the Protégé for description of ontology belong:
   –classes (or notion);
   –relation (or properties, attributes);
   –functions;
   –axioms,
   –copies (or individuals).

Classes—it is abstract groups, collections or sets of objects. They can include the copies, other classes, or halving both that and second. *The relations* give a type to co-operation between notions domain. *Functions*—it is the special case of relations, in which an n-element of relation is simply determined by the n-1 previous elements. *Axioms* are used for determination of complex limitations on the value of attributes, arguments of relations, for verification of information correctness, or for inference of new information.

By these facilities Protégé forming an ontological model to the LC domain is conducted.

The classes answer the types of artifacts, which, in same queue, answer the roles of program components in system and in the functional properties product/Classes are reflected in Protégé as an inheritance (inheritance hierarchy) hierarchy, which is disposed in to the window navigator of classes (Class Browser). By root of tree of classes in Protégé, by default, appointed class THING (thing, something). All created classes are to be inherited immediately or mediocre.

The protégé will be use for presentation CL testing processes.

It are a new type of description LC and testing processes, which are very necessary for e-learning students for practice preparing some tests for testing the programs [3] [5] [11].

4. Description of Ontology of Process Testing LC

The conceptual model of process testing of the PS has a kind [4] [5] [7] [8]:

$$SFT = \{TM, TD, TA, Env\}$$

where *TM*—subprocess of management by testing;

TD and *TA*—subprocesses of testing accordingly domains and applications;
Env—conceptual and informative environment of testing process of the PS.
To all three subprocesses will give the compatible formal presentation:

$$TM = \{Task(TM, TD, TA), CM(TA, TD), Env\}$$

where *Task*—tasks of correspond under process;

$$Env = En(TM) \cup En(TD) \cup En(TA)$$

En—conceptual and informative environment of correspond under process;
CM—under model of co-ordination of operations of correspond under process.
Environment composition is determined by expression:

$$Env = TG \cup SG \cup T \cup P \cup RG \cup RP$$

where *TG* and *SG*—test active voices and prepared programs;
T and *P*—tests and application for testing;
RG and *RP*—reports about implementation of the tests of programs.

Ontological description of testing process. For description of this process used ontological system Protégé. In her knowledge about the process model are given by *classes, slots, facets* and *axioms*. Similar possibility give also and other instruments. For example, diagrams of classes in the UML Rational Rose, which can translate in the program code of a few languages of programming.

For presentation of testing ontology use two groups of notions: *simple* and *complex.*

Testing—simple notions. It such: Tester (*Tester*), Context (*Context*), Action (*Activity*), Method (*Method*), Artifact *and Environment.*

Can have simple notion attributes. In quality *attributes* such are selectable under notions, which characterize base (paternal) notion and can accept the concrete values. Will give short maintenance of basic concepts.

Tester—the subject or object, which executes testing determines. The group of testing has a leader, which is a notion attribute, and him name—by the value of attribute. Attributes are been by *name, type, duties.* Tester attribute-duties-describes, that can do a tester in the process of testing. Notion duties–complex notion, which is determined on the basic of simple notions. For this notion it is possible to select next attributes: tester name, tester type, duties. Tester attribute-duties-describes actions, which can be done by tester in the process of testing.

Example to the tester XML-fragment:

```
<! -- TESTER -->
<xs: element name = "TESTER">
  MaxOccurs = "unbounded" ref = "TESTER"/>
    </xs: sequence>
    <xs:attributename = "TESTER_TYPE" use = "required">
    <xs:simpleType>
        </xs:attribute>
    <xs:attributename = "TESTER_NAME" use = "required"/>
```

Context determines the proper levels, methods of testing, entrances and going out tasks of testing. In ontology this notion determines one attribute: Context type (Level of testing) on form

Level of testing = {module, integration, system, regressive}.

Action consists of notions, that go into detail the steps of process of testing: planning testing, development (generation) of tests, implementation of tests, estimation of results, measuring test coverage, generation of reports and others like that. For this notion one attribute is inflicted-type of action (Activity type) with the possible values: type of action = {planning, development of tests, implementation of tests, and verification of results, coverage estimation, and preparation of report}.

Method—this notion, which is answered by a few methods of testing. For example, the module testing—methods of the structural and functional testing. Every method in relation to the initial code can be classified as a "white small box", "black small box" or based on specification of testing (specification-based). Fragment of method notion XML–chart:

```
<!-- METHOD -->
<xs:element name = "METHOD">
 <xs:complexType>
    <xs:attribute name = "METHOD_NAME" use = "required">
     <xs:simpleType>
       <xs:restriction base = "xs:token">
         <xs:enumeration value = "CONTROL_FLOW_TESTING"/>
         <xs:enumeration value = "DATA_FLOW_TESTING"/>
         <xs:enumeration ...
```

The methods based on coda subdivide on: structural; over seeding of errors; mutational. The structural methods subdivide on: testing a stream of management and testing a data flow. The methods of testing a management (control-flow methods) stream include coverage of operators, coverage of branches and different criteria of coverage of ways. This concrete methods testing is copies of different class of methods of testing.

By the similar rank methods of "black small box" are classified or based on specification: functional; on supposition about the errors; heuristic and so on.

From other side, in relation to process of search of errors and refusals, it is possible to divide all methods into systematic (search of errors) and stochastic (statistical)–exposure of refusals.

Thus, for description of method of testing will enter next attributes:

–Name (method name), "laying out on category";

–Method type (structural, based on the errors);

–Approach, based on code, on specifications, statistical.

Such lying out of methods allows simply classifying every method of testing and extending ontology.

Artifacts. Every action from testing can include a few artifacts, such as an object of testing, intermediate data, results of testing, plans, sets of tests, scripts and others like that. Name them "test active voices". The objects of testing can be different types: initial code, the HTML files, the XML files, built-in images, sound, video, documents and so on. All this artifacts mapping in ontology. Every artifacts is also associated with place of its saving, data, history of creation and revision (for example, creator, upgrade time, version number and others like that).

Environment. Program environments, where testing is executed, as a rule notion such given: name, type and product version. Given notion is broken up on two under notion: vehicle and program with attributes. Attributes of hardware environment are: *device name, model, and producer.*

Attributes of software environment are: *product name, product type and version.* The possible values of attribute can be seen by such:

Environment = {ОС, БД, Compiler, web-browser}.

Complex notions of process of testing. Such belong to the complex notions: tester (capability) duties and task (task). They are determined by simple notions.

In the distributed system co-operation between components is executed by interfaces (reports). After treatment of report, the component which got him returns the *answer.* That is why in ontology expediently to enter additional notions of report and answer. With every report it is possible to link the attributes *Type* and *Value.* With every answer it is possible to link its state, which is set as an attribute with two possible values:

The State answer = {Success, Refusal}.

Tricking into result to description of basic terms ontology of testing it will present an ontological model of process of testing with the use of led notions is given on the **Figure** 7.

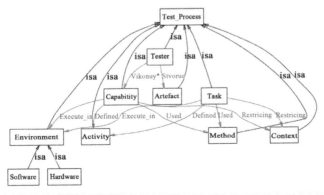

Figure 7. Count of ontology of testing.

For transformation this count to XML gets out format in windows Protege system (**Figure 8**).

Fragment of ontology of testing in the XML, automatically generates Protege 3.4 and is presented in the UNICODE terms:

```
<class>
        <name>: STANDARD-SLOT</name>
        <type>: STANDARD-CLASS</type>
        <own_slot_value>
                <slot_reference>: ROLE</slot_reference>
                <value value_type="string">Concrete</value>
        </own_slot_value>
        <superclass>:SLOT</superclass>
        <template_slot>: DOCUMENTATION</template_slot>
        <template_slot>: SLOT-CONSTRAINTS</template_slot>
        <template_slot>: SLOT-MAXIMUM-CARDINALITY</template_slot>
        <template_slot>: SLOT-MINIMUM-CARDINALITY</template_slot>
        <template_slot>: SLOT-NUMERIC-MAXIMUM</template_slot>
        <template_slot>: SLOT-NUMERIC-MINIMUM</template_slot>
        <template_slot>: SLOT-INVERSE</template_slot>
        <template_slot>: SLOT-DEFAULTS</template_slot>
        <template_slot>: SLOT-VALUES</template_slot>
        <template_slot>: ASSOCIATED-FACET</template_slot>
        <template_slot>: DIRECT-SUBSLOTS</template_slot>
        <template_slot>: DIRECT-SUPERSLOTS</template_slot>
        <template_slot>: DOCUMENTATION</template_slot>
        <template_slot>: SLOT-CONSTRAINTS</template_slot>
        <template_slot>: SLOT-MAXIMUM-CARDINALITY</template_slot>
        <template_slot>: SLOT-MINIMUM-CARDINALITY</template_slot>
        <template_slot>: SLOT-NUMERIC-MAXIMUM</template_slot>
        <template_slot>: SLOT-NUMERIC-MINIMUM</template_slot>
        <template_slot>: SLOT-INVERSE</template_slot>
        <template_slot>: SLOT-DEFAULTS</template_slot>
        <template_slot>: SLOT-VALUES</template_slot>
        <template_slot>: ASSOCIATED-FACET</template_slot>
        <template_slot>: DIRECT-SUBSLOTS</template_slot>
        <template_slot>: DIRECT-SUPERSLOTS</template_slot>
```

Using these notions, the KNU students on the practical getting by busy created a variant of ontology of process of testing and realization of the program of testing by the Ruby (**Figure 9**). Erroneous characters are marked on the checked program (**Figure 9**) on the right, and a correct record is on the left given.

Model of testing ontology and this program made two students in magister works and are placed on web-site http://sestudy.edu-ua.net. It is necessary to do the appeal to, which by pressing on the name "Ontology" word at the main panel of this site.

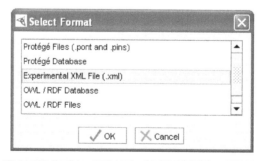

Figure 8. Saving ontology in the XML format.

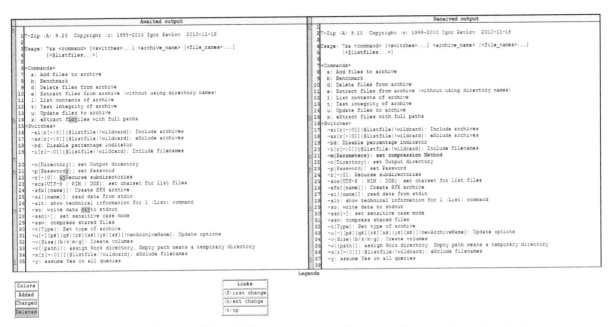

Figure 9. Testing program with the marked errors in it.

5. Life Cycle Ontology on Site

Complex technology that includes a spectrum of technologies, facilities, instruments of planning and reuses specification is realized in ITK of web-site [6]. (http://sestudy.edu-ua.net)

This site is based on standard systems (Eclipse, Protégé, CORBA, MS.Net and others), systems of support of co-operation of the programs, systems and environments between itself VS.Net "Eclipse" Java [6] [11]-[15].

The main menu of web-site has a few sections: TECHNOLOGIES, INTERPRABILITY, INSTRUMENTS, TEACHING and others. Realization of specified operations from class of operations of components development, assembling, change and their configuring is led in the "Technology" section. On this section it is given such position:

–Generation of DSL description to the LC domain;

–Ontology of presentation of the standard LC domain and domain of calculable geometry;

–Beb-services for interconnection different components in environment MS.Net, IBM, Eclipse;

–Transformation of general types of GDT data to fundamental FDT and others.

Web-site is oriented on realization by LC ontological facilities with the use of the Protege system. After its help by the student T Litho of departments the "Informative systems" KNU are developed ontology of calculable geometry, which behaves toward the normative course. Web-site is developed by three languages (Ukrainian, Russian, and Eng.). As Google statistics show, to web-site apply from the different countries (more 35,000 users–teachers and students). This site contains a textbook the "Software Engineering" and is used by author for the E-teaching to all aspects of this discipline. By me lecture at the ICTERI-2012 conference were done, in which mapping new approaches to teaching students of SE.

6. Conclusions

The essence of this work focuses on the automation LC by ontological description conceptual model. It is new approaches to the description of domain SE Standard ISO/IEC 12207-2007. Perform three basic tasks: to develop a conceptual model LC and describe this model in terms of language (DSL, OWL); to generate variants LC for development different systems; to consider the training of students scheme using LC by described ontology.

The formal terms for describing the conceptual model LC of the domain ontology are given. The table description of general, organizational processes and support processes of the standard LC is used for presentation processes in the language of DSL. The characteristic domain model and process model LC in DSL is done. A scheme describing LC in DSL is transformed to a lower level XML for processing systems in the environment (IBM, VS.Net, JAVA and so on).

Submission LC processes graphically DSL Tool VS.Net, and in the language XML is described. Conception of automation of the LC and realization testing process is discussed. As a practical implementation process is selected by process testing. A formal description of the conceptual model testing in terms of Protégé systems and algorithm testing in the language Ruby is realized.

It is noted that the ontological model of LC and computational geometry is implemented by the MIPT, KNU students. Technology of work with that ontology is presented on the website, which gives an access to realize ontology. (http://sestudy.edu-ua.net)

References

[1]   Gomes-Perez, A., Fernandez-Lopez, M. and Corcho, O. (2004) Ontological Engineering. Springer-Verlag, London, 403 p.

[2]   Mernik, M., Heering, J. and Sloane, A.M. (2006) When and How to Develop Domain—Specific Languages. *ACM Computing Surveys*, **37**, 316-344.

[3]   Lavrischeva, E.M. (2014) Software Engineering Computer Systems. Paradigms, Technologies, CASE-Tools Programming. Nauk, Dumka, 284 p. (In Russian)

[4]   Lavrischeva, E.M. (2013) Ontological Representation for the Total Life Cycle of AC Line Production of Software Product. *Proceedings Conf.TAAPSD'*2012, *Theoretical and Applied Aspects of Building Software Systems*, Yalta, 25 May-2 June 2013, 81-90.

[5]   Lavrischeva, E.M. (2013) The Approach to the Formal Submission of Ontology Life Cycle of Software Systems, Vesnik KNU, a Series of Physical and Math. *Sciences*, **4**, 140-149.

[6]   Lavrischeva, E.M., Zinkovich, V., Kolesnik, A., *et al.* (2012) Instrumental and Technological Complex for Development and Learning Design Patterns of Software Systems. State Intellectual Property Service of Ukraine, Copyright Registration Certificate No. 45292, 103 p. (In Ukrainian)

[7]   Korotun, T.M. and Lavrischeva, E.M. (2002) Construction of the Testing Process of Software Systems. *Problems of Programming*, **2**, 272-281. (In Ukrainian)

[8]   Korotun, T.M. (2005) Models and Methods Testing Engineering Programs Systems in Resource-Limited Settings. Autoref Dissertation, Kiev, 23 p. (In Ukrainian)

[9]   (2005) Walkthrough. Domain–Specific Language (DSL) Tools.

[10] Protégé—Frames User's Guide. http://protege.stanford.edu/doc/index.php/PrF_UG

[11] Mens, C., Van Gorp, P. and Czarnecki, K.A. Taxonomy of Model Transformation. http://drops.dagstuhl.de/2–5/11

[12] Lavrischeva, E.M. (2013) Generative and Composition Programming: Aspects of Developing Software System Families. *Cybernetics and Systems Analysis*, **49**, 110-123.

[13] Lavrischeva, E.M. and Ostrovski, A. (2013) New Theoretical Aspects of Software Engineering for Development Application and E-Learning. *Journal of Software Engineering and Application*, **6**, 34-40. http://www.crirp.org/journal/jsea

[14] Lavrischeva, E.M., Stenyashin, A. and Kolesnyk, A. (2014) Object-Component Development of Application and Systems. Theory and Practice. *Journal of Software Engineering and Applications*, **7**, 14. http://www.scirp.org/journal/jsea

[15] Lavrischeva, E.M. (2013) Conception of Programs Factory for Presentating and E-Learning Disciplines Software Engineering. 10*th International Conference on ICT in Education, Research and Industrial Applications*, Ukraine, 16 June 2013, 15. http://senldogo0039.springer-sbm.com/ocs/

[16] Lavrischeva, E., Ostrovski, A. and Radetskyi, I. (2012) Approach to E-Learning Fundamental Aspects of Software Engineering. 8*th international Conf. ICTERI—ICT in Education, Research and Industrial Applications*, Kherson, 6-10 June 2012. http://ceur-ws.org/Vol-848/ICTERI-2012-CEUR-WS-p-176-187

18

Alternatives Selection Using GORE Based on Fuzzy Numbers and TOPSIS

Arfan Mansoor, Detlef Streitferdt, Franz-Felix Füßl

Software Architectures and Product Line Group, Ilmenau University of Technology, Ilmenau, Germany
Email: arfan.mansoor@tu-ilmenau.de

Abstract

Context and Motivation: The notion of goal and goal models is ideal for the alternative systems. Goal models provide us different alternatives during goal oriented requirements engineering. Question/Problem: Once we find different alternatives, we need to evaluate these alternatives to select the best one. Ideas: The selection process consists of two main parts. In first part of the selection process among alternatives, we will use techniques in which we establish some evaluation criteria. The evaluation criteria are based on leaf level goals. Stakeholders are involved to contribute their opinions about the evaluation criteria. The input provided by various stakeholders is then converted into quantifiable numbers using fuzzy triangle numbers. After applying the defuzzification process on fuzzy triangle numbers we get scores (weights) for each criteria. In second part, these scores are used in the selection process to select the best alternative. Contribution: The two steps selection process helps us to select the best alternative among many alternatives. We have described the process and applied it to "cyclecomputer" selection case study.

Keywords

Decision Making, GORE, TOPSIS, Fuzzy Numbers

1. Introduction

Decision making process is about the selection of best option among all the alternatives. In almost all decision making problems, we have multiple criteria for selection among the alternatives. The problems involving multiple criteria are called Multi Criteria Decision Making (MCDM) problems. Decision making can be challenging because of conflicting stakeholders interests there is the uncertainty and vagueness of selected criteria. There may be different criteria but some are more important than others and tend to dominate the decision [1]. In general fuzzy set theory is adequate to deal with multi criteria problems [2].

In Goal Oriented Requirements Engineering (GORE), there is a great emphasis on alternative system proposals. Goal refinements help us in finding alternatives and during requirements elaboration process many alternatives are considered. The qualitative and quantitative analysis of these alternatives helps to choose the best one. In alternative selection we have to decide about the best option according to stakeholders needs.

In the context of GORE we need the support and methodology for identifying and managing the criteria for alternative's selection process. Finding the criteria based on GORE require high level goals to be analyzed till leaf goals are achieved *i.e.*, requirements. These leaf level goals help us in establishing the criteria which are used in the selection process among alternatives. The criteria are based on stakeholders needs and preferences and therefore stakeholders opinions need to be involved in selection process. It helps to identify the importance of requirement according to stakeholders understandings and needs. Based on these criteria we apply qualitative and quantitative reasoning techniques for the selection of alternative system proposals.

The general procedure of selection among alternatives consists of the following steps:
1. Finding acceptance criteria;
2. Involving stakeholders opinions;
3. Finding scores of each criteria;
4. Evaluating alternatives based on accepted criteria scores;
5. Making a selection.

In this paper we consider the case study of selecting one among four alternatives of "cyclecomputer". We use GORE to explore and establish the acceptance criteria. The acceptance criteria are then prioritized based on the stakeholders interests for determining which of these are more important than others. It serves two purposes: first involving the stakeholders opinions in selection process and second finding the relative importance of these criteria. The output is then given as input to Technique for Order of Preference by Similarity to Ideal Solution (TOPSIS) which selects the best alternative among the candidates.

The remainder of this paper is organized in the following sections: next section gives the literature review on topics used in our approach. Section 3 describes the proposed methodology. Section 4 introduces the "cyclecomputer" project and gives details of implementing proposed methodology for mentioned project. Section 5 discusses the related work on decision making and alternatives selection in GORE. Finally, last section concludes this paper.

2. Literature Review

2.1. GORE Review

The idea of goals emphasizes the understanding of organizational context for a new system [3]. Goal based requirements engineering is concerned with the identification of high level goals to be achieved by the system envisioned, the refinement of such goals, the operationalization of goals into services and constraints and the assignment of responsibilities for the resulting requirement to agents such as human, devices and programs [4].

Requirements engineering must address the contextual goals, functionalities to achieve these goals and constraints restricting how these functions are to be designed and implemented [5]. These goals, functions, and constraints have to be mapped to precise specifications of software behaviours [6]. From the 10th requirement engineering conference, the notion of goal has been explicitly stated in requirements engineering "Requirements Engineering (RE) is the branch of systems engineering concerned with the 'real-world goals' for, functions of, and constraints on software-intensive systems. It is also concerned with how these factors are taken into account during the implementation and maintenance of the system, from software specifications and architectures up to final test cases".

GORE concerns are classified into two major categories *i.e.*, goal analysis and goal evolution. Goal analysis is the process of exploring gathered documents, ranging from information about the organization, (*i.e.*, enterprise goals) to system specific information (*i.e.*, requirement) for the purpose of identifying, organizing and classifying goals [7]. Goal evolution concerns how the goals are changed from when they were identified to when they are operationalized. Goal evolution process is further refined into goal refinement and goal elaboration. Because stakeholders change their minds and goals have to be operationalized into requirements the goals and their priorities are likely to change. Based on goal refinement and goal elaboration we select the criteria which are used for alternative selection.

2.2. Fuzzy Numbers

Fuzzy numbers have been widely used in engineering disciplines because of their suitability to represent imprecise and vague information. Fuzzy numbers depict the physical world more realistically than single-valued numbers. Among the fuzzy number Triangular Fuzzy Number (TFN) is capable of aggregating the subjective opinions [8].

A triangular fuzzy number (TFN) is described by a triplet (L, M, H), where M is the modal value, L and H are the left (minimum value) and right (maximum value) boundary respectively. We use TFN to represent stakeholder opinions for criteria which are established through goal models.

2.3. TOPSIS Review

The Technique for Order of Preference by Similarity to Ideal Solution (TOPSIS) is a multi criteria decision analysis method. It is used to compare a set of alternatives based on weighted scores of each criterion. In this method two alternatives are hypothesized: positive ideal alternative and negative ideal alternative and then best alternative is selected which is close to the positive ideal solution and farthest from negative ideal alternative [9]. TOPSIS consist of following steps [10]:
1. Constructing a decision matrix;
2. Normalizing the decision matrix;
3. Finding the positive ideal and negative ideal alternatives;
4. Calculating the separation measures for each alternative;
5. Calculating the relative closeness to the ideal alternative.

3. The Proposed Method

First of all we have to explore different alternatives during GORE and for this we use goal models obtained during GORE. AND/OR diagrams which are the essential output artefact of these goal models are used in the exploration phase of alternatives. Once we found different alternatives, we need to evaluate these alternatives to select the best one. The alternatives are compared based on the weighted criteria. The criteria are weighted using fuzzy numbers and stakeholders opinions are taken as input and then converted to fuzzy numbers. By using the fuzzy numbers we can convert the qualitative information of stakeholders into quantitative one. The proposed methodology consist of following steps and is shown in **Figure 1**.

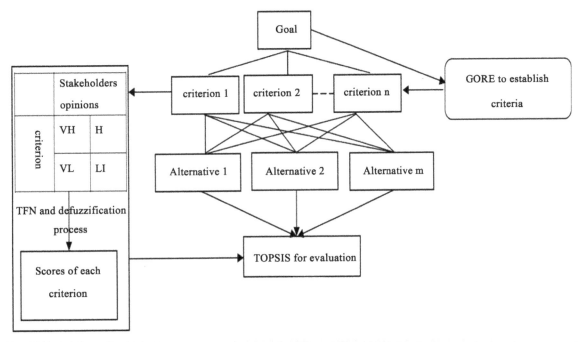

Figure 1. Proposed methodology.

1. Establishing high level goal(s);
2. Establishing the criteria based on leaf level goals (directly assignable to agents: humans or system agents);
3. Identify relevant stakeholders and take their opinions for above established criteria as inputs;
4. Calculate relative importance of each criterion by applying TFN and defuzzification process;
5. Normalize the scores;
6. Identifying the alternatives;
7. Evaluate alternatives using TOPSIS based on scores of each criteria;
8. Rank alternatives.

4. Case Study

The "cyclecomputer" system is used as case study for our work which is developed in our research group. This system will be attached to a bicycle, will process data from various sensors, and will communicate with a standard PC. A cyclist will be supported while riding the bike, for maintenance issues, for tour preparations, or to enhance the safety using the bike e.g., besides the normal cycling activities one could use the "cyclecomputer" as a medical device which will support people having of health problems. It can be used for professional cyclist or just for entertainment purposes. One of the results of the requirements engineering phase is a goal model [11].

Step 1 Establishing High level Goals: Though there are many goals related to "cyclecomputer" but for space and simplicity considerations we take following identified goals for high level "cyclecomputer" goal:

Achieve [Entertainment Service Satisfied], Achieve [Compition Service Satisfied],

Achieve[Training Service Satisfied], Achieve[Tour Management Service Satisfied].

Step 2 Refine Goals to Leaf Levels (establish criterion for each goal): The above mentioned goals are refined using GORE until they are assignable to agents *i.e.*, human agents or software agents. These leaf levels goals are used as criteria for alternative selection. Quality goals which include non-functional requirements and often serve selection criteria are also refined using GORE. The goals along with their subgoals and short description are presented in **Table 1**. It is only partial description of "cyclecomputer" goals.

Step 3(a) Identifying Stakeholders: Though there are number of stakeholders in "cyclecomputer" but the relevant stkeholders for our goals described in **Table 1** are shown in **Figure 2**.

1. Medical Cyclist: People who need a defined training/exercise due to any disease e.g., a heart disease. Medical cyclist can use pulse measurement, blood pressure, calory consumption by "cyclecomputer" device.

2. Doctor (medical): The doctor will cooperate with a patient to set-up the correct training cycles. The cycles are dependant on the patients constitution.

3. Touring Cyclist: People who like to ride the bicycle for long trips (>100 km) and they need specific services for their tours. The trips might take more than one day.

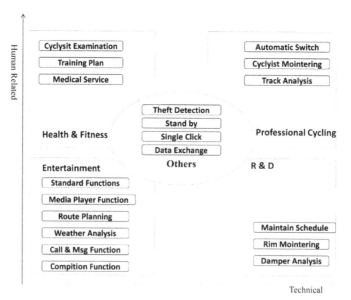

Figure 2. Relevant stakeholders.

Table 1. Partial goal subgoal description.

Goals	Sub goals till leaf level goals	Description
Entertainment Service Satisfied	Mic	The cycle computer should support Mic service.
	Data storage	The cycle computer should support data storage for fun services.
	Audio service	The cycle computer should record and play audio data.
Competition Service Satisfied	User accounts	• The cycle computer should have a user management *i.e.*, Many cyclists should be able to use the same physical device. • User specific data needs to be password protected
	Transferable to web	Track data should be transferred to a Web-portal to enable online competition/comparison.
	Online modus	The competition mode should be used "online" (while riding the bike).
	Offline modus	The competition mode should be used offline
Training Service Satisfied	Initial checkups	The cycle computer should offer an initial check-up to assess the drivers capabilities.
	Technical riding capabilities	• Frame quality level should be analyzable and visible *i.e.*, show the condition of the frame, interpret the frame condition by a coloured icon. • The quality level should be visualized by the time until the frame might break. • The cyclist should see the current speed of the cycle. • The cyclist should be informed when the oil in the shocks should be changed
	Fitness level	• The cycle computer should analyze the cyclist. • The cyclist should be informed about his heart beat.
	Calories consumption	The calorie consumption should be shown e.g., current calorie consumption, calorie consumption per tour, the calorie consumption for a specified time frame
Tour Management Service Satisfied	Route planning	• The cycle computer should offer route planning. • The planning should be done based on topographic maps. • Routing should consider the current weather forecast
	Weather info	• The cyclist should see the current environmental temperature. • The temperature of the last 5 days should be analyzable.
	Tour details	• The cycle computer should provide complete details of the tours • The cyclist should be informed about the current height (above sea level). A cumulative value should be shown by ascended and descended meters.
	Navigation	The cyclist should be able to navigate to a given location. The location could be a point of interest, e.g., a hotel. The cyclist should be informed about his global position on a map.
	Trip suggestions	The cycle computer should offer trip tips for professional sports cyclists e.g., gear change tips, speed tips based on the (known) route.

4. Trainer (sports): Create training plans, follow training plans, analyse the cyclist.

Step 3(b) Stakeholders Opinions Accumulation: We take three stakeholders, professional cyclist(SH1), fun cyclist (SH2), health and fitness cyclist (SH3). These stakeholders are asked to give their judgements against each criterion in **Table 1**. Their judgements are used to elicit the importance degree of each criterion. To enhance the user-friendliness for interacting with stakeholders ordinal scale is used. The scale values are same as given in [8]. In next step the ordinal scale values are converted to actual numerical numbers to apply TFN. **Table 2** shows the ordinal scale and their respective actual numerical values while **Table 3** shows stakeholders ordinal scale and numerical values against criteria identified in **Table 1**.

Step 4(a) Calculate the Relative Importance Using TFN: The different importance degrees of each criterion assigned by stakeholders is calculated using TFN. TFN is used to aggregate the subjective opinions of a stakeholder using fuzzy set theory. The TFN is represented by triplet (L, M, H) L being the smallest value, H being the largest value and M represents the geometric mean.

$$\text{TFN} = (L, M, H) \tag{1}$$

Step 4(b) Apply Defuzzification Process on TFN: After calculating TFN for each criterion we apply

Table 2. Ordinal scales and their numerical values.

Ordinal scale	Actual numbers
Very high importance (VHI)	1
High importance (HI)	0.75
Low importance (LI)	0.5
Very low importance (VLI)	0.25
No importance (NI)	0.001

Table 3. Stakeholder judgements according to ordinal scales and their numerical values.

Goals	Sub goals till leaf level goals	Ordinal scale			Numerical values		
		SH1	SH2	SH3	SH1	SH2	SH3
Entertainment Service Satisfied	Mic	H	VH	H	0.75	1	0.75
	Data storage	H	VH	H	0.75	1	0.75
	Audio service	LI	VH	LI	0.75	1	0.75
Compition Servie Satisifed	User accounts	VH	H	H	1	0.75	0.75
	Transferable to web	VH	H	H	1	0.75	0.75
	Online modus	VH	H	H	1	0.75	0.75
	Offline modus	VH	H	H	1	0.75	0.75
Training Service Satisfied	Initial checkups	H	H	VH	0.75	0.75	1
	Technical riding capabilities	VH	LI	VH	1	0.5	1
	Fitness level	H	LI	VH	0.75	0.5	1
	Calories consumption	H	LI	VH	0.75	0.5	0.75
Tour Management Service Satisfied	Route planning	VH	H	LI	1	0.75	0.5
	Weather info	H	H	H	0.75	0.75	0.75
	Tour details	H	LI	LI	0.75	0.5	0.5
	Navigation	VH	H	H	1	0.75	0.75
	Trip suggestions	H	VLI	H	0.75	0.25	0.75

defuzzification process. Defzzuification process is used to convert calculated TFN values into quantifiable values. Defuzzificatio process is represented by the Equation (2) which is derived from [12]:

$$D^{\alpha}\left(x_i\right) = \alpha f_R\left(x_i\right) + \left(1 - \alpha\right) f_L\left(x_i\right) \tag{2}$$

where $x_i = \text{TFN}_i$ representing triangular fuzzy number. The developer is involved in the process by representing his preference. α in the above equation represents the preference value of developer and it's value is in the range [0,1]. When $\alpha = 1$ it shows the optimistic view of developer resulting in the Equation (3):

$$D^1\left(x_i\right) = f_R\left(x_i\right) \tag{3}$$

When $\alpha = 0$ it shows the pessimistic view of developer resulting in the Equation (4):

$$D^0\left(x_i\right) = f_L\left(x_i\right) \tag{4}$$

where $f_L\left(x_i\right)$ represents the left end value of TFN$_i$ $i.e.$, pessimistic value while $f_R\left(x_i\right)$ represents the right end value of TFN$_i$ $i.e.$, optimistic value and are represented by the Equations (5) and (6) respectively:

$$f_L\left(x_i\right) = L_i + \left(M_i - L_i\right)\beta \tag{5}$$

Equation (5) represents left end boundary value:

$$f_R\left(x_i\right) = H_i + \left(M_i - H_i\right)\beta \tag{6}$$

Equation (6) represents right end boundary value.

β in the above equations represents the risks tolerance for particular criterion and it's value is in the range [0,1]. To keeps things simple we have chosen value 0.5 of preference and risk against each TFN calculated.

If we take only preference value and ignore the risk tolerance, defuzzification value can be calculated using the Equations (7) or (8):

$$D^\alpha\left(x_i\right) = \frac{1}{2}\alpha\left(M_i + H_i\right) + \frac{1}{2}(1-\alpha)\left(L_i + M_i\right) \tag{7}$$

$$D^\alpha\left(x_i\right) = \frac{1}{2}\left[\alpha H_i + M_i + (1-\alpha)L_i\right] \tag{8}$$

Step 5 Normalizing Values Obtained by Defuzzification Process: After defuzzification process the values are normalized by using the Equation (9):

$$ND_i = D_i \bigg/ \sum_{i=1}^{m} D_i \tag{9}$$

where "m" represents number of criteria.

Table 4 represents TFN, defuzzification and final normalized defuzzification values that give the importance of degrees of each criterion. The defuzzification normalized values give the prioritized list of criteria which is used in TOPSIS to evaluated alternatives.

Step 6 Cyclecomputer Alternatives: We selected four alternatives for evaluation: CM213C, CM404, HAC4Pro, Germin Edge 305. The preliminary analysis results of these selected alternatives are given in **Appendix**.

Table 4. TFN, Defuzzification and normalized scores.

Criteria	TFN	Defuzzification	Normalized scores
Mic	(0.75, 0.825, 1)	0.84	0.067
Data storage	(0.75, 0.825, 1)	0.84	0.067
Audio service	(0.75, 0.825, 1)	0.84	0.067
User accounts	(0.75, 0.825, 1)	0.84	0.067
Transferable to web	(0.75, 0.825, 1)	0.84	0.067
Online modus	(0.75, 0.825, 1)	0.84	0.067
Offline modus	(0.75, 0.825, 1)	0.84	0.067
Initial checkups	(0.75, 0.825, 1)	0.84	0.067
Technical riding capabilities	(0.5, 0.793, 1)	0.771	0.062
Fitness level	(0.5, 0.721, 1)	0.735	0.059
Calories consumption	(0.5, 0.655, 0.75)	0.639	0.051
Route planning	(0.5, 0.721, 1)	0.735	0.059
Weather info	(0.75, 0.75, 0.75)	0.75	0.060
Tour details	(0.5, 0.572, 0.75)	0.598	0.048
Navigation	(0.75, 0.825, 1)	0.84	0.067
Trip suggestions	(0.25, 0.520, 1)	0.569	0.046

Step 7 Evaluate Alternatives Using TOPSIS

Step 7(a) Constructing Decision Matrix: For "*m*" number of alternatives and "*n*" number of criteria we construct a $m * n$ matrix. Values in the matrix are entered according to **Table 5**. For four alternatives we randomly selected four criteria along with their scores from **Table 4** and a decision matrix is constructed.

Step 7(b) Normalizing Decision Matrix and Constructing Weighted Normalize Decision Matrix: The decision matrix is normalized according to Equation (10):

$$r_{ij} = x_{ij} \Big/ \sqrt{\left(\sum_i x_{ij}^2\right)} \quad \text{for } i = 1,\cdots,m;\ j = 1,\cdots,n \tag{10}$$

and then multiplied with each criterion score to get the weighted normalized decision matrix. **Figure 3** shows the resultant matrices.

Step 7(c) Determine the Positive Ideal and Negative Ideal Alternatives: Positive ideal and negative ideal alternatives are determined using the Equations (11) and (12) respectively:

$$A^* = \left(v_1^*,\cdots,v_n^*\right), \text{ where } v_j^* = \max_i \left(v_{ij}\right) \tag{11}$$

positive ideal alternative: (0.04, 0.05, 0.03, 0.02)

$$A' = \left(v_1',\cdots,v_n'\right), \text{ where } v_j' = \min_i \left(v_{ij}\right) \tag{12}$$

negative ideal alternative: (0.01, 0.01, 0.01, 0.01)

Step 7(d) Calculating the Separation Measures: separation measures for both positive and negative ideal alternatives are measured using Equations (13) and (14):

$$S_i^* = \left[\sum_j \left(v_j^* - v_{ij}\right)2\right]^{1/2}, \quad i = 1,\cdots,m \tag{13}$$

$$S_i' = \left[\sum_j \left(v_j' - v_{ij}\right)2\right]^{1/2}, \quad i = 1,\cdots,m \tag{14}$$

Figure 4 shows results for separation measure for positive ideal alternative and **Figure 5** shows results for negative ideal alternative.

$$\begin{array}{c|cccc} & 0.067 & 0.067 & 0.059 & 0.051 \\ & C1 & C2 & C3 & C4 \\ \hline A1 & 9 & 7 & 9 & 7 \\ A2 & 7 & 9 & 7 & 7 \\ A3 & 3 & 3 & 3 & 7 \\ A4 & 9 & 3 & 7 & 3 \end{array}$$

(a)

$$r_{ij} = \begin{array}{c|cccc} & 0.067 & 0.067 & 0.059 & 0.051 \\ & C1 & C2 & C3 & C4 \\ \hline A1 & 0.60 & 0.57 & 0.65 & 0.56 \\ A2 & 0.47 & 0.74 & 0.51 & 0.56 \\ A3 & 0.20 & 0.24 & 0.21 & 0.56 \\ A4 & 0.60 & 0.24 & 0.51 & 0.24 \end{array}$$

(b)

$$v_{ij} = \begin{array}{c|cccc} & C1 & C2 & C3 & C4 \\ \hline A1 & 0.04 & 0.03 & 0.03 & 0.02 \\ A2 & 0.03 & 0.05 & 0.03 & 0.02 \\ A3 & 0.01 & 0.01 & 0.01 & 0.02 \\ A4 & 0.04 & 0.01 & 0.03 & 0.01 \end{array}$$

(c)

Figure 3. Decision matrices. (a) decision matrix; (b) normalized decision matrix; (c) weighted normalized decision matrix.

$$S_i^* = \begin{array}{c} A1 \\ A2 \\ A3 \\ A4 \end{array} \begin{pmatrix} (0.04-0.04)^2 + (0.03-0.05)^2 + (0.03-0.03)^2 + (0.02-0.02)^2 \\ (0.03-0.04)^2 + (0.05-0.05)^2 + (0.03-0.03)^2 + (0.02-0.02)^2 \\ (0.01-0.04)^2 + (0.01-0.05)^2 + (0.01-0.03)^2 + (0.02-0.02)^2 \\ (0.04-0.04)^2 + (0.01-0.05)^2 + (0.03-0.03)^2 + (0.01-0.02)^2 \end{pmatrix}^{1/2} \qquad S_i^* = \begin{pmatrix} 0.02 \\ 0.01 \\ 0.06 \\ 0.14 \end{pmatrix}$$

Figure 4. Separation measure for positive ideal alternative.

Table 5. Alternative fulfilling criteria scores.

Alternative fulfilling criterion	9
Alternative partially fulfilling criterion	7
Alternative minimally fulfilling criterion	3
Alternative not fulfilling criterion	0.25

$$S_i' = \begin{array}{c} A1 \\ A2 \\ A3 \\ A4 \end{array} \left[\begin{array}{l} (0.04\text{-}0.01)^2 + (0.03\text{-}0.01)^2 + (0.03\text{-}0.01)2 + (0.02\text{-}0.01)^2 \\ (0.03\text{-}0.01)^2 + (0.05\text{-}0.01)^2 + (0.03\text{-}0.01)^2 + (0.02\text{-}0.01)^2 \\ (0.01\text{-}0.01)^2 + (0.01\text{-}0.01)^2 + (0.01\text{-}0.01)^2 + (0.02\text{-}0.01)^2 \\ (0.04\text{-}0.01)^2 + (0.01\text{-}0.01)^2 + (0.03\text{-}0.01)^2 + (0.01\text{-}0.01)^2 \end{array} \right]^{1/2} \quad S_i' = \left[\begin{array}{c} 0.042 \\ 0.078 \\ 0.02 \\ 0.037 \end{array} \right]$$

Figure 5. Separation measure for negative ideal alternative.

Step 7(e) Calculating Closeness to Ideal Solution: the relative closeness to the ideal solution is calculated using the Equation (15):

$$C_i^* = S_i' / \left(S_i^* + S_i' \right), 0 < C_i^* < 1 \tag{15}$$

Step 7(f) Ranking and Selecting: Finally the ranking is done and the alternative closet to 1 is selected as the best alternative. **Figure 6** gives results for our selected alternatives and alternative A2 is selected as an ideal solution.

5. Discussions

Alternatives selection is ongoing research in the area of GORE. On the other hand methods like AHP [13], TOPSIS [14], Fuzzy AHP, Fuzzy TOPSIS [1] and VIKOR are used in classical Multi-Criteria Decision Making (MCDM) problems. Multi-criteria decision making (MCDM) has been widely used in selecting or ranking decision alternatives characterized by multiple and usually conflicting criteria [15]. The approach of these methods is useful for alternatives selection and stakeholders involvement in GORE.

[16] also emphasises the importance of decision support in GORE but it differs from our work as it uses Analytic Hierarchy Process (AHP) for prioritization and it deals with only soft goals. AHP [13] involves pair-wise comparison. All pair of requirements is compared to determine the priority level of one requirement over another requirement. Requirements are arranged in matrix form, that is, rows and columns. Then priority is specified to each pair of requirements by assigning a preference value between 1 and 9, where 1 expresses equal value while 9 indicates extreme value. After that, AHP converts these scales to numerical values and a numerical priority is derived for each requirement. AHP is more suitable for small number of stakeholders and if alternatives are increased to seven are more it becomes difficult to handle them with AHP because it involves pair-wise comparison. In contrast our method involves stakeholders opinions and take into consideration both functional and non-functional requirements. In our method importance of criteria is evaluated using fuzzy set concepts, weight for each criterion is calculated based on stakeholder opinions. When a new criterion is added it is easy to extend, we don't need to change the previous calculations because newly added criterion is independent from others. These weights are then used in TOPSIS avoiding the cumbersome pair-wise comparisons of AHP.

[17] [1] use qualitative approaches for choosing the best alternative. They use temporal logic and label propagation algorithm. Our method differs from them by using quantitative approach for evaluating the alternatives. [8] deals with prioritizing software requirements, it considers prioritization of both functional and non-functional requirements at same level. This method produces two separate prioritized lists of functional and non-functional requirements. Like our approach their work also used the concepts from [9] but their work is only used for prioritization of functional and non-functional requirement while in our work the scores obtained after prioritization are used as an input to TOPSIS method for evaluation of alternatives.

Wiegers [18] method is semi-quatitative method which focused on customer involvement. Requirements are prioritized based on four criteria defined as benefit, penalty, cost, and risk. The attributes (criteria) are assessed on a scale from 1 (minimum) to 9 (maximum). The customer determines the benefit and penalty values whereas the developers provide the cost and risk values associated with each requirement. Then, by using a formula, the relative importance value of each requirement is calculated by dividing the value of a requirement by the sum of the costs and technical risks associated with its implementation.

AGORA [17] is another quantitative approach for alternatives extending the goal oriented requirements analysis but the focus of AGORA is on requirements elicitation. The method focuses on alternative among subgoals, that is, selection of subgoal among many subgoals of same parent. Furthermore AGORA attaches a matrix called preference matrix to nodes of goal graph. It is suitable if number of stakeholders is small in number.

$$C_i^* = \begin{pmatrix} A1 & 0.042/0.02 + 0.042 = 0.67 \\ A2 & 0.078/0.01 + 0.078 = 0.88 \\ A3 & 0.02/0.061 + 0.02 = 0.24 \\ A4 & 0.037/0.104 + 0.037 = 0.26 \end{pmatrix}$$

Figure 6. Relative closeness to ideal solution.

When stakeholders are more (plus four) and have to select among many alternatives, this method becomes difficult to handle and goal graph becomes cumbersome.

We used the Fuzzy set concepts to evaluate the importance of criteria for each goal. Weight for each criterion is calculated based on stakeholder opinions. These weights display stakeholder priorities for all requirements. The interaction of stakeholders at early phase of requirements engineering helps to capture the rational (by documenting the preferences) for the decisions and to identify inconsistencies at the early phase of requirements engineering. The method gives a systematic structure to calculate the fuzzy weight of each criterion. The subjecttive weights assigned by stakeholders are normalized into a comparable scale. The performance measures of all alternatives on criteria are visualized using TOPSIS which accounts for both the best and worst alternatives simultaneously.

6. Conclusions

In this paper an approach is presented to use the goal model of goal-oriented requirements engineering to establish the acceptance criteria. After that we apply the TFN and defuzzification process to get scores for each criterion. In the final step TOPSIS method is used to evaluate the alternatives and for selection of the best alternatives. TOPSIS method uses the score obtained by TFN and defuzzification process. The proposed methodology can be used against both the functional and non-functional requirements.

The methodology is explained by "cyclecomputer" case study where we establish 16 acceptance criteria and stakeholders opinions are collected for these criteria. After calculating the score of each criterion we take four criteria (for space considerations) and based on these evaluated four alternatives. This approach is promis- ing for ranking the criteria and using this ranking for alternative selection because we take the stakeholders opinions and most importantly developers' considerations for preference and risk tolerance into account. The formalization of the approach, its full integration into goal oriented requirements engineering and the validation by additional examples are future research topics.

Acknowledgements

We acknowledge support for the Article Processing Charge by the German Research Foundation and the Open Access Publication Fund of the Technische Universit Ilmenau.

References

[1]   Erturul, R. and Karakaolu, N. (2008) Comparison of Fuzzy Ahp and Fuzzy Topsis Methods for Facility Location Selection. *The International Journal of Advanced Manufacturing Technology*, **39**, 783-795.

[2]   Chen, C.-T. (2000) Extensions of the Topsis for Group Decision-Making under Fuzzy Environment. *Fuzzy Sets and Systems*, **114**, 1-9.

[3]   Lapouchnian, A. (2005) Goal-Oriented Requirement Engineering. An Overview of the Current Research, Technical Report, University of Toronto, Toronto.

[4]   Darimont, R. and van Lamsweerde, A. (1996) Formal Refinement Patterns for Goal-Driven Requirements Elaboration. *Proceedings of the 4th ACM Symposium on the Foundation of Software Engineering*, San Francisco, October 1996, 179-190.

[5]   van Lamsweerde, A. (2000) Requirements Engineering in the Year 00: A Research Perspective. *Proceedings of the 2000 International Conference on Software Engineering*, Limerick, 4-11 June 2000, 5-19.

[6]   Zave, P. (1997) Classi Cation of Research Eorts in Requirements Engineering. *ACM Computing Surveys*, **29**, 315-321.

[7] Anton, A.I. (1996) Goal-Based Requirements Analysis. *Proceedings of the 2nd International Conference on Requirements Engineering*, Colorado Springs, 15-18 April 1996, 136-144. http://dx.doi.org/10.1109/icre.1996.491438

[8] Mohammad Dabbagh, S.P.L. (2014) An Approach for Integrating the Prioritization of Functional and Nonfunctional Requirements. *The Scientic World Journal*, **2014**, Article ID: 737626.

[9] Goli, D. (2013) Group Fuzzy Topsis Methodology in Computer Security Software Selection. *International Journal of Fuzzy Logic Systems*, **3**, 29.

[10] Olson, D.L. (2004) Comparison of Weights in Topsis Models. *Mathematical and Computer Modelling*, **40**, 721-727.

[11] Mansoor, A. and Streitferdt, D. (2011) On the Impact of Goals on Long-Living Systems. *Workshop*: *Evolutionäre Software- und Systementwicklung-Methoden und Erfahrungen*, Karlsruhe, February 2011, 133-138.

[12] Liou, T.-S. and Wang, M.-J. (1992) Ranking Fuzzy Numbers with Integral Value. *Fuzzy Sets and Systems*, **50**, 247-255.

[13] Saaty, T.L. (2008) Decision Making with the Analytic Hierarchy Process. *International Journal of Services Sciences*, **1**, 83-98.

[14] Wang, T.-C. and Lee, H.-D. (2009) Developing a Fuzzy Topsis Approach Based on Subjective Weights and Objective Weights. *Expert Systems with Applications*, **36**, 8980-8985.

[15] Vinay, S., Aithal, S. and Sudhakara, G. (2012) Integrating Topsis and Ahp into Gore Decision Support System. *International Journal of Computer Applications*, **56**, 46-53.

[16] Castro, J., Kolp, M. and Mylopoulos, J. (2002) Towards Requirements-Driven Information Systems Engineering: The Tropos Project. *Information Systems*, **27**, 365-389. http://dx.doi.org/10.1016/S0306-4379(02)00012-1

[17] Wiegers, K. (1999) First Things First: Prioritizing Requirements. *Software Development Online*, **7**, 48-53.

[18] Kaiya, H., Horai, H. and Saeki, M. (2002) Agora: Attributed Goal-Oriented Requirements Analysis Method. *IEEE Joint International Conference on Requirements Engineering*, Essen, 2002, 13-22. http://dx.doi.org/10.1109/icre.2002.1048501

Appendix

Table 6. Comparison of cyclecomputers.

Feature	CM213C	CM404	HAC4Pro	Germin Edge 305
Price [€]		12	70	250
Speed [Miles]	yes	yes	yes	yes
Speed [KM]	yes	yes	yes	yes
Speed digits [xxx]	3	3	3	3
Speed digits [xxx]	1	1	1	1
Average speed			yes	yes
Wireless Speed Sensor	no	no	yes	n/a
Daytime AM/PM	yes	yes	yes	yes
Daytime 24h	yes	yes	yes	yes
Date day/month/year	no	no	yes	yes
Alarm clock			yes	
Stopwatch			yes	
Tire 1 Size	yes	yes	yes	yes
Tire 2 Size	yes	no	yes	yes
Sum-up Tire 1 and Tire 2	yes	no	yes	
Tire Size digits	4	4	4	
Tire Size min [mm]			500	
Tire Size max [mm]			3000	
Overall distance	5	5	5	
Overall distance digits [xxx,]	5	5	5	
Overall distance digits [,xxx]	1	1	1	
Overall riding time			yes	
Set overall distance	no	no	yes	Set overall distance
Daily distance	yes	yes	yes	Daily distance
Daily distance digits [xxx]	3	3	3	Daily distance digits [xxx]
Daily distance digits [xxx]	2	2	2	Daily distance digits [xxx]
Daily distance reset after [h]	12	12		Daily distance reset after [h]
Daily riding time	no	no	yes	Daily riding time
Distance digits	5	5		Distance digits
Distance [Miles]	yes	yes	yes	Distance [Miles]
Distance [KM]	yes	yes	yes	Distance [KM]
Distance backup, battery change	yes	no	no	Dist backup, battery change
Max battery Change time [sec]	15	0		Max battery Change time [sec]
Low battery warning	no	no	yes	Low battery warning
Battery life [months]			10	
Pedal Frequency	yes	no	yes	

Continued

Max. Pedal Frequency	no	no	yes	
Min. Pedal Frequency	no	no	yes	
Auto Turn off after [sec]	300	300	300	
Auto Turn on, on tire turn	yes	yes	yes	
Heartbeat Sensor	no	no	yes	
No of Buttons	2	4	5	
Height Sensor	no	no	yes	
Height min [m]			−200	
Height max [m]			9000	
Height in m			yes	
Height in feet			yes	
Daily height			yes	
Daily ascend			yes	
Daily descend			yes	
Set overall height			yes	
Show gradient (up/down)			yes	
Set Gradient min			0.0%	
Set Gradient max			99.0%	
Show average gradient			yes	
Show max gradient			yes	
Show min gradient			yes	
Varo-meter ...				
Current ascend value			yes	
Current descend value			yes	
Max ascend			yes	
Max descend			yes	
Average ascend			yes	
Average descend			yes	
No of ascends			yes	
No of descends			yes	
GPS	no	no	no	yes
Auto Lap	no	no	no	yes
Virtual partner	no	no	no	yes
Temp Sensor			yes	
Temp Celsius			yes	
Temp Fahrenheit			yes	
Max Temp			yes	
Min Temp			yes	
PC-Connection	no	no	yes	

Continued

PC Analysis SW	no	no	yes
Fitness …			
Sex	no	no	yes
Body weight	no	no	yes
Complete weight	no	no	yes
Age	no	no	yes
Set heartbeat 1 min. level	no	no	yes
Set heartbeat 1 max. level	no	no	yes
Set heartbeat 2 min. level	no	no	yes
Set heartbeat 2 max. level	no	no	yes
Ride by heartbeat zone	no	no	yes
Heartbeat alarm (outside zone)	no	no	yes
Check cool down heartbeat	no	no	yes
Time in riding zone	no	no	yes
Time above riding zone	no	no	yes
Time below riding zone	no	no	yes
Fitness level	no	no	yes
Current calorie consumption	no	no	yes
Overall calorie consumption	no	no	yes
Current performance in Watts	no	no	yes
Average performance	no	no	yes
Max. performance	no	no	yes
Compare training sessions	no	no	yes
Countdown timer 1	no	no	yes
Countdown timer 1 max [min: sec]	no	no	99:59
Countdown timer 2	no	no	yes
Countdown timer 2 max [min: sec]	no	no	99:59
Firmware upgradeable	no	no	yes
Sleep mode	no	no	yes
Ski mode (use device for skiing)	no	no	yes
Backlight	no	no	yes
Display size			128 × 160 4-level-grayscale
Waterproof [m]			30
Operation temp min [°C]			−20
Operation temp max [°C]			+60
Algorithms …			
Calculate heartbeat zone by Sex, age, fitness level			yes
Measure, Ruhepuls"			yes

19

Towards Knowledge Management in RE Practices to Support Software Development

Mamoona Humayoun, Asad Masood Qazi

University Institute of Information Technology, PMAS-University Institute of Information Technology, Rawalpindi, Pakistan
Email: mamoona@uaar.edu.pk, asad.masood@dpskw.com

Abstract

Requirement engineering in any software development is the most important phase to ensure the success or failure of software. Knowledge modeling and management are helping tools to learn the software organizations. The traditional Requirements engineering practices are based upon the interaction of stakeholders which causes iteratively changes in requirements and difficulties in communication and understanding problem domain etc. So, to resolve such issues we use knowledge based techniques to support the RE practices as well as software development process. Our technique is based on two prospective, theoretical and practical implementations. In this paper, we described the need of knowledge management in software engineering and then proposed a model based on knowledge management to support the software development process. To verify our results, we used controlled experiment approach. We have implemented our model, and verify results by using and without using proposed knowledge based RE process. Our resultant proposed model can save the overall cost and time of requirement engineering process as well as software development.

Keywords

Knowledge Management, Software Requirement Engineering, Software Development Methodologies, Knowledge Modeling

1. Introduction

1.1. Requirement Engineering

Software requirement engineering involves requirements elicitation, requirements specification, requirements validation and requirements management [1] [2]. Requirements elicitation involves the ways of gathering the requirements which include many traditional, cognitive, model based etc. techniques.

Whereas, the requirements specification (where analysis and negotiation of requirements are performed), and requirements of users are specified to make them understandable and meaningful for developers. Specifications can be formal as well as non-formal [3]. Formal techniques include the set of tools and techniques based on mathematical models whereas informal techniques are based on modeling the requirements in diagrams or making architecture of system. There are many and many techniques in both types of specification. Like in formal techniques of specifications, we have different formal specification languages like Z, VDM etc. and in In-formal or non-formal techniques, we have UML diagrams which include use-cases, sequence diagrams, collaboration and interaction diagrams etc.

In Requirements validation the completeness of the requirements is checked which means either gathered requirements are correct, complete or not. The main objectives are to analyze the validation and verification of RE process, to identify and resolve the problems and highly risk factors of software in early stages, and to make strengthen the development cycle [4].

Finally in requirements management phase, issues and conflicts of users are resolved. According to Andriole [5], the requirement management is a political game. It is basically applied in such cases where we have to control the expectations of stakeholders from software, and put the requirements rather than in well-meaning by customers but meaning-full by developers, so they can examine that, and actually full fill the user's requirements.

Authors of [6] include the Requirement change management under the Requirement Engineering process. RCM is a term which is used according to the history or previous development of the similar software product(s). On the basis of historical development, we investigate the need of RCM or not.

Software Requirement Specification (SRS) is a standard and official document which describes what the developers will develop. It includes detailed requirements specifications [7]. A standard IEEE format of SRS [8] describes the recommendations for a good SRS document.

1.2. Knowledge Management in Software Requirement Engineering

Many definitions of Knowledge modeling and knowledge management can be found in literature by authors having different background. The one of them is: "A method that simplifies the process of sharing, distributing, creating, capturing and understanding of company's knowledge" [9]. The summary of knowledge management in Software Engineering refers to this definition which says that the main purpose of knowledge modeling is to learn the software organizations. The more elaborated definition is: "A software organization that promotes improved actions through better knowledge and understanding" [10].

A knowledge model may contain multiple attributes. Many authors describe different knowledge attributes and factors. In [11], the six activities are been discussed which includes capturing, storing, sharing, learning, exploring and exploiting. In [12], the major four types of attributes are present in study which describes that there a knowledge model should describe the 4 types of knowledge which includes Domain Knowledge, Control Knowledge, System Knowledge and Explanatory Knowledge as presented in **Figure 1**.

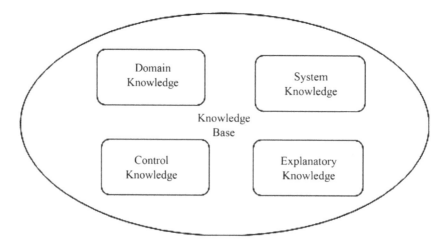

Figure 1. Attributes of knowledge modeling and management.

2. Related Work

Knowledge modeling is not a new area, a lot of work has been done using knowledge modeling techniques in last some decades. In software engineering, knowledge management techniques are used to provide an easy way to learn the software organizations. In software engineering there using of software development process or life cycle is used and it is called an "Experience Factory" in terms of Software engineering. In knowledge management, we collect these experiences from different resources like past papers, case studies etc. and store them into a single repository to easy reuse of software life cycle or development process [13].

In [14], we can see that the authors describe the knowledge based requirement engineering process which has to be implemented in the requirement elicitation phase. Authors define a way to use knowledge management on a strategy of Requirement engineering phase. In this paper the tacit knowledge is being converted into explicit knowledge to save additional cost as well as additional development time, which is described in [15]. Authors also claims that, there are many problems and situation in software industry, in which informal as well as formal techniques are not helpful, also there are no such algorithms defined which may help to tackle the solution. These create an ambiguity and inconsistency in the requirements, so we should focus on the knowledge management. Which can help the software engineers to obtain an acceptable solution?

By referencing [16], we can say that knowledge modeling and management can be helpful in software engineering by understanding the business needs correctly, better decision making process, accessing domain knowledge and sharing knowledge about local policies and practices.

In [17], authors have proposed a distributed and cloud computing based knowledge model as a service framework. This model will help to resolve the GSD (Global Software Development) issues. A central knowledge repository has been used as KM Server to store the knowledge in cloud environment.

In [18] a complete procedure to develop the knowledge model and run a complete knowledge based process has been described. The results of this case study have been implemented in some software organizations to observe the importance of knowledge modeling. Some activities of KM also has been described in this study, which includes the knowledge application, knowledge distribution, knowledge organization, knowledge adaptation, knowledge identification, knowledge acquisition and knowledge creation.

Authors in [19] argue that software process is essentially a knowledge process and it is structured in a knowledge management framework. In study [20] authors describes the issues faced by small and medium organizations by proper implementing knowledge management in Software Engineering area.

In [21], the authors describe the need of knowledge management in education of software engineering field. There is a big challenge still for organizations to develop a model to support effectively the knowledge management model. This paper also found some key factors which can make an impact on success of knowledge management practices in education.

A technology oriented knowledge model is been described in [22], which basically describes the complete procedure of sharing and creating knowledge in software engineering and software organizations.

An Ontology based knowledge management software development model has been proposed in the study given in [23]. Three types of packages have been described in this study, which are generic package, Ontology package and specific package. Authors basically try to analyze the instantiations in Ontology.

In [24], the authors defined a requirement engineering solution based on the natural language semantics solution. Natural language based solution can be helpful in the requirements discovery, requirements analysis and requirements specifications in form of requirements creation, requirements classification and requirements formalization.

In [25] authors identified the areas where knowledge management lies. In traditional software engineering, conceptual specifications and design phase were separate, but knowledge modeling bridge a gap between these phases. Also they talk about the generations of knowledge modelling in software engineering, which are:

In G1 the rules and frames are defined.

In G2 a symbolic representation is used to abstract the design phase. And then convert these abstractions into a model based system development.

A knowledge model can be based on the principle of task oriented, problem-solving and domain oriented. In task oriented the input and output of system is analyzed. Problem is then transformed in tree based architecture. On the other hand, in problem solving technique, a major task or goal is divided into sub tasks. Knowledge is transformed in hierarchical architecture. And in domain oriented, an Ontology is being used to explicit the domain elements.

KSM, a knowledge modelling tool is used to model the knowledge. In KSM the important thing is Knowledge area, which is further divided into supporting sub knowledge areas (also called supporting knowledge bodies) and their functionality. There are two languages used by the KSM to formulate the common terminologies and strategies of reasoning. Common terminologies are explained in Concel Language and the strategies are defined in Link Language.

It can also be observed from the study given in [26] that a major problem in requirement engineering is a communication, especially, when there is a communication between participants having different language and culture. So to tackle the issues, a knowledge modelling is used. A cycle/Spiral view of knowledge is proposed to solve the communication issue in RE Process. In this process the requirements are elicited and then specified. The elicited requirements are then tacit through socialization process. After elicited, the requirements are externalized or specified and after completion of circle the finalized requirements are documented, and unclear requirements again return back to specification stage.

In another paper given in [27], KMOS-RE is proposed, which is a knowledge model on a strategy to requirements engineering. In this proposed solution, the author(s) claims that the complexity of requirement engineering based on an application domain. In informal structured domain, the entities, functions, events and behavior of system is explained. However there are some issues in these informal structured domains which are symmetry of ignorance, situated actions and ambiguities. To solve such issues we use knowledge management in RE. A solution is based on the tacit and explicit. Tacit involves the socialization techniques like JAD, Interviews and externalization through knowledge representation and discourse analysis etc. And in explicit we have combination through data mining etc. and internalization through the knowledge management. Proposed KMOS-RE also defines the two phenomena's machine and world. In world phenomena side we have domain experts who have domain knowledge, and in the machine phenomena side, we have requirement engineers who have knowledge of software development. When both phenomena's are being gathered, with the help of software knowledge and domain knowledge, requirements specifications can be produced.

In [28] the author(s) emphasizes on the need of knowledge modelling in requirement engineering process. They claim that the requirement engineers should be able to understand the human's action in which the developed system will be implemented. Also, a requirement engineer should be able to understand the history which will help to develop project. Similarly requirement engineer should consider cultural norms of client (client's organization) and have an access to organization directories or social network to become known about the knowledge and its source.

To be able to above mention qualities, a requirement engineer may use the knowledge modelling. In this study, authors relate the requirement engineering with cognitive theories. As RE is a team work, so a process should be well defined, use of prototypes, use of common vocabulary for communication, supportive environment and address the issues in form of notations and symbols to resolve them separately [29].

A knowledge has four dimensions; current situation of environment, experienced knowledge, group knowledge and cultural knowledge [30]. So by focusing all these pre requisites authors of [28] compare the cognitive theories and examine the improvements in the requirement engineering process.

3. Proposed Work

Our proposed methodology is based on the existing model of Faxiang Chen, Burseitn F given in [11]. However, we have integrated this model by taking its attributes to just model the knowledge. Our main focus is on complete knowledge acquisition model which has proper semantic rules for elaborating the complete problem domain. The main steps of our proposed knowledge model are:

Knowledge Learning Stage
Knowledge Exploring
Knowledge Capturing
Knowledge Storing
Knowledge Sharing
Knowledge Exploitation

After these steps, we will merge our proposed model into a complete knowledge management model. Here, we did not involve the users or its basic requirements about the system, here we just focus on the techniques which we will use after getting the basic requirements from users. The input of this model can be a UML Diagram as well as the requirements in descriptive form. The knowledge model is illustrated in **Figure 2**.

3.1. Knowledge Learning Stage

In proposed model, the activities which are being defined in this learning stage are helpful to learn about the problems. Employees can learn knowledge of domain, system, control and explanatory from past papers, historical related software problems, previous coding and development methodologies, books and case studies etc. In next section of experiment design, we are using the case study of Police station automation system, which were developed by university students. The experiment group, go through the whole learning stage by getting knowledge of manual system from their own resources like internet, columns, manuals, relatives etc.

3.2. Knowledge Exploring

In above mentioned proposed knowledge model, we have presented the knowledge exploring phase in shape of database storage. Basically, in knowledge exploring phase, we explore the existing knowledge or related knowledge using case studies to achieve competitive advantage. In our scenario, we have been search about different approaches of implementation of Police station system, and then we come to know about an easy approach using

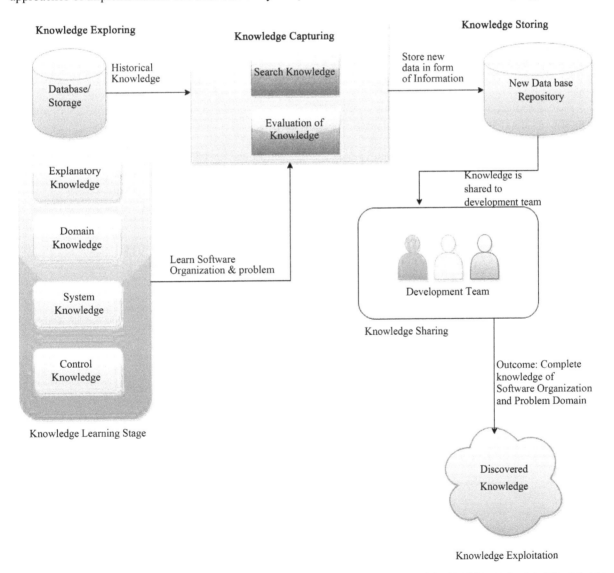

Figure 2. The proposed knowledge based model for requirement engineering.

knowledge model. Many automated systems or projects can be found on internet with named as E-Justice, Automated police station system etc. but our focus is to learn the implementation techniques to solve the situation according to our scenario and requirement.

3.3. Knowledge Capturing

The input of this phase is the knowledge which employees have learned as well as knowledge that has been explored related to software organizations as well as in our case about the software system, which has to be developed. In this phase we focus on "what". What knowledge is required etc.? In our particular scenario of Police station automation system, we have identified the methods, roles and privileges etc. in this stage.

3.4. Knowledge Storage

The input of this phase is captured knowledge from learning and exploring stage. We store all the required knowledge in our database. Most researchers use RDBMS [31] in this stage to store the knowledge. In our case we have store knowledge related to police station automation system in database.

3.5. Knowledge Sharing

In knowledge sharing phase, tasks in form of knowledge are divided into the project team. In our implementation phase we suggest one student group member to make knowledge model of the police station system, he/she will store the knowledge in their particular database in form of textual or descriptive data as well as in form of UML diagrams. Similarly, a developer has implemented the police station automated system in Micro Soft Visual Studio 2013 using C# as programming language. And the third member will assist both members as well as make the project documentation. A sharing of knowledge can be presented in form of simple use case diagram to identify the user's interaction with the system (see **Figure 3**).

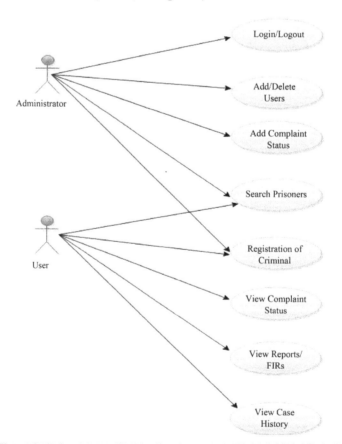

Figure 3. A simple use case diagram of police station automation system.

3.6. Knowledge Exploitation

In this last phase of knowledge model, the output in our case was a UML diagram of whole project. The group of students who develop this project previously, without any restriction of using RE or software development model was facing difficulties in this particular area, because they did not get any domain knowledge properly, and they were not clear about what to do.

4. Design of Experiment

For experiment design, the guidelines given by Kitchenham *et al.* [32] and Wohlin *et al.* [33] were used. In study of Kitchenham, we can see that the guidelines for experiment in Software engineering are being represented to analysis, data collection in a brief way, not in a detailed. However, Wohlin *et al.* uses some statistical techniques in experiment to analyze the results in more detailed form.

4.1. Goal and Variables

The goal of this experiment is to empirically investigate the proposed knowledge model. By implementing it on a particular case study, which we can analyze its maximum features and attributes in the first stage. Our experiment based on small project named as Police Station Automation system, of graduate students.

During experiment, we have identified following variables (see **Table 1**).

4.2. Participants

As we have two groups (Controlled and Experiment), so in each group we have 3 students, each group has 1 supervisor or expert and 1 reviewer. Participants are responsible to develop a program, documentation as well as testing. Because the basis of all steps, we can analyze the proposed model (its complexity, benefits and obstacles).

4.3. Objects

The software system which is being developed during this experiment is named as "Police Station Automation System". Each group is restricted to use same development platform Microsoft Visual Studio 2012 and Programming language C# with MS SQL Server as database storage.

4.4. Division of Participants

The division of participants, according to the above mentioned criteria for both groups (controlled as well as experiment) is given below.

4.5. Questionnaire from Participants

To check the correctness and verification, we have designed a questionnaire for all participants of both groups as well as their supervisors. The questionnaire contains following questions (see **Table 2**).

5. Execution of Experiment

To execute the experiment we have assigned the tasks to two groups of students. One group is performing the

Table 1. Identifying variables of experiment.

Sr. #	Description	Unit	Possible Values/Range
1	Time Taken by Group/Individual	Hours	20 Hours.
2	Programming Experience	Months	12 months (Max)
3	Group	-	Controlled/Experiment
4	Affiliation	-	Academia, Industry
5	Architecture/Design Experience	Months	12 months (Max)

Table 2. Questionnaire to be filled by participants of both groups (control and experiment).

Sr. #	Question
Q1	Does the proposed model complete the correctness?
Q2	Is the knowledge management model full fill ease of use property for all stakeholders?
Q3	Is this Flexible?
Q4	Does it hold enhancement of Usability property
Q5	Is the proposed model is also good for the understanding of User's? (User's Satisfaction)
Q6	Is Knowledge Management complex?

role of control group and the other is experiment.

5.1. Sample and Preparation

As said earlier, there are two groups of students of University located in Rawalpindi, Pakistan. To analyze the results, there are 3 members and 1 supervisor (Manager/Professor). In figure **Chart 1** and **Chart 2** we have mentioned the experience and knowledge of participants. Further, we allow control group to develop a software by using their existing knowledge and experience and collect the requirements from either station or by else. But the experiment group is restricted to follow the complete proposed knowledge management model to elicit the requirements. Knowledge management helps the participants in software reuse, software maintenance, evolution and quality control of software system.

5.2. Data Collection Performed

Data collection procedure was performed as it is defined in the section Design of Experiment. Questionnaire is filled by all the participants after the completeness of software development. No participant was left to fill the questionnaire and to give feedback about the proposed knowledge management practices.

5.3. Validation of Results

To ensure the validity of results, we conduct the experiment in a controlled environment. No participant was allowed to leave the room/Lab before completion of Questionnaire. Also, as mentioned earlier, both the developments were made one by one not at the same time or at the front of each other. Group 1 was unknown about the Group 2 activities and vice versa. Also, groups were designed in such a way, so they were not aware about the experiment. Basically it was a surprised experiment.

The results of questionnaire of both groups are mentioned in **Chart 3**.

6. Result Analysis

We analyze the results of experiment by using following steps:

6.1. Descriptive Statistical Analysis

We conduct two developments of same project from different group. One is control group and other is experiment group. After complete the requirement gathering and completion of software development we can analyze the results in a statistical way: (see **Table 3**).

Now we will analyze the results according to the experience of the participants. Our hypothesis of this step is: The results will shows that the experience of participants is a main factor in software development, but by using proper methodology we can overcome the minor differences in experiment in development (**Table 4**).

The experience of participants have small variation because some students usually starts internship during the studies. That's why some participants have affiliation with industry and others.

6.2. Analysis on Opinion of Participants

As mentioned above, after the development the software system, participants were asked to fill the questionnaire

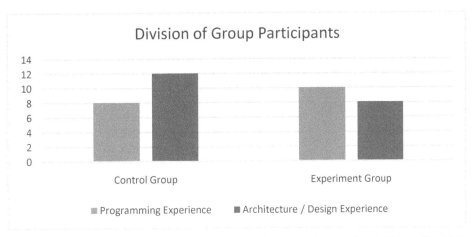

Chart 1. Distribution of participants according to their experience (In months).

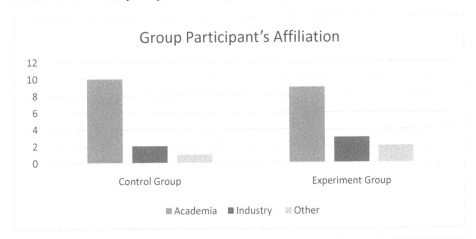

Chart 2. Distribution of participants according to their experience in different affiliation (In months).

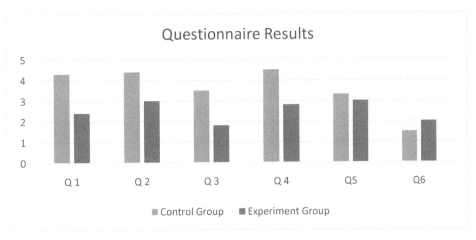

Chart 3. Average questionnaire results comparison by both groups.

to give the feedback about the proposed knowledge management based methodology of requirements gathering. The results show that the experiment group gives better results. Experiment group is go through with all the steps proposed in a Proposed solution section. Later on, when the control group compares their results with experiment group, they also give their positive remarks about that knowledge management based solution.

Table 3. Statistical analysis of time taken in development.

Sr. #	Time Taken in Requirements Engineering		Time Taken in Development	
	Control Group	Experiment Group	Control Group	Experiment Group
1.	40 Hours	50 Hours	60 Hours	20 Hours
Mean of Control Group		50	Mean of Experiment Group	35
Median of Control Group		50	Median of Experiment Group	35
S.D of Control Group		14.14	S.D of Experiment Group	21.21

Table 4. Influence of participants on basis of experience.

Group Affiliation	Arch./Design Experience	Programming Experience	Participants	Participants having both knowledge
Control Group	3	2	4	1
Experiment Group	4	2	4	2

6.3. Limitations of the Study

The study is implemented in an academic environment and has a small industry contribution. However we can further extend our work by implementing the proposed solution to an industry level. As there are small number of participants which is also a limitation of the study. Because if we have large number of participants, we can analyze the results in more better way.

7. Conclusion and Future Work

This paper is about presenting a knowledge based model to support the software requirement engineering phase which will definitely be a supportive material or supportive product for a complete software development methodology. Our proposed model is based on the study of Faxiang Chen, Burseitn F. [11], but more explanatory and detailed form. We present a knowledge model, which will help the software engineers to learn deeply about the software organization as well as the problem domain. Also, in our proposed model, the feedback of customer is also included continuously to get better and efficient results.

To implement proposed model, we use controlled experiment approach by using guidelines given in [32] [33]. We give a small task of simple police station automation system to graduate students of university located in Rawalpindi. Later on, we give a same project assignment to graduate students of another university located in Islamabad, and they were restricted to learn problem domain by using steps of proposed knowledge based model. Later on, we get a feedback from both groups as well as their supervisors about proposed methodology. Similarly, to refine the results more, we use experts review session to get feedback and comments about our proposed methodology. The resultant of our research is a well-defined and well structure problem domain as well as a proper knowledge model which will help the software engineers to learn about organization.

In the future, we can analyze this model by changing different experiment objects which are basically other software systems of real enterprises and more complex. By changing objects, our variables will also change, like in this case we apply it on graduate students, further we can apply it on software engineers having rich experience. Another future work of this study is use of ontologies, experiencing different data sets and including some other emerging things.

Acknowledgements

I am very Thank full to my Professor Dr. Mamoona Humayoun for her support in this study. I also thank to all the participants as well as their professors who take part in this experiment.

References

[1]   Chikh, A. (2011) A Knowledge Management Framework in Software Requirements Engineering Based on SECI Model. *Journal of Software Engineering and Applications*, **4**, 718-728. http://www.SciRP.org/journal/jsea

http://dx.doi.org/10.4236/jsea.2011.412084

[2]   Flores, F. and Fransico, M.M. (2010) Towards a Systematic Service Oriented Requirement Engineering Process (S-SoRE). In: Varajão, J.E.Q., Cruz-Cunha,M.M., Putnik, G.D. and Trigo, A., Eds., *ENTERprise Information System*, Springer, Berlin, 111-120. http://dx.doi.org/10.1007/978-3-642-16402-6_12

[3]   Batra, M., Malik, A. and Dave, M. (2013) Formal Methods: Benefits, Challenges and Future Direction. *Journal of Global Research in Computer Science*, **4**.

[4]   Boehm, B.W. (1984) Verifying and Validating Software Requirements and Design Specifications. *IEEE Software*, **1**, 75-88.

[5]   Andriole, S, and Safeguard Sci. Inc. (1998) The Politics of Requirements Management. *IEEE Software*, **15**, 82-84. http://dx.doi.org/10.1109/52.730850

[6]   Flores, F., Mora, M., Álvarez, F., O'Connor, R. and Macias, J. (2008) Handbook of Research on Modern Systems Analysis and Design Technologies and Applications. In: Global, I.G.I., Ed., *Chap. VI: Requirements Engineering: A Review of Processes and Techniques*, Minnesota State University, Mankato, 96-111. http://www.igi-global.com/book/handbook-research-modern-systems-analysis/490

[7]   Sommerville, I. (2011) Software Engineering. Pearson Education, Upper Saddle River.

[8]   IEEE Std. 830-1998 (1998) IEEE Recommended Practice for Software Requirements Specifications. IEEE Computer Society Software Engineering Standards Committee, No. SH94654.

[9]   Davenport, T.H. and Prusak, L. (1998) Working Knowledge: How Organizations Manage What They Know. Harvard Business School Press, Boston.

[10]   Dybå, T. (2011) Enabling Software Process Improvement: An Investigation on the Importance of Organizational Issues. PhD Thesis, Department of Computer and Information Science, Norwegian University of Science and Technology, Trondheim.

[11]   Chen, F.X. and Burseitn, F. (2006) A Dynamic Model of Knowledge Management for Higher Education Development. *The Proceedings of the 7th International Conference on Information Technology Based Higher Education and Training*, Ultimo, 10-13 July 2006, 173-180. http://dx.doi.org/10.1109/ithet.2006.339762

[12]   Devedzic, V. (2011) Knowledge Modeling—State of the Art. *Journal of Integrated Computer-Aided Engineering*, **8**, 1-27.

[13]   Basili, V.R., Caldiera, G. and Rombach, H.D. (1994) The Experience Factory. In: Marciniak, J.J., Ed., *Encyclopedia of Software Engineering*, John Wiley, Hoboken, 469-476.

[14]   Olmos, K. and Ordas, J. (2013) A Strategy to Requirements Engineering Based on Knowledge Management. *Requirements Engineering*, **19**, 421-440.

[15]   Gacitua, R., Ma, L., Nuseibeh, B., Piwek, P., de Roeck, A., Rouncefield, M., Sawyer, P., Willis, A. and Yang, H. (2009) Making Tacit Requirement Explicit. *Proceedings of the 2nd International Workshop on Managing Requirements Knowledge (MARK)*, Atlanta, 1-1 September 2009, 40-44.

[16]   Rus, I. and Lindvall, M. (2002) Knowledge Management in Software Engineering. *Journal of Software*, **19**, 26-38.

[17]   Khalid, S., Shehryar, T. and Arshad, S. (2015) The Role of Knowledge Management in Global Software Engineering. *Proceedings of the 2015 International Conference on Industrial Engineering and Operations Management*, Dubai, 3-5 March 2015, 1-5.

[18]   Ward, J. and Aurum, A. (2004) Knowledge Management in Software Engineering-Describing the Process. *Proceedings of the 2004 Australian Software Engineering Conference*, Washington DC, 13-16 April 2004, 137-146. http://dx.doi.org/10.1109/aswec.2004.1290466

[19]   Kess, P. and Haapasalo, H. (2002) Knowledge Creation through a Project Review Process in Software Production. *International Journal of Production Economics*, **80**, 49-55. http://dx.doi.org/10.1016/S0925-5273(02)00242-6

[20]   Dingsøyr, T., Brede Moe, N. and Nytro, O. (2001) Augmenting Experience Reports with Lightweight Postmortem Reviews. *Proceedings of the 3rd International Conference on Product Focused Software Process Improvement*, Kaiserslautern, 10-13 September 2001, 167-181.

[21]   Aurum, A., Parkin, P. and Cox, K. (2004) Knowledge Management in Software Engineering Education. *Proceedings of the IEEE International Conference on Advanced Learning Technologies (ICALT'04)*, Joensuu, 30 August-1 September 2004, 370-374. http://dx.doi.org/10.1109/icalt.2004.1357439

[22]   Li, J.J. (2007) Sharing Knowledge and Creating Knowledge in Organizations: The Modeling, Implementation, Discussion and Recommendations of Web-Log Based Knowledge Management. *Proceedings of the 2007 International Conference on Service Systems and Service Management*, Chengdu, 9-11 June 2007, 1-6.

[23]   Wongthongtham, P. and Chang, E. (2007) Ontology Instantiations for Software Engineering Knowledge Management. *Proceedings of the 2007 IEEE International Symposium on Industrial Electronics*, Vigo, 4-7 June 2007, 1859-1863.

[24] Georgiades, M.G., Andreou, A.S. and Pattichis, C.S. (2005) A Requirement Engineering Methodology Based on Natural Language Syntax and Semantics. *Proceedings of the* 13*th IEEE International Conference on Requirements Engineering* (*RE'*05), Paris, 29 August-2 September 2005, 473-474.

[25] Cuena, J. and Molina's, M. (2000) The Role of Knowledge Modeling Techniques in Software Development: A General Approach Based on Knowledge Management Tools. *International Journal of Human-Computer Studies*, **52**, 385-421. http://www.idealibrary.com

[26] Pilat, L. and Kaindl, H. (2011) A Knowledge Management Perspective of Requirement Engineering. *The Proceedings of the* 5*th International Conference on Research Challenges in Information Science* (*RCIS*), Gosier, 19-21 May 2011, 1-12.

[27] Olmos, K. and Rodas, J. (2014) KMoS-RE: Knowledge Management on a Strategy to Requirements Engineering. *Journal of Requirements Engineering*, **19**, 421-440.

[28] White, S.M. (2010) Application of Cognitive Theories and Knowledge Management to Requirements Engineering. *Proceedings of the* 4*th Annual IEEE of Systems Conference*, San Diego, 5-8 April 2010, 137-142.

[29] Rouse, W.B., Cannon-Bowers, J.A. and Salas, E. (1992) The Role of Mental Models in Team Performance in Complex Systems. *IEEE Transactions on Systems, Man, and Cybernetics*, **22**, 1296-1308.

[30] Lambe, P. (2007) Organizing Knowledge and Organizational Effectiveness. Chandos Publishing Ltd., Oxford.

[31] Ahsan, M., Hafeez, Y., Anwar, A. and Azeem, M.W. (2014) Knowledge Management Model for Support of Requirement Engineering. *Proceedings of the* 2014 *International Conference on Emerging Technologies* (*ICET*), Islamabad, 8-9 December 2014, 7-12.

[32] Kitchenham, B.A., Pfleeger, S.L., Pickard, L.M., Jones, P.W., Hoaglin, D.C., El Emam, K. and Rosenberg, J. (2002) Preliminary Guidelines for Empirical Research in Software Engineering. *IEEE Transactions on Software Engineering*, **28**, 721-734. http://dx.doi.org/10.1109/TSE.2002.1027796

[33] Jedlitschka, A., Hamann, D., Gohlert, T. and Schroder, A. (2005) Adapting PROFES for Use in an Agile Process: An Industry Experience Report. *Product Focused Software Process Improvement*, **3547**, 502-516.

20

Fuzzy Logic Inference Applications in Road Traffic and Parking Space Management

Ahmed Tijjani Dahiru

Department of Electrical/Electronics Technology School of Technical Education, Federal College of Education (Technical) Bichi, Kano, Nigeria
Email: babanbushra@hotmail.co.uk

Abstract

In modern motoring, many factors are considered to realize driving convenience and achieving safety at a reasonable cost. A drive towards effective management of traffic and parking space allocation in urban centres using intelligent software applications is currently being developed and deployed as GPS enabled service to consumers in automobiles or smartphone applications for convenience, safety and economic benefits. Building a fuzzy logic inference for such applications may have numerous approaches such as algorithms in Pascal or C-languages and of course using an effective fuzzy logic toolbox. Referring to a case report based on IrisNet project analysis, in this paper Matlab fuzzy logic toolbox is used in developing an inference for managing traffic flow and parking allocation with generalized feature that is open for modification. Being that modifications can be done within any or all among the tool's universe of discourse, increment in the number of membership functions and changing input and output variables etc, the work here is limited within changes at input and output variables and bases of universe of discourse. The process implications is shown as plotted by the toolbox in surface and rule views, implying that the inference is flexibly open for modifications to suit area of application within reasonable time frame no matter how complex. The travel time to the parking space being an output variable in the current inference is recommended to be substituted with distance to parking space as the former is believed to affect driving habits among motorist, whom may require the inference to as well cover other important locations such as nearest or cheapest gas station, hotels, hospitals etc.

Keywords

Fuzzy Logic Inference, Universe of Discourse, Membership Functions, Parking Space, Traffic, Simulations, Surface Views, Rule Views

1. Introduction

In the last two decades, the world has recorded high increase in use of automobiles. In fact about 32.6% increases are recorded between 2005 and 2013 [1]. This is indeed a serious challenge to parking space management and other related infrastructures. While road network expansions and extensions on one hand and urban centre restructuring on the other can be a good approach in solving the problem, yet effective and efficient utilization of the available parking space is a better approach. This is for the cost involved and time required in changing the face of urban structures. Artificial intelligence applications such as fuzzy logic inferences can optimize space allocation and management for motorists while flying in the roads and parking areas, in addition to other road traffic guides.

A number of GPS enabled solutions arrive at, such as Retschers pedestrian navigation project, NAVIO [2], which emphasizes the concepts of fusion of multiple intelligent sensors for building an inference for guiding visitors into university departments, which can probably be embedded on smartphones, PDAs etc. The emphasis on smart devices here is influenced by extreme smartness of today's mobile devices and their cognitive capabilities [3]. Socio-economic factors are considered in developing Nericell [4] for the application in developing societies for guidance against road conditions, such as potholes, bumpy roads etc.

The work presented here considers the principle of using intelligent multi-sensor fusion in fuzzy logic approach using Matlab toolbox as against algorism based solutions, to be applied in management of traffic and allocation of parking space in cities and major towns similar to the pedestrian navigation [2] and Nericell [3] projects. It should be clear that the sensors to be fused here can be camera, proximity sensors, gyroscopes, GPS, microphones, etc. thereby detecting presence of packed and moving vehicles, shown as illustration in **Figure 1** [5].

In a fuzzy logic inference based approach, factors such as traffic intensity, distance between pedestrian and parking lot and availability of parking space are taken into account for building system's inference [6]. The Matlab fuzzy toolbox can be used to facilitate the work in determining an available parking space for customers. The inference system can as well be built by programming using languages such as C or Pascal [7]. This simply implies that decision can be made by customers by using the inference guided system on the direction to follow to avoid traffic and use the most convenient available parking space within the shortest possible distance, a development seen to be as energy saving strategy and improved driving convenience. The Matlab fuzzy logic toolbox thus posses three turning points where such decisions can be modified to influence the system's inference. The turning points are:

○ *The input and output variables*: This can be achieved by redefining the variables;
○ *Fuzzy sets*: This involves introduction of additional sets on the universe of discourse. There should be adequate overlap at the sets bases (usually 25% - 50%);
○ *The rules*: This can be done by the addition of new rule sets.

Any of the three points above can be taken into account when determining an inference system, yet the three can be considered simultaneously depending upon system requirements. The implication of considering rules in building fuzzy logic inference in this case is that it solidly applies to a particular location's specific requirements (expert knowledge). Thus, for general purpose fuzzy inference and particularly for this paper, only input and output variables are considered modification.

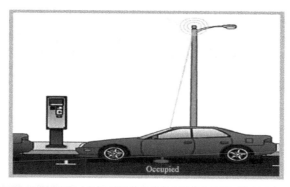

Figure 1. Sensor Networks at parking space [5].

2. The IrisNet Case Report

In Neagu's IrisNet project perception [8], the rules were set as well as input and output variables. Changing the rules, or input and output variables, or both, modifies or improves the work. Thus, decision in this case is changing only the input and output variables while the rules are not modified. Modification of rules are therefore reserved for location based purposes and expert knowledge (**Table 1**).

Applying the set rules without modification in Matlab fuzzy toolbox based on the current decision we have portion of the rules shown in **Figure 2**. Changing rules can be implemented using the rule editor.

The modifications done at the input and output variables are as follows:

o *Titles of some input variables*: Title changes to some membership functions were done to match the input variables correctly, e.g. to an average occupancy factor where we have three membership functions *vs* (very short), *s* (short) and *m* (medium) not being balanced and does not qualify the term factor very well. Thus the three membership functions titles given as *low*, *medium* and *high* to qualify the term and balance the title of the variables;

o *Bases of membership functions were adjusted for the input variables universe of discourse*: Titles to other input variables were considered appropriate and were maintained but given full titles *short*, *medium* and *long* for average distance instead of *S*, *M* and *L*. The same is applicable to the traffic intensity where we have *low*, *medium* and *high* instead of *L*, *M* and *H*;

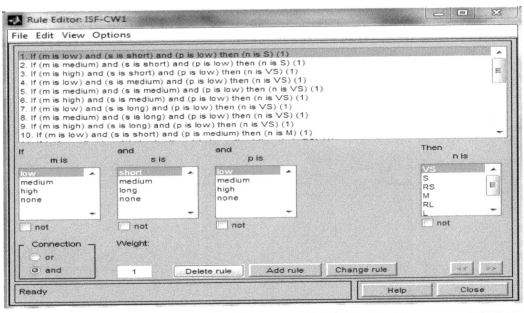

Figure 2. Matlab's rule editor (with no change to initial rules) [8].

Table 1. Initial base rules (IrisNet Project) [8].

Rule	*m*	*s*	*ρ*	*n*	Rule	*m*	*s*	*ρ*	*n*	Rule	*m*	*s*	*ρ*	*n*
1	VS	S	L	VS	10	VS	S	M	S	19	VS	S	H	VL
2	S	S	L	VS	11	S	S	M	VS	20	S	S	H	L
3	M	S	L	VS	12	M	S	M	VS	21	M	S	H	M
4	VS	M	L	VS	13	VS	M	M	RS	22	VS	M	H	M
5	S	M	L	VS	14	S	M	M	S	23	S	M	H	M
6	M	M	L	VS	15	M	M	M	VS	24	M	M	H	S
7	VS	L	L	S	16	VS	L	M	M	25	VS	L	H	RL
8	S	L	L	S	17	S	L	M	RS	26	S	L	H	M
9	M	L	L	VS	18	M	L	M	S	27	M	L	H	RS

o *Bases of membership functions were adjusted for the output variables universe of discourse:* The bases of the membership functions universe of discourse were adjusted to balance the input variables, most especially that they are termed to be average, hence balance is struck in this case to have an average result with consideration given to the bases of adjacent membership functions overlapping between 25% to 35%, as pointed out by Neagu's IrisNet project analysis.

Modification on rules as discussed earlier depends on experts knowledge (findings from research conducted on for example road users, authorities traffic rules and standardizations, the location based culture and traditions, climatic conditions, road networks etc.). Number of fuzzy sets is not hereby increased and shapes are not being changed for the fact that fuzzy systems are highly tolerant of shape approximation [8]. Thus, modifications done here are reflected to only input and output variables.

3. Surface View of the Inference System

Applying the modified input and output variables in the Matlab fuzzy toolbox, surface views are generated to facilitate the system's performance analysis, as well as managing complex problems within a reasonable period of time using a surface viewer of a fuzzy toolbox. The surface viewer is a three-dimensional mapping upon which any two sets or combinations of inputs and outputs are plotted. The developed inference system in this case has three inputs and the surface view displays any two sets of inputs and outputs. To have good representation of the surface, therefore we present the surface in three sets of input combinations below. The surface views shown in **Figures 4(a)-(c)** showcase the systems performance of input and output variables of **Figures 3(a)-(d)**.

4. The Rule Viewer

The rule viewer of the Matlab toolbox GUI below shows the developed view of the whole system. It is a Platform upon which the inference implication process can be viewed and interpreted for analytical purposes. If such an inference implication process is analyzed, then decision can be taken to either modify further or implement the decision.

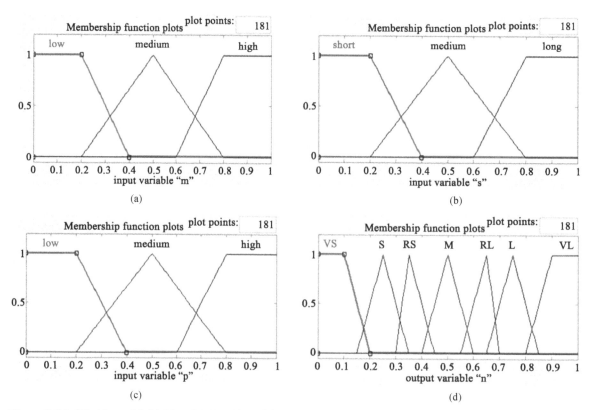

Figure 3. Modified input (a) (b) (c) and output (d) variables.

5. Discussions

The fuzzy inference system being developed here was based on Neagu's conception with a major modifications at the input and output variables. The surface view of **Figure 4** as a 3-D GUI display of any one or two combinational inputs and an output where the inference could be analyzed only with no room for modifications, thus it is merely read only. The three factor input combinations makes the design a little bit complex, thus the average distance to the parking space s, seems to contribute insignificantly to the decision making as it indicates longer travel time before parking space is reached. There could be a risk of the inference output being inaccurate or ambiguous. This can be inconsistent with road users' differing driving habits, implying that a driver could habitually be fast, slow or moderate. The road they use or environment which they drive may not be favorable to the time constraints of the designed fuzzy inference system. The simulated results shown in **Figures 5(a)-(c)** and **Figure 5** clearly showcases the process and operational implications of the inference with all possible combinations (m, s and ρ) at the input against output n. Among the three-factor input combinations, the simulation results indicates that it takes much shorter time "n" for a motorist to locate a parking space when average occupancy factor "m" and traffic intensity factor "ρ" are considered in building the inference. The rule view in this simulation case therefore indicates that for a distance of 50 km, occupancy factor of 50% and traffic intensity factor of 50%, it will take a motorist 2 hrs 30 minutes to reach a parking lot and pack. Any change in the input variables will end up changing the travel time. From a rule view, modifications can as well be effected and analyzed. Whereas the surface viewer facilitates management of complex problems within a reasonable time frame. It is a good system to be relied upon for predicting the situations ahead. It could be better if the recommendations prescribed are considered towards developing a perfect system. For instance substituting travel time as output with travel distance could be more meaningful. For the driver to be informed about the various distances to the available parking spaces may allow the driver to decide how to travel. Information about the time of journey as plotted above by the rule viewer (**Figure 5**), to the destination may not offer much in terms of decision making or convenience [9].

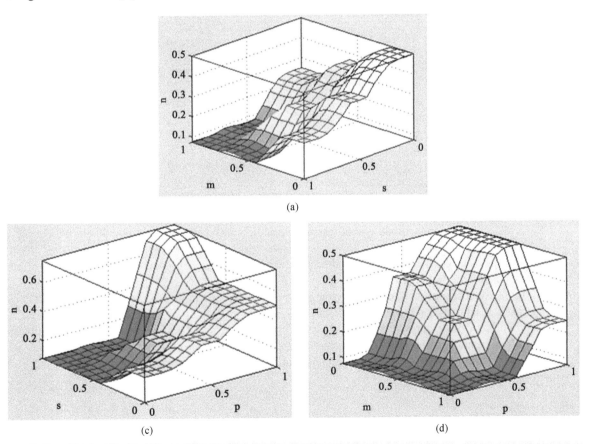

Figure 4. Surface views of the systems inference performance (a), (b) and (c).

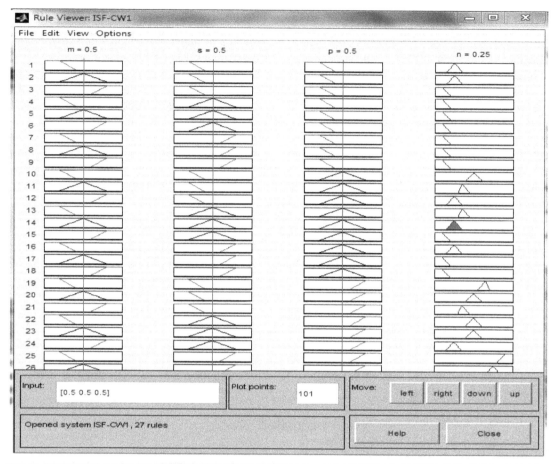

Figure 5. The rule viewer of the parking space fuzzy inference.

Based on the identified shortcomings of the currently developed inference the following could be recommended as basis towards perfection:

o   Increase the input membership functions from three to four or five so that good representations and clearer definition of the input system variables could be arrived at;

o   The rules need careful re-organizations which may depend on the environment the inference system is designed to be implemented;

o   There is need for the simplification of the system by using only two inputs instead of three, as the traffic intensity factor in this case seems to contribute insignificantly to the system;

o   The travel time as output of the system inference can be better substituted with length of journey to the parking lot. This is for the fact that travel time could change due un-expectations. Knowledge of where to pack and the distance in advance reduce the frustrations to the drivers as more energy and time are consumed to trace convenient parking spaces;

o   Similar fuzzy inference work can be carried out and implemented to locate similar important locations such as gas stations, hotels and restaurants, hospitals etc. [5];

o   It is important to consider duration of parking for individual vehicles (as vehicle sizes and weights differ) so that correct billing may be assigned to different parking spaces as one parking space may have more value in terms of security, sensitivity, importance than another etc. This could further influence drivers' decision on selection of parking spaces.

6. Conclusion

For fuzzy inference implications in this case, the toolbox provides flexible features for the adjustment whenever desirable. The modifications being done in this case therefore have improved the system in areas, such as balancing the universe of   discourse within the input and output variables, such that better defined three-dimensional surface views are obtained. The rule view as well is such simple and comprehensive enough to predict accurately and adjust conveniently. However this is subject to shortcomings such as inconsistencies with the environment which the system may be applied. Another implication is that the number of input membership functions of three in each case for m, s and ρ, are not adequate to give a better representation of the systems input variables.

Acknowledgements

The author appreciates the efforts of Dr John Readle and Mukhtar Ibrahim Bello of Faculty of Engineering and Informatics, University of Bradford, United Kingdom for their invaluable guidances and supports in this field. The author is also grateful to authors/editors/publishers of all those articles, journals and books from where the literature for this article has been reviewed and discussed.

References

[1]   International Organisation of Motor Vehicle Manufacturers (2015) World Vehicles in Use.
http://www.oica.net/category/vehicles-in-use

[2]   Retscher, G. (2006) An Intelligent Multi-Sensor System for Pedestrian Navigation. *Journal of Global Positioning Systems*, **5**, 110-118. http://dx.doi.org/10.5081/jgps.5.1.110

[3]   Campbell, A. and Choudhury, T. (2012) From Smart to Cognitive Phones. *IEEE Pervasive Computing*, **11**, 7-11.

[4]   Mohan, P., Padmanabhan V.N. and Ramjee, R. (2008) Demo Abstract: Nericell—Using Mobile Smartphones for Rich Monitoring of Road and Traffic Conditions. Microsoft Research India, Bangalore.

[5]   Ross, V. (2012) Smart Parking System Steer Drivers to Open Spaces. Popular Mechanics.
http://www.popularmechanics.com/technology/gadgets/news/smart-parking-systems-steer-drivers-to-open-spaces

[6]   Build Mamdani Systems (GUI) (2015) How to Build Mamdani Systems Using Fuzzy Logic Toolbox Graphical User Interface Tools. http://www.mathworks.com/help/fuzzy/building-systems-with-fuzzy-logic-toolbox-soft

[7]   Ibrahim, A.M. Introduction to Applied Fuzzy Electronics. Eastern Economy Edition, PHI. DeVry Institute of Technology, Toronto, Canada.

[8]   Neagu, D. (2012) Building Fuzzy Inference System: A Case Study. School of Informatics and Media, University of Bradford, Bradford.

[9]   Buckley, P. (2012) Smart Parking Sensor Platforms Helps City Motorist Save Time and Fuel. EE Times News and Analysis, UBM Tech.
http://www.eetimes.com/electronics-news/4216891/Smart-parking-sensor-platform-helps-city-motorists-save-time-and-fuel

21

Productivity Monitoring of Land Pipelines Welding via Control Chart Using the Monte Carlo Simulation

Pedro Mattos Tabim[1], Miguel Luiz Ribeiro Ferreira[2]

[1]Department of Graduation in Civil Engineering, Federal Fluminense University, Niterói, Brazil
[2]Mechanical Engineering Department, Federal Fluminense University, Niterói, Brazil
Email: pedro.tabim@gmail.com

Abstract

This article evaluates the efficacy of a tool developed in the Monte Carlo simulation and referred to as control chart. This tool is used in order to detect changes in productivity resulting from the occurrence of a given event during the welding of land pipelines with self shielded flux cored wire (FCAW). The elaboration of this control chart is based on the data from the Cumulative Probability Density Function (CDF) curve, and generated in the Monte Carlo simulation using version 6 of the Palisade Corporation's @Risk software for Excel, in a sample with productivity data from 29 welded joints, gathered through direct observation which considers the productive and unproductive times. In order to evaluate the control chart efficacy, the performance of welding productivity with a FCAW process with low alloy steels has been assessed during 29 days, summing up to 842 welded joints registered on "Relatórios Diários de Obras" (Construction Works Daily Reports). The results show that the model developed for the control chart elaboration is effective in monitoring the productivity of the observed welding procedure.

Keywords

Monte Carlo Simulation, Welding, Land Pipelines, Productivity

1. Introduction

Welding is the main productive process in construction works of land pipelines. Thus, the purpose of this paper is to develop a productivity monitoring methodology for the semi-automatic welding process with self shielded flux cored wire (FCAW) process of low alloy steel land pipelines. In this study, productivity data about a sample composed of 29 welded joints at a construction work in the Brazilian Northeast have been gathered in the field by direct observation.

On the gathering of these data, the times of the activities related to the welding productive process and associated downtimes during production have been measured in order to define the welding productivity. The unit used was joints/day, bearing in mind the employment in the land pipeline construction industry [1]. Virtual data and the Cumulative Probability Density Function (CDF) of Welding Productivity (WP), which takes into consideration the productive and unproductive welding times in this construction work, have been generated from actual productivity data of this sample, through Monte Carlo Method and @Risk 6 software.

A control chart for the monitoring of the productivity behavior of welding during construction has been elaborated, inspired by the traditional control charts for statistical processes control and based on the simulation CDF, aiming to detect eventual deviations of the productive process and allowing corrective action taking by the construction management. In order to check the effectiveness of such chart on production deviation detection during the construction work, production data about welded joints have been gathered during 29 days and registered in the Construction Work Daily Reports. We try to identify abnormalities for the days when the productivity is out of the limits established in the control chart.

2. Background Literature

2.1. Productivity Indicators

It is possible to define productivity as the value of the results, being those products or services, divided by the value of goods or resources [2]-[4]. In construction industries [5], working time quantity is estimated in menhour to yield a production or service unit. Productivity can be defined as the efficiency on transforming inputs—workforce, materials and equipment—in outputs or construction work product compliant to the required objectives [6].

The activities that compose the work process are described as: direct or productive work, support work and unproductive work [7] [8]. Another classification [9], the activities may be categorized in direct work, preparatory work, tools and equipment, material handling, waiting, travel, personal. In this article, direct work comprises welding and grinding activities and all the other activities are considered as nonproductive time. These activities are: wire changing, column positioning, idle time between activities, waiting time and handling of tools. A comparison between the concepts of work activities adopted in this paper with the authors aforementioned is presented in **Table 1**.

A data survey in a construction work at Duque de Caxias Refinery (REDUC) in Rio de Janeiro state [10], the total indicators of equivalent joints/day, welding volume in cm^3/day and couple joints/day have been considered for welding productivity. The most used method to measure welding productivity in pipeline constructions in the United States consists on the number of completed joints divided by the time span, *i.e.* the welding process output [1]. The joints/day unit, which is one of the most used indicators in the Brazilian industry in land pipelines construction, has been adopted for this paper.

2.2. Simulation by Monte Carlo Method

The Probability and Density Functions (PDF) and Cumulative Probability Density Function (CDF) curves are compared in order to estimate the welding productivity of carbon steel pipe tops joints achieved through the generation of random numbers via Monte Carlo simulation with parametric distributions from small samples with 10, 15 and 20 elements and the generated results originated from a 160 elements actual sample [11]-[13].

Table 1. Work activities concept comparative.

Time	Classification		
	[9]	[7]	[8]
Welding	Direct work	Direct work	Direct work
Griding	Direct work	Direct work	Direct work
Nonproductive	preparatory work, tools and equipment, material handling, waiting, travel, personal	Support work and unproductive work	Support work and unproductive work

As shown in these works, it is possible to determine that the Monte Carlo simulation is a suitable method to assess the welding productivity behavior.

The Monte Carlo simulation employment, according to most authors, consists in five steps: group the gathered data in class intervals in order to generate a frequency histogram; define a distribution for the probability density function, being a random variable that best represents the sample; implement the simulations with N repetitions; assess whether the number of simulations is suitable; after performing the simulations, generate the cumulative probability density function for results analysis [14]. @Risk software allows the modeling of functions and performing Monte Carlo simulations, presenting the simulation results graphically [15].

The Monte Carlo method consists in generating virtual data from an actual sample. The simulation is useful to achieve a model that imitates the random sample of a population or to perform statistical experiments, but the success of this method depends on the model capacity to reproduce the distribution achieved based on the actual sample data. Whether the parameter uncertainty is defined by technical literature or data gathering, parametric distributions are used and, when it is not possible, non-parametric distributions may be used, such as triangular and uniform ones, with the aid of experts. The use of non-parametric distributions is applicable to the simulation in many segments [16]. The Monte Carlo simulation has many applications with non-parametric distributions. [17] tested and validated the uniform, triangular and Beta (PERT) non-parametric distributions in air, rail and land transportation projects. [18] used the uniform distribution in order to estimate a modern municipal solid waste landfill life, once the quality of the data did not suffice to adjust the parametric distributions. [19] developed a simulation model based on the uniform distribution in order to adjust the heterogeneity of oil production scenarios around the world. [20] applied the triangular distribution in order to select the cementing method type to be used in a construction work due to its ease of use and supported by technical literature on construction planning.

3. Experimental Procedure

3.1. Sample

Two kinds of samples have been used on conducting the study. One was composed of welding data from a real time field gathering consisting of 29 joints by direct observation. The productive and unproductive times have been registered. The productive times correspond to the estimated activities in the welding procedure where the open arc and cleaning by grinding time spans are calculated, taking into consideration the time spans passed on measuring the negligible interpasses temperatures and attributing a zero value. The unproductive time spans are the ones when the welding was in downtime for any reasons. For the joint performance on the root pass the electrode E6010 has been used and for the rib, the consumable E8010-P1. The 2mm diameter flux cored wire E-91T8-G, AWS specification 5.29 [21], has been used on the four filling and finishing passes.

The welded pipes main characteristics are:
- Carbon steel API 5L X70 - PSL2;
- 28 inches or 711.2 millimeters diameter;
- 0.406 inches or 10.3 millimeters thickness.

The second sample is composed of 842 welded joints production during 29 days, using the same procedure as the sample described in the last paragraph, registered in the Construction Work Daily Report.

3.2. Data Gathering

The field data gathering took place in two steps: phase 1—data gathering during welding in the worksite forming the basis for the Monte Carlo simulation and elaboration of control chart; phase 2—welding productive data registered during 29 production days in the Construction Work Daily Reports.

The field data gathering on phase 1 took place during three workdays, from the beginning to the end of the workday, following monitoring by the welding team in the site where the pipes have been welded. The joint runtimes, which are referred to as production time, and the unproductive times where, for any reason, the welding activity was in a downtime have been registered in this process. The weather in this region was good, sunny and around 25°C. Accordingly, during the gathering of those data, no exceptional incidence such as rain, strike, accidents, among other incidents have been registered at the worksite. In this sense, it is possible to conclude that the performance conditions were normal.

On the other hand, these data have been gathered taking into consideration that the construction work was in a normal production stage, corresponding to a physical progress above 20%, having already surpassed the learning curve [22]. It is worth highlighting that the runtimes registers concern flux cored arc welding (FCAW) during the joint filling and finishing stages. Runtimes of root passes and rib with coated electrode process have not been considered in this paper.

On conducting this process 5 welding teams, each composed of two welders, two grinders and two helpers, have been monitored. In order to determine the timespan spent on welding each joint, it was required to define all the activities involved in this operation, that are: filler metal deposition, interpasses temperatures determination and cleaning between passes. Between these three activities a runtime has been associated, but the time spent in the interpasses temperatures determination activity was considered negligible and, thus, not measured. Thereby, the runtimes calculated were the ones related to filler metal deposition, referred to as welding time, and cleaning between passes, where the griding method was used and referred to as grinding time. To register the time spent in these activities, timing started on the opening of the welding electric arc in the filling phase and ended on the grinding after the finishing of all the welding passes with FCAW.

On the other hand, the gathering of these data prioritized the largest number of joints welded in a random manner, i.e. not prioritizing specific welders or pipeline stretches, aiming to avoid the influence of certain welders with distinguished skills, who could present a higher or lower performance. Besides the time spans considered productive, which are the welding and grinding times, the times when the workers, for any reason, were stopped and not performing any activity related to the welding process were also registered. The time spent in the start and end of the workday were not considered here. These time spans were considered unproductive in this paper.

A total of 29 welded joints runtimes have been gathered, encompassing the productive and unproductive times. **Table 2** presents the statistical parameters of the sample.

The workday at the jobsite stretched from 7 AM to 5 PM. However, it was observed that a given time was spent, on starting the activities, for the mobilization and displacement to the work position of the joint to be welded and for the same movement backwards at the end of the day. In order to calculate these displacement and mobilization times at the start and end of the workday, to be deducted from the hours of working, the minimum, probable and maximum values for the effective start and end of the workday have been attributed. Accordingly, 1 hour for lunch is deducted from the workday. **Table 3** presents these times in order to calculate the effective workday.

In order to determine the productivity in joints/day, we have proceeded like the following:

1) Sum of the welding and grinding runtimes and unproductive times;

2) Definition of the effective workday, where we have considered the lunch break and work start and finish times;

3) Definition of the Standard Team;

Table 2. Statistical parameters of the sample runtimes.

Parameter	Time (in seconds)		
	Welding	Griding	Unproductive
Maximum	2174	1320	1509
Minimum	1110	320	64
Mean	1516.72	797.79	304.69
Standard deviation	254.92	247.98	281.88
Coefficient of variation (standard deviation/mean)	0.17	0.31	0.92

Table 3. Start and end times of the effective workday.

Turn	Workday		
	Minimum	Likely	Maximum
Start	7:30 AM	8:00 AM	8:30 AM
End	3:40 PM	4:00 PM	5:00 PM

4) Definition of the number of team involved in the process;

5) Productivity calculation in joints/day of all teams in the work front.

The calculation of productivity in joints is expressed through the Equation (1) below:

$$WP = \text{Number of teams} \times \left(\text{Effective workday}/\text{Time per completed joint}\right) \tag{1}$$

- Welding Productivity (WP): considers the time per completed joint per welding team. This time is the denominator of the division by effective workday, producing the unit joints/day per team. To assess the productivity of the construction work with all teams, it is necessary to multiply it by the number of teams.

- Effective workday: is the 10 daily hours of working of the studied construction work subtracted from the mobilization and displacement times where the team did not effectively started the service and the 1 hour lunch break.

- Time per completed joint: is the sum of the opened arc time, grinding time and the unproductive times from the start of the open arc welding until the final grinding of finishing pass, in hours.

- Joint: top, with a chamfering angle between $60°$ and $64°$, root opening between 2 mm and 2.5 mm. The weld volume deposited by FCAW is 86.7×10^{-3} dm^3, calculated in similar procedure as [23].

- Welding team: is the composition of the team working to weld a joint. The team of the studied work was composed of 2 welders, 2 grinders and 2 helpers.

- Number of teams—in the construction work there were 5 welding teams with the same composition.

On phase 2 we aimed at gathering the productivity values in joints/day of the studied work taking into consideration a longer production period. These data have been achieved through registers of the Construction Work Daily Report document, which is used by the contracting party and the contractor to report the main occurrences. The productive data of 29 production days have been gathered following the aforementioned procedures.

3.3. Elaboration of the Productivity Control Chart

Aiming to develop a practical monitoring tool, quick in obtaining results and easy to understand, we chose to develop a control method similar to those based on the general theory of Shewhart's control chart rules, that esablishes a central limit, to which corresponds the sample mean, and the upper and lower limits adding or subtracting the mean of a k constant multiplied by a sample standard deviation. The control charts quickly detect anomalies in the process, once it is a real time monitoring technique [24]. Although inspired by the control charts already mentioned, the methodology developed in this work adopted its own criteria, which have been considered more suitable for productivity monitoring.

The control chart has been elaborated in the following steps: definition of the productivity model equation; conduction of a Monte Carlo simulation on the productivity model established in the Equation (1) from the productivity data gathered at the worksite via monitoring of the productive runtimes, unproductive times, start and end in order to obtain the CDF curve; definition of the control chart upper and lower limits.

The simulation of the productive model established in the Equation (1) is ran by the version 6 of the Palisade Corporation's @Risk software for Excel [25]. **Figure 1** represents a flow chart of the Monte Carlo simulation to produce the control chart.

The simulation procedure with the Monte Carlo method is conducted as in the following steps:

1st) Definition of the model input data. The input data are: welding time, grinding time, unproductive time, start time, end time, workday time deducted from lunch break, number of teams. The last two items are constant.

2nd) Definition of the output data, which in this case is the Welding Productivity (WP) defined in Equation (1).

3rd) Definition of the generating functions for the following variables: welding time, grinding time, unproductive time, start time and end time.

4th) After the definition of the generating functions and their input in the productivity model, a simulation with the Monte Carlo method is made with 1000 iterations.

5th) After the simulation, it has been verified whether the number of iterations was sufficient through convergence analysis made available by the computing software. In this case the result was positive and we proceeded to the next step. It is worth highlighting that, if the number of iterations was not sufficient, it would be necessary to raise it until a positive analysis of the convergence analysis took place, because, if it is not achieved, it is re-

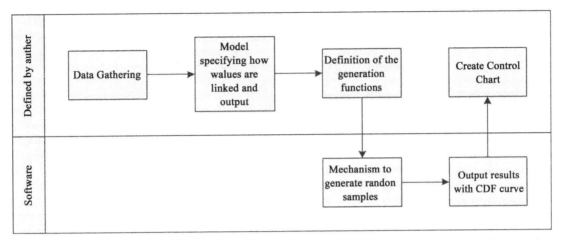

Figure 1. Flow chart of the simulation.

quired the assessment of the possibility to select another generating function of each variable considered in the productivity model. Otherwise, a non-parametric distribution is used.

66th) Once the previous steps have been conducted, a CDF curve is elaborated and the statistical parameters of the data obtained via simulation calculated.

On defining the generating functions in order to conduct the productivity model simulation, 3 different criteria have been adopted for each activity, taking into consideration the specific characteristics of each of them. Thereby, on defining the generating function of the welding times, a qui-square test, tool available in the @Risk6 software, was used. The function that showed the highest compliance was the Lognormal function for a significance level of 5% with the following main parameters: $\mu = 747.65$ and $s = 253.13$. Regarding the grinding time, the Weibull function presented the best compliance with the sample data, for a significance level of 5% with parameters $\alpha = 2.5198$ and $\beta = 645.79$.

For unproductive times, it was impossible to adjust the data with a CDF, because there was not compliance in the Qui-square test for any function presented by the version 6 of the @Risk software [25]. In **Table 2**, it is possible to notice a great value dispersion, resulting in a relevant amplitude between maximum and minimum, elevated dispersion attested by the analysis of the coefficient of variation and a bimodal behavior observed on the analysis of the distribution graph of the data gathered. The coefficient of variation is a meaningful way to determine which variable, in this case unproductive, has great dispersion. The variable with the smaller coefficient of variation, near 0, is less dispersed than the variable near 1.

It has been observed that the unproductive times result from many situations, for example, idleness, consumption materials waiting time, interruptions in order to reposition the tools, among others. In this sense, it has been concluded that the differentiated nature of the generating causes for the unproductive times is the main reason for the heterogeneous behavior in the sample and the difficulty on defining a generating function that would comply with the analyzed sample. Thereby, the solution adopted was to use the uniform distribution as a generating function, which attributes the same occurrence probability for the considered events. This function, which represents the behavior of the unproductive times due to various reasons, has been defined in the interval that corresponds to the minimum of 64 seconds and maximum of 1509 seconds, which respectively correspond to the shortest and longest unproductive time registered in this case.

The triangular function has been defined as generating factor for start and end times, which correspond to the preparations for the start and end of workday activities, taking into consideration the modeling impossibility of these processes. In this case, the main parameters of this distribution are: likely time, minimum time and maximum time, both for the start times and end times, presented in **Table 3**.

After defining the generating functions of the times considered in the welding process, the Monte Carlo simulation was ran in with the version 6 of the @Risk software for Excel with 1000 iterations, where the CDF and the generated data main statistics were obtained.

On the other hand, in order to define the control chart Lower and Upper Limits, the Probability criterion > 0% was adopted for the first one and Probability < 90% for the second one. These values have been extracted from the CDF curve. The upper limit setting in 90% aims at avoiding the use of data generated in the CDF, where the possibility of a discrepancy between the virtual data generated in a simulation and the ones originating from a real productive process increase. On the other hand, on setting the lower limit in 0%, the minimum positive value obtained in the simulation is attributed to the minimum productivity. We would also like to highlight that a similar criterion was used successfully by [12].

3.4. Control Chart Effectiveness Test

We gathered the production of welded joints during 29 days in the Construction Work Daily Reports in order to verify the possibility of using the productivity control chart, which has been elaborated with data resulting from real time direct observation and register of the times considered in the welding operation in the workforce. Thereby, the production from each workday in joints/day has been registered and entered in the control chart. In case the productivity registered in a given day was out of both the upper and lower limits of the control chart, it was verified if any incident or occurrence has been registered in the Construction Work Daily Report. A comparison between the construction work productivity CDF curve in joints/day and the curve obtained through simulation, respectively presented in **Figure 3** and **Figure 4**, was conducted to complement this analysis.

4. Results Analysis

From the CDF curve—**Figure 2**—obtained through simulation built based on direct observation and registration of both productive and unproductive times of the productive process, establishing the 0% quota of the CDF as lower limit corresponding to a productivity of 21 joints/day, 90% of the CDF, equivalent to 49 joints/day and the mean of 39 joints/day have been inserted as control chart limits presented in **Figure 3**.

The establishment of the upper quota in 90% of the CDF is due to the fact that values near 100% in the curve generated in the simulation present productivity results that do not represent a real productive process. In this article it has been established that this is the maximum value for the welding productivity as it is possible to note in **Table 4**.

The productivity data from the Construction Works Daily Report gathered during 29 production days have been inserted to assess the Control Chart capacity to detect variations in the welding productivity. **Table 5** represents

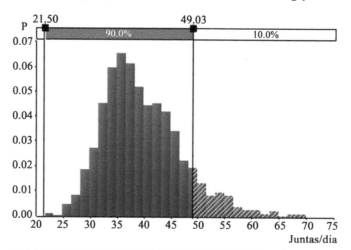

Figure 2. CDF of the welding productivity indicator.

Table 4. Statistical parameters for the WP simulation.

Parameter	Joints/Day
Maximum	49
Minimum	21
Mean	39
Standard deviation	6
Coefficient of variation	0.15

the statistical parameters originated in the construction report and the result of the simulation. These data have been inserted in the Control Chart presented in **Figure 3**.

The analysis of **Figure 3** shows that 86% of the elements of the productivity measured in the construction work are between the control chart minimum and maximum values and 14% of the elements are below minimum. Also, it is possible to notice that most values are below central limit.

During the analysis of the occurrence of points out of the lower limit and tending to be below the simulated mean, logistics problems in the construction work, deformations on the pipes to be welded, among other problems caused by the contractor management malpractices that were affecting the welding performance have been registered in the Construction Work Daily Reports. These problems are due to factors impossible to be encompassed by the experimental data gathering, because they are either special causes or welding process anomalies. From this result it is possible to conclude that this tool is effective on detecting the productivity variations, allowing corrective actions to be taken towards problems. On the other hand, it is possible to notice the effectiveness of the Monte Carlo simulation use in predicting the welding productivity behavior in accordance to what [11]-[13] have determined, once this control chart has been built from the CDF generated from the simulation obtained through data gathered by direct observation of the productive process of 29 joints. The evaluation period that encompasses the example of the control chart corresponded to the production of 824 joints registered in the Construction Work Daily Reports. Accordingly, it has been verified that the productivity model adopted in the Monte Carlo simulation, as well as the premises adopted in its building, both in the behavior of the productive times and unproductive times, presented adequate results. This analysis is reinforced when comparing the behavior of the WP obtained through Monte Carlo simulation CDF (**Figure 2** and **Table 4**) and of the 29 days production corresponding sample, registered in the Construction Work Daily Reports (**Figure 4** and **Table 5**).

It is possible to determine that in **Figure 2**, which presents the CDF built from the simulation based on the 29 joints experimental data gathered through direct observation and measurement of the productive and unproductive times of the productive process, the occurrence probability of the productivity data gathered in the construction work, which vary from 11 to 44 joints/day, is placed around 75%. **Figure 4** represents the behavior of the productivity registered in 29 workdays and, in this case, the occurrence probability of the productivity

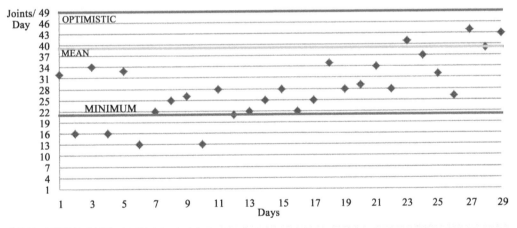

Figure 3. Control chart.

Table 5. Statistical parameters of 29 days productivity in the construction work.

Parameter	Joints/Day
Maximum	44
Minimum	11
Mean	28
Standard deviation	9
Coefficient of variation	0.30

Source: Construction Work Daily Report.

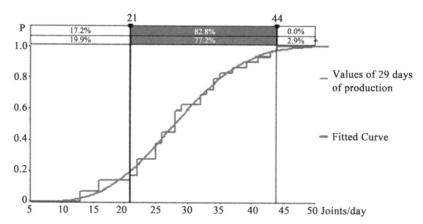

Figure 4. The welded joints productivity CDF during 29 days in the construction work registered in the CWDR

between the values from 21 to 44 joints/day is around 77%. Thereby, on comparing **Figure 2** and **Figure 4**, it is possible to state that the curve generated in the simulation expresses the behavior of the productive process with reasonable precision.

5. Conclusions

By the results being achieved, it is possible to determine that the CDF curve generates through Monte Carlo simulation from the small samples gathered through direct observation of the productive process represents, with a good precision margin, the productivity of low alloy steels land pipelines welding process with the shielded flux cored wire process in the construction work.

The welding productivity model develops from the worksite welding direct observation with the registration of the productive and unproductive times, as well as the distribution models adopts in it in order to conduct the Monte Carlo simulation and welding productivity CDF building is successful in representing the productivity behavior in the construction work for the welding procedure being studied in this article.

The control chart, built from the CDF generated through a Monte Carlo simulation based on the productivity model and limits established in this work, has proven to be an effective tool on monitoring the welded joints productivity during construction work.

References

[1]   Miller, C. and Crawford, M.H. (2002) Welding-Related Expenditures, Investments, and Productivity Measurement in U.S. Manufacturing, Construction, and Mining Industries. Technical Report, American Welding Society, Miami.

[2]   Ritzman, L.P. and Krajewski, L.J. (2003) Foundations of Operations Management. 2nd Edition, Prentice Hall, Upper Saddle River.

[3]   Slack, N., Chambers, S. and Johnston, R. (2002) Operations Management. 2nd Edition, Atlas, São Paulo.

[4]   Gaither, N. and Frazier, G. (2002) Production and Operations Management. Thomson Learning, São Paulo.

[5]   Diekmann, J.E. and Heinz, J. (2001) Determinants of Jobsite Productivity. Construction Industry Institute, Austin.

[6]   de Souza, U.E.L. (2006) How to Increase Labor Efficiency: Productivity Management Manual in Construction. 1st Edition, Pini, São Paulo.

[7]   Adrian, J.J. (2004) Construction Productivity: Measurement and Improvement. Stipes Publishing, Champaign.

[8]   Schwartzkoft, W. (2004) Calculating Lost Labor Productivity in Construction Claims. Aspen, Austin.

[9]   Construction Industry Institute (2010) Guide to Activity Analysis. University of Texas, Austin.

[10]   Gioia, A.L.S., Silva Júnior, I.F. (2007) Assessment of Methodology for Productivity Measurement in Pipe Instalation Activity in Industrial Works. Graduation, Monograph, University Federal Fluminense, Niterói.

[11]   Martins, J.L.F. (2011) Application of Simulation with Monte Carlo and Latin Hypercube Methods to Estimate Productivity in the Welding Process of SMAW. PhD Thesis, University Federal Fluminense, Niterói.

[12]   Martins, J.L.F., Ferreira, M. and Saraiva, J.M.F. (2011) Productivity Estimation in Welding by Monte Carlo Method.

Soldagem e Inspeção, **16**, 204-212.

[13] Constâncio, D.S., Ferreira, M. and Freire, I.J. (2009) Welding Productivity's Estimate of Industrial Piping, Being Used Monte Carlo's Method. *Proceedings of the XXXV CONSOLDA—Congresso Nacional de Soldagem*, Piracicaba, 26-29 Outubro 2009, 26-29.

[14] Morano, C.A.R. (2003) Application of Risk Analysis Techniques in Construction Projects. Master's Dissertation, University Federal Fluminense, Niterói.

[15] Grey, S. (1995) Practical Risk Assessment for Project Management. John Wiley & Sons, Chichester.

[16] Vose, D. (2000) Risk Analysis: A Quantitative Guide. 2nd Edition, John Wiley & Sons, Chichester.

[17] Salling, K.B. (2008) Assessment of Transport Projects: Risk Analysis and Decision Support. PhD Thesis, Technical University of Denmark, Lyngby.

[18] Bieda, B. (2013) Stochastic Approach to Municipal Solid Waste Landfill Life Based on the Contaminant Transit Time Modeling Using the Monte Carlo (MC) Simulation. *Science of the Total Environment*, **442**, 489-496. http://dx.doi.org/10.1016/j.scitotenv.2012.10.032

[19] Voudouris, V., Stasinopoulos, D., Rigby, R. and Di Maio, C. (2011) The ACEGES Laboratory for Energy Policy: Exploring the Production of Crude Oil. *Energy Policy*, **39**, 5480-5489. http://dx.doi.org/10.1016/j.enpol.2011.05.014

[20] Chou, J. and Ongkowijoyo, C.S. (2015) Reliability-Based Decision Making for Selection of Ready-Mix Concrete Supply Using Stochastic Superiority and Inferiority Ranking Method. *Reliability Engineering and System Safety*, **137**, 29-39. http://dx.doi.org/10.1016/j.ress.2014.12.004

[21] AWS A5.29/A5.29M (2010) Specification for Low-Alloy Steel Electrodes for Flux Cored Arc Welding. 4th Edition, American Welding Society, Miami.

[22] Anzanello, J.M. and Fogliatto, F.S. (2007) Learning Curves: Literature Review and Further Research. *Gestão e Produção*, **14**, 109-123. http://dx.doi.org/10.1590/s0104-530x2007000100010

[23] Modenesi, P.J. (2001) Estimation of Welding Costs. University Federal de Minas Gerais. http://www.infosolda.com.br/images/Downloads/Artigos/industrial/estimativa-dos-custos-de-soldagem.pdf

[24] Montgomery, D.C. and Runger, G.C. (2007) Applied Statistics and Probability for Engineers. 4th Edition, John Wiley & Sons, New York.

[25] Palisade Corporation (2013) @Risk Users Guide. Version 6, Palisade Corporation, New York.

22

A Novel Triangular Chaotic Map (TCM) with Full Intensive Chaotic Population Based on Logistic Map

Mahmoud Maqableh

Management Information Systems, Faculty of Business, The University of Jordan, Amman, Jordan
Email: maqableh@ju.edu.jo

Abstract

Chaos theory attempts to explain the result of a system that is sensitive to initial conditions, complex, and shows an unpredictable behaviour. Chaotic systems are sensitive to any change or changes in the initial condition(s) and are unpredictable in the long term. Chaos theory are implementing today in many different fields of studies. In this research, we propose a new one-dimensional Triangular Chaotic Map (TCM) with full intensive chaotic population. TCM chaotic map is a one-way function that prevents the finding of a relationship between the successive output values and increases the randomness of output results. The tests and analysis results of the proposed triangular chaotic map show a great sensitivity to initial conditions, have unpredictability, are uniformly distributed and random-like and have an infinite range of intensive chaotic population with large positive Lyapunov exponent values. Moreover, TCM characteristics are very promising for possible utilization in many different study fields.

Keywords

Chaos, Chaotic Maps, Triangular Chaotic Map, Logistic Map, Lyapunov Exponent

1. Introduction

Over the last few years, many researchers have studied chaos theory in several fields, such as electronic systems, fluid dynamics, lasers, weather and climate [1]-[5]. Chaos theory is implementing today in many different fields of studies such as: engineering, computer science, mathematics, physics, geology, microbiology, biology, economics, finance, algorithmic trading, meteorology, philosophy, politics, population dynamics, psychology, and robotics [6]. Moreover, Chaos theory has attracted the cryptography field due to its characteristics, such as its deterministic nature, unpredictability, random-look nature and its sensitivity to initial value [7].

Cryptographers have utilized dynamic chaotic maps to develop new cryptographic primitives by exploiting chaotic maps, such as logistic maps, Henon maps, and Tent maps. There are similarities and differences between cryptography algorithms and chaotic maps [8]. The parameters in chaotic maps are meaningful, if they are real numbers, which can be used in the cryptographic algorithms as encryption and decryption keys. Chaotic systems are sensitive to any change or changes in the initial condition(s) and are unpredictable in the long term, thus representing the diffusion in cryptographic encryption algorithms. Iterations of a chaotic map lead to the spreading of the initial region over the entire phase space, and this can be achieved in cryptographic algorithms by designing the algorithm based on rounds. The main difference between chaos and cryptography is that encryption transformations are defined on finite sets, whereas chaos has meaning only in real numbers.

Since 1990, many studies on digital chaotic cryptography have been proposed to provide secure communications based on chaotic maps including chaotic block ciphers [9]-[34], chaotic cryptography hash functions [7] [31] [35]-[49], and chaotic pseudorandom number generators [11] [50]-[65]. In general, chaos theory has been proved a secure algorithm against known cryptanalysis techniques. Recently, various studies have been conducted on chaotic cryptographic algorithms [7] [66]-[87]. Some of the proposed chaotic cryptographic algorithms that have been analysed have had weak internal designs and incorrect exploitation of chaotic maps. In this research, we propose novel triangular chaotic map.

The rest of this research paper is organized as follows. Section 2 introduces chaos theory. The details of chaotic maps are discussed in Section 3. Section 4 describes details of Logistic map and Lyapunov exponent. In Section 5, details of the new Triangular Chaotic map are given. Finally, the conclusion is given in Section 6.

2. Chaos Theory

Chaos is derived from a Greek word "Χαos", meaning a state without order or predictability [2]. A chaotic system is a simple, non-linear, dynamical, and deterministic system that shows completely unpredictable behaviour and appears random [88]. Moreover, it is a deterministic system with great sensitivity to initial conditions, such that a computer system can give an amazingly different result when the value of an input parameter is changed. On the other hand, in classical science small changes in an initial value might generate small differences in the result [89] [90]. A system is called a chaotic system if it is sensitive to initial conditions, topology mix, and if periodic orbits are dense.

According to Alligood et al. (1996), a dynamical system contains all the possible states and regulations that control the next state from the current state. On the other hand, the deterministic regulations are those that determine the current state uniquely from the previous states, whereas there is always a mathematical equation to determine the system evolution [91]. From the previous definitions of deterministic and dynamical systems, we cannot say that the randomness is not allowed. The bifurcation in dynamic differential equation changes the number of solutions as the parameters is changed [92].

In 1890, Poincaré published his article [89] (on the equations of the dynamics and the three-body problem) of 270 pages, which simplified the way of looking at the complicated continuous trajectories from differential equations [2]. Then, in 1898, Hadamard observed the sensitivity to initial conditions and unpredictability of special systems, calling this the geodesic flow [2]. Later, in 1908, Poincaré noted that chaos sensitivity depends on initial conditions and gives unpredictable results [90] [93]. Later on, Edward Lorenz (1963) examined chaos theory and described a simple mathematical model of weather prediction [91]. Lorenz's model was the first numerical model to detect chaos in a non-linear dynamical system [3] [94]. Lorenz's findings were very interesting in that some equations rise to some surprisingly complex behaviour and chaos behaviour dependent on the initial condition [2]. In 1975, Li and Yorke were the first to introduce the word 'chaos' into mathematical literature, where system results appear random [1]-[5] [95] [96].

Chaotic maps have been the subject of an extremely active research area due to their characteristics, such as sensitivity to the initial value, complex behaviour, and completely deterministic nature. The chaotic behaviour can be observed in many different systems, such as electronic systems, fluid dynamics, lasers, weather, climate and economics [2] [88] [89] [97]. Our intuition tells us that a small change in input parameters should give a small change in output, but chaotic systems show us that this is not necessarily the case. Usually, chaotic maps define infinitely large fields of real numbers. The most important characteristics of chaotic systems are as follows:

1. Apparently random behaviour but completely deterministic: The behaviour of chaotic systems seems to be random but actually it is purely deterministic. Hence, if we run the chaotic system many times with the same initial value, we will obtain the same set of output values. Furthermore, the chaotic systems are dynamical systems that are described by differential equations or iterative mappings, and the next state is specified from the previous state (see Equation 3-1 [5] [98] [99]).

$$\frac{d}{dt} x_i = F_i\left(x_1, \cdots, x_n\right) \quad i = 1, 2, \cdots, n \tag{1}$$

2. Sensitivity dependence on the initial conditions (The state from which the system starts): Dynamical systems evolve completely differently over time with slight changes in the initial state [88] [90].

3. Unpredictable (difficult or impossible to predict the behaviour in the long term): In chaotic maps, even if one knows the current state of the chaotic system it is useless trying to predict the next state of the system. In other words, it is very difficult to predict the future states of the chaotic system in the long term [89] [100].

3. Chaotic Maps

According to Alligood *et al.* (1996), a chaotic map is a function of its domain and range in the same space, and the starting point of the trajectory is called the initial value (condition) [101]. Chaotic dynamics have a unique attribute that can be seen clearly by imagining the system starting twice with slightly different initial conditions [102]. Chaos theory attempts to explain the result of a system that is sensitive to initial conditions, complex, and shows unpredictable behaviour. Chaotic dynamical systems increase communication security with higher dimensions and more than one positive Lyapunov exponent [91]. A Lyapunov exponent is used to help select the initial parameters of chaotic maps that fall in chaotic areas. A chaotic system exhibits some chaotic behaviour and often occurs in the study of dynamical systems. In the following subsections, we will give a brief induction to some chaotic systems: Logistic map, Lorenz attractors, Rossler attractors, Henon map, Tent map, and Piecewise linear chaotic map.

3.1. Logistic Map

In 1845, Pierre Verhulst proposed a logistic map, which is a simple non-linear dynamical map. A logistic map is one of the most popular and simplest chaotic maps [103]. Logistic maps became very popular after they were exploited in 1979 by the biologist Robert M. May [89]. The logistic map is a polynomial mapping, a complex chaotic system, the behaviour of which can arise from very simple non-linear dynamical equations, as shown in **Figure 1** [104]. The logistic map equation is written as:

$$g\left(x_n\right) = x_{n+1} = r \times x_n \times \left(1 - x_n\right) \tag{2}$$

where x_n is a number between zero and one, x_0 represents the initial population, and r is a positive number between zero and four.

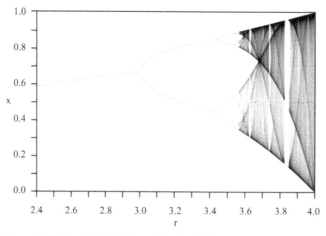

Figure 1. Bifurcation diagram of the Logistic map [105].

The logistic map is one of the simplest chaotic maps; it is highly sensitive to change in its parameter value, where a different value of the parameter r will give a different map f [89]. Its transformation function is F: $[0,1] \rightarrow [0,1]$ which is defined in the above equation. From the onset of chaos, a seemingly random jumble of dots, the behaviour of the logistic map depends mainly on the values of two variables (r, x_0); by changing one or both variables' values we can observe different logistic map behaviours. The population of a logistic map will die out if the value of r is between 0 and 1, and the population will be quickly stabilized on the value $(1-r)/r$ if the value of r is between 1 and 3 [89]. Then, the population will oscillate between two values if the value of parameter r is between 3 and 3.45. After that, with values of parameter r between 3.45 and 4 the periodic fluctuation becomes significantly more complicated. Finally, most of the values after 3.57 show chaotic behaviour.

In the logistic map $g(x_n) = r \times x_n \times (1 - x_n)$, the function result depends on the value of parameter r, where different values of r will give quite different pictures. We can note that $g(x_1) = x_2$ and $g(x_2) = x_1$, that mean $g(g(x_1)) = x_2$ and $g(g(x_2)) = x_1$. According to Alligood *et al.* (1996) the periodic fluctuation between x_1, x_2 is steady and attracts orbits (trajectories). Therefore, there are a minimum number of iterations of the orbit to repeat the point. There are obvious differences between the behaviour of the exponential model and the logistic model's behaviour. To show the difference between the two functions, we take an example of the exponential function $f(x_{n+1}) = 2x_n$ and an example of logistic function $g(x_{n+1}) = 4x_n(1 - x_n)$; the initial value for both functions is 0.0090, and we then calculate the population for $n = 0, 1, 2, \cdots, 10$ resulting in an accuracy of five decimal places. We can notice that the output values of the exponential function are always increasing as time progresses, while the output values of the logistic function are fluctuating with a finite limited size between zero and one [88] [89] [93].

3.2. Lorenz Attractor

The Lorenz attractor is one of the most popular three-dimensional chaotic attractors; it was examined and introduced by Edward Lorenz in 1963 [2]. He showed that a small change in the initial conditions of a weather model could give large differences in the resulting weather. This means that a slight difference in the initial condition will affect the output of the whole system, which is called sensitive dependence to the initial conditions. The non-linear dynamical system is sensitive to the initial value and is related to the system's periodic behaviour [90]. Lorenz's dynamic system presents a chaotic attractor, whereas the word chaos is often used to describe the complicated manner of non-linear dynamical systems [106]. Chaos theory generates apparently random behaviour but at the same time is completely deterministic, as shown in **Figure 2**. The Lorenz attractor is defined as follows:

$$dx/dt = a * (y - x)$$
$$dy/dt = r * x - y - x * z \qquad (3)$$
$$dz/dt = x * y - b * z$$

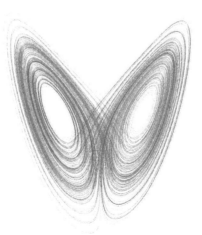

Figure 2. A plot of the trajectory of the Lorenz system, (modified from [107])

3.3. Rossler Attractors

In 1976 [88] [89], O. Rossler created a chaotic attractor with a simple set of non-linear differential equations [88]. Rossler attempted to write the simplest dynamical system that exhibited the characteristics of a chaotic system [89] [108]. The Rossler attractor was the first widely-known chaotic attractor from a set of differential equations; defined by a set of three non-linear differential equations, the system exhibits a strange attractor for a = b = 0.2 and c = 5.7 (see Equation (4)) [108]. The Rossler attractor is a rather nice but not famous attractor, which draws a nifty picture of a non-linear three-dimensional deterministic dynamical system, as shown in **Figure 3**.

$$dx/dt = -y - z$$
$$dy/dt = x + Ay \qquad (4)$$
$$dz/dt = B + xz - Cz$$

A, B, and C are constants.

3.4. Henon Attractors

The Henon map is one of the dynamical systems that exhibit chaotic behaviours. The Henon map is defined by two equations; the map depends on two parameters a, b, and the system exhibits a strange attractor for a = 1.4 and b = 0.3 (see Equation (5)). A Henon map takes one point (x, y) and maps this point to a new point in the plane, as shown in **Figure 4** [108].

$$x_{n+1} = y_n + 1 - ax_n^2$$
$$y_{n+1} = bx_n \qquad (5)$$

3.5. Tent Map

A Tent map is an iterated function of a dynamical system that exhibits chaotic behaviours (orbits) and is governed by Equation (6). It has a similar shape to the logistic map shape with a corner (**Figure 5** and **Figure 6**)

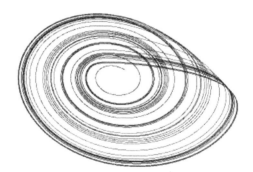

Figure 3. Rossler attractor [89].

Figure 4. Henon attractor for a = 1.4 and b = 0.3 [89].

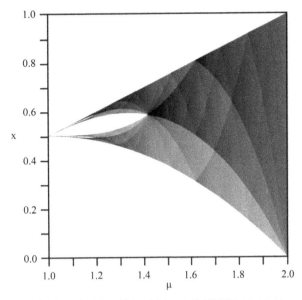

Figure 5. Bifurcation diagram for the tent map [110].

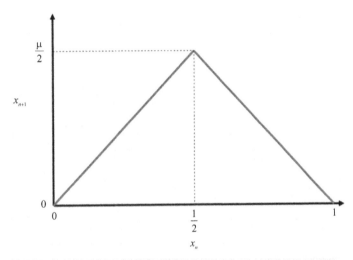

Figure 6. Graph of tent map function.

[109]. The Tent map exhibits the Lyapunov exponents on the unit interval $T(x) \in [0,1]$ and $\mu \in [0,2]$. It is a simple one-dimensional map generating periodic chaotic behaviour similar to a logistic map.

$$T_\mu(x) = \begin{cases} \mu x, & x \leq 1/2 \\ \mu(1-x), & 1/2 \leq x \end{cases} \qquad (6)$$

3.6. Piecewise Linear Chaotic Maps

Piecewise linear chaotic maps (PWLCMs) are simple non-linear dynamical systems with large positive Lyapunov exponents. In [111], they are shown to have several brilliant chaotic properties that can be exploited in chaotic cryptographic algorithms. PWLCM has perfect behaviour and high dynamical properties such as invariant distribution, auto-correlation function, periodicity, large positive Lyapunov exponent, and mixing property [112]. Iterations of PWLCM with initial value and control parameters generate a sequence of real numbers between 0 and 1, which is called an orbit. A large positive Lyapunov exponent means that the system shows chaotic behaviour over large orbits [110]. The periodicity property indicates that the system behaviour is average over time and space. Correlation functions are a very important test of the correlation over time and space between random variables at two different points, thus indicating correlation statistical properties [2].

PWLCMs are the simplest kind of chaotic systems, which need one division and few additions. A skew Tent map is a PWLCM defined by a generalized form of Tent map that is very similar to a Tent map with small differences (see Equation (7)). A more complex example of PWLCMs is defined by Equation (8). It is very clear from Equation (8) that $f(0, p) = 0$, $f_2(0.5, p) = 0$, $f_3(1, p) = 0$ for any $P \in (0, 0.5)$. Thus, we should avoid those values as initial parameters of x_n.

$$x_{n+1} = f\left(x_n, p\right) = \begin{cases} x_n/p, & x_n \in [0, p) \\ (1 - x_n)/(1 - p), & x_n \in [p, 1] \end{cases} \tag{7}$$

$$x_{n+1} = f\left(x_n, p\right) = \begin{cases} x_n/p, & x_n \in [0, p) \\ (x_n - p)/(0.5 - p), & x_n \in (p, 0.5] \\ f(1 - x_n, P), & x_n \in [0.5, 1] \end{cases} \tag{8}$$

where x_0 is the initial condition value, P is the control parameter, $x_n \in [0, 1]$, and $P \in (0, 0.5)$.

4. Logistic map and Lyapunov Exponent

Chaos theory is a simple non-linear dynamical system that shows completely unpredictable behaviour [88]. A chaotic system is a deterministic system with great sensitivity to initial conditions that can give amazingly different results on a computer when one or both input parameters' values are changed. In contrast, small changes in the initial value of classical science equations tend to generate small differences in the result [7]. Chaotic maps have been an active research area due to their characteristics such as deterministic nature, unpredictability, random-look nature, and sensitivity to initial value [7] [11] [19] [34] [52] [53] [55] [113]-[123]. In the last decade, researchers have noticed a relationship between chaos theory and cryptography. Chaotic systems' properties are analogous to some cryptography systems' properties; for example, sensitivity to initial conditions is analogous to diffusion, iterations are analogous to rounds in encryption systems, and chaotic system complexity is analogous to complexity of cryptography algorithms. Cryptographers have utilized dynamical chaotic maps to develop new security primitives by exploiting some chaotic maps [89] [100]. Some of the well-known chaotic maps are Logistic map, Tent map and Henon map.

A Lyapunov number is the divergence rate average of very close points along an orbit and it is the natural algorithm of the Lyapunov exponent (see Equation (9) [91]). Therefore, the Lyapunov exponent is used with chaotic behaviour to measure the sensitivity dependence on the initial condition [88]. This means that, in one-dimensional chaos maps, the Lyapunov numbers are used to measure separation rates of nearby points along the real line. The Lyapunov exponent is used to help in choosing the initial parameters of chaotic maps that fall in chaotic areas. The Lyapunov exponent has three different cases of dynamics as follows [89]:

1. If all Lyapunov exponents are less than zero, there is a fixed point behaving like an attractor.

2. If some of the Lyapunov exponents are zero and others are less than zero, there is an ordinary attractor, which is simpler than a fixed point.

3. If at least one of the Lyapunov exponents is positive, the dynamical system is not stable (chaotic) and vice versa.

$$h\left(x_1\right) = \lim_{n \to \infty} (1/n)\left[\ln\left|f'\left(x_1\right)\right| + \cdots + \ln\left|f'\left(x_n\right)\right|\right] \tag{9}$$

A logistic map shows a chaotic behaviour that can arise from very simple non-linear dynamical equations (see **Figure 7** [124]). Logistic map behaviour seems to be a random jumble of dots and mainly depends on two parameters (x_0 and r). We can observe different logistic map behaviours by changing the value(s) of one or both of these parameters. The general idea of a logistic map was built based on an iterations function, where the next output value depends on the previous output value (see Equation (1)). **Figure 8** shows the calculated Lyapunov exponent value of a logistic map with different values of parameter $r \in [0, 4]$. In a logistic map equation, x_0 and r represent the initial conditions, $x_0 \in [0, 1]$ and $r \in [0, 4]$. Chaotic behaviour is exhibited with $3.57 > r \geq 4$, but it shows non-chaotic behaviour with some values of parameter r (see **Figure 9** and **Figure 10**). In this section, we refer to x_0 and r parameters as the initial conditions of a logistic map.

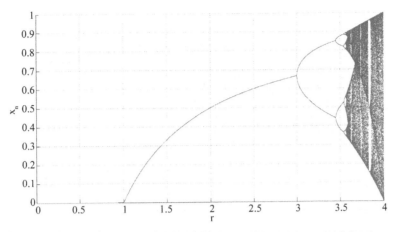

Figure 7. Bifurcation diagram of logistic map.

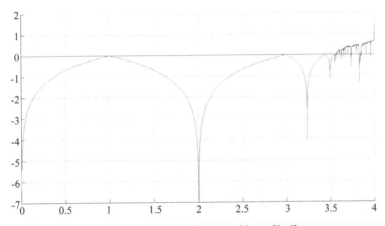

Figure 8. Lyapunov exponent of Logistic map with $t \in [0, 4]$.

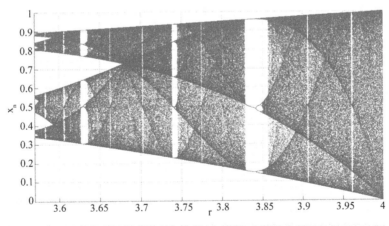

Figure 9. Logistic map bifurcation diagram of a periodic window.

A small range of logistic map parameters are consider as valid values to show chaotic behaviour [69]. In general, chaotic behaviour is exhibited with values of parameter r greater than 3.57 and less than or equal to 4. It is very clear from **Figure 9** that the logistic map periodic window becomes significantly complicated with $3.57 > r \geq 4$. In **Figure 9** and **Figure 10**, we plotted a portion of logistic map bifurcation and its Lyapunov exponent, respectively, using MATLAB software, to give a clear picture of the chaotic areas. There are non-chaotic areas with some values of parameter r over the chaotic interval, which are called stability or islands. It is very clear

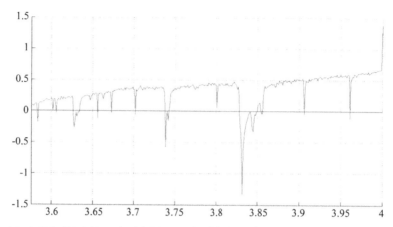

Figure 10. Lyapunov exponent of Logistic map with $t \in [3.575, 4]$.

that there is a 3-periodic window between 3.828429 and 3.841037 [69]. The value of $r = 3.840$ falls in the 3-periodic window and the value of $r = 3.845$ fall in the 6-periodic window. Therefore, after a small number of iterations with different initial values of x, (x_0) will end up in one of these periodic. The cryptosystems fall within the 3-perodic and the 6-periodic windows with $r = 3.840$ and 3.845, respectively, and were utilized for the purpose of attacking them [125]. Moreover, the logistic map population will cover the full interval of x, ([0,1]), only with $r = 4$.

5. Novel Triangular Chaotic Map (TCM)

In this section, a novel Triangular Chaotic map (TCM) is proposed. TCM is a one-dimensional chaotic map of degree two with full chaotic population over infinite interval of parameter t values (see Equation (10)). The Triangular Chaotic Map behaviour mainly depends on the initial values of parameters y_0 and t. TCM behaviour seems to be a random jumble of dots, and depends on initial conditions (y_0 and t). The y_0, y_n are positive real numbers between 0 and 1, $y_n \in [0, 1]$, and t can be any positive real number $t \in [0, \infty]$. **Figure 11** shows a TCM map bifurcation diagram and Figure 11 shows the calculated Lyapunov exponent value over $r \in [0, 4]$. It is very clear from the figures that TCM shows perfect chaotic behaviour over the full interval. **Figure 12** shows a TCM diagram with initial value of t very close to zero and random number of y_0, iterating TCM map many times, and then plotting the t series of values of y_n using MATLAB software. In other words, we plotted corresponding points of y_n to a given value of t and increased t to the right. TCM is very sensitive to any change(s) in one or both initial conditions and is unpredictable in the long term, as shown in **Figure 11** and **Figure 12**. In this paper, we refer to y_0 and t parameters as the initial conditions of TCM map.

$$f(y_n) = y_{n+1} = \begin{cases} (t \times y_n \times (1 - y_n))\%1 & n\%2 = 0 \\ (\pi \times y_n \times \beta)\%1 & n\%2! = 0 \end{cases} \quad (10)$$

where y_n is a number between zero and one, y_0 represents the initial population, t is a positive real number, n is a number of iterations, β: is a positive odd number between 3 and 99.

The general idea of a TCM map was built based on an iteration function. The result of the next output value (y_{n+1}) in TCM depends on the previous output value (y_n) (see Equation (3)). A TCM map over a different range of parameter t values will give different f maps. To show TCM sensitivity we plotted the behaviour of three nearby initial values of y_0 and three nearby initial values of t. Three nearby initial values of y_0 (0.990000, 0.990001, and 0.990002) for $t = 1$ started at the same time and rapidly diverged exponentially over time with no correlation between each of them (see **Figure 13**). Moreover, we plotted populations of three slightly different parameter values of t (4.000000, 4.000001, and 4.000002) and $y_0 = 0.5$ to show great sensitivity to initial conditions of the TCM map (see **Figure 14**).

TCM diagram and population distribution histograms have been plotted for population of TCM over the $t \in [32, 36]$. TCM iterated 43686 times with initial conditions values of $t_0 = 32$ and $y_0 = 0.5$. We draw the TCM diagram by plotting corresponding points of y_n to a given value of t and increasing t to the right (see **Figure 15**).

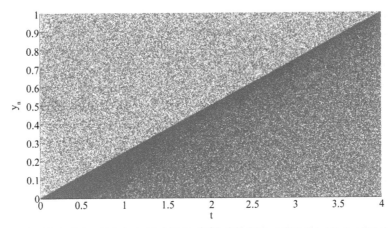

Figure 11. TCM chaotic map bifurcation diagram with $t \in [0, 4]$.

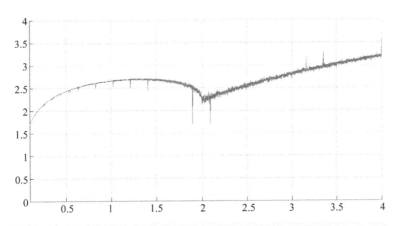

Figure 12. Lyapunov exponent of TCM chaotic map with $t \in [0, 4]$.

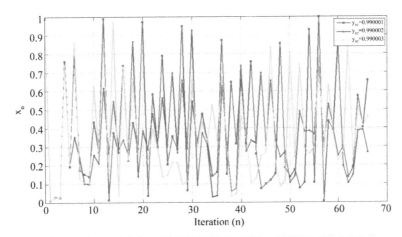

Figure 13. TCM iterations with $t = 1$ and three different initial values of y_0.

TCM population interval, $[0, 1]$, is divided into 10 equal sub-intervals and the number of points in each interval has been counted for each sub-interval and plotted (see **Figure 16**). It is very clear from **Figure 15** and **Figure 16** that TCM population is uniformly distributed over the interval $[0, 1]$ with $t \in [32, 36]$. We draw the TCM diagram and population distribution histogram with different initial t values $(0, 4, 8, 12, \cdots$ etc.$)$ and the overall results confirm that the TCM population distributions are uniformly distributed with $t \geq 12$ and interval size 4. In conclusion, TCM is a new one-dimensional chaotic map with perfect chaotic behaviour over infinite interval,

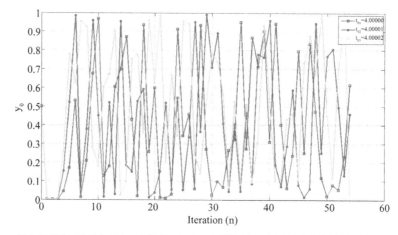

Figure 14. TCM iterations with $y_0 = 0.5$ and three different initial values of t.

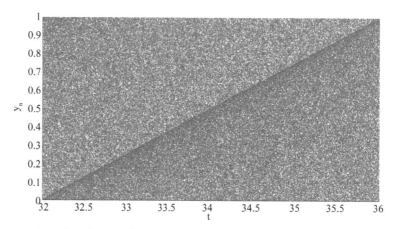

Figure 15. TCM chaotic map bifurcation diagram with $t \in [32, 36]$.

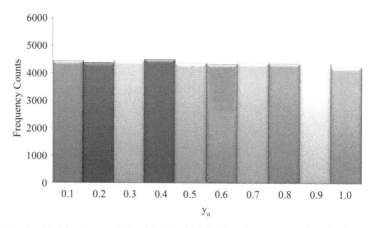

Figure 16. TCM distribution of y_n values over $t \in [32, 36]$.

high positive Lyapunov exponent value, uniform distribution, and great sensitivity to any change(s) in the initial condition or the control parameter.

As we explained earlier, a small range of logistic map parameters are considered valid values to show chaotic behaviour $r > 3.57 \geq 4$. In addition, the logistic map population will cover the full interval of x, $x_n \in [0, 1]$, only with $r = 4$. Therefore, we propose to use a modified version of the logistic map defined in Equation (8). We used the remainder of dividing the logistic map by 1 to ensure that all the output values will be between zero and one,

$x_n \in [0, 1]$, and we added a small real number ($\beta \leq 0.001$) to ensure $x_n \neq 0$ or 1. Consequently, in the modified version the value of parameter r can be any value greater than 0, $r \in [0, \infty]$. We plotted the modified version of logistic map bifurcation and its Lyapunov exponent over different intervals using MATLAB software (see **Figure 17** and **Appendix A**). It is very clear from **Figure 18** that the modified version has bigger intervals of chaotic behaviour and it covers the full x interval over many different values of parameter r. Unfortunately, it still shows non-chaotic areas over different values within the intervals: [0, 4], [4, 8], [8, 12] and [12, 16], which are known as stability or islands. In contrast, the TCM map shows perfect chaotic behaviour and covers the entire range of y for every value of t (see **Figure 18** and **Appendix B**). In other words, in the Triangular Chaotic Map at every value of $f(x)$ there is at least one image value, but in the logistic map and modified logistic map there are no image values.

6. Conclusion

In this research, we propose a new Triangular Chaotic Map (TCM) with high-intensity chaotic areas over infinite interval. The tests and analysis results of the proposed chaotic map show that it has very strong chaotic properties such as very high sensitivity to initial conditions, random-like, uniformly distributed population, deterministic nature, unpredictability, high positive Lyapunov exponent values, and perfect chaotic behaviour over infinite positive interval. TCM chaotic map is a one-way function that prevents the finding of a relationship between the successive output values, which increases sophistication and randomness of the proposed chaotic map. Therefore, TCM is considered as an ideal chaotic map with perfect and full population chaotic behaviour over the full interval. TCM characteristics are promising for possible utilization in many different fields of study to optimize exploitation chaotic maps.

Acknowledgements

This research work was conducted at the School of Engineering and Computer Sciences in Durham University,

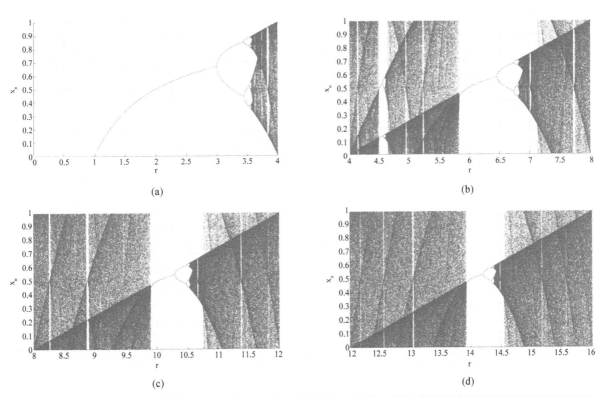

Figure 17. Modified logistic map bifurcation diagrams over different intervals. (a) Modified logistic map diagram for $a \in [0, 4]$; (b) Modified logistic map diagram for $r \in [4, 8]$; (c) Modified logistic map diagram for $a \in [8, 12]$; (d) Modified logistic map diagram for $r \in [12, 16]$.

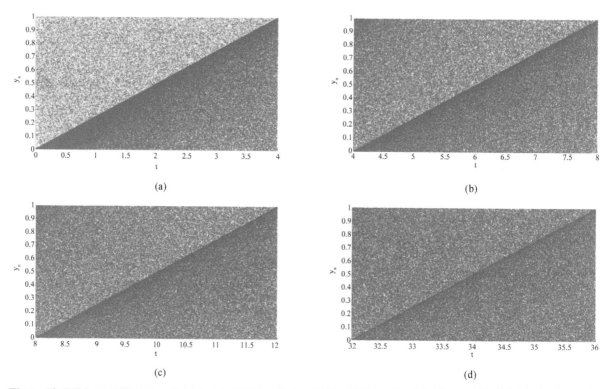

Figure 18. TCM map bifurcation diagrams over different intervals. (a) TCM diagram for $t \in [0, 4]$; (b) TCM diagram for $t \in$ [4, 8]; (c) TCM diagram for $t \in$ [8, 12]; (d) TCM diagram for $t \in$ [12, 16].

Durham—UK.

References

[1]   Sneyers, R. (1997) Climate Chaotic Instability: Statistical Determination and Theoretical Background. *Environmetrics*, **8**, 517-532. http://dx.doi.org/10.1002/(SICI)1099-095X(199709/10)8:5<517::AID-ENV267>3.0.CO;2-L

[2]   Zeng, X., Pielke, R.A. and Eykholt, R. (1993) Chaos Theory and Its Application to the Atmosphere. *Bulletin of the American Meteorological Society*, **74**, 631-639. http://dx.doi.org/10.1175/1520-0477(1993)074<0631:CTAIAT>2.0.CO;2

[3]   Wikipedia. Chaos Theory. Cited 17 January 2009. http://en.wikipedia.org/w/index.php?title=Chaos_theory&oldid=264934743

[4]   Serletis, A. and Gogas, P. (2000) Purchasing Power Parity, Nonlinearity and Chaos. *Applied Financial Economics*, **10**, 615-622. http://dx.doi.org/10.1080/096031000437962

[5]   Serletis, A. and Gogas, P. (1997) Chaos in East European Black Market Exchange Rates. *Research in Economics*, **51**, 359-385. http://dx.doi.org/10.1006/reec.1997.0050

[6]   Wikipedia (2015) Chaos Theory. https://en.wikipedia.org/w/index.php?title=Chaos_theory&oldid=693847517

[7]   Maqableh, M., Samsudin, A.B. and Alia, M.A. (2008) New Hash Function Based on Chaos Theory (CHA-1). *IJCSNS International Journal of Computer Science and Network Security*, **8**, 20-26.

[8]   Kocarev, L. (2001) Chaos-Based Cryptography: A Brief Overview. *IEEE Circuits and Systems Magazine*, **1**, 6-21. http://dx.doi.org/10.1109/7384.963463

[9]   Pareek, N.K., Patidar, V. and Sud, K.K. (2003) Discrete Chaotic Cryptography Using External Key. *Physics Letters A*, **309**, 75-82. http://dx.doi.org/10.1016/S0375-9601(03)00122-1

[10]   Pareek, N.K., Patidar, V. and Sud, K.K. (2005) Cryptography Using Multiple One-Dimensional Chaotic Maps. *Communications in Nonlinear Science and Numerical Simulation*, **10**, 715-723. http://dx.doi.org/10.1016/j.cnsns.2004.03.006

[11]   Xiang, T., Liao, X.F., Tang, G.P., Chen, Y. and Wong, K.W. (2006) A Novel Block Cryptosystem Based on Iterating a

Chaotic Map. *Physics Letters A*, **349**, 109-115. http://dx.doi.org/10.1016/j.physleta.2005.02.083

[12] Chen, S., Zhong, X.X. and Wu, Z.Z. (2008) Chaos Block Cipher for Wireless Sensor Network. *Science in China Series F: Information Sciences*, **51**, 1055-1063. http://dx.doi.org/10.1007/s11432-008-0102-5

[13] Peng, J., You, M.Y., Yang, Z.M. and Jin, S.Z. (2007) Research on a Block Encryption Cipher Based on Chaotic Dynamical System. *3rd International Conference on Natural Computation, ICNC* 2007, Haikou, 24-27 August 2007, 744-748. http://dx.doi.org/10.1109/ICNC.2007.612

[14] Yang, H.Q., Liao, X.F., Wong, K.W., Zhang, W. and Wei, P.C. (2007) A New Block Cipher Based on Chaotic Map and Group Theory. *Chaos, Solitons & Fractals*, **40**, 50-59. http://dx.doi.org/10.1016/j.chaos.2007.07.056

[15] Peng, J., Jin, S.Z., Chen, G.R., Yang, Z.M. and Liao, X.F. (2008) An Image Encryption Scheme Based on Chaotic Map. *4th International Conference on Natural Computation, ICNC* '08, Jinan, 18-20 October 2008, 595-599. http://dx.doi.org/10.1109/icnc.2008.227

[16] Lian, S. (2009) A Block Cipher Based on Chaotic Neural Networks. *Neurocomputing*, **72**, 1296-1301. http://dx.doi.org/10.1016/j.neucom.2008.11.005

[17] Wang, F.J., Zhang, Y.P. and Cao, T.J. (2009) Research of Chaotic Block Cipher Algorithm Based on Logistic Map. *2nd International Conference on Intelligent Computation Technology and Automation*, 2009, *ICICTA* '09, Changsha, 10-11 October 2009, 678-681. http://dx.doi.org/10.1109/ICICTA.2009.169

[18] Peng, J., Jin, S.Z., Liu, H.L. and Liu, Y.G. (2009) A Block Cipher Based on a Hybrid of Chaotic System and Feistel Network. *5th International Conference on Natural Computation, ICNC* '09, Tianjin, 14-16 August 2009, 427-431. http://dx.doi.org/10.1109/icnc.2009.663

[19] Amin, M., Faragallah, O.S. and Abd El-Latif, A.A. (2010) A Chaotic Block Cipher Algorithm for Image Cryptosystems. *Communications in Nonlinear Science and Numerical Simulation*, **15**, 3484-3497. http://dx.doi.org/10.1016/j.cnsns.2009.12.025

[20] Huang, J.-H. and Liu, Y. (2010) A Block Encryption Algorithm Combined with the Logistic Mapping and SPN Structure. 2010 *2nd International Conference on Industrial and Information Systems* (*IIS*), Dalian, 10-11 July 2010, 156-159. http://dx.doi.org/10.1109/indusis.2010.5565655

[21] Zhao, G., Chen, G.R., Fang, J.Q. and Xu, G. (2011) Block Cipher Design: Generalized Single-Use-Algorithm Based on Chaos. *Tsinghua Science & Technology*, **16**, 194-206. http://dx.doi.org/10.1016/S1007-0214(11)70030-X

[22] Masuda, N., Jakimoski, G., Aihara, K. and Kocarev, L. (2006) Chaotic Block Ciphers: From Theory to Practical Algorithms. *IEEE Transactions on Circuits and Systems I: Regular Papers*, **53**, 1341-1352. http://dx.doi.org/10.1109/TCSI.2006.874182

[23] Habutsu, T., Nishio, Y., Sasase, I. and Mori, S. (1991) A Secret Key Cryptosystem by Iterating a Chaotic Map. In: Davies, D.W., Ed., *Advances in Cryptology—EUROCRYPT* '91, Springer, Berlin, 127-140. http://dx.doi.org/10.1007/3-540-46416-6_11

[24] Gutowitz, H.A. (1993) Cryptography with Dynamical Systems, in Cellular Automata and Cooperative Phenomena. Kluwer Academic Press, Dordrecht. http://dx.doi.org/10.1007/978-94-011-1691-6_21

[25] Kotulski, Z. and Szczepanski, J. (1997) Discrete Chaotic Cryptography (DCC). *Annalen der Physik*, **6**, 381-394. http://dx.doi.org/10.1002/andp.19975090504

[26] García, P. and Jiménez, J. (2002) Communication through Chaotic Map Systems. *Physics Letters A*, **298**, 35-40. http://dx.doi.org/10.1016/S0375-9601(02)00382-1

[27] Masuda, N. and Aihara, K. (2002) Cryptosystems with Discretized Chaotic Maps. *IEEE Transactions on Circuits and Systems I: Fundamental Theory and Applications*, **49**, 28-40. http://dx.doi.org/10.1109/81.974872

[28] Baptista, M.S. (1998) Cryptography with Chaos. *Physics Letters A*, **240**, 50-54. http://dx.doi.org/10.1016/S0375-9601(98)00086-3

[29] Wong, W.-K., Lee, L.-P. and Wong, K.-W. (2001) A Modified Chaotic Cryptographic Method. *Computer Physics Communications*, **138**, 234-236. http://dx.doi.org/10.1016/S0010-4655(01)00220-X

[30] Alvarez, E., Fernández, A., García, P., Jiménez, J. and Marcano, A. (1999) New Approach to Chaotic Encryption. *Physics Letters A*, **263**, 373-375. http://dx.doi.org/10.1016/S0375-9601(99)00747-1

[31] Wong, K.W. (2002) A Fast Chaotic Cryptographic Scheme with Dynamic Look-Up Table. *Physics Letters A*, **298**, 238-242. http://dx.doi.org/10.1016/S0375-9601(02)00431-0

[32] Machado, R.F., Baptista, M.S. and Grebogi, C. (2004) Cryptography with Chaos at the Physical Level. *Chaos, Solitons & Fractals*, **21**, 1265-1269. http://dx.doi.org/10.1016/j.chaos.2003.12.094

[33] Guan, Z.-H., Huang, F. and Guan, W. (2005) Chaos-Based Image Encryption Algorithm. *Physics Letters A*, **346**, 153-157. http://dx.doi.org/10.1016/j.physleta.2005.08.006

[34] Gao, T. and Chen, Z. (2008) Image Encryption Based on a New Total Shuffling Algorithm. *Chaos, Solitons & Fractals*, **38**, 213-220. http://dx.doi.org/10.1016/j.chaos.2006.11.009

[35] Wong, K.W. (2003) A Combined Chaotic Cryptographic and Hashing Scheme. *Physics Letters A*, **307**, 292-298. http://dx.doi.org/10.1016/S0375-9601(02)01770-X

[36] Xiao, D., Liao, X. and Deng, S. (2005) One-Way Hash Function Construction Based on the Chaotic Map with Changeable-Parameter. *Chaos, Solitons & Fractals*, **24**, 65-71. http://dx.doi.org/10.1016/S0960-0779(04)00456-4

[37] Lian, S.G., Liu, Z.X., Ren, Z. and Wang, H.L. (2006) Hash Function Based on Chaotic Neural Networks. 2006 *IEEE International Symposium on Circuits and Systems*, ISCAS 2006, Island of Kos, 21-24 May 2006. http://dx.doi.org/10.1109/iscas.2006.1692566

[38] Peng, F. and Qiu, S.-S. (2007) One-Way Hash Functions Based on Iterated Chaotic Systems. *International Conference on Communications, Circuits and Systems*, ICCCAS 2007, Kokura, 11-13 July 2007, 1070-1074. http://dx.doi.org/10.1109/ICCCAS.2007.4348231

[39] Khan, M.K., Zhang, J. and Wang, X. (2008) Chaotic Hash-Based Fingerprint Biometric Remote User Authentication Scheme on Mobile Devices. *Chaos, Solitons & Fractals*, **35**, 519-524. http://dx.doi.org/10.1016/j.chaos.2006.05.061

[40] Xiao, D., Liao, X. and Deng, S. (2008) Parallel Keyed Hash Function Construction Based on Chaotic Maps. *Physics Letters A*, **372**, 4682-4688. http://dx.doi.org/10.1016/j.physleta.2008.04.060

[41] Song, Y.R. and Jiang, G.P. (2008) Hash Function Construction Based on Chaotic Coupled Map Network. *The 9th International Conference for Young Computer Scientists*, ICYCS 2008, Hunan, 18-21 November 2008, 2753-2758. http://dx.doi.org/10.1109/ICYCS.2008.134

[42] Deng, S., Xiao, D., Li, Y.T. and Peng, W.B. (2009) A Novel Combined Cryptographic and Hash Algorithm Based on Chaotic Control Character. *Communications in Nonlinear Science and Numerical Simulation*, **14**, 3889-3900. http://dx.doi.org/10.1016/j.cnsns.2009.02.020

[43] Guyeux, C. and Bahi, J.M. (2010) Topological Chaos and Chaotic Iterations Application to Hash Functions. *The 2010 International Joint Conference on Neural Networks* (*IJCNN*), Barcelona, 18-23 July 2010, 1-7. http://dx.doi.org/10.1109/ijcnn.2010.5596512

[44] Huang, Z. (2011) A More Secure Parallel Keyed Hash Function Based on Chaotic Neural Network. *Communications in Nonlinear Science and Numerical Simulation*, **16**, 3245-3256. http://dx.doi.org/10.1016/j.cnsns.2010.12.009

[45] Wang, Y., Wong, K.-W. and Xiao, D. (2011) Parallel Hash Function Construction Based on Coupled Map Lattices. *Communications in Nonlinear Science and Numerical Simulation*, **16**, 2810-2821. http://dx.doi.org/10.1016/j.cnsns.2010.10.001

[46] Yi, X. (2005) Hash Function Based on Chaotic Tent Maps. *IEEE Transactions on Circuits and Systems II: Express Briefs*, **52**, 354-357. http://dx.doi.org/10.1109/TCSII.2005.848992

[47] Zhang, J., Wang, X. and Zhang, W. (2007) Chaotic Keyed Hash Function Based on Feedforward-Feedback Nonlinear Digital Filter. *Physics Letters A*, **362**, 439-448. http://dx.doi.org/10.1016/j.physleta.2006.10.052

[48] Amin, M., Faragallah, O.S. and Abd El-Latif, A.A. (2009) Chaos-Based Hash Function (CBHF) for Cryptographic Applications. *Chaos, Solitons & Fractals*, **42**, 767-772. http://dx.doi.org/10.1016/j.chaos.2009.02.001

[49] Xiao, D., Shih, F.Y. and Liao, X. (2010) A Chaos-Based Hash Function with both Modification Detection and Localization Capabilities. *Communications in Nonlinear Science and Numerical Simulation*, **15**, 2254-2261. http://dx.doi.org/10.1016/j.cnsns.2009.10.012

[50] Kocarev, L. and Jakimoski, G. (2003) Pseudorandom Bits Generated by Chaotic Maps. *IEEE Transactions on Circuits and Systems I: Fundamental Theory and Applications*, **50**, 123-126. http://dx.doi.org/10.1109/TCSI.2002.804550

[51] Tong, X.-J., Cui, M.-G. and Jiang, W. (2006) The Production Algorithm of Pseudo-Random Number Generator Based on Compound Non-Linear Chaos System. *International Conference on Intelligent Information Hiding and Multimedia Signal Processing*, 2006, IIH-MSP '06, Pasadena, 18-20 December 2006, 685-688. http://dx.doi.org/10.1109/IIH-MSP.2006.265094

[52] Chen, S. and Zhong, X.-X. (2007) Chaotic Block Iterating Method for Pseudo-Random Sequence Generator. *The Journal of China Universities of Posts and Telecommunications*, **14**, 45-48. http://dx.doi.org/10.1016/s1005-8885(07)60054-5

[53] Zheng, F., Tian, X.-J., Song, J.-Y. and Li, X.-Y. (2008) Pseudo-Random Sequence Generator Based on the Generalized Henon Map. *The Journal of China Universities of Posts and Telecommunications*, **15**, 64-68. http://dx.doi.org/10.1016/S1005-8885(08)60109-0

[54] Qi, A.X., Han, C.Y. and Wang, G.Y. (2010) Design and FPGA Realization of a Pseudo Random Sequence Generator Based on a Switched Chaos. *International Conference on Communications, Circuits and Systems* (*ICCCAS*), Chengdu, 28-30 July 2010, 417-420. http://dx.doi.org/10.1109/ICCCAS.2010.5581965

[55] Yoon, J.W. and Kim, H. (2010) An Image Encryption Scheme with a Pseudorandom Permutation Based on Chaotic Maps. *Communications in Nonlinear Science and Numerical Simulation*, **15**, 3998-4006. http://dx.doi.org/10.1016/j.cnsns.2010.01.041

[56] Dabal, P. and Pelka, R. (2011) A Chaos-Based Pseudo-Random Bit Generator Implemented in FPGA Device. 2011 *IEEE* 14*th International Symposium on Design and Diagnostics of Electronic Circuits & Systems* (*DDECS*), Cottbus, 13-15 April 2011, 151-154. http://dx.doi.org/10.1109/ddecs.2011.5783069

[57] Forré, R. (1991) The Hénon Attractor as a Keystream Generator. In: Davies, D.W., Ed., *Advances in Cryptology—EUROCRYPT* '91, Springer, Berlin, 76-81.

[58] Matthews, R.A.J. (1989) On the Derivation of a "Chaotic" Encryption Algorithm. *Cryptologia*, **13**, 29-42. http://dx.doi.org/10.1080/0161-118991863745

[59] Li, S., Mou, X. and Cai, Y. (2001) Improving Security of a Chaotic Encryption Approach. *Physics Letters A*, **290**, 127-133. http://dx.doi.org/10.1016/S0375-9601(01)00612-0

[60] Wolfram, S. (1985) Cryptography with Cellular Automata. In: Williams, H.C., Ed., *Advances in Cryptology—CRYPTO* '85 *Proceedings*, Lecture Notes in Computer Science, Spinger-Verlag, Berlin, 429-432.

[61] Lee, P.-H., Pei, S.-C. and Chen, Y.-Y. (2003) Generating Chaotic Stream Ciphers Using Chaotic Systems. *Chinese Journal of Physics*, **41**, 559-581.

[62] Sang, T., Wang, R. and Yan, Y. (2000) Constructing Chaotic Discrete Sequences for Digital Communications Based on Correlation Analysis. *IEEE Transactions on Signal Processing*, **48**, 2557-2565. http://dx.doi.org/10.1109/78.863058

[63] Kwok, H.S. and Tang, W.K.S. (2007) A Fast Image Encryption System Based on Chaotic Maps with Finite Precision Representation. *Chaos, Solitons & Fractals*, **32**, 1518-1529. http://dx.doi.org/10.1016/j.chaos.2005.11.090

[64] Patidar, V., Pareek, N.K. and Sud, K.K. (2009) A New Substitution-Diffusion Based Image Cipher Using Chaotic Standard and Logistic Maps. *Communications in Nonlinear Science and Numerical Simulation*, **14**, 3056-3075. http://dx.doi.org/10.1016/j.cnsns.2008.11.005

[65] Patidar, V., Pareek, N.K., Purohit, G. and Sud, K.K. (2010) Modified Substitution-Diffusion Image Cipher Using Chaotic Standard and Logistic Maps. *Communications in Nonlinear Science and Numerical Simulation*, **15**, 2755-2765. http://dx.doi.org/10.1016/j.cnsns.2009.11.010

[66] Biham, E. (1991) Cryptanalysis of the Chaotic-Map Cryptosystem Suggested at EUROCRYPT'91. In: Davies, D.W., Ed., *Advances in Cryptology—EUROCRYPT* '91, Springer, Berlin, 532-534. http://dx.doi.org/10.1007/3-540-46416-6_49

[67] Wheeler, D.D. (1989) Problems with Chaotic Cryptosystems. *Cryptologia*, **13**, 243-250. http://dx.doi.org/10.1080/0161-118991863934

[68] Alvarez, G., Montoya, F., Romera, M. and Pastor, G. (2000) Cryptanalysis of a Chaotic Encryption System. *Physics Letters A*, **276**, 191-196. http://dx.doi.org/10.1016/S0375-9601(00)00642-3

[69] Alvarez, G., Montoya, F., Romera, M. and Pastor, G. (2003) Cryptanalysis of a Discrete Chaotic Cryptosystem Using External Key. *Physics Letters A*, **319**, 334-339. http://dx.doi.org/10.1016/j.physleta.2003.10.044

[70] Wei, J., Liao, X.F., Wong, K.W. and Zhou, T. (2007) Cryptanalysis of a Cryptosystem Using Multiple One-Dimensional Chaotic Maps. *Communications in Nonlinear Science and Numerical Simulation*, **12**, 814-822. http://dx.doi.org/10.1016/j.cnsns.2005.06.001

[71] Li, C.Q., Li, S.J., Alvarez, G., Chen, G.R. and Lo, K.-T. (2008) Cryptanalysis of a Chaotic Block Cipher with External Key and Its Improved Version. *Chaos, Solitons & Fractals*, **37**, 299-307. http://dx.doi.org/10.1016/j.chaos.2006.08.025

[72] Wang, X. and Yu, C. (2009) Cryptanalysis and Improvement on a Cryptosystem Based on a Chaotic Map. *Computers & Mathematics with Applications*, **57**, 476-482. http://dx.doi.org/10.1016/j.camwa.2008.09.042

[73] Yang, J., Xiao, D. and Xiang, T. (2011) Cryptanalysis of a Chaos Block Cipher for Wireless Sensor Network. *Communications in Nonlinear Science and Numerical Simulation*, **16**, 844-850. http://dx.doi.org/10.1016/j.cnsns.2010.05.005

[74] Álvarez, G., Montoya, F., Romera, M. and Pastor, G. (2004) Keystream Cryptanalysis of a Chaotic Cryptographic Method. *Computer Physics Communications*, **156**, 205-207. http://dx.doi.org/10.1016/S0010-4655(03)00432-6

[75] Jakimoski, G. and Kocarev, L. (2001) Analysis of Some Recently Proposed Chaos-Based Encryption Algorithms. *Physics Letters A*, **291**, 381-384. http://dx.doi.org/10.1016/S0375-9601(01)00771-X

[76] Li, S.J., Mou, X.Q., Ji, Z., Zhang, J.H. and Cai, Y.L. (2003) Performance Analysis of Jakimoski-Kocarev Attack on a Class of Chaotic Cryptosystems. *Physics Letters A*, **307**, 22-28. http://dx.doi.org/10.1016/S0375-9601(02)01659-6

[77] Çokal, C. and Solak, E. (2009) Cryptanalysis of a Chaos-Based Image Encryption Algorithm. *Physics Letters A*, **373**, 1357-1360. http://dx.doi.org/10.1016/j.physleta.2009.02.030

[78] Maqableh, M.M. and Dantchev, S. (2009) Cryptanalysis of Chaos-Based Hash Function (CBHF). 1*st International Al-*

ternative Workshop on Aggressive Computing and Security—iAWACS, Laval, 23-25 October 2009, 20-30.

[79]   Yang, Q.-T., Gao, T.-G., Fan, L. and Gu, Q.-L. (2009) Analysis of One-Way Alterable Length Hash Function Based on Cell Neural Network. *5th International Conference on Information Assurance and Security, IAS '09*, Xi'an, 18-20 August 2009, 391-395. http://dx.doi.org/10.1109/ias.2009.87

[80]   Xiao, D., Liao, X. and Wang, Y. (2009) Improving the Security of a Parallel Keyed Hash Function Based on Chaotic Maps. *Physics Letters A*, **373**, 4346-4353. http://dx.doi.org/10.1016/j.physleta.2009.09.059

[81]   Deng, S., Li, Y. and Xiao, D. (2010) Analysis and Improvement of a Chaos-Based Hash Function Construction. *Communications in Nonlinear Science and Numerical Simulation*, **15**, 1338-1347. http://dx.doi.org/10.1016/j.cnsns.2009.05.065

[82]   Li, C.Q., Li, S.J., Chen, G.R. and Halang, W.A. (2009) Cryptanalysis of an Image Encryption Scheme Based on a Compound Chaotic Sequence. *Image and Vision Computing*, **27**, 1035-1039. http://dx.doi.org/10.1016/j.imavis.2008.09.004

[83]   Rhouma, R., Solak, E. and Belghith, S. (2010) Cryptanalysis of a New Substitution-Diffusion Based Image Cipher. *Communications in Nonlinear Science and Numerical Simulation*, **15**, 1887-1892. http://dx.doi.org/10.1016/j.cnsns.2009.07.007

[84]   Li, C., Li, S. and Lo, K.-T. (2011) Breaking a Modified Substitution-Diffusion Image Cipher Based on Chaotic Standard and Logistic Maps. *Communications in Nonlinear Science and Numerical Simulation*, **16**, 837-843. http://dx.doi.org/10.1016/j.cnsns.2010.05.008

[85]   Maqableh, M.M. (2011) Fast Parallel Keyed Hash Functions Based on Chaotic Maps (PKHC). *Western European Workshop on Research in Cryptology*, Weimar, 20-22 July 2011, 33-40.

[86]   Maqableh, M.M. (2010) Secure Hash Functions Based on Chaotic Maps for E-Commerce Application. *International Journal of Information Technology and Management information System (IJITMIS)*, **1**, 12-19.

[87]   Maqableh, M.M. (2010) Fast Hash Function Based on BCCM Encryption Algorithm for E-Commerce (HFBCCM). *5th International Conference on e-Commerce in Developing Countries: With Focus on Export*, Le Havre, 15-16 September 2010, 55-64.

[88]   Bertuglia, C.S. and Vaio, F. (2005) Nonlinearity, Chaos & Complexity: The Dynamics of Natural and Social Systems. Oxford University Press.

[89]   Alligood, K.T., Sauer, T.D. and Yorke, J.A. (1996) Chaos an Introduction to Dynamical Systems. Springer-Verlag, New York.

[90]   Solari, H.G., Natiello, M.A. and Mindlin, G.B. (1996) Nonlinear Dynamics A Two-Way Trip from Physics to Math. Institute of Physics Publishing, Bristol.

[91]   Baker, G.L. and Gollub, J.P. (1990) Chaotic Dynamics an Introduction. Press Syndicate of the University of Cambridge, New York.

[92]   Poincaré, J.H. (1890) Sur le problème des trois corps et les équations de la dynamique. Divergence des séries de M. Lindstedt. *Acta Mathematica*, **13**, 1-270.

[93]   Lorenz, E.N. (1963) Deterministic Nonperiodic Flow. *Journal of Atmospheric Sciences*, **20**, 130-141. http://dx.doi.org/10.1175/1520-0469(1963)020<0130:dnf>2.0.co;2

[94]   Pritchard, J. (1996) The Chaos Cookbook. Butterworh-Heinemann, Oxford.

[95]   Rahimi, A., Mohammadi, S. and Rahimi, R. (2009) An Efficient Iris Authentication Using Chaos Theory-Based Cryptography for E-Commerce Transactions. *International Conference for Internet Technology and Secured Transactions (ICITST 2009)*.

[96]   Serletis, A. and Gogas, P. (1999) The North American Natural Gas Liquids Markets Are Chaotic. *The Energy Journal*, **20**, 83-103. http://dx.doi.org/10.5547/ISSN0195-6574-EJ-Vol20-No1-5

[97]   Gilmore, R. (2004) Chaos and Attractors. Encyclopedia of Mathematical Physics, EMP MS 93.

[98]   Tullaro, N.B., Abbott, T. and Reilly, J.P. (1992) An Experimental Approach to Nonlinear Dynamics and Chaos. Vol. 1, Addison-Wesley, Boston.

[99]   Parker, T.S. and Chua, L.O. (1989) Practical Numerical Algorithms for Chaotic Systems. Springer-Verlag, New York. http://dx.doi.org/10.1007/978-1-4612-3486-9

[100] Schmitz, R. (2001) Use of Chaotic Dynamical Systems in Cryptography. *Journal of the Franklin Institute*, **338**, 429-441. http://dx.doi.org/10.1016/S0016-0032(00)00087-9

[101] Maqableh, M.M. (2012) Analysis and Design Security Primitives Based on Chaotic Systems for eCommerce. Doctoral Thesis, Durham University, Durham.

[102] Grassi, G. and Mascoio, S. (1999) Synchronizing Hyperchaotic Systems by Observer Design. *IEEE Transactions on*

Circuits and Systems II: Analog and Digital Signal Processing, **46**, 478-483. http://dx.doi.org/10.1109/82.755422

[103] May, R.M. (1976) Simple Mathematical Models with Very Complicated Dynamics. *Nature*, **261**, 459-467. http://dx.doi.org/10.1038/261459a0

[104] Wikipedia. Logistic Map. Cited 20 February 2009. http://en.wikipedia.org/w/index.php?title=chaotic_maps&oldid=261864353

[105] Naess, A. (2000) Chaos and Nonlinear Stochastic Dynamics. *Probabilistic Engineering Mechanics*, **15**, 37-47. http://dx.doi.org/10.1016/S0266-8920(99)00007-7

[106] Contributors, W. (2005) Chaos Theory. http://en.wikipedia.org/w/index.php?title=Chaos_theory&oldid=264934743

[107] Rössler, O. (1976) An Equation for Continous Chaos. *Physics Letters A*, **57**, 397-398. http://dx.doi.org/10.1016/0375-9601(76)90101-8

[108] Ho, A. (2006) Chaos Introduction. http://www.zeuscat.com/andrew/chaos/chaos.html

[109] Wikipedia. Tent Map. Cited 25 February 2009. http://en.wikipedia.org/w/index.php?title=Tent_map&oldid=186656075

[110] Li, S., Chen, G. and Mou, X. (2005) On the Dynamical Degradation of Digital Piecewise Linear Chaotic Maps. *International Journal of Bifurcation and Chaos*, **15**, 3119-3151. http://dx.doi.org/10.1142/S0218127405014052

[111] Jun, P., Jin, S.Z., Liu, Y.G., Yang, Z.M., You, M.Y. and Pei, Y.J. (2008) A Novel Scheme for Image Encryption Based on Piecewise Linear Chaotic Map. 2008 *IEEE Conference on Cybernetics and Intelligent Systems*, Chengdu, 21-24 September 2008, 1012-1016.

[112] Rhouma, R., Arroyo, D. and Belghith, S. (2009) A New Color Image Cryptosystem Based on a Piecewise Linear Chaotic Map. 6th *International Multi-Conference on Systems, Signals and Devices*, 2009, *SSD '09*, 23-26 March 2009, 1-6. http://dx.doi.org/10.1109/SSD.2009.4956666

[113] Yang, H.Q., Wong, K.-W., Liao, X.F., Zhang, W. and Wei, P.C. (2010) A Fast Image Encryption and Authentication Scheme Based on Chaotic Maps. *Communications in Nonlinear Science and Numerical Simulation*, **15**, 3507-3517. http://dx.doi.org/10.1016/j.cnsns.2010.01.004

[114] Yang, H.Q., Wong, K.-W., Liao, X.F., Wang, Y. and Yang, D.G. (2009) One-Way Hash Function Construction Based on Chaotic Map Network. *Chaos, Solitons & Fractals*, **41**, 2566-2574. http://dx.doi.org/10.1016/j.chaos.2008.09.056

[115] Lian, S., Sun, J. and Wang, Z. (2005) A Block Cipher Based on a Suitable Use of the Chaotic Standard Map. *Chaos, Solitons & Fractals*, **26**, 117-129. http://dx.doi.org/10.1016/j.chaos.2004.11.096

[116] Li, P., Li, Z., Halang, W.A. and Chen, G.R. (2007) A Stream Cipher Based on a Spatiotemporal Chaotic System. *Chaos, Solitons & Fractals*, **32**, 1867-1876. http://dx.doi.org/10.1016/j.chaos.2005.12.021

[117] Ali-Pacha, A., Hadj-Said, N., M'Hamed, A. and Belgoraf, A. (2007) Lorenz's Attractor Applied to the Stream Cipher (Ali-Pacha Generator). *Chaos, Solitons & Fractals*, **33**, 1762-1766. http://dx.doi.org/10.1016/j.chaos.2006.03.009

[118] Tong, X. and Cui, M. (2008) Image Encryption with Compound Chaotic Sequence Cipher Shifting Dynamically. *Image and Vision Computing*, **26**, 843-850. http://dx.doi.org/10.1016/j.imavis.2007.09.005

[119] Gao, H., Zhang, Y.S., Liang, S.Y. and Li, D.Q. (2006) A New Chaotic Algorithm for Image Encryption. *Chaos, Solitons & Fractals*, **29**, 393-399. http://dx.doi.org/10.1016/j.chaos.2005.08.110

[120] Chee, C.Y. and Xu, D. (2006) Chaotic Encryption Using Discrete-Time Synchronous Chaos. *Physics Letters A*, **348**, 284-292. http://dx.doi.org/10.1016/j.physleta.2005.08.082

[121] Gao, T. and Chen, Z. (2008) A New Image Encryption Algorithm Based on Hyper-Chaos. *Physics Letters A*, **372**, 394-400. http://dx.doi.org/10.1016/j.physleta.2007.07.040

[122] Sun, F. and Liu, S. (2009) Cryptographic Pseudo-Random Sequence from the Spatial Chaotic Map. *Chaos, Solitons & Fractals*, **41**, 2216-2219. http://dx.doi.org/10.1016/j.chaos.2008.08.032

[123] Li, P., Li, Z., Halang, W.A. and Chen, G.R. (2006) A Multiple Pseudorandom-Bit Generator Based on a Spatiotemporal Chaotic Map. *Physics Letters A*, **349**, 467-473. http://dx.doi.org/10.1016/j.physleta.2005.09.060

[124] Arroyo, D., Li, C.Q., Li, S.J. and Alvarez, G. (2009) Cryptanalysis of a Computer Cryptography Scheme Based on a Filter Bank. *Chaos, Solitons & Fractals*, **41**, 410-413. http://dx.doi.org/10.1016/j.chaos.2008.01.020

[125] Kanso, A. and Smaoui, N. (2009) Logistic Chaotic Maps for Binary Numbers Generations. *Chaos, Solitons & Fractals*, **40**, 2557-2568. http://dx.doi.org/10.1016/j.chaos.2007.10.049

Appendix A

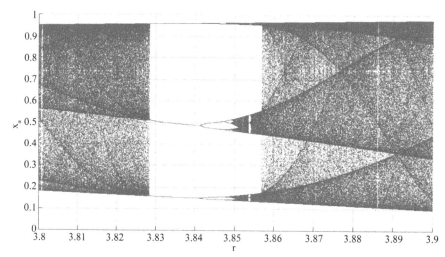

Figure A1. Logistic map bifurcation diagram with $t \in [3.8, 3.9]$.

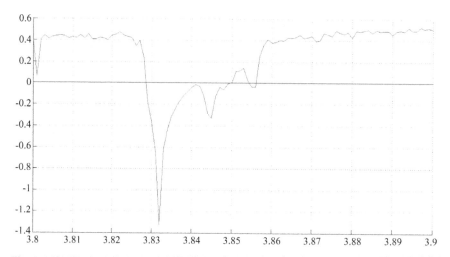

Figure A2. Lyapunov exponent of logistic map with $t \in [3.8, 3.9]$.

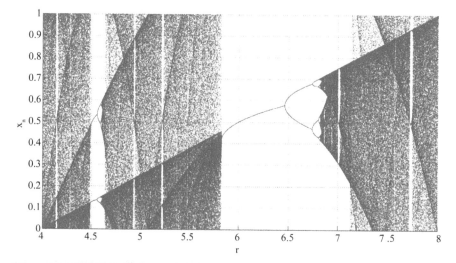

Figure A3. Modified logistic map bifurcation diagram with $t \in [4, 8]$.

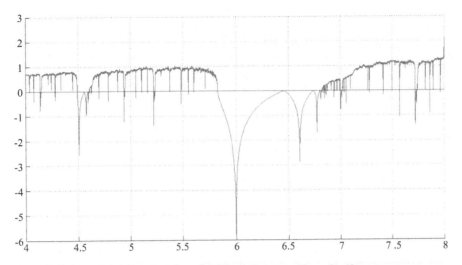

Figure A4. Lyapunov exponent of modified logistic map with $t \in [4, 8]$.

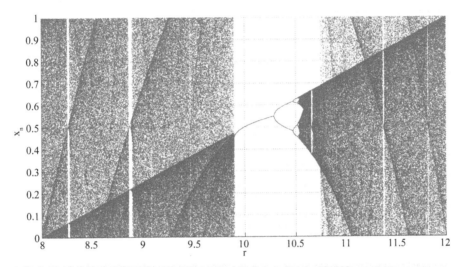

Figure A5. Modified logistic map bifurcation diagram with $t \in [8, 12]$.

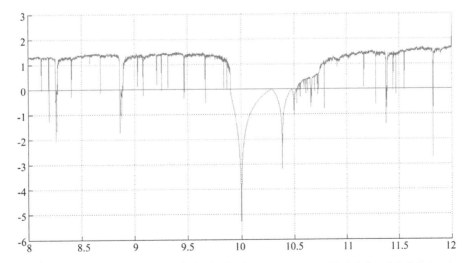

Figure A6. Lyapunov exponent of modified logistic map with $t \in [8, 12]$.

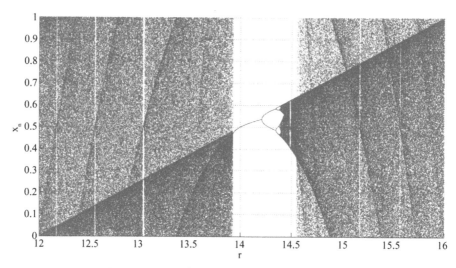

Figure A7. Modified logistic map bifurcation diagram with $t \in [12, 16]$.

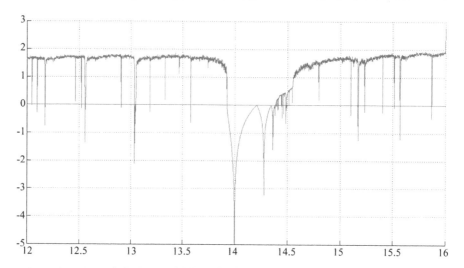

Figure A8. Lyapunov exponent of modified logistic map with $t \in [12, 16]$.

Appendix B

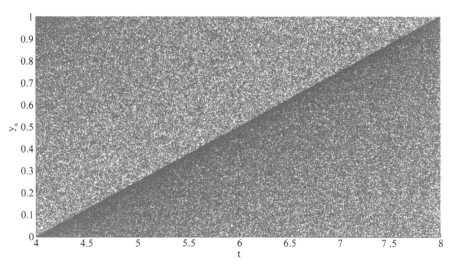

Figure B1. TCM chaotic map bifurcation diagram with $t \in [4, 8]$.

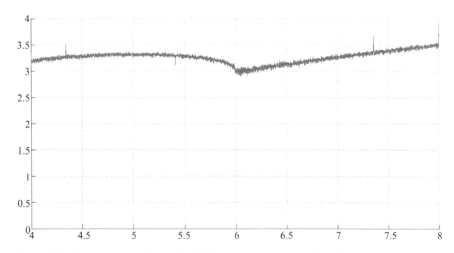

Figure B2. Lyapunov exponent of TCM chaotic map with $t \in [4, 8]$.

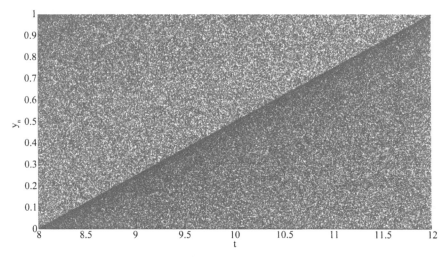

Figure B3. TCM chaotic map bifurcation diagram with $t \in [8, 12]$.

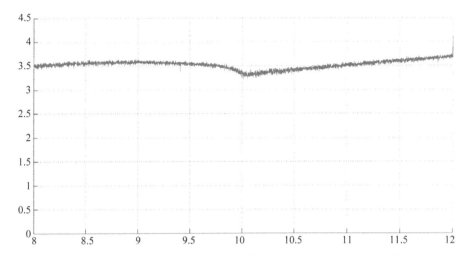

Figure B4. Lyapunov exponent of TCM chaotic map with $t \in [8, 12]$.

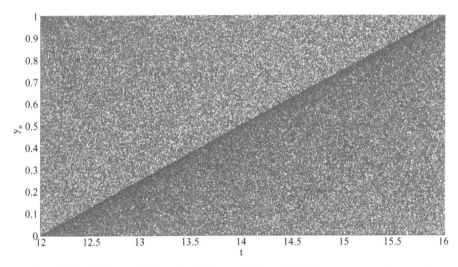

Figure B5. TCM chaotic map bifurcation diagram with $t \in [12, 14]$.

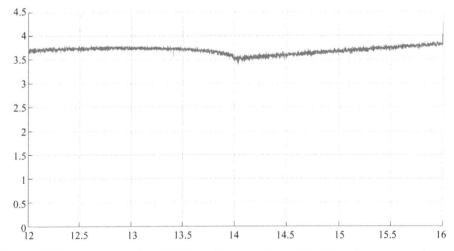

Figure B6. Lyapunov exponent of TCM chaotic map with $t \in [12, 14]$.

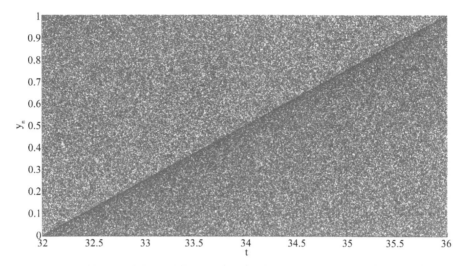

Figure B7. TCM chaotic map bifurcation diagram with $t \in [32, 36]$.

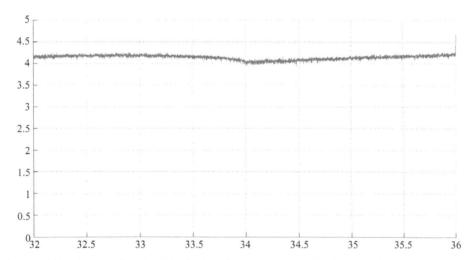

Figure B8. Lyapunov exponent of TCM chaotic map with $t \in [32, 36]$.

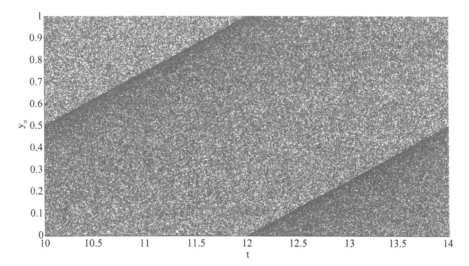

Figure B9. TCM chaotic map bifurcation diagram with $t \in [10, 14]$.

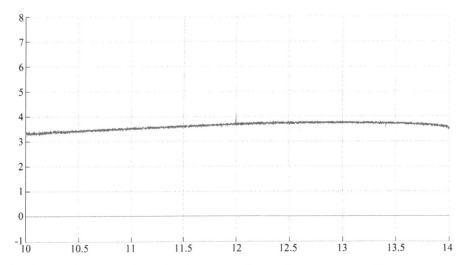

Figure B10. Lyapunov exponent of TCM chaotic map with $t \in [10, 14]$.

Permissions

The contributors of this book come from diverse backgrounds, making this book a truly international effort. This book will bring forth new frontiers with its revolutionizing research information and detailed analysis of the nascent developments around the world.

We would like to thank all the contributing authors for lending their expertise to make the book truly unique. They have played a crucial role in the development of this book. Without their invaluable contributions this book wouldn't have been possible. They have made vital efforts to compile up to date information on the varied aspects of this subject to make this book a valuable addition to the collection of many professionals and students.

This book was conceptualized with the vision of imparting up-to-date information and advanced data in this field. To ensure the same, a matchless editorial board was set up. Every individual on the board went through rigorous rounds of assessment to prove their worth. After which they invested a large part of their time researching and compiling the most relevant data for our readers.

The editorial board has been involved in producing this book since its inception. They have spent rigorous hours researching and exploring the diverse topics which have resulted in the successful publishing of this book. They have passed on their knowledge of decades through this book. To expedite this challenging task, the publisher supported the team at every step. A small team of assistant editors was also appointed to further simplify the editing procedure and attain best results for the readers.

Apart from the editorial board, the designing team has also invested a significant amount of their time in understanding the subject and creating the most relevant covers. They scrutinized every image to scout for the most suitable representation of the subject and create an appropriate cover for the book.

The publishing team has been an ardent support to the editorial, designing and production team. Their endless efforts to recruit the best for this project, has resulted in the accomplishment of this book. They are a veteran in the field of academics and their pool of knowledge is as vast as their experience in printing. Their expertise and guidance has proved useful at every step. Their uncompromising quality standards have made this book an exceptional effort. Their encouragement from time to time has been an inspiration for everyone.

The publisher and the editorial board hope that this book will prove to be a valuable piece of knowledge for researchers, students, practitioners and scholars across the globe.

List of Contributors

Andreas Nascimento and Mauro Hugo Mathias
Departamento de Mecânica, Faculdade de Engenharia, Câmpus de Guaratinguetá (FEG), Universidade Estadual Paulista (UNESP), Guaratinguetá, Brazil

Edson Da Costa Bortoni, José Luiz Gonçalves and Pedro Antunes Duarte
Universidade Federal de Itajubá (UNIFEI), Itajubá, Brazil

Fayed F. M. Ghaleb
Faculty of Science, Mathematices Department, Ain Shams University, Cairo, Egypt

Ebrahim A. Youness, Mahmoud Elmezain and Fatma Sh. Dewdar
Faculty of Science, Computer Science Division, Tanta University, Tanta, Egypt

Nasir Mehmood Minhas, Asad Masood Qazi, Sidra Shahzadi and Shumaila Ghafoor
University Institute of Information Technology, PMAS-University Institute of Information Technology, Rawalpindi, Pakistan

Abhinandan H. Patil and Neena Goveas
Department of Computer Science and Information Systems, Birla Institute of Technology and Science, Goa, India

Krishnan Rangarajan
Department of Information Science, Dayanand Sagar College of Engineering, Bangalore, India

Sheetal R. Vij and Amruta More
Department of Computer Engineering, Maharashtra Institute of Technology, Pune, India

Debajyoti Mukhopadhyay
Department of Information Technology, Maharashtra Institute of Technology, Pune, India

Avinash J. Agrawal
Department of Computer Science and Engineering, Ramdeobaba College of Engineering and Management, Nagpur, India

Alhussain Akoum and Nour Al Mawla
Department GRIT, Lebanese University, Beirut, Lebanon

Jun Qu
Logistics Department, Tongji University, Shanghai, China

Chang-Qing Yin
School of Software Engineering, Tongji University, Shanghai, China

Shangwei Song
College of Design and Innovation, Tongji University, Shanghai, China

Vipul Vashisht and Manohar Lal
SOCIS, IGNOU, New Delhi, India

G. S. Sureshchandar
ASQ India Pvt Ltd., Chennai, India

Monika Singh and Ashok Kumar Sharma
Faculty of Engineering & Technology (FET), Mody University of Science & Technology, Sikar, India

Ruhi Saxena
Computer Science & Engineering, Thapar University, Patiala, India

M. J. Escalona, F. J. Domínguez-Mayo, J. A. García-García and N. Sánchez, J. Ponce
Web Engineering and Early Testing Research Group, IWT2, University of Seville, Seville, Spain

Reema Patel and Dhiren Patel
Computer Engineering Department, NIT, Surat, India

André Ribeiro, Afonso Silva and Alberto Rodrigues da Silva
INESC-ID/Instituto Superior Técnico, Lisbon, Portugal

Agaji Iorshase and Onyeke Idoko Charles
Department of Mathematics/Statistics/Computer Science, Federal University of Agriculture, Makurdi, Nigeria

Panos Fitsilis and Vyron Damasiotis
Technological Educational Institute of Thessaly, Larissa, Greece

Saher Manaseer, Warif Manasir and Mohammad Alshraideh
1Department of Computer Science, The University of Jordan, Amman, Jordan

Nabil Abu Hashish
Al Israa University, Amman, Jordan

Omar Adwan
Department of Computer Information Systems, The University of Jordan, Amman, Jordan

Raúl Beltrán Ramírez, Rocío Maciel Arellano and Adauto Casas Flores
Departamento de Sistemas de Información, Universidad de Guadalajara Periférico Norte, Zapopan, México

Carlos González Sandoval
Centro de Enseñanza Técnica Industrial, Guadalajara, México

Ekaterina M. Lavrischeva
Moscow Physics-Technical Institute, Dolgoprudnuy, Russia

Arfan Mansoor, Detlef Streitferdt and Franz-Felix Füßl
Software Architectures and Product Line Group, Ilmenau University of Technology, Ilmenau, Germany

Mamoona Humayoun and Asad Masood Qazi
University Institute of Information Technology, PMAS-University Institute of Information Technology, Rawalpindi, Pakistan

Ahmed Tijjani Dahiru
Department of Electrical/Electronics Technology School of Technical Education, Federal College of Education (Technical) Bichi, Kano, Nigeria

Pedro Mattos Tabim
Department of Graduation in Civil Engineering, Federal Fluminense University, Niterói, Brazil

Miguel Luiz Ribeiro Ferreira
Mechanical Engineering Department, Federal Fluminense University, Niterói, Brazil

Mahmoud Maqableh
Management Information Systems, Faculty of Business, The University of Jordan, Amman, Jordan

Printed in the USA
CPSIA information can be obtained
at www.ICGtesting.com
JSHW051429221024
72173JS00006B/1415

9 781632 384805